Phenomenology and the Transcendental

"*Phenomenology and the Transcendental* provides a wide-ranging and thought-provoking exploration of the transcendental character of phenomenology. Encompassing historical and contemporary discussions, and including important essays by key figures such as Carr, Crowell, and others, it is a fine collection that demonstrates the enormous strength of phenomenology as a continuing and expanding domain of inquiry as well as its increasing interdisciplinary significance and engagement."

—*Jeff Malpas*, Distinguished Professor, University of Tasmania, Australia

The aim of this volume is to offer an updated account of the transcendental character of phenomenology. The main question concerns the sense and relevance of transcendental philosophy today: What can such philosophy contribute to contemporary inquiries and debates after the many reasoned attacks against its idealistic, aprioristic, absolutist, and universalistic tendencies—voiced most vigorously by late-twentieth-century postmodern thinkers—as well as attacks against its apparently circular arguments and suspicious metaphysics launched by many analytic philosophers? Contributors also aim to clarify the relations of transcendental phenomenology to other post-Kantian philosophies, most importantly to pragmatism and Wittgenstein's philosophical investigations. Finally, the volume offers a set of reflections on the meaning of post-transcendental phenomenology.

Sara Heinämaa is a professor of philosophy in the Department of Social Sciences and Philosophy at the University of Jyväskylä, Finland, and a senior lecturer in the Department of Philosophy, History, Culture and Art Studies at the University of Helsinki, Finland.

Mirja Hartimo is a docent of theoretical philosophy at the University of Helsinki and University of Tampere, Finland.

Timo Miettinen is a postdoctoral researcher in the Network for European Studies, Department of Political and Economic Studies at the University of Helsinki, Finland.

Routledge Research in Phenomenology

Edited by Søren Overgaard, *University of Copenhagen, Denmark,*
Komarine Romdenh-Romluc, *University of Nottingham, UK,* and
David Cerbone, *West Virginia University, USA*

Phenomenology and the Transcendental

Edited by Sara Heinämaa,
Mirja Hartimo, and
Timo Miettinen

Routledge
Taylor & Francis Group

LONDON AND NEW YORK

First published 2014 by Routledge

2 Park Square, Milton Park, Abingdon, Oxon OX14 4RN
711 Third Avenue, New York, NY 10017, USA

Routledge is an imprint of the Taylor & Francis Group,
an informa business

First issued in paperback 2016

Library of Congress Cataloging-in-Publication Data

Phenomenology and the transcendental / edited by Sara Heinamaa,
   Mirja Hartimo, and Timo Miettinen.— 1 [edition].
      pages cm. — (Routledge research in phenomenology ; 1)
   Includes bibliographical references and index.
   1. Transcendentalism.   2. Phenomenology.   I. Heinamaa, Sara, 1960–
editor of compilation.
   B823.P44 2014
   141′.3—dc23
   2013045053

ISBN: 978-0-415-86988-1 (hbk)
ISBN: 978-1-138-21056-1 (pbk)

Typeset in Sabon
by Apex CoVantage, LLC

Contents

PART III
Mind and the World

PART IV
Beyond Correlation

Introduction

Methodological, Historical, and Conceptual Starting Points

*Sara Heinämaa, Mirja Hartimo,
and Timo Miettinen*

Since the turn of the millennium, phenomenology has become one of the major approaches in contemporary philosophy of the mind and cognition. Phenomenological results and innovations have influenced not only theories of perception and cognition but also our views on social emotions and human coexistence. Consequently, contemporary phenomenology is well known for its contributions to the philosophy of selfhood and preconceptual perception, for its explications of empathy, shame, and guilt, and for its emphasis on the facticity and plurality of human life. Phenomenological analyses have broadened our view of the interface between the mental and the physical, and they have contributed to our understanding of the classic division between the animal and the human as well as that between nature and culture. These insights have had considerable effects on present-day theorization of subjectivity and intersubjectivity and on the related discourses on personal and social identities, from philosophical anthropology to theories of gender and ethnicity.

In this development, phenomenology has entered into close exchanges with the empirical studies of the human psyche and human signification, most prominently with experimental psychology, neuroscience, cognitive science, psychiatry, psychoanalysis, anthropology, and social theory.[1] Consequently, there is a growing interest to integrate phenomenological investigations with the empirical sciences. Moreover, the novel interdisciplinary attitude is not evident merely in inquiries into the human psyche or mind. Parallel developments manifest themselves in contemporary discussions of a number of other topics, such as the topics of action, embodiment, nature, language, and gender.[2] Consequently, the conceptual innovations of phenomenology now often combine with and contribute to a variety of empiricist and naturalistic theoretical enterprises.

Contemporary naturalism, however, is not a single philosophical position. It includes a variety of different approaches to mental and cultural phenomena, ranging from extreme physicalist and eliminativist approaches to nonreductive postpragmatic and neo–Aristotelian theories. These approaches differ significantly in their accounts of human experience and its relation to the material world. However, they all share one characteristic that may prove problematic in the attempt to naturalize phenomenology or to combine phenomenology with the positive sciences: they take for granted the senses of nature and the world, which are operative in the theoretical discourses of the natural world and the human being, and do not offer tools that would enable us to problematize these senses radically enough for constitutive inquiries that concern their institution and reinstitution. According to the classic phenomenological argument, the idea of science as a theoretical practice implies the task of examining the senses of the world and nature operative in all naturalization projects. We do not need to assume an all-encompassing viewpoint external to human capacities in order to execute such inquiries but can rely on our human capacities of critique, discrimination, and reflection.

This book is an attempt to answer these shortcomings. It argues for the indispensability of the transcendental standpoint for phenomenology and philosophical reasoning in general. The concept of the transcendental, however, is not understood here as referring to a pregiven domain of experience, sense, or inquiry. Instead, it denotes a general motive of philosophical reflection that does not take for granted the everyday attitude or the results of the special sciences but asks for their foundation in our basic experience of the world. To put it in the language of modern philosophy, transcendental inquiries concern those *conditions of possibility* that allow us to constitute the world as true, valid, and objective and ourselves as beings in this world. Transcendental knowledge, in contrast to a common misconception, is not something that transcends our lives and our understanding; instead, it is an investigation into the senses operative in our experiences.

In his groundbreaking work *Ideas: General Introduction to Pure Phenomenology and to a Phenomenological Philosophy* (1913), Edmund Husserl argued for the necessity of establishing the phenomenological method on a universal suspension of all conviction about the reality of nature and the world, implicated in our theoretical and practical, scientific, and everyday beliefs and cognitions.[3] The aim, he explained, was not to doubt or negate the world or to establish another foundation for human knowledge but to interrupt our natural belief in the presence and reality of the world for the single purpose of clarifying transcendentally the conditions and the origin of this belief and everything that depends on it. Husserl wrote:

> If I do this, as I am fully free to do, I do not then deny this "world," as though I were a sophist, I do *not doubt that it is there* as though I were a skeptic; but I use the "phenomenological epoché" which *completely bars me from using any judgment that concerns spatio-temporal existence* (. . .) The whole world as placed within the nature-setting and presented in experience as real, taken completely "free from all theory," just as it is in reality experienced, and made clearly manifest in and through the linkings of our experience, has now no validity for us, it must be set in brackets, untested indeed but also uncontested. Similarly

all theories and sciences, positivistic or otherwise, which relate to the world, however good they may be, succumb to the same fate.

(Hua 3, 56–57/100)

The epoché makes possible the crucial step that Husserl called "the phenomenological reduction" and that consists of the thematization of the correlation between our conscious state and the world. Together these two steps allow us to interrupt our natural attention to the world and focus our studies on our sense-constitutive activities and passivities. Thus the main function of the reduction is to enable the explication of the constitutive operations that are responsible for the sense and comprehensibility of the world.

Husserl's radical philosophical aspiration does not just demarcate phenomenology from those theoretical approaches that call themselves "naturalistic." The very same radicalism separates Husserlian phenomenology also from those constructivist approaches that study the ideas of nature, the natural world, and human nature by inserting them in social, historical, or social-historical circumstances. The shortcomings of all such approaches, Husserl explains, are fundamentally similar. As they trace the sense of nature or the natural back to historical and social processes, they necessarily presuppose the world as a framework or horizon in which the relevant circumstances prevail and events proceed.[4] The fundamental presupposition of the world is left intact even if the senses of nature and the natural world are investigated as social or historical accomplishments since these accomplishments are still conceptualized as *worldly* events or processes. In other words, on Husserl's analysis, the social and historical constructivist approaches are not radical enough for philosophical purposes.[5]

From a phenomenological standpoint, no factual construction, be it naturalistic or historicist, can settle philosophical questioning. Philosophy, in this view, charts possibilities, not realities.[6] It is not a logical construction but establishes itself as a transcendental inquiry into the conditions of possibility of our experience of the world and everything within it (including logic).

The volume at hand is motivated by the insight that the novel interdisciplinary situation in which phenomenology conducts fruitful exchanges with several empirical sciences demands that we reconsider thoroughly the fundamental methodological questions concerning the transcendental character of phenomenological inquiries. *Phenomenology and the Transcendental* brings together original articles that together clarify the transcendental aspects of phenomenology and outline new transcendental versions of phenomenology in distinction from the naturalistic, vitalist, and poststructuralist approaches that dominate philosophy at the moment.[7] The volume thus contributes to the development of contemporary phenomenology in two related ways: it deepens the topical debates by offering fresh methodological and metaphilosophical insights and extends the established topical range by arguing that phenomenology is not tied to any specific topics, whether in perception and cognition, in empathy and social emotions, or in our mental lives as wholes. Accordingly, phenomenology defines a methodology that can be applied in multiple topical areas. This way, phenomenology broadens significantly the scope of classic transcendental philosophy toward new domains of experience, including the temporal development of personhood, mortality and generativity, animality, and materiality.

1 ON THE CLASSIC CONCEPT OF THE TRANSCENDENTAL

Although the idea of transcendental philosophy is associated with philosophical ideas that are characteristically modern, the concept of the transcendental dates back to medieval thought. The notions of *transcendentia* and later *transcendentalia* were first used during the thirteenth century to denote those properties that characterize being in all of its instances and thus "transcend" all individual categories. This idea had its background in the Aristotelian doctrine of "being" (*to on*) and "one" (*to hen*) as the universal characteristics of all being—real or ideal, sensed or intuited—that are needed for any sense of "meaning" or "reality" to come about.

The medieval authors, and particularly St. Thomas Aquinas, followed Aristotle in emphasizing the fundamental role of the concepts of *res* and *unum*, being and unity, as the primary transcendentals. However, they also broadened the scope of transcendental attributes to include the relationality of beings to each other and to the intellect. According to Thomas, every being is also defined by its difference from all other beings—that is, as something (*aliquid*)—as well as by its "trueness" (*verum*) and "goodness" (*bonum*).

This broadened notion of the transcendental served as the basic point of departure for the modern reformulation of transcendental philosophy in the works of Immanuel Kant. According to the classic definition provided by Kant's *Critique of Pure Reason*, the expression 'transcendental' is to refer to "all cognition which is occupied not so much with objects as with the mode of our cognition of objects in so far as this mode of cognition is to be possible *a priori*" (Kant CPR A11–12/B25).

Thus the domain of transcendental reflection was to be relocated in experience rather than the experienced reality, and, accordingly, transcendental philosophy was supposed to constitute a system of such knowledge with a clear demarcation between necessary and contingent aspects of human cognition. While Kant acknowledged that the history of the notion of transcendental dated back already to "the ancients," he nevertheless maintained that the medieval doctrine of the *transcendentalia* could only amount to tautological propositions of mutually convertible definitions (CPR B113). Instead of mere tautological or "analytic" definitions, the new domain of the transcendental was to consist of *synthetic a priori* judgments that genuinely reveal something novel about the structures of cognition and thus add to our knowledge.

Kant characterized his method of discovering the transcendentals by the term 'deduction.' This term that was adopted from the legal context of the time referred basically to the idea of justification that was at the heart of Kant's philosophical method. While the *a priori* principles of cognition serve as the basis for all of our knowledge, they are not themselves beyond all proof: they, too, require justification in order to be operative (CPR A148/ B188). We cannot assume the amount of categories, their types, or any other *a priori* principles beforehand, nor can we simply apply them to reality. Their legitimacy must be demonstrated in a way that excludes all other ideas, concepts, or principles as possible explanations of the phenomena. Despite the radical character of his approach, Kant nevertheless took it for granted that we can, and must, derive the categories from logic. He argues that because logic had not progressed since Aristotle, it was "a closed and complete body of doctrine" and could thus serve as the model for categories (CPR Bviii).

The core of Kant's method of transcendental deduction was based on his argument for the unity of conscious life. Not only do we judge the appearing things as being of certain qualities and quantities, but our experiencing is always accompanied by certain "mineness." Kant turned back to Descartes and emphasized the representation "I think" (*cogito*) as something that accompanies all experiencing. He termed this representation "pure apperception" or "original apperception"—literally, the surplus of perception—and he argued that it also constituted the foundation of all self-consciousness *per se*: "I also call its unity the *transcendental unity of self-consciousness* in order to designate the possibility of a priori cognition from it" (CPR B132).

Although Kant was favorable to the Cartesian idea of *cogito*, he followed Hume in rejecting Descartes's solution according to which the transcendental self can be characterized and understood in terms of *res cogitans*, a thinking thing or substance. Instead of a mental entity, the necessary self of all experiencing was to be understood as a nonintuitable pole of experience that lacks "any quality whatsoever" (CPR A355). Thus, in its apperceived form, Kant argued, the transcendental ego "contains nothing manifold" (CPR B135)—as human beings, we all are instantiations of the same transcendental ego.

These arguments constitute the kernel of Kant's doctrine of *transcendental idealism*. Thus in its Kantian sense, idealism does not depend on the notion of the subject as the creator or producer of the world but instead asserts and argues for the indispensable role of self-consciousness in the constitution of a meaningful experience of transcendence, that is, of the world and its objects.

Kant's transcendental idealism was notoriously haunted by the ambiguous surplus element of worldly transcendence, that is, the "things themselves," that helped guarantee the distinction between appearance and reality. Although Kant's appeal to "things in themselves" allows several different interpretations and although this idea can be supported by multiple arguments, its perplexing and ambiguous character was one of the main reasons that lead the German idealists, Fichte and Hegel, to refute Kant's doctrine of transcendental idealism in favor of "absolute idealism," which emphasized the ultimate unity of thinking and being and traced the development of self-consciousness through (historical) time.

Despite this critical reaction, transcendental philosophy was not completely abandoned by the nineteenth-century philosophers. It was further developed by a wide variety of thinkers often referred to as "neo-Kantians," who emphasized the need to turn back to study and work on the Kantian problematics of the possibility of knowledge. Critical epistemology, not metaphysics or ontology, was to be located at the heart of philosophical reflection. In the works of Hermann Cohen, Paul Natorp, and Ernst Cassirer, however, the classical Kantian problematics of cognition was set free from its strictly logical aspects that concerned the general conditions of possible knowledge. The Kantian task of executing transcendental inquiries into such conditions merged with the interest to accommodate the structures of human cognition with the rapid development of the modern natural sciences as well as with the multiplicity of human cultures and their symbolic forms. Here, the debate concerning the transcendental approach and its proper character became the decisive point for the autonomy of philosophical knowledge, its separation from the mere idea of a "world-view" (*Weltanschauung*), but also for the very unity of the scientific enterprise in general: What is the relation between the natural-scientific and the human-scientific knowledge? Do they share a common foundation in the cognitive structures of the human subject?

The stimulating role of neo-Kantianism in regard to the emergence of the phenomenological movement can hardly be exaggerated. Both Husserl and Heidegger were deeply influenced by the two main strands of the neo-Kantian movement: the Marburg school of Cohen, Natorp, and Cassirer, as well as the Baden school of Wilhelm Windelband and Heinrich Rickert. The antimetaphysical and antispeculative connotations of phenomenology were in line with the epistemological interest of the neo-Kantians. The explicitly Kantian nomenclature of Husserl—ego, subject, and self-consciousness—as well as the emphasis on "factical life" of the early Heidegger both alluded to the neo-Kantian problematic.[8]

However, as the historical development of the phenomenological movement shows, the relation between the idea of phenomenological inquiries on the one hand and the idea of transcendental inquiries on the other hand is far from being clear. Husserl's late problematic of the lifeworld, Heidegger's turn to the history of being, Merleau-Ponty's discourse on the element of the flesh, as well as Sartre's interest in the Hegelian problematic of recognition can all be interpreted as critical confrontations with the basic theses of the Kantian tradition: the primacy of consciousness over the world, of epistemology over ontology, of theory over praxis, of mind over body, and of cognition over affection. Still, giving up completely on making the distinction between transcendental and empirical inquiries would mean that we renounce many of the central themes and arguments of classical phenomenologists, and this risks that we miss altogether what they conceived of as the *differentia specifica* of philosophical reflection as such.

2 HUSSERL AND THE POSSIBILITY OF TRANSCENDENTAL PHENOMENOLOGY

Husserl's first seminal work, *Logical Investigations*, the "breakthrough of phenomenology," was published in two volumes in 1900 and 1901. Its relation to Kantian transcendental philosophy was highly ambiguous. On the one hand, Husserl's rejection of contemporary psychologism seemed to refer to the need for a strict transcendental investigation. The central role of the notion of "intuition" (*Anschauung*) rang the bells of any Kantian, and in the *Prolegomena* Husserl explicitly argued that the role of pure logic is to give us conditions of the possibility of theory in general. On the other hand, Husserl explicitly rejected the Kantian doctrine of the pure ego that had been promoted by Natorp; moreover, his famous exposition on the "categorial intuition" was in clear opposition to the Kantian division between sensibility and understanding. What is certain, however, is that the unclarities relating to the transcendental problematic—its foundation, method, and scope—influenced the development of Husserl's thought all the way to his late works.

In Husserl scholarship, it has become usual to speak of the so-called "transcendental turn" in Husserl's thinking, a development that took place between the first edition of the *Logical Investigations* and the first volume of *Ideas* (1913). This development was marked by the explication of the method of the transcendental-phenomenological reduction and by the discovery of the transcendental ego.[9] A new Kantian motive emerged in Husserl's philosophy and opened a new set of research tasks. The Kantian and Cartesian terms 'transcendental ego,' 'self,' and 'subject' received radical redefinitions in the novel "critique of reason" that Husserl proposed in a Kantian line.[10] The transcendental ego was not to be arrived at via speculation or transcendental deduction but by holding fast to the principle of intuition. Thus, whatever structures or features we may label as transcendental, they must be straightforwardly *given* in experience. For this reason, Husserl was able to consider Descartes the true originator of the transcendental motive of modern philosophy:

> I should like to note the following right away: the expression "transcendental philosophy" has been much used since Kant, even as a general title for universal philosophies whose concepts are oriented toward those of the Kantian type. I myself use the word "transcendental" in the

broadest sense for the original motif, discussed in detail above, which through Descartes confers meaning upon all modern philosophies, the motif which, in all of them, seeks to come to itself, so to speak—seeks to attain the genuine and pure form of its task and its systematic development.

(Hua 6, 100/97)[11]

Transcendental phenomenology, accordingly, was to found itself as a *descriptive* science—although its scope was not to be restricted in the domain of descriptive statements or theoretical reason. Especially in his later works on the crisis of the European sciences, Husserl emphasized the role of transcendental thought in the unification—or reunification—of the domains of theory and praxis and the rearticulation of philosophical self-responsibility on the basis of their union.

Husserl's relation to the very content of transcendental philosophy can be viewed as a radicalization, a rearticulation, and a distention of the Kantian concept of the transcendental. It was a radicalization insofar as Husserl extended the transcendental critique also to logic that Kant had taken for granted. It was a rearticulation insofar as Husserl, by emphasizing the idea of givenness rather than deduction, located the domain of transcendental within the individual ego, thus making the transcendental ego inextricably *personal* and *singular*. But it was also a distention, as Husserl significantly broadened the scope of transcendental investigation to include the temporal development of the ego, its bodily existence, and intersubjective relations. Moreover, instead of focusing solely on the inner life of the subject, the scope of the transcendental was to be extended to its historical, social, and geographical conditions in the lifeworld. Even the topics of culture and communal life were to be framed as transcendental. Let us shortly focus on the character of the transcendental ego, its singularity, and its facticity.

The primary justification for Husserl's use of the notion of "transcendental" was based on the "Cartesian" discovery according to which the mode of being characteristic of consciousness differs essentially from that of worldly beings. It is possible to imagine a consciousness without a world, but not a world without an ego to which it is given: hence, consciousness is the transcendental condition of all transcendence, the world. However, we do not infer this condition from individual experiences, but we are constantly living it through, which makes the transcendental ego something Kant never saw it to be: an inextricably singular being. But if the transcendental ego is singular, then it means that the domain of transcendentality is really nothing separate from the concrete, worldly person; rather, the transcendental and the empirical refer to two different *aspects* of the conscious life of the individual.

This insight becomes clear as we focus on the topic of embodiment. On the one hand, it is quite obvious that as empirical beings in the world, we are similar to other concrete things, such as trees and tables—we have "bodies" or *Körper*, as Husserl would have put it. On the other hand, it is equally clear that our conscious bodily existence differs radically from the bodily existence of material objects; we are not mere physical things but "living bodies" (*Leibe*) that are able to see, hear, and touch things and to discover the limits of our body through self-affection.[12] As Husserl insists, it is impossible to imagine perception without a living bodily existence, which makes bodily existence a transcendental condition. But this idea does not do away with our empirical being in the world—the empirical and the transcendental are thus two sides of the same coin. We are, as Husserl put it in his later works, defined by this complex "paradox of subjectivity."[13]

The same goes for our relations to other experiencing subjects. The others are there in my field of experience as fellow human beings—parents, siblings, friends, and strangers—with whom I can interact and communicate in multiple ways. However, I am also linked with others simply by my capacity of grasping the world: the very sense of the world as an infinite and exhaustible whole implies the infinity of possible observers with perspectives and horizons that transcend my individual perceptions. In other words, the objectivity of the world necessitates, as its condition, the multiplicity of different perspectives and horizons of experiencing. As Husserl put it in his *Cartesian Meditations*, it is actually the "transcendental we" that deserves to be called the genuine subject of the world, or what he elsewhere termed the "concrete absolute." Thus the phenomenon of intersubjectivity, too, bears transcendental significance.[14]

There are, of course, points in which Husserl's definition of the transcendental resembled significantly that of Kant's. For one, Husserl credited Kant for his unique attempt of describing the field of sensuous intuition not only as a raw data-like givenness but as a *productive activity,* which founds the predicative forms of experience. In other words, Kant demonstrated that receptivity is not merely a subject matter of psychology but also a topic for transcendental investigations. However, since Kant conceived of the transcendental ego to be atemporal and unchanging, he failed—and this from a Husserlian perspective—to investigate into the essential laws and elementary facts of this productive activity (Hua 11, 119). Kant did not bring together the associative synthesis with the temporal structure of transcendental consciousness: his account was unable to question how individual associations provide the transcendental life with its peculiar shape.[15]

This lack motivated Husserl to develop his unique theory of *transcendental person.* I do not merely "live through" individual acts, but these acts have the tendency of creating lasting tendencies, patterns, and intentions, which become part of my personal history. These tendencies may manifest themselves, for instance, in the form of lasting "convictions" (*Überzeugungen*), "decisions" (*Entscheidungen*), or "resolutions of the will" (*Willenentschlüsse*; e.g., Hua 39, 47). As such, such convictions endow my transcendental ego with its essential uniqueness, its personal history and character. This is why Husserl stresses that the notions of habitus and style should not be taken in their everyday sense of custom and routine, nor should they be equated with memory or recollection.[16] Instead, they should be understood as transcendental features that belong primordially to the sphere of pure ego (Hua 4, 111).

3   HUSSERL'S LEGACY

The development of phenomenology after Husserl has been significantly guided by the question of the possibility of the transcendental standpoint. While it is evident that Heidegger, already in his earliest lectures, framed his conceptual approach in clear contrast to the Cartesian-Kantian vocabulary of ego, subject, and consciousness, it is nevertheless clear that the ideas of "factical life" and *Dasein* did not entail a breakaway from the transcendental problematic. As emphasized in the introduction to the *Being and Time,* an investigation into the fundamental structures of *Dasein* as transcendence—as a being that constantly exceeds itself both temporally and to the world—constitutes essentially a "transcendental knowledge." The analyses of worldliness and practical being at hand as well as the three-fold division between "disposedness" (*Befindlichkeit*), "understanding" (*Verstehen*), and "discourse" (*Rede*) can easily be located within a transcendental framework. The same cannot be as easily said of Heidegger's later thinking, which can be interpreted, at least partially, as a resolute attempt at distancing oneself from the subjectivist outlook of modern transcendental philosophy toward a new philosophy that articulates the fundamental receptivity of the human being (for whom "there is being," *es gibt Sein*).

Existential phenomenologists, most prominently Jean-Paul Sartre and Maurice Merleau-Ponty, developed further Husserl's and Heidegger's transcendental inquiries. They combined phenomenology effectively with methods, concepts, and insights stemming from several intellectual movements, from French Cartesianism and vitalism (Malebrance, Maine de Biran, and Bergson), from structuralist anthropology and linguistics (Saussure and Lévi-Strauss), from the twentieth-century interpretations of Hegel (Kojève and Hyppolite), and from the critiques that Kierkegaard and Nietzsche directed against Hegel's universalism and finalism. Despite the synthetic character of their discourses, the French existentialists pursued transcendental investigations that concerned the conditions of perception and communication, the limits of selfhood and personhood, and the intentional operations that egoic and personal subjects can perform.

Merleau-Ponty's analyses of embodiment and expressivity in *Phenomenology of Perception* (1945) aimed at articulating the conditions of objective perception and disclosing the dynamic structures of preconceptual and affective consciousness.[17] His later ontology of flesh, as outlined in *The Visible and the Invisible* (1964)[18] and related manuscripts and lectures, is today commonly associated with Bergson's vitalism, Schelling's or Spinoza's monism, and Whitehead's philosophy of nature. But despite such classically metaphysical resonances, Merleau-Ponty still formulates his philosophical aims in terms of the reductive method of Husserlian phenomenology: "I will finally be able to take a position in ontology (. . .) and specify its theses exactly, only after the series of reductions (. . .) which are all in the first one, but also are truly accomplished only in the last one" (1964, 233/179; cf. 1964, 207–208/156–157, 219/165–166).[19]

Following Eugen Fink's sixth Cartesian Meditation, Merleau-Ponty argued that the radical character of phenomenology remains a promise unless phenomenology incorporates an account of its own motivations and its reflective and conceptual-linguistic operations. What is needed is a "phenomenology of phenomenology," and this, Merleau-Ponty contended, can and must be grounded in a new intensified or deepened type of reflection, that is, a "hyper-reflection" (*sur-réflexion*), that is conscious of its living roots in prereflective experience and of the changes that it introduces in experience (Merleau-Ponty 1964, 61/38; cf. [1945] 1993, 75–76/61–63). As reckoned already in *Phenomenology,* this requires that phenomenology realizes the temporal character of its own analyses of sense constitution and the *eide* of experiencing and proceeds to a genetic stage:

> Until some means has been discovered whereby we can link the origin and the essence or meaning of the [experience]; until some definition is found for a concrete essence, a structure of [experience] which shall express both its generality and its particularity, until phenomenology becomes genetic phenomenology, unhelpful reversions to causal thought and naturalism will remain justified.
> (Merleau-Ponty [1945] 1993, 146–147/126)[20]

Expanding on this line of thought, the volume at hand takes seriously the dynamic character of phenomenology.[21] The authors of this work understand the concept of the transcendental primarily in terms of a movement or a motive that does not simply leave behind the empirical reality but asks for its conditions of possibility in the experiencing subject, its correlates, and its manifold intentional layers. The task of transcendental reflection is to make explicit how the world, its objectivity and validity, depends on the constitutive functions of subjectivity and intersubjectivity. Correlatively, it must also ask to what extent these functions themselves are embedded in different worldly structures.

***

The volume at hand consists of four parts. Part I of *Transcendental Phenomenology* includes principled discussions on the nature of transcendental phenomenology, its main variations, and its relation to the tradition of transcendental philosophy. It outlines the historical development that starts with Kant and continues to present-day debates about the proper tasks and methods of phenomenological philosophy. Finally, Part I presents new interpretations of transcendental phenomenology, and thus it demonstrates how contemporary phenomenologists work to continue and develop transcendental inquiries without falling back on any form of metaphysical foundationalism.

The volume opens with the article "Transcendental Life," in which Steven Crowell discusses Husserl and Heidegger as paradigms of transcendental thinking. The chapter argues for the indispensability of the transcendental phenomenological point of view when approaching normativity. Thus it gives a detailed answer to why the naturalist approaches cannot adequately address the questions of logic, epistemology, aesthetics, and ethics. In his chapter, "Categories of Experience and the Transcendental," Laszlo Tengelyi clarifies the way in which Husserl's notion of the transcendental relates to Kant's notion. Most importantly, in contrast to Kant's transcendental deduction of categories that proceeds on *a priori* grounds, the phenomenologist's transcendental argument is based on the contingent fact that the world exists. Tengelyi locates the main difference between Kant's and the phenomenologist's approaches to their respective notion of necessity, which in phenomenology is not *a priori* necessity but *factual necessity* that arises from experience. His chapter also importantly suggests that Husserl's notion of the transcendental should be understood in the framework of Kant's Third Critique rather than the First. While the two previous chapters study and discuss the nature of transcendental phenomenology, Bernhard Obsieger's article, "The Transcendental Nature of Experience," dives into the phenomenological way of philosophizing and actually carries out a transcendental phenomenological analysis of temporality and intersubjectivity.

Part II, *Subjectivity and Intersubjectivity*, further clarifies the structures of transcendental subjectivity and intersubjectivity and the Husserlian concepts of activity and passivity. The essays in this part demonstrate that transcendental phenomenology is not mere epistemology but also analyzes dependencies that are relevant to social philosophy, political philosophy, and ethics. The constituting self, as disclosed in the essays, is not an empty pole, a formal principle or solitary agent, but has a temporal character, a bodily dimension, and communal linkages. By emphasizing the temporal character of constitution, this part also brings to the view the constitutive function of passivity. It argues that, rather than an immutable and amorphous mass from which conscious acts lade or bail, passivity can and must be conceived in dynamic terms as the developing source and result of activity. The first chapter in the second section takes us first into the conception of the human being in the naturalistic attitude, then in the personalistic attitude, and eventually in the transcendental attitude. In "Transcendental Subjectivity and the Human Being," Hanne Jacobs thematizes the basic difference between two main attitudes that we can take to human beings: the naturalistic attitude of the natural sciences that theorize human beings as physicalistic systems or psycho-physical wholes, and the personalistic attitude in which the human being is apprehended as a communicating and expressive subject of actions and passions. Jacobs emphasizes that the two realms of being delineated in these attitudes are not ontologically distinct, and she argues that the naturalistic attitude presupposes the personalistic pregivenness of the human being as a communicating and expressive subject. On the basis of these explications, Jacobs then reconsiders the nature or character of transcendental subjectivity and its self-constitution as a human being. In "Husserl on the Factical and Historical Grounds of the Transcendental Subject," Simo Pulkkinen argues that while passivity founds our actual attentive acts, these acts, on the other hand, come to form a "secondary passivity" by the processes of association and habituation. The accomplishment of an act does not vanish with the ceasing of the act but pertains and participates as a habitual formation in subsequent meaning constitution. Thus transcendental subjectivity is affected by its own historicity, and this makes it dynamic and embedded in the world and in the intersubjective community. Pulkkinen's chapter thus shows in detail how the embeddedness of an agent comes about.

In "The Animal and the Infant: From Embodiment and Empathy to Generativity," Sara Heinämaa argues that the Husserl's discourse of transcendental intersubjectivity includes an important analysis that binds the full sense of the world to a specific form of intersubjectivity organized into generations and chains of generations. The figures of the infant and the animal are crucial to this analysis. By explicating Husserl's line of thought on this point and by developing it further, Heinämaa argues that language has a central role in the constitution of the crucial form of intersubjectivity that correlates with the full sense of the world. This helps us distinguish between the constitutive functions of linguistic and nonlinguistic communities. In the article "Transcendental Social Ontology," Timo Miettinen discusses the significance of the transcendental approach for Husserl's theory of intersubjectivity. According to his reading, Husserl did not conceive communities merely as derivative phenomena of the individual ego; instead, his phenomenology of intersubjectivity was able to afford communities a transcendental status. The problem of sociality cannot thus be returned to the idea of shared intentions or common mental states, but it entails a fundamental relation to *transcendence,* that is, to the constitution of a common world. Phenomenological social ontology, Miettinen concludes, must be approached from the idea of transcendental correlation, that is, the relation between constituting subjectivity and constituted accomplishments.

Part III, *Mind and the World,* switches the focus and studies the concepts of the world and the body and the role of the object in transcendental phenomenology. In his contribution, "The Emergence and Transformation of Husserl's Concept of World," David Carr traces the development of Husserl's conception of the world from its first appearance as the commonsense view of the world to lifeworld that is prior to any scientific or practical attitudes. Carr argues that once the concept of world moves into a central position in Husserl's formulation of the phenomenological method, it undergoes a series of transformations that culminate in the concept of the lifeworld in the 1930s. As the last publication *The Crisis of European Sciences* shows, two related research tasks ensue from these transformations: the task of establishing the ontology of the lifeworld and the task of inquiring into the transcendental grounds of this ontology. In the next chapter, "Phenomenological Sources, Kantian Borders: An Outline of Transcendental Philosophy as Object-Guided Philosophy," Sophie Loidolt discusses the transcendental attitude towards the world and argues for an object-guided transcendental phenomenology. Loidolt emphasizes the Kantian kernel of transcendental philosophy and points out that this kernel does not just include the idea of correlation but also implies that the possible objects of experience have necessary transcendental structures. Based on this, Loidolt argues that, instead of being conceived and practiced as a philosophy of pure subjectivity, phenomenology can and must be developed as an inquiry into the very structures of objectivity. Joona Taipale's chapter "The Bodily Feeling of Existence in Phenomenology and Psychoanalysis" continues with a detailed examination of the transcendental phenomenological account of the body and compares and contrasts it to the notions of the body in Freudian psychoanalysis. Despite the fact that psychoanalysis remains a nontranscendental discipline, Taipale illustrates important connections between these two discourses on human embodiment. His contribution thus explores the margins of transcendental phenomenology and argues that "factical" necessity, as Tengelyi would put it, makes transcendental phenomenology continuous with certain empirical approaches. In "William James on Consciousness and the Brain: From Psycho-Physical Dualism to Transcendental Philosophy," Richard Cobb-Stevens then explores the borderline between Husserlian phenomenology and William James's pragmatism highlighting transcendental features in James's thought. In particular, he argues that James's conception of pure experience should be understood along the transcendental lines as explicated by Husserl, in which the dualisms between mind and body as well as appearance and reality are overcome. The same world is examined within the transcendental attitude that enables us to pay attention to the ways in which the world presents itself. Thus the phenomena thematized in phenomenology must be understood as manifestations of things themselves— a notion whose roots can be traced back to Antiquity.

Part IV, *Beyond Correlation*, discusses recent criticisms that motivate the move beyond transcendental phenomenology and demonstrates that this move cannot mean a step back to pretranscendental inquiries but must rather proceed forward. Rather than naturalizing phenomenology or inserting phenomenological inquiries into some positive ontology, this final part of the volume argues that transcendental philosophy can and must be developed by a radicalization of its questions. Thus traditional transcendental inquiries concerning the limits of human experience and knowledge are subordinated to questions that concern the roots of our present interest in the limitations or the unlimitedness of knowledge.

First, in "What Is a Transcendental Description?" Fredrik Westerlund discusses two principal objections that have been presented against phenomenology: subjectivism and essentialism. He argues that the former form of criticism can be countered but the latter cannot. Consequently, he holds, transcendental phenomenology should be conceived as the delineation of the general paradigms of meaning whose range and force lie in their de facto capacity to clarify individual cases of intending and should not be assimilated with any pursuit for the essential features of experiencing. The question is whether such an enterprise still can or should be called "transcendental." In his chapter, "Transcendental Idealism and Strong Correlationism: Meillassoux and the End of Heideggerian Finitude," Jussi Backman discusses Quentin Meillassoux's recent interpretation and critique of Heidegger's philosophical position. The chapter emphasizes the fact that Meillassoux situates Heidegger in the post-Kantian tradition of transcendental idealism that he defines by the idea of correlation between being and thinking. Backman then argues that Meillassoux's "speculative" attempt to overcome the Kantian philosophical framework in the name of absolute contingency should be understood as a further development of its ultimate contemporary form, the Heideggerian philosophy of finitude. Niall Keane's chapter, "*Die Kehre spielt im Sachverhalt selbst*—Making Sense of the Twists and Turns in Heidegger's Thought," discusses the influential notion that there is a groundbreaking "turn" in Heidegger's thought. Keane argues that the Heideggerian turn, which is usually delineated as the dividing line between Heidegger's early and late periods, should not be understood simply as a shift of position. Rather, the "turn" unfolds as a topical motive in Heidegger's thinking, and this motive explains the transition from the early analytic of *Dasein* toward the history of being. The turning, however, does not entail a renouncement of transcendental philosophy but its rearticulation.

NOTES

1. See, for example, Petitot and colleagues 1999, and the recent discussions in the journal *Phenomenology and Cognitive Science*.
2. See, for example, Zahavi (ed.) 2012.
3. Originally *Ideen zu einer reinen Phänomenlogie und phänomenologischen Philosophie*.
4. This argument is spelled out in a compact way in the so-called *Logos* essay, "Philosophy as rigorous science" (originally *Philosophie als strenge Wissenschaft* (1911).
5. Similar argument has been voiced by philosophers working in the analytical tradition of modern philosophy, for example, by Hilary Putnam. In his article, "Why reason cannot be naturalized" (1983), Putnam distinguished between two main senses of "naturalism," reductive physicalistic on the one hand, motivated by the success of the modern natural sciences, and cultural relativism on the other hand, motivated by the findings of contemporary anthropology. Paradoxically, these two forms of naturalism tend toward opposite attitudes in epistemology and metaphysics, one toward absolutism and monism and

the other toward relativism and pluralism. What is common to both of them, according to Putnam, is that they give up making sense of normativity in its genuine sense, the sense that is imperative to logic, epistemology, and ethics.

For phenomenology of normativity, see Crowell 2013. For naturalist attempts to account for normativity, see, for example, De Caro and Macarthur 2010 and Milkowski and Talmont-Kaminski 2010. For how some philosophers turn to transcendental philosophy, although not to phenomenology, in response to different kinds of shortcomings of the naturalist point of view, see Smith and Sullivan 2011.

6. In the essay "Philosophy and sociology" (1960), Merleau-Ponty formulates this idea as follows: "History, Husserl used to say (. . .) cannot judge an idea; and when it does, this 'evaluating' (*wertende*) history borrows surreptitiously from the 'ideal sphere' the necessary connections which it pretends to bring forth from the facts" (Merleau-Ponty 1960, 129/103).

7. By contemporary "vitalist approaches," we mean ontological and epistemological approaches that are based on or motivated by Spinozist, Nietzschean, or Bergsonian metaphysics of forces and objects, such as Deleuze's transcendental empiricism or contemporary traits of "speculative materialism."

8. In regard to the topic of facticity, Heidegger was influenced especially by Dilthey's treatises on the historicity of human life. See Bambach 1995. Cf. Also Steven Crowell's article in this volume.

9. Whether the change in Husserl's thinking should be viewed as a turn away from his earlier work or as an expansion of it is intensively debated in the secondary literature. The readings that emphasize the transcendental character of his reflections avoid the fruitless debate whether his philosophy is realistic or idealistic. Some scholars argue that already Husserl's *Logical Investigations* can be read as a transcendental philosophical work. Such an interpretation is favored especially among those who emphasize the continuity of the development of Husserl's views (cf. Cobb-Stevens 2003). For example, Sokolowski (2000, 211) holds that the first truly phenomenological work is Husserl's *Logical Investigations* (1900–1901), and by "truly phenomenological" he refers to the philosophical reflection in the transcendental as opposed to all naturalistic reflections. The idea seems to be that already in the *Logical Investigations*, prior to the explication and development of the method of reduction, Husserl performs a reduction via the "ontological way," that is, he starts with the sciences and turns into a transcendental reflection on their conditions of possibility. According to Sokolowski, Husserl gave the name "reduction" to mark the distinction between phenomenology and psychology that was already brewing in the *Logical Investigations* (Sokolowski 2008, 171–172). Along these lines, John Drummond has also argued that Husserl's turn to transcendental phenomenology is not a departure from the approach of the *Logical Investigations* but is an extension of this approach (Drummond 2002). Husserl himself has characterized his own analyses in the *Philosophy of Arithmetic* as phenomenological-constitutional in their attempt at making "'categorical objectivities' [. . .] understandable on the basis of the 'constituting' intentional activities" (Hua 17 §27a). This suggests that Husserl's project could be understood, at least retrospectively, to be in some sense transcendental already in the 1890s.

10. HuaDok 3/5, 14. Cf. Mohanty 1996. In the second edition of the *Logical Investigation* published in 1913, contrary to his earlier position, Husserl claimed to have discovered the domain of the pure ego while distancing himself from the "corrupt forms of ego-metaphysic" (Hua 19/1, 374).

11. See also Husserl's emphasis on the Cartesian dimension of the transcendental problematic in the *Crisis*: "What the modern period calls the theory of the understanding or of reason—in the pregnant sense "critique of reason,"

transcendental problematic—has the roots of its meaning in the Cartesian Meditations. The ancient world was not acquainted with this sort of thing, since the Cartesian *epoché* and its ego were unknown. Thus, in truth, there begins with Descartes a completely new manner of philosophizing which seeks its ultimate foundations in the subjective" (Hua 6, 83/81).

12. On the topic of the living body, See Sara Heinämaa's, Hanne Jacobs's, and Joona Taipale's articles in this volume.
13. Hua 6, 182/178. See also Carr 1999.
14. Cf. Timo Miettinen's article in this volume.
15. See, for example, Kant's *Critique:* "Actual experience, which is constituted by apprehension, association (reproduction), and finally recognition of appearances, contains in recognition, the last and highest of these *merely empirical elements of experience,* certain concepts which render possible the formal unity of experience, and therewith all objective validity (truth) of empirical knowledge" (CPR A124–125).
16. Here Husserlian phenomenology parallels interestingly with William James's classic pragmatist theory of habits.
17. Originally *Phénoménologie de la perception.*
18. Originally *Le visible et l'invisible.*
19. Cf. Fink [1988] 1995, 71–76; Bruzina 2004, 151–152.
20. Cf. Merleau-Ponty 1964, 70–71/46–47; Fink [1988] 1995, 77–84.
21. Cf. Laszlo Tengelyi's chapter in this volume.

REFERENCES

Bambach, C. 1995. *Heidegger, Dilthey and the Crisis of Historicism.* Ithaca, NY: Cornell.
Bruzina, R. 2004. *Edmund Husserl and Eugen Fink: Beginnings and Ends in Phenomenology, 1928–1938.* New Haven, CT, and London: Yale University Press.
De Caro, M. & Macarthur, D. eds. 2010. *Naturalism and Normativity.* New York: Columbia University Press.
Carr, D. 1999. *The Paradox of Subjectivity: The Self in the Transcendental Tradition.* New York, Oxford: Oxford University Press.
Cobb-Stevens, R. 2003. "The other Husserl and the standard interpretation." Review of *The Other Husserl: Horizons of transcendental phenomenology* by Donn Welton. *Research in Phenomenology* 33 (1): 315–328.
Crowell, S. 2013. *Normativity and Phenomenology in Husserl and Heidegger.* Cambridge: Cambridge University Press.
Drummond, J. J. 2002. "The logical investigations: Paving the way to a transcendental logic." In *One Hundred Years of Phenomenology*, eds. D. Zahavi & F. Stjernfelt, 31–40. Dordrecht: Kluwer Academic Publishers.
Fink, E. 1988. VI. *Cartesianische Meditation, Teil 1: Die Idee einer transzendentalen Methodenlehre,* eds. H. Ebling, J. Holl, and G. van Kerckhoven. *Teil 2: Ergenzungsband,* ed. G. van Kerckhoven. *Husserliana Dokumente II/1–2.* Dordrecht, Boston, London: Kluwer Academic Publishers. In English *Sixth Cartesian Meditation: The Idea of a Transcendental Theory of Method,* trans. R. Bruzina. Bloomington and Indianapolis: Indiana University Press, 1995.
Husserl, E. Hua 3. *Ideen zu einer reinen Phänomenlogie und phänomenlogischen Philosophie. Erstes Buch: Allgemeine Einführung in die reine Phänomenologie,* ed. W. Biemel. The Hague: Martinus Nijhoff, 1950. In English 1962. *Ideas: General Introduction to Pure Phenomenology,* trans. W. R. Boyle Gibson. New York, London: Macmillan.

————. Hua 4. *Ideen zur einer reinen Phänomenologie und phänomenologischen Philosophie. Zweites Buch: Phänomenologische Untersuchungen zur Konstitution*, ed. M. Biemel. The Hague: Martinus Nijhoff, 1952. In English *Ideas Pertaining to a Pure Phenomenology and to a Phenomenological Philosophy, Second Book: Studies in the Phenomenological Constitution*, trans. R. Rojcewicz and A. Schuwer, Dordrecht, Boston, London: Kluwer Academic Publishers, 1993.

————. Hua 6. *Die Krisis der europäischen Wissenschaften und die transzendentale Phänomenologie: Eine Einleitung in die phänomenologischen Philosophie*, ed. W. Biemel. The Hague: Martinus Nijhoff, 1954. In English *The Crisis of European Sciences and Transcendental Phenomenology: An Introduction to Phenomenological Philosophy*, trans. D. Carr. Evanston, IL: Northwestern University, 1988.

————. Hua 11. *Analysen zur passiven Synthesis. Aus Vorlesungs und Forschungsmanuskripten, 1918–1926*, ed. M. Fleischer. The Hague: Martinus Nijhoff, 1966. In English *Analyses Concerning Passive and Active Synthesis: Lectures on Transcendental Logic*. trans. A. J. Steinbock. Dordrecht: Kluwer, 2001.

————. Hua 17. *Formale und transzendentale Logik. Versuch einer Kritik der logischen Vernunft*, ed. P. Janssen. The Hague: Martinus Nijhoff, 1974. In English *Formal and Transcendental Logic*, trans. D. Cairns. The Hague: Martinus Nijhoff, 1969.

————. Hua 19. *Logische Untersuchungen. Zweiter Teil: Untersuchungen zur Phänomenologie und Theorie der Erkenntnis*, ed. U. Panzer. Halle, 1901, rev. ed. 1922. The Hague: Martinus Nijhoff, 1984. In English *Logical Investigations, Vol. 2*, trans. J. N. Findlay. Routledge: London and New York, 1970.

————. Hua 39. *Die Lebenswelt. Auslegungen der vorgegebenen Welt und ihrer Konstitution. Texte aus dem Nachlass (1916–1937)*, ed. R. Sowa. New York: Springer, 2008.

————. HuaDok3/5. *Briefwechsel*. Band V: Die Neukantianer, ed. Karl Schuhmann. The Hague: Kluwer Academic Publishers, 1994.

Kant, I. 1965. *Critique of Pure Reason*, trans. N. K. Smith. St. Martin's Press: New York.

Merleau-Ponty, M. [1945] 1993. *Phénoménologie de la perception*. Paris: Gallimard. In English *Phenomenology of Perception*, trans. C. Smith, New York: Routledge & Kegan Paul, 1995.

————. 1960. *Signes*. Paris: Gallimard. In English *Signs*, trans. R. C. McCleary. Evanston, IL: Northwestern University Press.

————. 1964. *Le visible et l'invisible*. Paris: Gallimard. In English *The Visible and the Invisible*, trans. A. Linguis. Evanston, IL: Northwestern University Press, 1968.

Milkowski, M. & Talmont-Kaminski K. eds. 2010. *Beyond Description: Naturalism and Normativity*. King's College London: College Publications.

Mohanty, J. N. 1996 "Kant and Husserl." *Husserl Studies* 13: 19–30.

Petitot, J., F. Valera, B. Pachoud, and J.-M. Roy. eds. 1999. *Naturalizing Phenomenology: Issues in Contemporary Phenomenology and Cognitive Science*. Stanford, CA: Stanford University Press.

Putnam, H. 1983. "Why reason can't be naturalized." *Synthese* 52 (1): 3–23.

Smith, J. & Sullivan, P. eds. 2011. *Transcendental Philosophy and Naturalism*. Oxford, New York: Oxford University Press.

Sokolowski, R. 2000. *Introduction to Phenomenology*. Cambridge: Cambridge University Press.

————. 2008. "Husserl's Discovery of Philosophical Discourse." *Husserl Studies* 24: 167–175.

Zahavi, D., ed. 2012. *The Oxford Handbook of Contemporary Phenomenology*. Oxford: Oxford University Press.

Part I
Transcendental Philosophy

1 Transcendental Life

Steven Crowell

1 METAPHYSICS AND TRANSCENDENTAL PHILOSOPHY

As Hegel knew, philosophical beginnings are hard. One cannot say everything at once, but to say anything is already to take a stand on issues that require justification, to presuppose something that should already have been said and justified. If one could presuppose certain things as given—quantum theory, say, or the validity of the Mosaic law—one could simply deduce the consequences, according to the problem at hand. But even if, for pragmatic reasons, this is how much philosophy is done, it just postpones the day of reckoning. In philosophy, nothing is simply given.

At least, that's the presupposition with which I will begin here, and since it forms the background of my approach to transcendental life, it deserves some preliminary discussion.

Viewed at a sufficiently high level of abstraction, there are two ways to think about the kind of inquiry that philosophy is: the "metaphysical" way and the "transcendental" way. The metaphysical way is characterized by methodological monism. The goal of such thinking is, as Rorty (following Sellars) aptly put it, to see how "things, in the largest sense of the term, hang together, in the largest sense of the term" (1982, 29). The fact that one of those things, the philosopher, is carrying out that very inquiry is an interesting fact that will be woven into the account of things in various ways, but it will not have any *methodological* significance. That is, it will not constrain the resulting account in the sense of providing, in advance, a characterization of the subject matter of the inquiry. Thus, that human beings do philosophy will just be part of human "nature," where the nature of "nature" will be filled in by the metaphysical account itself: in terms of monads or entelechies or *Potenzen* or atoms in the void or whatever. Both Aristotle and Quine are metaphysicians in this sense. In what follows, I will argue that this way of doing philosophy leads to deep ambiguities, taking aim at that naturalism which, in both Continental and analytic philosophy, seems to be the metaphysical consensus of our time.

The "transcendental" way of thinking about the kind of inquiry philosophy is, on the other hand, characterized by methodological pluralism. In this approach, the fact that human beings do philosophy places a methodological constraint on how we must conceive the *topic* of philosophy. Whatever may become the theme of philosophical interest must, on the transcendental view, be understood as the *correlate* of a specific sort of inquiry, an inquiry whose structure, rules, and aims provide necessary conditions without which we cannot so much as identify what it is we are inquiring into. And if there are different sorts of inquiry—everyday, scientific, philosophical—then it will not be possible simply to identify the things at issue in one with the things at issue in the others. That human beings do philosophy, for instance, will have different *essential* features, depending on whether one approaches that fact biologically, psychologically, sociologically, or philosophically. In what follows, I will defend a version of this transcendental way, arguing that a *philosophical* approach to human beings doing philosophy precludes the sort of metaphysical naturalism I mentioned earlier.

Specifically, if there are (philosophical, transcendental) conditions that make inquiry into nature or life possible, then these conditions define what it is to be the inquirer in question; they make up its "nature." And if there are other ways of inquiring into the entity who inquires—for instance, scientific or metaphysical ones—then the relation between their findings and transcendental philosophy will be determinable only through the latter, precisely because metaphysical and scientific inquiries are *inquiries*. It is therefore not possible to treat the inquirer simply as part of a whole—"nature," "life"— that is given, somehow, independently of the inquiry. To put it in the form of a thesis: in philosophy, what it is to be a human being cannot be determined independently of the ability to philosophize, and that means independently of *my own* ability to philosophize, since a general concept, human being, is not available in advance. The transcendental conditions of inquiry thus have some deep connection to the first-person stance, where the latter cannot be defined as part of some greater whole accessible in third-person terms.

This last point leads us to phenomenology, the philosophical movement inaugurated by Edmund Husserl and developed significantly by Martin Heidegger, both of whom I will treat here as paradigms of the transcendental way of thinking. The term 'transcendental life' in my title refers to the determination of the philosophical inquirer that should allow us to understand the connection between philosophical inquiry and science, the inquirer and the human being.

In turning to the phenomenological approach, it will be quite impossible to explicate all the concepts that would bear on this question. I will instead try to bring out its distinctive features by constructing a schema of transcendental phenomenology that can encompass both Husserl and Heidegger, one that holds even in the face of their undeniable differences. To do so, I will consider three related questions: What constitutes the methodological indispensability of the first-person stance (section 2)? How does this determine a phenomenological approach to the polysemic notion of life (section 3)? What response does this allow to positions that reject the transcendental standpoint? Examples of the latter can be found in both Continental and analytic philosophy. In section 4, I will discuss some recent developments in postpositivist philosophy of science that seem to authorize a nonscientistic naturalism as the ultimate context for approaching philosophical questions, and in section 5, I will take up Renaud Barbaras's "biocentric," but still supposedly phenomenological, attempt to determine the concept of life as desire.

2   INTENTIONALITY: THE INDISPENSABILITY OF THE FIRST-PERSON POINT OF VIEW

In what, then, does the methodological priority of the first-person point of view consist? As is well known, Husserl arrived at his transcendental phenomenology through a critique of logical psychologism—the view that the validity of logical laws can be explained by treating them as functions of thinking conceived as a mental process, the sort of thing studied by the natural science of psychology. Though there have been many sophisticated versions of this idea, Husserl's general objection is that any such approach leads to skepticism or relativism, since it entails that logical laws could change. As nothing but high-level empirical generalities, such laws might, through further psychological research, be found not to exist, or else they might evolve into other laws as the species changes over time.[1] In either case, Husserl argues, such a theory undermines its own coherence as a theory, since its status as scientific knowledge depends not only on individual propositions but also on the explanatory form in which those propositions stand toward one another, a form that presupposes the validity of logical laws. In contrast to those like Thomas Nagel (1997, 55–76)—or, in Husserl's time, Paul Natorp—who conclude from this that no philosophical clarification of logical validity is possible, Husserl proposed that the "holding" (*Geltung*) of logical laws can be clarified if one reflects phenomenologically on mental processes of thinking; that is, if one takes the first-person experience of thinking and reasoning as the starting point for an elucidation of logic under the normative perspective of claims to *truth*.

To Natorp, Husserl's position here seemed psychologistic, but Husserl insisted that reflection on the field of mental processes could yield *necessities*. For instance, to judge that "the rose bush on my porch has red blossoms" may, in a given empirical case, be nothing more than to formulate some words in a language, to think "signitively" and thus emptily about something about which I have no direct knowledge. However, when considered in what Husserl calls its "essence" as a judgment, such a mental process *normatively* entails a possible fulfillment—one that (in this case) would take place in direct perception of the rose bush. Thus, while there is no necessary empirical connection between the signitive mental process and some perceptual mental process that might or might not occur subsequently in my stream

of consciousness, there is nevertheless a necessary connection of *meaning*—
a normative law—that links such signitive processes to perceptual ones.[2]
When grasped as governed by the norm of truth, an act of thinking is, as
Husserl puts it, "teleologically" oriented toward what fulfills it, and it is
only this normative aspect that allows such a signitive act to fail—that is, to
be incorrect. Such normative assessment would be unintelligible if thinking
were considered solely as an empirically occurring mental process.

This is the basic idea behind Husserl's notion of intentionality or "intentional content," and from it he develops a universal transcendental phenomenology of consciousness. For it is a small step from the idea that signitive
acts (such as thinking) have a sense that is teleologically oriented toward
fulfillment to the idea that *all* conscious acts can be understood in this way.
Consider perception, for instance. When I perceive that the rose bush on my
porch has red blossoms, my perception has a certain content: it is *about* the
rose bush, not in some general way but precisely *as* having red blossoms—
"under a certain description" we might say, though no act of description
need be involved. Though only part of the bush is directly visible to me, the
perceptual content presents the bush as a whole. Such content is thus norm
governed in a very specific way: it can fail. What it purports to present in
that way can prove not to be so. A closer look can show that it is not a *real*
rose bush (but a hallucination, or plastic), or that it is not determined as
it seemed (its blossoms are brown). What makes this possible belongs to
the phenomenological essence of perception, namely, that it is teleologically
oriented toward further acts of perception that would either fulfill (confirm)
its content or alter or destroy (disconfirm) it. This is not a contingent fact; it
constitutes what it is to *be* perceptual content. Considered first-personally,
any perceptual content is oriented normatively toward certain determinate
possibilities of success or failure, and if that is so, then there are not merely
empirical regularities governing first-person experience but normative necessities. I cannot have the perceptual experience as of a rose bush without
being in some sense beholden to the norms that establish what subsequent
experience must be like if the thing actually is a rose bush.

Husserl made this point the basis of his transcendental phenomenology.
As he put it in his programmatic essay of 1911, "Philosophy as Rigorous
Science," philosophy has a "critical" orientation toward experience; it is not
concerned with questions of fact but with questions of *possibility*: "How
can experience as consciousness give or contact an object? How can experiences be mutually *legitimated* or *corrected* by means of each other, and
not merely replace each other?" (1965, 87; Hua 25, 14). That mental processes have this feature is indisputable, as these examples show. Nor can
the answer to such questions be supplied by third-person theories—such
as a causal theory of reference or reliabilism—since the confirmation takes
place *within* experience. It must therefore belong to the essence of what
consciousness *is*. Later in the same essay, Husserl makes this point in a vivid
way: "Everything psychical [is . . .] ordered in an overall connection, in a

'monadic' unity of consciousness, a unity that in itself has nothing a\
do with nature, with space and time or substantiality and causality, b\
its thoroughly peculiar 'forms'" (1965, 107–108; Hua 25, 30).[3] A ps\
logical inquiry treats consciousness in its extrinsic relation to nature, t̶ ̶ ̶g̶\
mental processes as empirical occurrences, but another ("critical") point of
view is possible because consciousness is itself normatively ordered, thanks
to the "peculiar forms" that govern intentional content. Phenomenological
philosophy, then, thematizes consciousness as the locus of the constitution
of that content, that is, meaning (*Sinn*).

The distinctive character of the transcendental standpoint in phenomenology derives from this notion of meaning.

First, by showing how anything like confirmation and disconfirmation is
possible in experience—how there can be normative relations between entities of whatever sort—phenomenological reflection on meaning articulates
the validity conditions of all other inquiries. In order to express this point
methodologically, Husserl invokes the *epoché:* the "bracketing" of any
assumptions derived from other inquiries, whether scientific or everyday; the
refusal to assume their findings as the basis for philosophical constructions.

Second, the focus on meaning exemplifies the transcendental thesis that
entities can be considered only as correlates of the inquiries (or experiences)
in which they are given. As Husserl puts it: "In a certain way [. . .] we can say
that all real unities are 'unities of meaning'"—for instance, "reality and world
are names here precisely for certain valid unities of meaning [. . .] related to
certain concatenations of absolute, of pure consciousness" (1983, 128–9;
Hua 3, 134). If I can experience or inquire into it, it is there for me *as*
something, and I can reflect on the normative "forms" that constitute it precisely as the thing it is. In order to express this point methodologically, Husserl invokes the transcendental-phenomenological reduction, which focuses
reflection not on consciousness in the sense of "inner experience," nor on its
objects as things in the world, but precisely on the *correlation* in which the
phenomenon of meaning, the as-structure of experience, becomes salient.

Taken together, these features of transcendental phenomenology express
the methodological priority of the first-person point of view. What meaning
"is" shows up only for an inquirer who takes his or her own experience in
its intentional structure as the field of inquiry. And since meaning in this
sense is presupposed in all other inquiries as their enabling condition, it
cannot be directly identified with the entities thematized in those inquiries.
In particular, it cannot be identified with a mental entity or representation;
but neither can it be identified with a process in the brain, a social structure,
or language. Thus, despite its methodological commitment to first-person
experience, phenomenology is nothing subjective. There is no meaning without consciousness and its teleological correlations, but neither is there meaning without things in the world, since to speak of meaning is just to speak
of that very teleology in its function of disclosing what it is *to be* a thing
of such and such a sort, given in such and such a way. The transcendental

subject—the one who inquires in this way—is thus defined in terms of its disclosure ("constitution") of a world in which it too is somehow involved.

But this raises a significant question: Is Husserl's conception of consciousness—*phenomenal* consciousness—sufficient to characterize such a subject, such an inquirer? Heidegger, for instance, argued that it is inconceivable that phenomenal consciousness alone could possess the normative teleology Husserl attributed to it. On my reading, Heidegger accepted the main tenets of Husserl's transcendental turn: the methodological primacy of the first-person stance; the reduction to meaning (which he called "being"); and the corresponding insistence on correlation (in his language: no entity without an "understanding of its being").[4] But Heidegger made a crucial discovery about the kind of inquirer capable of experiencing teleological or normative relations of meaning: in addition to being conscious, such an inquirer must be *an issue* for itself. *Dasein*—Heidegger's name for the inquirer from the transcendental point of view—is "a being in whose very being that being is an *issue*" (1962, 32; GA 2, 16). In other words, for intentional *content* to be assessable in terms of success or failure, the "entity which is intentional" (Heidegger 1985a, 110; GA 20, 152) must, in being at all, be able to assess *itself* in that way. *Being*-a-self is thus a "success term." Consciousness simply is or is not; *Dasein*, in contrast, can succeed or fail at being itself. Let us briefly look at what this determination of the transcendental subject adds to Husserl's approach to meaning.

Heidegger's account of intentionality begins not with perception or judgment but with the way things show up for us in our everyday practical dealings with them. This has led some to claim that Heidegger substitutes the primacy of practice for Husserl's alleged emphasis on "theoretical" experience.[5] But Heidegger is quite clear that this is not the point. In *Metaphysical Foundations of Logic*, he writes that "one cannot pack transcendence [his term for the transcendental subject] into an intuition"—as Husserl apparently did in his conception of transcendental reflection—but "even less can it be packed into a practical comportment" (1984, 183; GA 26, 235). Rather, starting with practical comportment serves the purpose of revealing a condition on the content of experience that precedes both theory and practice, namely, existential death, a condition of the transcendental subject that enables it to disclose things not merely in accord with norms but *in light* of them. Intentional content, for Heidegger, depends on a being who is able to grasp the possible *as* possible, the normative *as* normative, measure *as* measure. This calls for a bit of explanation.

In my practical dealings with them, things show up as useful in various ways, and this instrumentality constitutes what they *are*. For instance, a hammer is good for driving nails, which in turn are good for joining boards, which in turn are good for constructing frames, and so on. The point of putting things this way is to emphasize *that* things show up as meaningful and that they do so *because* they are apprehended in light of norms. But what is the source of this normative ordering? It does not adhere to the things themselves considered in isolation; rather, it depends on what Heidegger calls the "work" to be done: because I am making a birdhouse, things show up as hammers, nails, slats—that is, as appropriate for the job.[6] If I were making a real house, this tiny little hammer and these tiny little nails that are perfect for the birdhouse would not be useful at all, they would not be "good for" the job; they would fail at being what they are supposed to be.

But even the work to be done does not *sufficiently* determine the kind of normativity that informs experience of something as an implement in this sense. Hammers and nails of a certain sort are appropriate for making a birdhouse because making one can itself be done well or badly—that is, because there can be good and bad birdhouses. But suppose I use a sledgehammer to drive a bunch of very large nails into some random pieces of wood in a shape that resembles a very ugly and drafty birdhouse. Have I failed in making a birdhouse or succeeded in making a piece of sculpture? Nothing in what I've produced can help us decide this. The only thing that decides what I'm *making* is what I am *trying* to make, and this in turn depends on what I am trying *to be*. As Heidegger puts it, the "totality of involvements" (the normative relational whole that includes the implements and the work being done) "itself goes back to a 'towards-which' in which there is *no* further involvement" (no further relation to other things that would determine what is good for what). Rather, it goes back to a "for-the-sake-of-which," which "always pertains to the being of *Dasein,* for which, in its being, that very being is essentially an *issue*" (1962, 116–117; GA 2, 113). What does all this mean?

What decides whether what I've produced is a bad birdhouse or a good sculpture is the fact that I am doing it either for the sake of being a carpenter or for the sake of being an artist; whether I am *trying to be* one or the other. And what I am trying to be does not depend on other entities in the world but only, as Heidegger puts it, on what is *at issue* in what I am doing. Only because being one or the other matters to me, is at stake for me, can things present themselves as good for this or that; and only thus can they "be" what they are. What it is or means to be a hammer or nails or whatever ultimately turns on relations of this kind; that is, on there being some entity in the world for whom its own being is *normatively* at stake. Because I can succeed or fail at being a carpenter or an artist, things can succeed or fail at being what they are.

This analysis of course raises many questions—for instance, about the relation between transcendental phenomenology and a certain "idealism"— but we cannot stop to consider them here. Rather, we must note that in Heidegger's phenomenology, the point is fully universal. It might appear that the analysis holds only for tools and other artefacts that are made for a purpose by human hands. Can it be said that things in general—things of nature, for instance—can succeed or fail at being what they are only because *Dasein* can succeed or fail at being this or that? To answer "yes" is precisely to acknowledge Heidegger's commitment to the transcendental way in philosophy, namely, the insistence that what things are—their meaning, the "truth" of their being—cannot be determined apart from a normative framework that allows them to show up as this or that *specific* thing. We shall consider some implications of this in the next section, but for now we simply note that *if* we experience something as something at all—whether as an event or mystery, a mere thing, a quark, a living thing or whatever—then it is thanks to a normative context that must go back to something I am trying to *be,* some way in which I—father, teacher, penitent, physicist, artist—am engaged with the stakes of success or failure, something in which it matters to me whether I do it well or badly. Only this mattering—what John Haugeland (1998) calls my being "beholden" to norms, my "commitment" to them—allows things to show up in ways that are either "acceptable" or "unacceptable," thus introducing into experience the very possibility of the kind of teleological orientation toward confirmation or disconfirmation upon which Husserl's account of intentionality is based.

But one further aspect must be addressed if we are to see how all this bears on the question of transcendental life. For one might object that Heidegger's is not a transcendental position at all, since the norms that govern trying to be a father, a physicist, a teacher, and so on are social facts, and thus that meaning is here reduced to something factual (and perhaps ultimately natural). But while it is true that such norms are indeed social—as Heidegger puts it, success or failure at being something (father, teacher, friend) cannot be divorced entirely from what "one" does—I myself am not identical to any of these roles, or "practical identities."[7] The deepest point about "self" being a success term lies in the fact that I am such that I can still *be* without being *anything*. This ultimately explains the indispensability of the first-person stance and is Heidegger's deepest contribution to the analysis of meaning.

Here I can only sketch the point.[8] That I can be without being anything is attested in the unitary phenomenon that Heidegger considers under the separate headings of *Angst,* death, and conscience. The upshot is that in anxiety, I confront myself as *not* beholden to any of the norms and practices that normally claim me. Affectively, nothing matters to me; I cannot gear into the world through my practical identities, and for this reason the world and things in the world lose all significance. The way I understand myself in such a situation—my ultimate "for-the-sake-of-which"—is what Heidegger calls existential death: not the demise of my organism but the "possibility of no longer being able-to-be-there" (1962, 294; GA 2, 333), the possibility of *being* without being *able*-to-be (*Seinkönnen*) *anything*. This sense of what it is for me to "be"—that for-the-sake-of-which I am in existential death—is articulated, in what Heidegger calls "conscience," as "guilt," which he glosses as "having to take over being-a-ground" (1962, 330; GA 2, 377). Thus when all my practical identities have fallen away, I still exist for-the-sake-of something at which I can succeed or fail: I am still *responsible* for *being*-a-ground. What this means, I suggest, is that I am called to take over my situation (thrownness) *in light of* what is best, that is, in light of normative *measure*. In *Vom Wesen des Grundes*, Heidegger makes this point explicit by referring to Plato's idea of the Good: "the essence of the *agathon* lies in its sovereignty over itself [. . .] as the for the sake of . . ." (1998b, 124; GA 9, 161). To be for-the-sake-of something at all is to be oriented toward a normative distinction between what merely is and what is best, to be *responsible* for that distinction.

What is ultimately at stake for *Dasein*, then, is a distinction between inauthentically inhabiting a practical identity by trying to live up to its norms as sheer "givens" (what "one" does) or else authentically trying to be what one is by acknowledging that in my commitment to those norms, I am responsible for their normative *force*. What it means to be a father or a friend is not something I merely try to conform to; it is at *issue,* in question, in what I do. In this way, as Haugeland (2000) has convincingly shown, I not only "let" things "be" (show up as) this or that; I am also open to the possibility that things can show up that are deemed "impossible" according to the prevailing norms in light of which I am acting, thus requiring me to give up or radically modify those very norms. The possibility of existential death is thus also the possibility of objectivity—that is, of distinguishing between the way things show themselves and the way things are, *despite* the fact that things can show up *as* they are only as the correlates of specific practices, inquiries, and other normative frameworks.

To summarize the claims I have argued for in this section: Heidegger advances over Husserl not by abandoning transcendental phenomenology but by showing that the normativity inherent in the teleological ordering of consciousness cannot derive from consciousness alone. As we shall see, the theme of "transcendental life" takes on importance for Husserl as he too moves away from a focus on phenomenal consciousness toward a transcendental subject that is embodied, practical, and social. But Heidegger goes further: the transcendentally determined subject must be characterized as intrinsically suspended between success and failure, *at issue* in everything it does. Intentional content is possible only for a being defined not by reason but by care (*Sorge*).

But aren't all living beings—or at any rate, all the higher ones—defined in this way? Don't all living beings care about their own being, concerned as they are with survival? And doesn't that concern carry over to concern for the success or failure of the construction of their nests, the raising of their offspring, and other such things? Isn't it clear that the teleological structures of consciousness derive from life itself? Shouldn't we then fold Heidegger's arcane existential phenomenology back into something much more familiar—a "philosophy of life"—thereby avoiding dubious transcendental theories and joining forces with the emerging metaphysical consensus that life and nature provide the horizon for understanding everything, including the inquiries into life and nature that Husserl held to be in need of transcendental-phenomenological clarification? It is time to take up our second guiding question. How is the polysemic concept of life to be approached phenomenologically?

3   DETERMINING LIFE TRANSCENDENTALLY

This question is all the more pressing since both Husserl and the early Heidegger sometimes adopt the term 'life' to characterize the transcendental subject itself. This is understandable since, in contrast to the Kantian idea of the transcendental subject as a *formal* "unity of apperception," phenomenology attains its notion of self or subject through nonformal reflection on consciousness (or being-in-the-world), on experience as it is lived. But if, as we have argued, transcendental phenomenology defines the subject wholly in terms of the conditions necessary for the constitution of meaning, what condition does the term 'life' add to that definition? What aspect, among all the candidates in the term's semantic field, comes into play when Husserl describes transcendentally reduced consciousness as transcendental *life?*[9]

In the *Crisis,* for instance, Husserl characterizes the distinction between transcendental philosophy and all other inquiry—everyday, scientific, metaphysical—by invoking Helmholtz's image of the "life of the plane," where two-dimensional creatures lead their lives entirely unaware of the third dimension that sustains them, and the "life of depth," which, on this image, is the transcendental consciousness that constitutes or discloses the meaning of what is experienced on the "plane" (1970a, 118–121; Hua 6, 120–123). To reflect phenomenologically on this dimension is to enjoy "a completely different sort of waking life" from the one in which I do not attend to the necessary correlation between consciousness and its objects. It is to become cognizant of "the universal accomplishing life in which the world comes to be as existing for us" (1970a, 145; Hua 6, 148). But what does the term 'life' add here to the transcendental determination of consciousness as a teleological unity? Does it entail that such consciousness must be an organism? Have a certain kind of DNA? Be part of nature conceived as a nexus of substances in space and time closed under causal laws? Be historical? If we are to avoid Rickert's judgment that life is "the concept for what lacks a concept," we must admit that the concept of life is extraordinarily vague (or polysemic)—precisely the sort of meaning that is supposed to be clarified phenomenologically by returning to its (no doubt complex) sources in the constitutive achievements of transcendental consciousness.

Husserl is quite clear that the "life" at issue here cannot be understood as though consciousness were "the human soul." Transcendental life is not defined by starting with consciousness as a part of the concrete *natural* unity, human being, since rejection of this idea is the crux of Husserl's solution to the "paradox of human subjectivity." Were life understood as human subjectivity, then the concept of transcendental life would entail that "the subjective part of the world swallows up, so to speak, the whole world and thus itself too. What an absurdity!" (1970a, 180; Hua 6, 183). If one sticks rigorously to the transcendental perspective, on the contrary, in which "human being" is a constituted meaning, then in "the transcendental subjects, i.e., those *functioning* in the constitution of the world," "nothing human is to be found, neither soul nor psychic life nor real psychophysical human beings" (1970a, 183; Hua 6, 187). This claim is nothing but a paradoxical way of expressing our thesis: a consistent transcendental phenomenology will not presuppose some conception of human being but will define the (transcendental) subject exclusively in terms of what shows itself as necessary for the constitution of meaning. Because this thesis introduces no metaphysical distinction, however, it might be argued that because the human inquirer is alive, the transcendental subject must also be alive. But this just allows the question to re-emerge: whence comes this determination, "life," and what does it add to our understanding?

Before addressing this point specifically, it should be noted that the same issue arises in Heidegger's earliest texts, and his way of handling it—more consistent than Husserl's—is instructive.

Much has been made of the fact that prior to writing *Being and Time*, Heidegger uses the term 'factic life' to distinguish the topic of his phenomenology from Husserl's reflection on consciousness. It is tempting to tell the following story about this: Heidegger dismisses Husserl's transcendental project, and with it its paradoxes, in favor of a metaphysical (in our sense) appeal to a simply "given" concept of life, that is, one that eludes any methodological preformation.[10] What is significant about such factic life is that it generates categories whose sense derives from living itself. The task of philosophy—an accomplishment of factic life—is to identify the categories in which life expresses *itself,* "comes to itself" interpretively: categories are "im Leben selbst am Leben" (1985b, 88). Life also accomplishes *science* through a kind of objectification, but since this differs from the (nonobjectifying) way in which life understands itself, philosophy cannot be the sort of "theoretical" inquiry that science is (Heidegger 1987, 84–94). Instead it is a (rather obscurely characterized) "hermeneutic intuition" that seeks to illuminate life from within by attending to the way it understands itself in all its other accomplishments (Heidegger 1987, 117). A closer look at Heidegger's approach to life here, however, reveals that the concept plays *no* role that could mark a break with the transcendental conception of phenomenology defended by Husserl.[11]

First, it might be expected that if Heidegger were adopting a nontranscendental (metaphysical) position, he would join forces with then-current "philosophical anthropology,"[12] which, drawing upon the life-sciences, tries to construct a speculative account of "man's place in nature" (Scheler), or to define man's "ex-centric positionality" (Plessner) *vis-à-vis* all other life-forms. But Heidegger is not drawn to this sort of project, since it starts with the positive sciences and so remains in the grip of the theoretical attitude, which, in its very "objectification" of life, misses life's defining character. For Heidegger, Husserl's objection to naturalism does not go far enough; the real problem, according to Heidegger, is the "general dominance of the *theoretical*" itself (1987, 87). The life sciences, no matter how construed, do not provide the basic categories for understanding life. In this respect,

Heidegger embraces *Lebensphilosophie* in a qualified way: though the concept of life is "confused" (*Verschwommen*) and "ambiguous" (*Vieldeutig*), the genuine tendency of philosophers like Nietzsche, Dilthey, and Bergson is correct (1985b, 80).[13] So how, then, does Heidegger propose to disambiguate the notion?

According to Heidegger, a phenomenological approach to life seeks the categories that render it intelligible, and the primary category that captures the oriented directedness of the "movement" of life is "world." What characterizes the specifically philosophical category of life is its *worldly* character. "World" here does not mean nature or cosmos; rather, it belongs to life itself, a thesis that Heidegger spells out in terms of a correlation between two further categories: care (*Sorge*) and significance (*Bedeutsamkeit*). Care is the "relational sense" (roughly, the "subjective" or noetic correlate) of life, and significance is its "content-sense" (roughly, the "objective" or noematic correlate; 1985b, 90ff.). When factic life grasps its own life in its everyday dealings, it is not as a biological kind but as concerned, troubled, caring about things in the world. Nor are the categories by which it pretheoretically grasps its world drawn from science; rather, they formally indicate the normative context of first-person experience: *significance*. But care and significance are the very terms in which Heidegger defines *Dasein* and world in *Being and Time*. Thus *conceptually* 'life' adds nothing to the transcendental approach Heidegger embraces explicitly in that later text.[14]

Once Heidegger defines *Dasein* in a strictly transcendental way as that being in whose being that very being is an issue for it, he drops the term 'life' altogether, and it never reappears in a philosophically significant role any of his subsequent writings. In *Being and Time*, Heidegger is adamant that the "analytic of *Dasein*" must be distinguished from all "biology, anthropology, and psychology"—that is, from any science of life. There is a connection between philosophy and life—the expression "philosophy of life" says "about as much as 'the botany of plants'"—but one cannot begin with the notion of life, since in so doing "'life' itself as a kind of being does not become ontologically a problem" (Heidegger 1962, 72; GA 2, 62). And, more generally, he connects "life" to "nature" and argues that, from the transcendental point of view, "the 'nature' by which we are 'surrounded' is [. . .] an entity within-the-world" (Heidegger 1962, 254; GA 2, 280) whose meaning thus always presupposes *Dasein*'s capacity to disclose the world through its normative commitments.[15]

Consideration of both Husserl and Heidegger thus leads to the following conclusion: Whatever 'life' means in the phrase 'transcendental life' must be determined from within the transcendental point of view itself.[16] It cannot be borrowed from any of the polysemic uses one finds in the natural attitude or the "life of the plane"—whether from biology or cybernetics, or from ordinary, poetical, or metaphysical (e.g., Aristotelian) conceptions of life and nature. *Transcendental* life will then be the ultimate basis upon which other notions of life can be determined. But while Heidegger was consistent

on this point, Husserl's approach involves an ambiguity that some later phenomenological projects have tried to exploit in an effort to circumvent the
transcendental altogether. Let us consider this ambiguity briefly.

Husserl clearly saw that most—if not all—the meanings that supported
the "life of the plane" refer to an *embodied* consciousness. For instance, to
be perceptually aware of my rose bush as such is to be aware of the side that
is not currently visible as that which *would be* visible were I to exercise my
ability to move around it to get a better look. This normative condition is
not a thought; *thinking* that I could move around to the back presupposes
the very meaning in question. It is an ability that I must be able to exercise.
In the "life of the plane," we will say that this ability belongs to my body,
but how is "body" understood here? On the one hand, we may think of
it ("theoretically") as what Husserl calls *Körper*—a physical thing among
others in nature. On the other hand, we may think of it as what Husserl
calls the "animate organism," the body taken as "ensouled," as "living."[17]
This too belongs to nature: lizards and cats, as well as human beings, are
animate organisms. But from the transcendental point of view, both of these
conceptions involve presuppositions that go beyond what is necessarily
entailed by the meaning-constituting ability that I, as transcendental subject, exercise. As Husserl demonstrates in *Ideas II,* both physical body and
animate organism are themselves constituted meanings. The body that is
involved in constitution, in contrast, is understood exclusively in terms of that
meaning-constituting ability itself. Husserl's term for the body in this sense
is '*Leib*' (lived body), the body as experienced in transcendentally reduced
first-person experience.[18]

This notion of the body is supremely important in Husserl's phenomenology, serving as the basis for his account of intersubjectivity and thus
the whole realm of socio-cultural meaning. But it raises questions about the
concept of transcendental life. To what extent does embodiment in this sense
authorize treating life as something like the horizon of the transcendental
project, something the latter presupposes but cannot get "back behind"?
Alternatively, if we say that the transcendental subject is embodied, social,
and practical, haven't we already located it within a conceptual field that
includes animals? Will this not entail that *animality* itself is a transcendental
condition on meaning?

The answer—as Heidegger recognized—must be no. One cannot infer
from the analysis of *Leib* that lizards or cats are indeed "embodied." One
cannot infer that they are *not* embodied either; rather, the whole question of
what it means to be embodied now takes on the contours of the distinction
between the life of the plane and the life of depth.[19] Cats and lizards show up
as animate organisms, and I too, as a human being, show up as an animate
organism. But this provides no grounds for asserting that any of us show
up as transcendentally constituting *Leib*, since *Leib* is defined in *functional*
terms as a necessary condition on a kind of normatively structured meaning. And, as Heidegger's analysis of existential death shows, such meaning

is possible only for a being who is oriented toward measure *as measure* and thus can succeed or fail at being a self. Thus embodiment—in the sense of *Leib* as a transcendentally constitutive condition—can provide no reason to think that the transcendental project must itself be understood within the horizon of a "metaphysics" of life. But how, then, are we to think about life phenomenologically?

If we adhere to the thesis that meaning can only be explicated from the transcendental standpoint, then there are two consistent approaches to take toward the polysemic notion of life, one of which leads inevitably to the other. The first we may call the "regional" approach and the second the "privative" approach. The first is found already in Kant. Just as Kant determined the root cognitive meaning of "nature" by uncovering the *a priori* principles presupposed in Newtonian physics, so one might turn to the life sciences to seek out the theoretical concepts and laws that define their object-field, life. Phenomenological analysis would then show how such concepts gain their validity. Both Husserl and Heidegger call this the project of "regional ontology."[20] The various sciences presuppose a certain meaning (or "regional essence") that defines what they take their object of study to be. Such meanings are not thematic objects of scientific inquiry but belong to what Kuhn would call the "paradigm" of the science in question. Phenomenology reflects on these mostly tacit "conceptual" connections, clarifying the logical and intentional implications that are at stake in their employment—as when, in *Ideas II*, Husserl reflects on the constitution of the domain of "material nature" (i.e., the regional ontology of physics). In this way, phenomenology spells out the normative commitments of the science in question.

A similar strategy can be pursued in less theoretically defined areas of experience as well. When we speak of the "life" of an accountant, for instance, we mean to pick out what normatively distinguishes this practice and role from others, and perhaps make a value judgment about its relative regimentation in contrast to other such roles.[21] And we can reflect on the way that "life" and "living" are understood in various cultures, or how "nature" is understood in different historical periods. All that is necessary for such regional ontologies is a sufficiently rich descriptive characterization of the beliefs and practices in which such meanings are embedded. This sort of broadly construed regional approach simply expresses the phenomenological commitment to correlation: meaningful reference—that is, identification of something as "alive" or as "natural"—always involves a context of practices and discourses whose normative forms make such reference possible.

In the case of the term 'life,' however, the regional approach raises an issue that cannot be addressed by its means, thus leading necessarily to the *privative* approach. Consider the case of a regional ontology of the science of biology. Unless it is a biology whose paradigm involves the idea that the biological can ultimately be reduced to physics and chemistry, its way of identifying its proper object—as life or organism—will invoke *teleological* concepts and explanations. But where does one find the phenomenological ground for this sort of meaning? Heidegger argued that a judgment that something is there "in-order-to" do something—that is, is "good for something"—can have a determinate meaning only if grounded in an entity that is intrinsically responsive to norms *as norms*. Only such a being is capable of the first-person responsibility for normative force upon which *definite* reference to something as something depends. But this suggests that observation of animate organisms cannot provide the ground for the teleological judgments that pervade the biological sciences. Rather, the "paradigm" or regional ontology of a biology that invokes teleological explanations must ultimately make reference to my own experience, my own transcendental life as a being for whom, in its being, that being is essentially an issue.

This is the essence of the privative approach: I can only think of phenomena of *non*transcendental life as privations (or perhaps better: modifications) of my own transcendentally determined life. I can employ teleological modes of explanation in understanding nonhuman animals *not* because I recognize that they and I share an ontological region, "life," but because I constitute them as possessing abilities that I possess, but privatively or in modified form—even if, objectively, I can know that they also possess certain abilities (sonar navigation, for instance) that I do not. Both Husserl and Heidegger employ this privative strategy. When reflecting on the lifeworld, for instance, Husserl argues that animals present themselves as "modifications [*Abwandlungen*] of my fully human being, which serves as a norm" (2008, 478). In order to grasp the "world" they inhabit, we start "from the primordial mode [*Urmodus*] 'human being'" and work "in an imperfect way, by means of intentional modifications," to an understanding of how their experiences and ours go to make up "the one world" (2008, 510). Husserl's remark entails that we *experience* the life around us in this privative way, that "animality" has *necessary connections of meaning* to what we experience ourselves as being. And if that is true, then any account that starts with phenomena of life in the hope of avoiding the supposed subjectivism of transcendental phenomenology will simply reflect, unknowingly, this privative constitution. It is built into the meaning of our experience.

The privative approach is clearly evident in Heidegger's work. In *Being and Time*, he writes that "[l]ife must be understood as a kind of being to which there belongs a being-in-the-world. Only if this kind of being is oriented in a privative way to *Dasein*, can we fix its character ontologically" (1962, 290; GA 2, 328). This approach led him, in 1930, to conceive animal life not as worldless but "world-poor" (Heidegger 1995, 185ff; GA 29/30, 273ff). Clearly, animals are not mere things—we experience them as "instinctively" responding to what we could call normative distinctions, acting in accord with something like a teleology—but we have no ground for thinking that these norms are *at stake in* their experience, and without that, a necessary condition for "world" is missing. Indeed, Heidegger argues that despite our embodiment, there is an "abyss" between us and animals: because of our orientation toward measure *as measure,* we are closer to the "divinities" than to the beasts (Heidegger 1998a, 248; GA 9, 326). Examples could be multiplied. Whether all this adds up to an objectionable humanism, as has been alleged,[22] cannot be decided here, but it is clear that Heidegger offers no approach to the phenomenon of life beyond the regional and the privative.

Thus we are at the point at which we must address our third leading question: What response can transcendental phenomenology offer to positions that reject transcendentalism and treat life metaphysically as the *unhintergehbar* horizon of all inquiry? One example of such a position is found in the "new" (nonphysicalistic) naturalism that is beginning to emerge from work in postpositivist history and philosophy of science.[23] My argument in the following section will be that even when it wants to reject scientism, postpositivism can determine its concepts of nature and life only by way of a regional-ontological or else a privative approach. A second example comes from phenomenology itself, in which the previously discussed move toward a "concretization" of the transcendental subject appears to authorize a similar "new" naturalism. In section 5, I will take up one such position, the "biocentrism" of Renaud Barbaras. Here too I will argue that the intended move beyond transcendental phenomenology is illusory: either it is no longer phenomenological, or else it fails to account for crucial features of the "life" that is ours.

4 TRANSCENDENTAL CRITICISM OF THE NEW POSTPOSITIVIST NATURALISM

With transcendental philosophy under suspicion—either as subjectivism or humanism—many philosophers have sought a path back to an encompassing context, nature, that would not succumb to the critique of naturalism that motivated both transcendental phenomenology and earlier analytic philosophy to do justice to what seemed distinctive about "conceptual" or normative claims—namely, their apparent irreducibility to matters of fact. In phenomenology, the touchstone for many of these efforts is Merleau-Ponty, who, in the *Phenomenology of Perception*, drew on Husserl's analysis of *Leib* to suggest a more complicated picture of how transcendental constitution differs from both standard rationalist and empiricist accounts of experience. In his late work, *The Visible and the Invisible*, however, he took the body's "chiasmic" structure to indicate a fundamental metaphysical reality, the "flesh of the world." Nature as such is a kind of *apeiron* (or "brute meaning")—the source of what comes to be abstractly considered as embodiment on the one hand and mental functioning, consciousness, on the other.

A similar desire to situate human rationality and normativity within the context of a "nature" that is understood as prior to any rigid opposition between fact and value, is and ought, can be found in some of the work being done in postpositivist philosophy of science. In a recent paper that nicely presents some of the issues, John Zammito argues that since postpositivism has "demonstrated convincingly that there are no 'facts' apart from theoretical frames and evaluative standards constructing them," the door is open to reconsidering "the idea of a normative naturalism"—that is, the idea that human nature is part of nature, and that there should be no call, philosophically, to step outside that context in an effort to understand rationality and normativity.[24] Such naturalism is thus a "refusal to take recourse to 'first philosophy' or *a priori* principles" (forthcoming, 9). But even if we refuse to adopt "some absolute transcendental norm" (forthcoming, 28), such naturalism must still provide a *positive* characterization of "nature" if, as Zammito recommends, we are to embrace "the idea that nature can be [. . .] normative for humans" (forthcoming, 27). So how does postpositivism understand "nature"?

Postpositivism gets its name by rejecting the positivist idea that the success of modern natural science can best be understood by rationally reconstructing scientific discourse into a purely factual language that exhibits strict logical entailments. The positivist program, oriented toward physics, thus shared Husserl's picture of nature as a value-free realm of facts closed under causal law. For postpositivism, however, this picture merely reflects the modern scientistic worldview, Weber's "disenchanted" nature from which one can expect no normative guidance. Against such scientism, philosophers such as Hilary Putnam and Thomas Kuhn argue that the concept of a pure fact is illusory. Facts are established only within a holistic context of discourses, practices, and theories from which no purely factual component can be distilled, and here postpositivism makes contact with transcendental phenomenology. Even perceptually, I can only grasp the *fact* "that the rose bush is in bloom" if I and the bush are involved in a norm-governed context in which subsequent experiences can be assessed as either confirming or disconfirming my perceptual intentional content. Thus both phenomenology and postpositivism reject the positivist idea of rational reconstruction of (knowledge of) nature on the basis of purely logical principles. However, in its stance toward normativity, postpositivism does not adopt phenomenology's first-person point of view. What stance does it adopt, then, in order to theorize a concept of nature that can sustain a "naturalist normativity" (forthcoming, 18)? Since, as Zammito (following William Rehg) argues, the rationality of science itself—its "criteria of judgment"—"*emerge immanently* in the discourse and practice of actual science" (forthcoming, 15), it seems plausible to think that the concept of nature in question will be gleaned from examining the discourses and practices of science itself.

But what do such sciences tell us? Is there really a scientific concept of nature other than the physicist's realm of entities closed under causal law? The postpositivist critique of the constructivist approach to the rationality of scientific knowledge goes hand in hand with a turn from physics toward biology as the paradigm of knowledge of nature (Zammito 2004). Perhaps the evolutionary and teleological thinking characteristic of biology has the resources—*independent* of the concept of first-person responsibility for the normative upon which phenomenological analysis of meaning insists—to clarify how norms belong to nature, thereby enabling the sort of "critically informed understanding of human nature and the natural world" (forthcoming, 23) that a normative naturalism would require. Zammito is sympathetic to something like this idea—which, as a philosophical project, clearly represents a version of the "regional-ontological" approach to determining what "nature" means—but, as his discussion of evolutionary ethics shows, he is rightly uncomfortable with its lingering scientism.

Evolutionary ethics draws directly on the biological sciences in its account of normativity and is, in this regard, "the straightforward extension of natural science to encompass human life as part of nature."[25] But Zammito does not believe that this appeal to natural science will do. Evolutionary biology purports to explain the causes that propel human conduct, thus yielding something like "imperatives" embedded in our genetic history. It argues, for example, that if altruistic desires are found to be an important human genetic inheritance such that "most human beings have deep and abiding interests in the interests of others," then "the existence of such distinctive desires *must* [my emphasis] inform our views about what kinds of lives we should seek for ourselves and others" (forthcoming, 25). But since we also seem to have a genetically deep and abiding interest in killing and cheating one another, it is hard to see why one of these "interests" should entail anything *imperative* for how to live. "Nature" in this scientifically determinable sense does provide a context for investigating human life, but it hardly seems to provide a "naturalist normativity." At best it provides the raw materials for the sort of responsibility for norms that a phenomenological approach to transcendental life insists is basic. From the phenomenological point of view, then, this concept of nature gains any cognitive authority it might possess from the science itself, and its extrapolation to ethics depends on whether *in fact,* as E. O. Wilson argues, "human life is primarily the result of evolution and that there is no purpose to human life beyond the 'imperatives' our genetic history provides" (Zammito forthcoming, 24–25). But such a view is really no different from the "disenchanted" nature of Max Weber and positivism: the normative is entirely absent, and the term 'imperative' is here used in a Pickwickian sense.

Zammito challenges such scientism. He joins Roger Smith in rejecting biological reductionism's commitment to treating the physical sciences as the best way to approach the normative in human life, since "it extrudes too much that is human from its consideration" (forthcoming, 25). And because what is "extruded" here is, at bottom, the fact that human conduct can only be understood in terms of reasons, not causes, biological reductionism renders its own existence unintelligible by "contradict[ing] the historical values that constituted natural science itself: it 'cannot sustain the way of life in which norms like objectivity and truth have authority and in which things and events have significance'" (forthcoming, 26). Taking the findings of biology at face value, scientistic naturalism runs afoul of the postpositivist insight into the *historical* emergence of science. Because the historical conditions of its genesis are not conceptually reducible to the sort of "genesis" that evolutionary biology thematizes, biological reductionism cannot be taken to provide exclusive access to knowledge of what it is to be human. But if Zammito embraces this historicist *reductio* of biological reductionism, what alternative remains for determining a naturalistic concept of nature?

Here Zammito turns back to the model of the philosophical anthropology of the 1920s, which, he contends, could acknowledge "both 'man's place in nature' and the emergent radical novelty of humans as a natural species" (forthcoming, 27). For Zammito, the important point is that philosophical anthropology was not reductive; it drew upon the most sophisticated biological thinking of its time, but it also incorporated the findings of the cultural and historical sciences to project "a theory of development which would recognize man as natural and nature as creative of something that is unique in the human" (forthcoming, 27). But does this appeal to the human *sciences*—to the third-person results of history, psychology, or anthropology—really get us any further? Why is this not simply to add a regional ontology of the cultural sciences to a regional ontology of the biological sciences—nature and human nature—in which it is not at all clear how the two "natures" are, or even can be, related? The normative force of the natural here is supposed to be a function of a broad and unified concept of nature, but that unity is nothing given; rather, it derives from the *projected* unification (through comparative and historical studies) of two notions of life and nature that, at the outset, are admitted to have very different regional characteristics. If they did not, then biological reductionism would have sufficed in the first place.

Thus we should not be surprised when, in describing the virtue of the approach through philosophical anthropology, Zammito gives voice to the phenomenological alternative to the regional approach: "Grasping being human should urge us to reconstruct what being natural is" (forthcoming, 28). What is this but a version of the *privative* approach? One determines what life or nature is by starting with what being human is, where being human is not to be defined by this or that science. Of course, this strategy has a long pedigree: In the *Physics*, Aristotle could conceive nature as teleologically ordered because he understood the teleological orientation of human rational agents: "The best illustration is a doctor doctoring himself: nature is like that" (1984, 341). That nature acts for reasons is not something that observation reveals; it is something that we may want to impute to nature because we *cannot but understand ourselves* in this way. Whether nature, so understood, has normative implications for us remains an open question.

Postpositivism wants to overcome the conundrums of traditional epistemology by seeing both subject and object as dynamic emergents from "natural" processes, but it offers no clear path toward an account of what this *unhintergehbar* nature is. Transcendental phenomenology, as I understand it, shares with postpositivism a rejection of constructivism and epistemological foundationalism, but for that very reason it *also* dispenses with any appeal to an overarching positive concept, such as "nature," that would bring with it independent constraints on how the transcendental subject, as the locus of responsibility for norms, must be conceived. When we "situate" the subject in "natural processes," we always do so already privatively, by conceiving those processes on the model of our first-person understanding of what it is for me *to be*. Thus the new naturalism of postpositivist science studies can be welcomed as a critique of the one-sided scientistic concept of nature that has dominated intellectual life in modernity. But it cannot serve as an alternative to the transcendental account of meaning, since the very experiences to which it appeals—meanings drawn from science, history, and even philosophical speculations about nature—either presuppose the regional ontologies (paradigms) of the sciences in question or else involve a privative extension of my first-person grasp of "transcendental" life to nature and life as a whole.

If analytic postpositivist philosophy of science's attempt to provide a compelling alternative to the transcendental way thus founders on its "theoretism" or objectivism—its failure to recognize the philosophical indispensability of the first-person stance in any account of normativity—perhaps a project that starts from within phenomenology itself may fare better. I shall conclude by considering one such.

5 TRANSCENDENTAL CRITICISM OF PHENOMENOLOGICAL "BIOCENTRISM"

We remarked above that many phenomenological approaches that wish to dispense with transcendentalism take their point of departure from Merleau-Ponty's concept of the body and its extension into the idea of the "flesh of the world." This is clearly not a transcendental phenomenology, neither a regional nor a privative approach to nature and life. Rather, it is an attempt to specify an elemental reality that underlies the categorial oppositions ("correlations") to which the transcendental stance is beholden. However, it is questionable whether this ontology of the flesh remains phenomenological at all. Indeed, it seems to exemplify a return to speculative *Naturphilosophie,* and this is certainly one of its contemporary attractions.

Nevertheless, even among those who criticize Merleau-Ponty on this point, the goal of attaining a concept of life or nature that will be phenomenologically attestable without entailing transcendentalism remains a beacon. An example is found in the "biocentric" phenomenology of Renaud Barbaras. Drawing upon Gondek and Tengelyi's superb *précis* of Barbaras's position, I will argue that the latter avoids the privative approach only by exceeding the limits of phenomenology.

Barbaras rejects Heidegger's privative approach to life, but he does not abandon the idea that there is a certain methodological "asymmetry" built into phenomenology. To identify the phenomenon of life in general, Barbaras does not turn to life as studied in biology (his is not a regional approach) but to subjectivity as "immediately lived life" (Gondek and Tengelyi 2011, 591). With Aristotle in the background, and drawing on Patočka's idea of the primacy of "phenomenality" as such, Barbaras determines life as "movement" (Barbaras 2006, 81–107). As Gondek and Tengelyi point out, in Aristotle "motion had a purely physicalistic or cosmological significance," whereas "in Heidegger it was applied to *Existenz*" (2011, 590). Barbaras, in contrast, identifies a kind of motion that characterizes life as such. The movement of life is not supposed to be a general metaphysical principle, nor a privative determination from the kind of existentiality that characterizes *Dasein*, but rather something that is attested in living itself. But how does one get to that phenomenologically?

Husserl had characterized life as "striving" (*Streben*), but as we saw, this was ultimately a privative determination of transcendental life as rational striving. Barbaras, in contrast, links the movement of life to the phenomenon of desire, a phenomenon that is (presumably) drawn from our own first-person experience (Barbaras 2006, 108–127). His task, as Gondek and Tengelyi put it, "is to grasp *Erleben*—and thus consciousness, intentionality, and indeed spirit—from out of *Leben* itself" (2011, 591). Thus his position is "biocentric" in the sense that it is the life within us—and not our transcendental ability to determine that life—that provides the ultimate point of reference for philosophical thinking.

But if the essence of life—desire—is accessible to us only through our own experience, in what sense is this not an example of the privative approach? Biocentrism could avoid the privative approach *if* it could phenomenologically isolate a concept of desire that is indifferent or neutral between the inquirer and other entities that the inquirer identifies as alive. But, Husserl might ask, how is this to be done? Once the transcendental capacity (call it "rationality") comes into play, the term 'desire' is equivocal, and only privative strategies can lead from the essence of desire as I experience it and what I *call* desire (or striving) in other creatures. If Barbaras does not go along with Husserl on this point, it is because he believes that, on the basis of a phenomenology of *my* desire, he can *reverse* the privative approach: it is not life that is a privative concept *vis-à-vis Dasein* or *Existenz;* the latter—and with it, intentionality, object-determination, and norm-responsiveness—is a privation of *life* conceived as desire.

What allows Barbaras to reverse the privative approach is his characterization, following Lévinas, of desire as different from need and lack. Desire is "not a circumscribed incompleteness to which there corresponds a definite object but an incompleteness that is hollowed out by what fulfills it and that experiences every satisfaction as the negation of what would truly fulfill it" (Barbaras 2006, 121). The desire that pervades and defines life is not desire for some determinate thing that would satisfy it, but rather a "dissatisfaction with the finite" as such, a movement that opens the living being onto the Infinite. "The living of the living subject is rooted ultimately in the fact that it aims to realize the unrealizable, to constitute a totality that is untotalizable since its own existence as living subject has as a condition the absence of this totality [. . .]" (Barbaras 2006, 120).

It is on this basis that the kind of object-consciousness characteristic of intentionality, the sort of meaning that Husserl and Heidegger made their point of departure, is supposed to become intelligible. But how? Gondek and Tengelyi ask: What explains the fact that a desire whose "orientation is ultimately toward the Open, the Infinite, and so precisely toward the non-given and non-objective" nevertheless "directs itself always precisely toward objects?" And they answer: "even though desire can never be entirely satisfied, it is nevertheless always directed toward that which—if only partly—can indeed satisfy it. It follows from this," they continue, "that desire is not so much out to fulfill itself as it is to *determine* itself" (Gondek and Tengelyi 2011, 601). This is the key to reversing the privative approach: Freedom—*Dasein*'s responsibility for the measures that allow things to show up *as* something—is the ground of our access to determinate objects only in that it is a *privation* of the general movement of life toward the Infinite, a mode of "determining oneself" through the relative satisfaction of an insatiable desire for what lies "beyond" the given.

Can this account convince us that Barbaras has been able to move beyond a privative approach to life while remaining phenomenological? A key point in deciding this question is whether an appeal to desire's ability to determine itself or establish its place in the world suffices to account for the experience of determinate things, that is, for intentionality and meaning. Here Barbaras seems to rely on a general concept of negation: "Correlative to the living subject's individuality, negation is constitutive of a totality such that it is simultaneously the positing of what it is the negation of" (2006, 120). That is, in opening onto the Infinite totality, desire simultaneously "negates" this totality as "unpresentable," thereby positing it as such. This very unpresentability of the totality is then the condition for the presentability of things, beings:

> Life is negativity, an unfulfillable lacking that opens up the field of transcendence within which being can appear: because it is dissatisfaction, life is also pure reception, open to presence as such. Hence negativity, which has been seen as constitutive of perception strictly speaking, is by no means the attribute of the human person and of its anguish; instead it emerges from the vital level (Barbaras 2006, 136).

But it is not clear that such a concept of negation can suffice. The slogan "every determination is a negation" cannot be reversed. It makes sense only if what is negated is determinate already, and so is a *determinate* negation, that is, only if it takes place already within a normative context in which the negation can yield the sort of experience that Husserl described in terms of intentional confirmation or disconfirmation. Negation as such determines nothing positively, gives rise to no particular intentional content, even if the free play of such "negation" is, as Barbaras rightly insists, a necessary condition for such content. But just this was Heidegger's point in tracing the possibility of normative determination to a being in whose being that being is essentially an issue, and so to existential death (or "anguish") and the "privative" approach to life that it entailed.

Both Lévinas and Heidegger also appeal to a movement that is oriented beyond the world as a whole and that makes intentional directedness to determinate objects possible. Heidegger analyzes this movement, "transcendence," not as desire but as the being-towards-death that takes over responsibility for grounding as such. Lévinas, in turn, identifies it precisely with desire as an "insatiable" metaphysical "trans-ascendance" that goes beyond all being and makes ontology possible (Lévinas 1969, 33–35). But the Heideggerian and the Levinasian phenomenologies of transcendence—both of which subscribe to the privative approach to life in general—recognize a crucial element that is absent in Barbaras's account of life as desire, namely, the fact that the transcendence in question cannot be understood as oriented to some vague Open or Infinite in the sense of the *indeterminate;* rather, it must be oriented toward the *Good.* This is crucial, since it attests phenomenologically to the sort of normative orientation without which nothing like determinate object- or thing-hood could be experienced.[26]

In the absence of such an orientation toward the Good (toward measure as such), it would be utterly inexplicable how intentionality in the full sense could be derived from life as desire, from the striving toward the infinite. This means that freedom and existence cannot be seen as privative modifications of a broader concept of life. Nothing in the concept of desire as striving for the Infinite allows us to understand how determinate object-orientation is possible. Rather, if we wish to call "desire" that transcendence which underlies intentionality, then it must include the peculiar "care" for measure and the normative without which no determinate content is possible. But in that case, the desire in question is always already *ours,* in the sense that it is transcendentally defined, and there can be no basis but the privative for attributing such desire to life in general. In ignoring this point, Barbaras offers a nonphenomenological concept of desire and simply helps himself to the idea of "determination" in a way that really gets us no further than Merleau-Ponty's concept of flesh. For Merleau-Ponty, too, leaves the genesis of the "invisible" from the "visible"— the clarification of how the normative space of reasons is grounded in the flesh of the world—as a mere promissory note, based on a nonphenomenological conviction, or dialectical argument, that it simply must be so.

NOTES

1. The *locus classicus* for Husserl's arguments is the *Prolegomena to Pure Logic,* Volume One of his *Logical Investigations* (Husserl 1970b, 53–247; Hua 18, 16–258).
2. Husserl believes that the reverse is also the case: perceptual mental processes point toward the possibility of being expressed signitively, but I won't go into that here. See Husserl (1983, 294–297; Hua 3, 303–307).

3. See also Crowell (2010).
4. For the argument, see Crowell (2001a).
5. See, for instance Figal (2010, chapter 1). Figal's belief that one must move beyond Heidegger's transcendentalism toward a more "hermeneutic" phenomenology derives from attributing to Heidegger something like the "primacy of practice" thesis, which he holds to be subjectivistic and idealistic.
6. There are, of course, socially typical uses for things, and it is essential that the norms involved be public in this sense, but I will not dwell on this point here. See the account in Dreyfus (1991, 151–162).
7. The term is Christine Korsgaard's. See Korsgaard (1996, 101).
8. For further discussion, see Crowell (2007, 2001b).
9. In a wide-ranging treatment of Husserl's relation to *Lebensphilosophie,* Andrea Staiti shows how deeply the theme of transcendental life permeates his thinking. Staiti highlights Husserl's response to Rickert's attack on *Lebensphilosophie,* in which Rickert argued that life is "der Begriff des Begriffslosen" (1920, 5) and thus not a philosophical basis for an account of anything (Staiti 2010, 62). According to Rickert, a philosophical account can begin only with the conceptually articulated realm of scientific cognition, and he insinuated that Husserl's phenomenology, with its emphasis on lived experience and "intuition," was dangerously close to an objectionable *Lebensphilosophie.* Rather than deny the charge, as Staiti shows (2010, 85), Husserl argued that the neo-Kantian approach to reason left out the "Lebensquelle" from which "alle Abstraktionen [. . .] geschöpft sind" (Husserl 2001, 239). Only phenomenology can uncover these "living sources" in a genuinely *scientific* way. Thus, although phenomenology "sich selbst nicht Lebensphilosophie nennt" in the modern sense, "in Erhaltung des echten antiken Sinnes von Philosophie als universaler Wissenschaft Lebensphilosophie ist" (Husserl 2001, 240; Staiti 2010, 86). As Staiti points out, however, what "life" means here is far from clear, especially when we consider that the scientific character of phenomenology's approach to the "living sources" of reason is established by the reduction, which transforms all everyday and scientific concepts of life into constituted meanings. Staiti does a good job of showing that there is a continuity between Husserl's early emphasis on the transcendental subject as "consciousness" and his later tendency to speak of it as "transcendental life," but his reasoning hints at the fundamental ambiguity here: "Hätte die Verwendung des Wortes 'Leben' auf etwas grundsätzlich Revolutionäres im Vergleich zu den früheren Forschungen verwiesen, so hätte Husserl sehr wahrscheinlich seine Einführung motiviert und aufgeklärt, wie er es sonst für zahlreiche Termini und Begriffe immer wieder tat [. . .]" Since he did not do that, Staiti argues, one should conclude "dass Lebensphilosophie genau das war, was er immer schon betrieben hatte, obwohl auf eine eigene, wissenschaftlich begründete Weise" (2010, 55–56). But this only returns us to the question of this section: Which, of all the meanings of the polysemic term 'life' governs this conclusion? Husserl's later work is a curious amalgam of genuine insight based on transcendental reflection and construction based on borrowings from ordinary and scientific (natural and social) conceptions of life and nature. A "scientific" phenomenology of life must be in a position to distinguish between these two. As we shall see, Heidegger's transcendental phenomenology is more consistent on this point.
10. Of course, Heidegger famously mounts a critique of the very concept of the given, following Natorp in targeting Husserl's appeal to the primacy of "intuitive givenness" to consciousness (1987, 63–76). But his appeal to life in these early lectures draws upon Dilthey's idea of the *Unhintergehbarkeit* of life, which brings it into the orbit of a metaphysical view. As I will argue,

Heidegger only gets a clear grasp of the issues when, in *Being and Time,* he drops the notion of life altogether in favor of a fully transcendental conception of *Dasein.*

11. I have argued these points extensively in Crowell (2001a).
12. For an exhaustive account of this movement, see Fischer (2009).
13. Here Heidegger, like Husserl, criticizes Rickert's neo-Kantian dismissal of *Lebensphilosophie,* since Rickert fails to distinguish between "life" as a term of intellectual fashion and as a philosophically necessary "basic category of phenomenology" (1985b, 80).
14. In a recent paper tracing the "configurations" of the concept of life in Natorp, Husserl, and Heidegger, Martina Roesner shows how Heidegger's early concept of life is governed by a search for the "originary" (*Ursprünglichkeit*). He tries to find a middle way between Natorp's idea of a "reconstruction" of the primordial dimension from which concepts emerge and the ambiguities of Husserl's concept of life as, on the one hand, that form of consciousness that takes the "world" for granted and, on the other, that "pure" or transcendental life responsible for the constitution of meaning. In so doing, Roesner argues, Heidegger develops a concept that is both "factical-concrete" insofar as it "is not subject to any transcendental or other methodological modifications," but also "transcendental" insofar as factical-concrete life itself, absorbed in various modes of world-engagement or de-worlding, "points toward a life-ground" (*Lebensgrund*) that is the "constitutive source" (in the sense of a prior "*Indifferenzpunkt*") of all the adumbrations in which factic life shows itself (2012, 78). Roesner's argument points to the purely *dialectical* character of the concept of life that appears in these early lecture courses—a concept that is fashioned exclusively to avoid problems with other views with which Heidegger wishes to take issue. In *Being and Time,* Heidegger rejects the dialectical expedient of positing some *Indifferenzpunkt* and subordinates all conceptions of life to the strictures of transcendental method, that is, to the "ontology of *Dasein*" which is "*superordinate* to an ontology of life" (1962, 291; GA 2, 328).
15. See also Heidegger (1962, 71–75, 94; GA 2, 61–67, 88). Many interpreters—for example, Krell (1992), van Buren (1994), Figal (2010)—have seen this move from *Lebensphilosophie* to transcendental phenomenology as a regrettable lapse in Heidegger's thinking. My argument in this chapter is meant to suggest why such a view is philosophically short sighted.
16. This would mean that the much-disputed "lifeworld" would have to be seen as falling within the scope of the concept of transcendental life. Contrary to what Nicholas de Warren (2012, 165) argues in his review of Staiti's book, then, the lifeworld cannot be invoked as "something akin to the 'not-known' or 'unthought' of transcendental life itself."
17. See, for instance, Husserl (1969, 90–92; Hua 1, 122–4).
18. On the constitution of *Körper,* see Husserl (1989, 3–95; Hua 4, 1–90). On the constitution of the animate organism, see Husserl (1989, 151–80; Hua 4, 143–71). Husserl does not always clearly distinguish between body as animate organism and the lived body, which leads to some of the ambiguities we are tracking here. I look at this issue more closely in Crowell (2012).
19. It is well known that Heidegger did not take up the question of "this 'bodily nature'" that "hides a whole problematic of its own" (1962, 143; GA 2, 145). Some interesting insights on how he might approach it from within the sort of transcendental framework I am defending here can be found in the *Zollikon Seminars* (Heidegger 2001).
20. See Husserl (1983, 18–23; Hua 3, 23–29) and Heidegger (1962, 28–31; GA 2, 12–15).

21. It is in this sense that Heidegger identifies one sense of "world" as "that 'wherein' a factical Dasein as such can be said to 'live'" (1962, 93; GA 2, 87).
22. The *locus classicus* here is Derrida (1982), but the idea has generated a large literature.
23. See, for instance, Rouse (2002) and the essays in de Caro and Macarthur (2004).
24. See Zammito (forthcoming, 9). For a full account of the history of postpositivist science studies and their impact on the self-conception of philosophy in the twentieth century, see Zammito (2004).
25. See Smith (2007, 107), quoted in Zammito (forthcoming, 24).
26. The ancient concept of desire—which Barbaras seems to trade on without making it explicit—registers this point in its thesis that desire is desire for the good. One has rightly rejected this: desire desires only what would fulfill it (something it can—and if Barbaras is right, must—fail to attain). There is no trace of the normative in this, which is why Heidegger's approach (which does not tie the normative to "desire") is phenomenologically more compelling than Lévinas's. But this is a topic for another paper.

REFERENCES

Aristotle. 1984. *Physics*. In *The Complete Works of Aristotle*. Vol. I., edited by J. Barnes. Princeton, NJ: Princeton University Press.
Barbaras, R. 2006. *Desire and Distance. Introduction to a Phenomenology of Perception*. Translated by P. B. Milan. Stanford, CA: Stanford University Press.
Crowell, S. 2001a. *Husserl, Heidegger, and the Space of Meaning: Paths Toward Transcendental Phenomenology*. Evanston, IL: Northwestern University Press.
———. 2001b. "Subjectivity: Locating the First-Person in *Being and Time*." *Inquiry* 44: 433–54.
———. 2007. "Conscience and Reason: Heidegger and the Grounds of Intentionality." In *Transcendental Heidegger*, edited by S. Crowell and J. Malpas, 43–62. Stanford, CA: Stanford University Press.
———. 2010. "Husserl's Subjectivism: The 'ganz einzigen "Formen"' of Consciousness and the Philosophy of Mind." In *Philosophy, Phenomenology, Sciences: Essays in Commemoration of Edmund Husserl*, edited by C. Ierna, H. Jacobs, and F. Mattens, 363–389. Dordrecht: Springer.
———. 2012. "Transcendental Phenomenology and the Seductions of Naturalism: Subjectivity, Consciousness, and Meaning." In *The Oxford Handbook of Phenomenology*, edited by D. Zahavi, 25–47. Oxford: Oxford University Press.
Derrida, J. 1982. "The Ends of Man." In *Margins of Philosophy*, 111–136, translated by A. Bass. Chicago: University of Chicago Press.
de Caro, M. and Macarthur, D., eds. 2004. *Naturalism in Question*. Cambridge, MA: Harvard University Press.
de Warren, N. 2012. "Review of Andrea Staiti, *Geistigkeit, Leben und geschichtliche Welt in der Transzendentalphänomenologie Husserls*." *Husserl Studies* 28: 161–66.
Dreyfus, H. L. 1991. *Being-in-the-World: A Commentary on Heidegger's Being and Time, Division I*. Cambridge: MIT Press.
Figal, G. 2010. *Objectivity. The Hermeneutical and Philosophy*. Translated by Th. George. Albany: SUNY Press.
Fischer, J. 2009. *Philosophische Anthropologie. Eine Denkrichtung des 20. Jahrhunderts*. Frankfurt: Alber.
Gondek, H.-D. and Tengelyi, L., eds. 2011. *Neue Phänomenologie in Frankreich*. Frankfurt: Suhrkamp.

Haugeland, J. 1998. "Truth and Rule Following." In *Having Thought: Essays in the Metaphysics of Mind,* 305–361. Cambridge: Harvard University Press.

———. 2000. "Truth and Finitude: Heidegger's Transcendental Existentialism." In *Heidegger, Authenticity, and Modernity. Essays in Honor of Hubert L. Dreyfus, Vol. I* Edited by M. Wrathall and J. Malpas, 43–77. Cambridge: MIT Press.

Heidegger, M. 1962. *Being and Time.* Translated by John Maquarrie and Edward Robinson. New York: Harper and Row; *Sein und Zeit* (Gesamtausgabe 2). Edited by W.-F. von Herrmann. Frankfurt: Vittorio Klostermann, 1977.

———. 1984. *Metaphysical Foundations of Logic.* Translated by M. Heim. Bloomington: Indiana University Press; *Metaphysische Anfangsgründe der Logik* (Gesamtausgabe 26). Edited by K. Held. Frankfurt: Vittorio Klostermann, 1978.

———. 1985a. *History of the Concept of Time: Prolegomena.* Translated by T. Kisiel. Bloomington: Indiana University Press; *Prolegomena zur Geschichte des Zeitbegriffs* (Gesamtausgabe 20). Edited by P. Jaeger. Frankfurt: Vittorio Klostermann, 1979.

———. 1985b. *Phänomenologische Interpretationen zu Aristoteles. Einführung in die phänomenologische Forschung* (Gesamtausgabe 61). Edited by K. Bröcker-Oltmanns. Frankfurt: Vittorio Klostermann.

———. 1987. *Zur Bestimmung der Philosophie* (Gesamtausgabe 56/57). Edited by B. Heimbüchel. Frankfurt: Vittorio Klostermann.

———. 1995. *The Fundamental Concepts of Metaphysics: World, Finitude, Solitude.* Translated by W. McNeill and N. Walker. Bloomington: Indiana University Press. *Die Grundbegriffe der Metaphysik. Welt-Endlichkeit-Einsamkeit* (Gesamtausgabe 29/30). Edited by F.-W. von Herrmann. Frankfurt: Vittorio Klostermann, 1983.

———. 1998a. "Letter on 'Humanism." In *Pathmarks,* edited by W. McNeill. Cambridge: Cambridge University Press; "Brief über den 'Humanismus'." In *Wegmarken* (Gesamtausgabe 9). Edited by F.-W. von Herrmann. Frankfurt: Vittorio Klostermann.

———. 1998b. "On the Essence of Ground." In *Pathmarks,* translated by W. McNeill. Cambridge: Cambridge University Press; "Vom Wesen des Grundes." In *Wegmarken* (Gesamtausgabe 9). Edited by F.-W. von Herrmann. Frankfurt: Vittorio Klostermann, 1976.

———. 2001. *Zollikon Seminars. Protocols-Conversations-Letters.* Edited by M. Boss. Translated by F. Mayer and R. Askay. Evanston, IL: Northwestern University Press.

Husserl, E. 1965. "Philosophy as Rigorous Science." In *Phenomenology and the Crisis of Philosophy,* translated by Q. Lauer. New York: Harper Torchbooks; *Aufsätze und Vorträge.* Edited by T. Nenon and H. R. Sepp. Dordrecht: Martinus Nijhoff, 1987. (Hua 25)

———. 1969. *Cartesian Meditations: An Introduction to Phenomenology.* Translated by D. Cairns. The Hague: Martinus Nijhoff; *Cartesianische Meditationen und Pariser Vorträge.* Edited by S. Strasser. Den Haag: Martinus Nijhoff, 1963. (Hua 1)

———. 1970a. *The Crisis of European Sciences and Transcendental Phenomenology.* Translated by D. Carr. Evanston, IL: Northwestern University Press; *Die Krisis der europäischen Wissenschaften und die transzendentale Phänomenologie.* Edited by W. Biemel. Den Haag: Martinus Nijhoff, [1954]. (Hua 6)

———. 1970b. *Prolegomena to Pure Logic.* In *Logical Investigations, Volume I,* translated by J. N. Findlay. London: Routledge & Kegan Paul; *Logische Untersuchungen, erster Band: Prolegomena zur reinen Logik.* Edited by E. Holenstein. Den Haag: Martinus Nijhoff, 1975. (Hua 18)

———. 1983. *Ideas Pertaining to a Pure Phenomenology and to a Phenomenological Philosophy, First Book.* Translated by F. Kersten. The Hague: Martinus Nijhoff;

Ideen zu einer reinen phänomenologie und phänomenologischen Philosophie, Erstes Buch. Edited by W. Biemel. Den Haag: Martinus Nijhoff, 1950. (Hua 3)

———. 1989. *Ideas Pertaining to a Pure Phenomenology and to a Phenomenological Philosophy, Second Book.* Translated by R. Rojcewicz and A. Schuwer. Dordrecht: Kluwer. (Hua 4)

———. 2001. *Natur und Geist. Vorlesungen Sommersemester 1927.* Edited by M. Weiler. Dordrecht: Kluwer Academic Publishers. (Hua 32)

———. 2008. *Die Lebenswelt. Auslegungen der vorgegebenen Welt und ihrer Konstitution. Texte aus dem Nachlass (1916–1937).* Edited by R. Sowa. Dordrecht: Springer. (Hua 39)

Korsgaard, C. 1996. *The Sources of Normativity.* Cambridge: Cambridge University Press.

Krell, D. 1992. *Daimon Life: Heidegger and Life-Philosophy.* Bloomington: Indiana University Press.

Lévinas, E. 1969. *Totality and Infinity.* Translated by A. Lingis. Pittsburgh: Duquesne University Press.

Nagel, T. 1997. *The Last Word.* Oxford: Oxford University Press.

Rickert, H. 1920. *Die Philosophie des Lebens. Darstellung und Kritik der philosophischen Modeströmungen unserer Zeit.* Tübingen: J. C. B. Mohr.

Roesner, M. 2012. "Zwischen transzendentaler Genese und faktischer Existenz. Konfigurationen des Lebensbegriffs bei Natorp, Husserl und Heidegger," *Husserl Studies* 28/1: 61–80.

Rorty, R. 1982. "Keeping Philosophy Pure. An Essay on Wittgenstein." In *Consequences of Pragmatism: Essays 1972–1980,* 19–36. Minneapolis: University of Minnesota Press.

Rouse, J. 2002. *How Scientific Practices Matter: Reclaiming Philosophical Naturalism.* Chicago: University of Chicago Press.

Smith, R. 2007. *Being Human: Historical Knowledge and the Creation of Human Nature.* New York: Columbia University Press.

Staiti, A. S. 2010. *Geistigkeit, Leben und geschichtliche Welt in der Transzendentalphänomenologie Husserls.* Würzburg: Ergon Verlag.

van Buren, J. 1994. *The Young Heidegger: Rumor of the Hidden King.* Bloomington: Indiana University Press.

Zammito, J. 2004. *A Nice Derangement of Epistemes: Post-Positivism in the Study of Science from Quine to Latour.* Chicago: University of Chicago Press.

Zammito, J. (forthcoming). "The 'Last Dogma' of Positivism: Historicist Naturalism and the Fact/Value Dichotomy."

2 Categories of Experience and the Transcendental

László Tengelyi

A new phenomenology has recently emerged in France. In the period from Emmanuel Lévinas and Michel Henry to Jean-Luc Marion and Marc Richir, it has become increasingly evident that the phenomenon as such cannot be derived from what Edmund Husserl described as a "constitution" by intentional consciousness but has to be considered as an event of appearing that establishes itself *by itself.*

This basic insight has some consequences of utmost importance. On the one hand, a new concept of the subject has been elaborated. Phenomenology never accepted the overhasty proclamation, according to which the subject was doomed to death, but it has now definitively broken with the idea of a self-sustained and self-possessed ego, characteristic of modern philosophy. It has been shown that, in self-awareness and self-perception, the subject finds itself originally in the dative case rather than in the nominative case, since the event of appearing happens *to* it, before it could grasp itself as an I. On the other hand, phenomenology has recently come to regain an access to effective reality and objectivity, which seemed to have been lost by transcendental philosophy. Since the event of appearing establishes itself *by itself,* effective reality and objectivity are encountered in experience, before a process of "constitution" in the Husserlian sense of the word could get hold of it. Consequently, it has become clear that a well-understood process of constitution does not imply any ontological dependence of effective reality on intentional consciousness. Nor are the conditions for the possibility of experience determined in advance by the structure of subjective faculties. Idealism is overcome; transcendentalism is revised and reinterpreted.

These changes have opened up the field of a new inquiry into what may be designated as "the categories of experience." In a phenomenological approach, categories of experience are not primarily considered as "modes of assertion" (i.e., as "categories" in the original sense of the word) but, so to speak, as "modes of experience," even if, at the same time, these modes of experience may be related to categories of predicative thinking as their prepredicative "counterparts." That is why they may be called "categories of *experience.*" Even more properly, they can be designated as "experientials." In a phenomenological approach, these categories—or quasi-categories—are not related to "being *qua* being," as Aristotelian categories are. Nor are experientials related to the "transcendental object" of experience, as Kantian categories are. What they are related to is rather the event of appearing that happens to us by itself. The well-known categories of philosophical tradition like substantiality, causality, necessity and contingency, possibility, and effective reality appear in a new light if they are no longer related to being *qua* being or to the "transcendental object" of experience but are interpreted as articulations and determinations of the event of appearing. Thus, phenomenology comes to establish itself as *"another* first philosophy" (Marion 2001, 16). On these grounds, it has become also possible to pick up Husserl's idea of a phenomenological metaphysics of "contingent facticity" (Hua 1, 182; Husserl 1999, 156),[1] distinguished so carefully at the end of *Cartesian Meditations* from every metaphysics "in the customary sense" (Hua 1, 166; Husserl 1999, 139). The main task of a phenomenological metaphysics may be said to consist in an inquiry into the categories of experience.

In what follows, such an inquiry into experientials will be outlined. The thesis I shall argue for is that experientials express mere tendencies to a concordance of experience (*"Einstimmigkeitstendenzen der Erfahrung"*). In order to elucidate this thesis, I shall first make clear that, in a certain sense, it assigns a transcendental status to the categories of experience. Second, it will be shown in which sense concrete experientials can be said to be necessary conditions for the very possibility of concordant experience. Finally, the following considerations will be closed by a reflection on the new meaning the term 'transcendental' is given in a phenomenological inquiry into the categories of experience.

1   EXPERIENTIALS AS TRANSCENDENTAL CONDITIONS OF CONCORDANT EXPERIENCE

The categories of experience may be seen as necessary conditions for the possibility of new experiences that remain in concordance with previous ones. Consequently, they have a transcendental status in phenomenology, just as well as, for instance, in Kantianism. However, Kant takes it for granted that the concordance of experience is itself necessary. Indeed, we are told in a famous passage of the *Critique of Pure Reason:* "There is one single experience in which all perceptions are represented as in thoroughgoing and orderly connection [. . .]" (A 110, Kant 1965, 138). On the contrary, phenomenology admits of diverging and conflicting experiences, and it does not even exclude the possibility that some antagonistic perceptions of the world can never be integrated into a single, all-embracing experience. Therefore, in phenomenology, concordant experience is taken to be contingent.

It does not follow from this that, in phenomenology, no kind of necessity can be attributed to the categories of experience. Of course, it is a question if there is a kind of necessity that is reconcilable with the contingency of concordant experience. The answer to this question, however, is unequivocally in the affirmative: the "necessity of a fact," by which Husserl characterizes the *cogito,* that means, the "actual present experiencing" of the subject (Hua 3/1, 98),[2] is clearly a case in point. According to Descartes, the contingent fact of *cogito* somehow implies or entails the necessity of *sum.* Assuredly, it remains to be seen what the expression "implies or entails" precisely means in this context. From a logical point of view, the relation of *cogito* to *sum* is, therefore, a problem.[3] It is, however, in any case clear that the proposition *cogito, ergo sum* is about a necessity that results from a contingent fact. It is, indeed, a contingent fact that, at the very moment, I exist and think; but as long as I actually think, my existence is necessary. That is why Husserl speaks of the "necessity of a fact."[4] Sartre picks up this Husserlian notion. He says: "The relation of the for-itself [. . .] to facticity can be correctly termed a factical necessity [*nécessité de fait*]. It is indeed this factical necessity which Descartes and Husserl seized upon as constituting the evidence of the cogito" (Sartre 1943, 122; 1956, 84, translation modified). The special character of the necessity Descartes, Husserl, and Sartre have in mind is due to the circumstance that this necessity is dependent on a contingent fact. In phenomenology, such a necessity can be attributed to experientials, which remain, indeed, dependent on the contingent fact of concordant experience.

From these considerations, it is clear that, in principle, a factical necessity *can* characterize the categories of experience. Is there, however, any argument ascertaining that the categories of experience *are* indeed characterized by such a factical necessity? Once more, the answer to this question is unambiguously in the affirmative. According to phenomenology, the factical necessity of experientials arises from the very existence of the world, which, at least in Husserl's eyes, remains ultimately a contingent fact.

This relationship between the categories of experience and the existence of the world requires some clarification. According to phenomenology, there is a world if there is a thoroughgoing and orderly connection that assures the possibility of concordant experience. It is commonly known that Husserl conceives of the world as a horizon of all horizons, that is, as a "universal horizon" or "a constant horizon of existing things, of values, of practical projects, of works, etc." (Hua 6, 110, 121).[5] Taken in this sense, however, the world is *pregiven* to every single experience of things. Indeed, in the *Crisis of European Sciences and Transcendental Phenomenology*, it is shown that "things, objects [. . .] are 'given' [. . .] as things, objects *in the horizon of the world*" (Hua 6, 146). Besides such a pregivenness to every experience of things, Husserl attributes to the world expressly a *unicity*: "On the other hand," he says, "the world is not existent like an entity, like an object, but it is existent in a unicity, for which a plural is meaningless" (Hua 6, 146). Moreover, in his lectures on *First Philosophy*, Husserl makes clear that the existence of the world is *indubitable,* because there is no experience that could motivate a doubt concerning the very existence of the world. In one of his research manuscripts on the lifeworld, which has recently been published in volume 39 of the series *Husserliana,* a reflection on the embodiment of the subject leads him to attribute to the existence of the world not only an indubitability but even an *apodictical* certainty, which stands on equal footing with the certainty of the cogito.[6] That is why, here, Husserl says: "By closer consideration, it is strictly impossible for the ego [. . .] to imagine the world as non-existent" (Hua 6, 146). However, if the world is nothing else but a thoroughgoing and orderly connection that assures the possibility of concordant experience, then the very conditions for such a concordance of experience are characterized by an incontestable necessity.

On the other hand, according to Husserl, no absolute necessity underlies the indubitability—or even apodictical certainty—of the world. Just as the evidence of the cogito, this certainty relies exclusively on "the necessity of a fact" or on a "factical necessity." A phenomenology that remains faithful to its methodological principles cannot assign to the world the status of an *ens necessarium.* Indeed, the indubitability or apodicticity of the world is dependent on the basic fact that there is an experience of things. That is why, even in his later works and research texts, Husserl abides by his conviction, according to which the existence of the world is ultimately a contingent fact, even if it is indubitable or apodictically certain.

In order to elucidate this paradoxical contingency of the world, we may quote an observation of Kant's, according to which, in principle, experience could be chaotic: "Appearances might very well be so constituted that the understanding should not find them to be in accordance with the conditions of its unity. Everything might be in such confusion that, for instance, in the series of appearances nothing presented itself which might yield a rule of synthesis und so answer to the concept of cause and effect" (B 123, Kant 1965, 124). A phenomenologist may entirely share Kant's view that, as a matter of fact, experience is not in such confusion. He or she may even continue to follow the main line of thought of the *Critique of Pure Reason* by drawing the conclusion that some categories or experientials like cause and effect apply to experience. This inference is clearly a *transcendental argument*, based on the insight that the categories of experience are necessary conditions for the very possibility of the world. However, a phenomenologist will inevitably dissent with Kant's "transcendental deduction" of the categories of experience, which is designed to prove on *a priori* grounds that experience is not chaotic but is necessarily submitted to a thoroughgoing categorial order. On the contrary, a transcendental argument that can be used in phenomenology must be based on the *contingent fact* that, actually, experience is not chaotic. It runs as follows: "Since, in fact, the world exists, some categories necessarily apply to experience." Such an argument conveys to the categories of experience only a *factical* necessity, which never can be proven on *a priori* grounds. In opposition to Kantianism, phenomenology admits of a necessity that is separated from aprioricity.

In my view, transcendental arguments for the necessity of experientials are the very pillars of a phenomenological inquiry into the categories of experience. The main task that can be ascribed to such an inquiry is indeed to show that certain modes of experience are necessary conditions for the very possibility of the world. A transcendental argument for the necessity of such a mode of experience is a regular proof, which has its cogency. However, the necessity of the whole argument remains dependent upon the contingent facticity of concordant experience.

In the next section, some concrete categories of experience will be considered. We shall try to show that they are, as a matter of fact, necessary conditions for the very possibility of the world.

2   SOME CONCRETE CATEGORIES OF EXPERIENCE

Appearance and horizon belong inseparably together. We find these two moments in every experience. Although every horizon can be transformed into a series of appearances, these appearances, in their turn, are surrounded by new horizons. In spite of its mobility, the demarcation line between appearance and horizon remains indelible. It determines the basic structure of experience. Therefore, this demarcation line can be used to divide experientials into two different kinds: there are experientials that are necessary conditions of appearances, and there are other experientials that are necessary conditions of the horizons of these appearances. This division of experientials into two different groups may remind us of Kant's distinction between mathematical and dynamic categories. However, a phenomenological inquiry into experientials diverges in several respects from Kant's doctrine of the categories of experience. One of these differences is that the obsolete distinction between mathematical physics and metaphysical dynamics is not renewed. Another difference is that, in phenomenology, space and time may be just as well considered as categories of experience as, for instance, causality. For, in phenomenology, categories—in the sense of experientials—are taken to be modes of experience rather than modes of assertion. Evidently, space and time are just as well modes of experience as causality. However, they are necessary conditions of the very appearance of things, whereas causality, as Kant has seen it correctly, is not. Therefore, in phenomenology, space and time can be characterized as categories of appearance. Causality, on the contrary, is neither implied not presupposed by appearances themselves.

It is not difficult to see that space and time are necessary conditions for the possibility of the world. Kant emphasizes that "we can represent to ourselves only one space; and if we speak of diverse spaces, we mean thereby only parts of one and the same unique space" (A25; Kant 1965, 69). He adds that "these parts cannot precede the one all-embracing space, as being, as it were, constituents out of which it can be composed; on the contrary, they can be thought only as *in* it. Space is essentially one; the manifold in it, and therefore the general concept of spaces, depends solely on [the introduction of] limitations" (A25; Kant 1965, 69). The case with time is similar. We are told: "Different times are but parts of one and the same time" (A 31; Kant 1965, 75). It is added that "every determinate magnitude of time is possible only through limitations of one single time that underlies it" (A32, Kant 1965, 75). According to the *Critique of Pure Reason,* these particularities unmistakably show that space and time are not general concepts but pure forms of sensible intuition. From this insight Kant deduces his double thesis of "empirical reality" and "transcendental ideality" of space and time. In a remarkable passage, he formulates this double thesis concerning space in an easily understandable way: "It is, therefore, solely from the human standpoint that we can speak of space, of extended things, etc."(A 26; Kant 1965, 71). Here, only space and extended things are mentioned, but, obviously, a similar statement is true of time and temporal entities. Furthermore, it is clear from the *Critique of Pure Reason* that the human standpoint, mentioned by Kant in this passage, is meant to be the standpoint of the human race as such. The question whether there is any difference between the standpoint of one human being and another one with respect to space and time does not arise for Kant.

In a phenomenological view, the legitimacy of such a generic approach to the subject is by no means obvious. Phenomenology breaks with the metaphysics of the subject characteristic of modernity. It does not commit itself to any thesis about a "death of the subject," but it discovers that the subject is, so to speak, split into the I and the Other. That is why phenomenology is not inclined to ascribe to the subject any generic structure or standpoint without deriving it from a concrete relationship between the I and the Other.

The consequences of this change can be clearly exhibited via the example of space. In Husserl's phenomenology of intersubjectivity, the subject considers itself as a functional center of orientation in space. It relates all appearances to itself, taking its own body—"the body in the absolute Here"—to be the "central body" or the "zero body" of their space (Hua 1, 152; Husserl 1999, 123). In other words, the subject grasps the space as a kinesthetic space of appearances that are correlated with its immediately felt bodily movements.

The Other is interpreted by the I as another functional center of orientation in the same space. Husserl describes this experience of the Other as follows:

> "After all, I do not apperceive the other ego simply as a duplicate of myself and accordingly as having my original sphere or one completely like mine. I do not apperceive him as having, more particularly, the spatial modes of appearance that are mine from here; rather, as we find on closer examination, I apperceive him as having spatial modes of appearance like those I should have if I should go over there and be where he is" (Husserl 1999, 120; 117).

Consequently, I apperceive the Other "such as I should be if I were there" (Husserl 1999, 122; 119), "as if I were standing over there where the Other's body is" (Husserl 1999, 126; 123).

In the German original of these two phrases, Husserl uses the particle *"wie wenn."* In a close study of the phenomenology of intersubjectivity, Klaus Held pointed out the ambiguity characteristic of this particle, which, on the one hand, expresses a potentiality (a *Wenn*), since, actually, I am able to go there where the Other's body is, but it expresses also an irreality (an *Als-Ob*), since my simultaneous presence there, where the Other's body is, is excluded by the very fact of our coexistence.[7] From this irreality it follows that my experience of space never coincides with the Other's experience of space. The space is given to the subject just as perspectivally as an appearance in the space. Therefore, phenomenologically speaking, the one single space talked about by Kant cannot be but a tendency to the concordance of different experiences of space. Yet irreality belongs here together with potentiality. However, from the potentiality of my being there, where the Other's body is, it follows that the experience of space the Other has is something like an "analogue" or a "modification" of my experience of space.[8] Husserl shows that this is precisely the condition for the possibility of a world common to the I and the Other. Accordingly, the idea of one single space expresses not simply a tendency to concordance discovered empirically, but it rather expresses an expectation of concordance belonging necessarily to every experience of space. The necessity of this expectation remains, however, dependent upon the ultimately contingent fact that there is a world. It remains, in other words, a factical necessity.

Similar reflections are pertinent to time as well. Even if this statement needs further elucidation and corroboration, we will take it for granted without further inquiry in order to leave room for a consideration on causality. As far as this classical problem of Hume and Kant is concerned, our task is the same as in the case of space and time: we have to show that causality expresses a necessary condition for the very possibility of the world. There is, however, an important difference between the two cases: whereas space and time are categories of appearance, causality is only a category of the horizons of appearance. As Kant puts it, space and time are "referred to the possibility of appearances" (A 178; Kant 1965, 210); causality, on the contrary, applies only "to the relations of existence" (A 179; Kant 1965, 210). Consequently, causality does not determine the internal structure and content of singular appearances but only their relations to each other. From a phenomenological point of view, these relations belong to the structure of the horizon, in which appearances are given to us.

To some extent, we can rely on the *Critique of Pure Reason* in order to make clear how causality expresses a tendency to the concordance of experience. Confronted with Hume's analysis of causality in the *Enquiry into the Principles of Human Understanding*, Kant sets himself the task of proving that, in the world of appearances, one event "follows in conformity with a rule, that is of necessity," upon another (A 194; Kant 1965, 222). Thereby, he tries to establish the principle of causality, according to which everything that happens in nature has a cause. He elaborates a transcendental argument, which, in his own words, can be summarized as follows: "The principle of the causal relation in the sequence of appearances is [. . .] valid of all objects of experience [. . .], as being itself the ground of possibility of such experience" (A 202; Kant 1965, 227).

How can it be shown that causality is a necessary condition for the very possibility of concordant experience? Kant adduces two examples in order to make clear what role causal relations play in experience:

1. If I see in front of myself a house, I grasp the different parts of my object after each other without taking a definite direction in the synthesis of apprehension. As Kant remarks, my perceptions "could begin with the apprehension of the roof and end with the basement, or could begin from below and end above; and I could similarly apprehend the manifold of the empirical intuition either from right to left or from left to right" (A 192; Kant 1965, 221).

2. The case is quite different with events or happenings in nature; thus, for instance, with a ship that I can see moving downstream: "My perception of its lower position follows upon the perception of its position higher up in the stream, and it is impossible that in the apprehension of this appearance the ship should first be perceived lower down in the stream and afterwards higher up. The order in which perceptions succeed one another in apprehension is in this instance determined, and to this order apprehension is bound down" (A 192; Kant 1965, 221).

The difference between the two cases is clear: whereas in the first example the synthesis of apprehension is reversible, in the second it is not. The irreversibility of apprehension entails a concordance in the experience of successive events or happenings, since the "compulsion" (Nötigung) to follow a definite order in apprehension results "in necessitating us to connect [our representations] in some one specific manner" (A 196–7; Kant 1965, 224). According to Kant, this compulsion and necessitation is due to the fact that a causal relation connects the successive events (for instance, the ship is moved by its engine downstream or it simply drifts with the tide).

In my opinion, nothing prevents a phenomenologist from accepting the main results of this analysis of causality. As a matter of fact, here Kant himself turns out to be a phenomenologist avant la lettre. The difference concerns only the question of which necessity is ascribed to a causal order of appearances. Kant attempts to prove on a priori grounds that experience is irreducible to a "rhapsody of perceptions" (A 156; Kant 1965, 193) without necessary order and all-embracing unity. Phenomenology dissents, maintaining that the undeniable difference of experience from a rhapsody of perceptions without necessary order and all-embracing unity is nothing but an ultimately contingent fact, which cannot be proven on *a priori* grounds. To be sure, phenomenology adds that a certain concordance of experience is not just one fact among others, but it is a basic—or even primordial—fact that provides causality and other categories of horizon with a factical necessity.

3   METHODOLOGICAL TRANSCENDENTALISM IN A PHENOMENOLOGICAL PERSPECTIVE

Our inquiry into experientials like space and time or causality has shown that, from a phenomenological point of view, just like in the perspective of critical philosophy, categories of experience are seen as transcendental conditions of concordant experience. However, a phenomenological approach to the categories of experience does not take the word 'transcendental' in the same sense as Kantianism, since it is not *a priori* necessity but only factical necessity, the necessity of a fact, that it ascribes to a "transcendental condition of concordant experience." In the remaining part of this chapter, I shall reflect on this difference.

Phenomenology relies on the basic or primordial fact that experience is characterized by necessary order and comprehensive unity, but it does not see in the concordance of experience any *a priori* necessity. Therefore, it does not even attempt to deduce it from the self-consciousness of the subject. It takes seriously the insight that even a basic or primordial fact could, in principle, be otherwise, since, like every fact, it is contingent. That is why we must admit that the categories of experience do not express any unbreakable laws of nature. They express nothing more than *mere tendencies* to a concordance of experience. Assuredly, Kant is right in saying the following: "If [. . .] we experience that something happens, we in so doing always presuppose that something precedes it, on which it follows according to a rule" (A 195; Kant 1965, 223). However, it cannot be proven on *a priori* grounds that this presupposition is correct. We can say nothing more than that we *expect* of everybody to share this assumption. The necessity and the universal validity of experientials manifest themselves in certain general expectations. Phenomenology can appropriate some of Kant's transcendental arguments, but it must restrict their conclusions to such expectations. It is, however, important to see that the word 'expectation' does not express here any normative claim.[9]

If we rely on a terminological distinction known from Kant's *Critique of Judgment,* we may formulate what has been just said also in a different way: for phenomenology, the categories of experience belong to the sphere of *reflective judgment* rather than to that of determinative judgment. In the sense of this distinction, it may be asserted that experientials are not *first* discovered as modes of assertion in predicative thinking and *then* applied to experience, but, as modes of experience, they are directly searched for in experience itself. In his analysis of causality, Kant himself shows how such a quest of categories in experience can methodically be established. Phenomenology adopts this procedure, and it extends it to other categories of experience as well. Such a quest of categories in experience does not start with the universal in order to arrive at the particular, but, conversely, it starts with the particular in order to arrive at the universal. Therefore, it can be considered as belonging to the realm of reflective judgment rather than to that of determining judgment.

Of course, this does not mean that a phenomenological inquiry into categories should be an affair of aesthetics or of teleology. It is certainly true that Kant's *Critique of Judgment* is dedicated to an investigation on these two domains of reflective judgment. However, from the "First Introduction to the *Critique of Judgment*," it is clear that, besides aesthetics and teleology, there is a third use of reflective judgment, called 'logical' and concerned with the applicability of concepts to natural things and events. It is this third use of reflective judgment that is relevant for our present considerations. In the "First Introduction to the *Critique of Judgment*," the question of how forms of nature can be brought into concepts turns out to be inseparable from the question of how particular laws of nature can be subordinated to universal ones. The necessary connection between the two questions can be illustrated by an example of fundamental importance. That we have a concept of mechanical movement equally applicable to celestial bodies and to sublunar phenomena is due to the fact that Newton's universal law of gravitation unites Kepler's special laws of planetary movement with Galilei's particular law of free fall. By this example and similar ones, Kant is led to assume that nature "qualifies itself by the affinity of its particular laws with more general ones as one experience in the sense of an empirical system" (Kant 1790, 209). In the "First Introduction to the *Critique of Judgment*," this assumption of a "*system according to empirical laws*" is described as the very "transcendental principle of judgment" (Kant 1790, 209). However, Kant adds that this principle is only "a subjectively necessary transcendental presupposition" (Kant 1790, 209); in other words, it is only a "heuristic principle" that, according to Kant, belongs "to the system of the critique of pure reason, but not to that of doctrinal philosophy" (Kant 1790, 206).

In my opinion, phenomenology can be distinguished from Kantianism by its conviction that there are no other transcendental principles than heuristic ones. If this is true, even the principle of causality expresses only a "subjectively necessary transcendental presupposition" of concordant experience; moreover, even space and time as necessary conditions for the very possibility of the world belong only to the territory of reflective judgment. The illusion that space and time in their singularity are immediate forms of intuition arises, in reality, from an entirely speculative and, in this sense, metaphysical conception of the subject, which disregards the difference between the I and the Other. Similarly, the illusion that experience as a thoroughgoing and orderly connection of perceptions can be proven on *a priori* grounds by being deduced from the necessity of transcendental apperception arises, in reality, from a no less speculative and, in this sense, metaphysical conception of consciousness, which, once again, abstracts from the split of the subject into the I and the Other. Phenomenology dissolves these illusions by maintaining that space and time, just as well as causality, express mere tendencies to a concordance of experience or even mere expectations with regard to such a concordance, and that they do not belong to the domain of determinative judgment but are relegated to the sphere of reflective judgment.

To sum up: I have been trying to show that transcendental arguments can be integrated into a phenomenological investigation on the categories of experience, provided that they are founded on "subjectively necessary transcendental presuppositions" of reflective judgment. Thus reinterpreted, these arguments assign to the categories of experience a necessity that is based on the contingent fact of the world. In my view, the critically revised and restricted transcendentalism I have been pleading for is entirely immune to the critique to which some new phenomenologists in France have recently submitted the idea of transcendental conditions. For instance, Marion may be right in reproaching Kant for having put forward a transcendental theory of experience, according to which "phenomena appear only on condition, alienated by imposed phenomenality" (Marion 1997, 257; 2002, 183.). However, this objection of "conditioned phenomenality" loses its validity and pertinence as soon as the necessary conditions for the very possibility of concordant experience are taken to express mere tendencies and expectations. Another point, which deserves to be mentioned here, is stressed even more by Richir than by Marion: from a phenomenological point of view, the very idea that the limits of possible experience are determined in advance by the subjective conditions of knowledge seems to be dubious, since every change in reality may open up the field of new possibilities that go beyond the limits of what is, in each case, foreseeable and predictable. However, also this objection loses its validity and pertinence, as soon as the necessary conditions for the very possibility of concordant experience are taken to express merely heuristic principles of reflective judgment. Therefore, it seems to me that we can continue to adhere unswervingly on a refined version of the transcendental method in phenomenology, even if we accept and adopt the new achievements of the last decades.

NOTES

1. Translated as "accidental factualness" in Husserl 1999, 156.
2. Husserl (1931, 131): "Obviously [. . .] the ontic necessity [*Seinsnotwendigkeit*] of the actual present experiencing is no pure essential necessity, that is, no pure eidetic specification of an essential law; it is the necessity of a fact (*Faktum*), and called 'necessity' because an essential law is involved in the fact, and here indeed in its existence as such."
3. See Hintikka 1962, 4.
4. See Tengelyi 2011, 124–132.

5. Cf., "Universalhorizont realer, wirklich seiender Objekte" (Hua 6, 147).
6. Hua 39, 256: "Apodiktisch ist die Gewissheit vom Sein der Welt [. . .]."
7. "Das 'wie wenn' ist die doppeldeutige Verquickung eines die Irrealität anzeigenden 'wie' (im Sinne von 'als ob') mit einem 'wenn' von temporaler Bedeutung" (Held 1972, 35).
8. In order to understand these notions properly, see Hua 1, 118; 1999, 115.
9. Its German equivalent is, therefore, not "*Erwartung*" in the sense of a "*Forderung*" (requirement) but "*Erwartung*" in the sense of "*Ansinnen*" or "*Zumuten*" (request).

REFERENCES

Held, K. 1972. "Das Problem der Intersubjektivität und die Idee einer phänomenologischen Transzendentalphilosophie." In *Perspektiven transzendentalphänomenologischer Forschung,* edited by U. Claesges & K. Held, 3–60. The Hague: M. Nijhoff.

Hintikka, Jaakko. 1962. "*Cogito, Ego Sum*: Inference or Performance?" In *The Philosophical Review* 71, 1 (January): 3–32.

Husserl, E. 1950. *Cartesianische Meditationen und Pariser Vorträge.* Edited by S. Strasser. The Hague: Martinus Nijhoff. (Hua 1). Translation: Husserl, E. 1999. *Cartesian Meditations. An Introduction to Phenomenology.* Translated by D. Cairns, Dordrecht, Boston, London: Kluwer.

———. [1954] 1962. *Die Krisis der europäischen Wissenschaften und die transzendentale Phänomenologie. Eine Einleitung in die phänomenologische Philosophie.* Edited by W. Biemel. The Hague: Martinus Nijhoff. (Hua 6). Translation: Husserl, E. 1970. *The Crisis of European Sciences and Transcendental Phenomenology: An Introduction to Phenomenological Philosophy.* Translated by D. Carr. Evanston, IL: Northwestern University Press.

———. 1976. *Ideen zu einer reinen Phänomenologie und phänomenologischen Philosophie I.* Edited by Karl Schuhmann. The Hague: Martinus Nijhoff. (Hua 3/1). Translation: Husserl, E. 1931. *Ideas. General Introduction to Phenomenology.* Translated by B. Gibson. London: Collier Macmillan Publishers.

———. 2008. *Die Lebenswelt. Auslegungen der vorgegebenen Welt und ihrer Konstitution. Texte aus dem Nachlass (1916–1937).* Edited by R. Sowa. Dordrecht: Springer. (Hua 39)

Kant, I. 1790. "Erste Einleitung zur *Kritik der Urteilskraft.*" Academy Edition, Vol. XX, 193–251. Berlin: W. de Gruyter.

———. 1904. *Kritik der reinen Vernunft,* First Edition ("A"): Academy Edition, Vol. IV. Berlin: G. Reimer, 1911; Second Edition ("B"): Academy Edition, Vol. III. Berlin: G. Reimer.

———. 1965. *Critique of Pure Reason.* Translated by N. K. Smith. New York: St. Martin's Press.

Marion, J.-L. 1997. *Étant donné.* Paris: Presses Universitaires de France.

———. 2001. *De surcroît.* Paris: Presses Universitaires de France.

———. 2002. *Being Given. Toward a Phenomenology of Givenness.* Translated by Jeffrey L. Kosky. Stanford, CA: Stanford University Press.

Sartre, J.-P. 1943. *L'être et le néant. Essai sur l'ontologie phénoménologique.* Paris: Gallimard.

———. 1956. *Being and Nothingness. An Essay on Phenomenological Ontology.* Translated by H. E. Barnes. New York: Philosophical Library.

Tengelyi, L. 2011. "Necessity of a Fact in Aristotle and in Phenomenology." In *Philosophy Today* 55 (SPEP Supplement): 124–132.

3 The Transcendental Nature of Experience

Bernhard Obsieger

1 PHENOMENOLOGY AS TRANSCENDENTAL PHILOSOPHY

There is something paradoxical about the fact that the world only appears to us through our first-person experience but, nevertheless, appears to us as being independent of this experience. My world of experience is at the same time a common objective world and a world that is relative to my own knowledge of it. Correspondingly, our experience of the world can be understood from two different points of view. We can understand it as a process that takes place within the common world and belongs to a subject that is itself just one worldly being among others. This point of view characterizes our natural attitude of everyday life, in which we simply accept the objective being of the world without caring about the fact that this objective being is only accessible through our subjective knowledge. The other possible attitude, which I will call transcendental, addresses the world as a correlate of our first-person perspective. From this point of view, our experience is not understood as a process that occurs within the world but as the process in which the world presents itself to us, and the subject is not understood as existing within the world but as the subjective correlate of the world as it appears from the experiential first-person point of view. Experience and the subject are thus understood as correlated to the "being there" of the world, not as something that belongs to the world that is there for us.

So we are faced with the question of how we are to understand the possibility and meaning of the "being there in itself" of the world *as* a "being there for me." This question is by nature a transcendental question, since it can only be asked within the transcendental attitude. Yet it is not just one transcendental question among others but, rather, concerns the very meaning of the transcendental attitude itself. I will address this question trying to understand the relation between the two interpretations of experience and the experiencing subject. The transcendental interpretation of experience characterizes phenomenology as transcendental philosophy. This kind of philosophy is not simply concerned with the nature of objects but with the correlation between objects and our knowledge of them.[1] Insofar as phenomenology addresses the structure of experience from a transcendental point of view, it can be regarded as a form of transcendental philosophy and thereby associated with Kantianism. On the other hand, it is by conceding a transcendental status to experience that phenomenology fundamentally differs from the classical Kantian conception of transcendental philosophy.

Whereas the common theme of Kantianism and transcendental phenomenology is the correlation between the world and our knowledge, these two kinds of transcendental philosophy address this correlation at different levels. Kant addresses it at the level of its conditions of possibility. The structure of our world of experience is correlated beforehand with the structure of our faculty of cognition, that is, of reason. "For reason is the faculty which furnishes us with the principles of knowledge a priori. Hence, pure reason is the faculty which contains the principles of cognizing anything absolutely a priori" (Kant 2011, B24). Since this faculty makes possible any concrete knowledge by experience, the correlation between reason and the possible objects of knowledge must be prior to experience. Accordingly, the structure of reason determines beforehand the structure of possible objects that can be known by us. According to Kant, these structures are not only determined in advance but are also manifest to us and can become the theme of a peculiar kind of knowledge. As Kant says, "though *all* our *knowledge begins with experience,* it by no means follows that *all* arises out of experience"(Kant 2011, B1).

Any particular experience reveals its object in its relation to the total horizon of possible experience and thereby manifests the necessary structures of any possible object of knowledge. For example, when I see a tree in the garden, its place and time are experienced as being localized within the totality of the spatio-temporal world. Moreover, I experience it as being one and not many and as being real and so forth. Thereby, this experience manifests to me not only the spatio-temporal structure of the world as a whole but also the totality of the possible quantitative and modal structures of objects. The reality of the tree has its meaning in contrast to the modalities of necessity and possibility; and the meaning of "being one" is only understandable in contrast to the other quantitative determinations such as "many" or "all." (Obviously, the same holds true for the other Kantian categories, which are also involved in the experience of the tree.) Due to this manifestation of the total horizon of our possible experience, which is part and parcel of every concrete experience whatsoever, we can possess a knowledge of the world that does not spring from experience without being limited to an analysis of concepts and judgments. The anticipation of the form of the world of experience, which is based upon the anticipatory givenness of its spatio-temporal structure, makes possible a knowledge that precedes our experience of the world and nevertheless tells us something about the world itself. The possibility and nature of this knowledge, which Kant calls synthetic *a priori*, is the theme of Kantian transcendental philosophy.

Therefore, we can see how the Kantian conception of transcendental philosophy is connected to his project of a critique of pure reason, that is, of an investigation of the possibility and status of a purely rational, nonexperiential knowledge of the world, as it was claimed by pre-Kantian rationalistic metaphysics. The interest in the possibility of a knowledge that does not have its source in any way in experience makes Kant consider the correlation of our knowledge and its object at the level of the *a priori* structures that determine beforehand the form of our possible experience. That interest also makes him neglect the correlation between the objects and experience itself. In contrast, it is precisely at the level of experience that transcendental phenomenology addresses the correlation of knowledge and its objects. In this manner, the concrete being of the world as it manifests itself in our experience becomes the theme of transcendental philosophy. The structures of the objects are addressed in their correlation to the structures of the acts of experience in which they are given. Also, this correlation is of an intrinsically necessary and intelligible kind, and therefore it is subject to *a priori* knowledge. Yet it is easy to see that this kind of *a priori* knowledge does not fit into the Kantian distinction of the *a priori* and the empirical, insofar as the source of our knowledge of the correlation between experience and its objects is experience itself. Husserl repeatedly criticizes Kant for ignoring or neglecting this sense of *a priori* as concerning essential or eidetic structures (see Kern 1966, 58 ff.).[2] One of the reasons for this neglect is of course that Kant takes as his point of departure the rationalistic conception of *a priori* knowledge as not having its source in experience, as we find it in the rationalists' efforts to prove the existence of innate ideas.

It is also partly for this reason that the correlation between experience and its object seems to Kant of no importance, despite the fact that this correlation is presupposed in his own considerations concerning its conditions of possibility. This becomes clear, for example, in his second formulation of his supreme principle of all synthetical judgments: "The conditions of the possibility of experience in general are at the same time conditions of the possibility of the objects of experience, and have, for that reason, objective validity in an a priori synthetical judgement" (Kant 2011, A158, B197). The wording of this statement can give rise to the impression that Kant is not so much speaking of a correlation between these conditions of possibility but of their identity. This impression is not completely mistaken, since Kant conceives of the relation between experience and its object very much as a unity. He understands the mutual correspondence between the appearances and the appearing object as the kind of correspondence that we find between a sensation and a quality. The sensation is in itself the presentation of the quality, and the latter is that which presents itself in the sensation. This correspondence seems self-evident, and there do not really seem to be two different terms involved. The sensation and the corresponding quality can be regarded as different ways or directions in which we can apprehend one and the same datum. My sensation of the blue sky and the blue color of the sky that I see are just the two sides of an identical datum, and their correlation appears to be founded on this identity. Consequently, the correspondence between a sensation and a quality does not seem to require any further investigation, and since sensation is at the very heart of our experiential knowledge of objects, it is understandable that Kant could consider the intrinsic relation between experience and its object as not deserving any special attention. For the same reason, Kant does not sharply distinguish between the two sides of this relation, speaking of "representation" (*Vorstellung*) as both the representing and the represented. Kant treats experience and its object as a unity, despite the fact that he does see their difference, as, for example, when he distinguishes in the Transcendental Aesthetic between the objects of inner and outer sense or when he points out the impossibility of reducing the latter to the former in his Refutation of Idealism (Kant 2011, B274–279). Consequently, he does not notice the necessity that links the two terms of the relation to each other, and he reduces their correspondence to the unity of one and the same two-sided fact.

In this manner, Kant assimilates the status of experience to the status of an object, assigning it to the realm of that which is there *for* the subject. What we know by experience is both our experience itself and its objects, since the knowledge of both is based on the same data, which are simply apprehended in different ways. For instance, we can be directed at an apple tree or at the appearance of the apple tree, but this only means a change in the manner in which we are directed at the same phenomenon.[3] If we reflect on our experience, this experience is converted into an "object of the inner sense," which according to Kant is an object in very much the same way as the object of the "outer sense" that appears through it. The givenness of the experience and of its object forms an inseparable unity. In this manner, Kant understands our experiences as the psychological objects of the "inner sense," that is, as objects of other possible acts of knowledge—the acts of reflection—thereby putting our experiences at the same level as their objects. By understanding the mode of being (given) of experience as that of an object, he considers experience from the point of view of the natural attitude.

As I pointed out, this is where transcendental phenomenology radically differs from Kantianism. From now on, I will call the way experience is related to its object the "intentional correlation." As we shall see, this correlation also involves the subject of experience. The next question I want to discuss is what it means to address experience as the transcendental dimension with which any kind of object is correlated.

2   THE INTENTIONAL CORRELATION

Experience is in itself correlated with that which is experienced. At first sight, the access to the intentional correlation does not seem to be a problem. We just have to take experience as it presents itself to us. As is easy to understand, to articulate the way in which something presents itself is to describe it. Therefore, the method of addressing the intentional correlation is the seemingly trivial task of describing how different kinds of objects present themselves in our experience of them and how this experience at the same time manifests itself. It is true that this description must be carried out from an eidetic or structural point of view, and this already requires a change of our direction of interest. This is of course a difficulty common to any philosophical inquiry, and the structures of the intentional correlation do not seem more difficult to discern than any other kind of general structures.

Although the access to the immediate self-givenness of our experience at first sight seems to be completely unproblematic, it is precisely this access that poses the main methodological problem of phenomenology. We are not used to addressing our experience in this way. The main reason the intentional correlation normally remains unnoticed is that we are not directed toward how the object is given but toward how it really is. We are not interested in our experience as such but in what it is adding to our knowledge of the object. We are only interested in the way the object appears insofar as its appearance tells us something relevant about its real being.

However, normally we are not seeking a *thematic* knowledge of the object and do not focus on its permanent properties but rather on momentary states of affairs, considering the object from the point of view of a very limited practical or theoretical interest. In everyday life, but also when I am guided by some theoretical interest, I will only attend to the properties of the object insofar as they are relevant in a given situation. My interest will also be of importance for the whole course that my experience will take. For instance, when I want to know if I forgot to close the kitchen window, I will look at my house in such a way that I will be able to discern whether the window is closed or not. This interest will not only determine which aspects of the house I will notice but also the course and content of my experience and the way this content is apprehended. In any case, although my interest is directed particularly at certain aspects of the objects, these objects are taken as I suppose them to be.

This directedness toward the objects "as they are in themselves" and as correlated to our general knowledge of them must be changed if we want to address the correlation between our experience and its objects. We must address the objects as they are correlated with our acts of experience, that is, as they are given and not as we believe them to be. Here we encounter the difficulty that we cannot simply leave aside the real being of the objects, since this directedness toward "real being" is in a certain manner an essential part of our experience, which is in itself experience *of a reality* that transcends it. Therefore the question arises of how we are to understand the givenness of transcendent being. In which way can something that transcends our experience nevertheless be present to us in this very experience? What makes it possible that we apprehend an appearance as the appearance of a transcendent object?

The meaning of the object *as it is intended* exceeds its intuitive presence in experience. The difference between these two kinds of givenness—as intended and as intuitively self-present—is the key to understanding how we can be directed in our experience toward an object as a whole without it being necessary for the object to present itself completely to us. The being of the object always transcends its intuitive presence and corresponds to a multiplicity of different possible modes of givenness, in which it can present itself as their identical correlate. This identical being of the object is accessible through the meaning or sense of our intention, by which it is directed at an identical and transcendent structure that never can coincide with any particular modes of givenness in which we experience it. Yet this still does not tell us what our intentional directedness to a perceptual object consists in. Intending the sense or meaning of an object is not sufficient to be aware of it as something whose presence transcends its appearance and whose being is more than a being-represented. How can we be directed at a transcendent object as presenting itself to us? By what kind of intentionality do we refer to an object as "being really there"?

As is well known, Husserl adopts from Hume the term 'belief' to characterize the peculiar mode in which we are conscious of the "real being" of something.[4] To be directed toward transcendent being means that we consider the objects not simply as we experience them but as we believe them to be. Because the character of belief is part of the very meaning of a transcendent object, our intending these objects transcends by itself their givenness in our experience. That which is intuitively given *motivates* an anticipation of the identical being of the object as it can be experienced through a series of different possible modes of givenness. Transcendent being, insofar as it is intended, is always correlated to such an anticipation of the series of experiences in which it could be given. This is why we relate to this being by believing (accepting) the anticipation unless other experiences motivate different anticipations. In this case, our belief in the real being of something can be modified; we can doubt or abandon it. Yet these are also modalities of belief in which we take a stance toward transcendent being.

Since it is belief by which we address the transcendent being of objects and overstep their being-given, we must suspend this belief if we want to consider the objects as they are correlated with our experience. This does not mean that we should adopt an attitude of *doubt* or disbelief instead but that it is necessary to suspend our interest in the "real being" of the object. We must abandon the whole point of view of belief if we want to address the object as it is correlated with our experience of it. This suspension of belief by which we direct our interest toward the being-given of the object is what Husserl calls the *epoché,* employing an ancient skeptical term that refers to the deliberate refraining from judgment. The epoché leads to a *reduction* of the being of the object to its being-given, and thereby it opens the way to the dimension of the correlation between experience and object. (It thus entails a reduction in the twofold sense of a restriction and a return.) This phenomenological reduction is therefore not so much a loss as the access to a new dimension of our experience, namely, the transcendental dimension (see Zahavi 2003, 46, and Kern 1966, 219).

The object side is not the only side of the intentional correlation that must be reduced if we are to address this correlation the way it is given in our experience. In our ordinary attitude, also the subject and experience itself are not taken as they manifest themselves but as we suppose them to be. When we reflect upon ourselves as the subject of a certain experience, we are not used to considering our subjectivity the way we are involved in this experience and are aware of ourselves in it. Instead, we apprehend our subjectivity as we generally believe it to be. As in the case of the object, the meaning with which we endow ourselves as subjects can belong to an experience in such a way that our self-interpretation is part of the descriptive content of the experience itself. But the fact that we *really are* how we are supposed to be by our ordinary self-apprehension is not part of the descriptive content of our self-awareness as the subjects of our experience. Through this self-apprehension, I am aware of myself in the same way as I am aware of a transcendent object. This kind of self-understanding must therefore be distinguished from my immediate self-awareness as the subject of my experience.

However, there is also another kind of self-awareness in which I am always present to myself without being the transcendent object of my self-apprehension but in which I am immediately aware of my being. This self-awareness is not part of the intentional correlation insofar as it is not limited to my involvement in a particular experience. I am never only the subject of an isolated experience on its own but am at the same time the subject of my stream of consciousness as a whole. As this subject, I am always immediately present to myself with my full being in an immediate non-thematic awareness that determines the whole style of my experience and action. This awareness is certainly not an awareness of myself as an object but rather as the subject of my experience. The immediate awareness of our being is not static but rather is always changing. We are present to ourselves in different ways depending upon which aspects of our being are of importance in a given situation. In this peculiar kind of immediate awareness, my convictions and potentialities are always present to me; I know of them without having to recall them. The presence of my habits is always influencing the way I act, not as a transcendent cause of my action but as a permanently present heritage of the tendencies and abilities I have acquired in the past and that can be actualized in a given situation as an immediate awareness of drives, abilities, convictions, and bodily or intellectual knowledge. My actions would not be what they are without this immediate awareness of my abilities (or inabilities), projects, and habits, which are continually present to me whether I want it or not. I am aware of their reality as part of my being, and this awareness has nothing to do with a transcendent self-apprehension.[5]

Nevertheless, as mentioned earlier, it is not the whole being of the subject that is correlated with a particular experience but only those aspects of this being that are immediately involved in it. If I see a mountain from below, I am aware of myself as being situated below the mountain and as seeing it. In contrast to this, when I am feeling angry, I am aware of myself as a subject of affectivity, volition, and moral judgment. Although it is true that the subject is with its whole concrete being the subject of each and every one of its particular experiences, it must be stressed that the subject is part of the intentional correlation only as the subject side of a particular experience, that is, insofar as every experience is not only experience *of* its object but is also in another sense experience of myself as experiencing the object. It is no accident that both the "subjective genitive" and the "objective genitive" are, after all, different uses of the same grammatical form of the genitive, and in the case of the subject's self-awareness, their meanings coincide. The manifestation of the ownership of an experience and the manifestation of the subject as its correlate are one and the same manifestation. The experience "belongs to" its subject by way of a correlation that has some similarity with the correlation with the object. Husserl expresses this analogy by speaking in both cases of a "pole" of experience.[6] Yet the manner in which we are aware of ourselves as the I-pole of our experience differs essentially from our awareness of its object-pole. The subject appears in a manner entirely different from that in which its object appears. Indeed, it appears as experiencing rather than as experienced.

Not only the object and the subject but also the being of the experience itself must be considered from the point of view of the epoché. When we reflect on an experience, we normally apprehend it with a meaning that transcends the way it is self-given as a part of the intentional correlation. We locate our experience in the objective time of the world and (indirectly) in objective space as a process that belongs to a bodily subject whose life takes place within a common natural and social world and is part of history. This self-understanding certainly can belong to the descriptive content of our experience and may play an important role in the intentional correlation itself (for example, in the way objective space and time appear to us), but all this belongs to the self-givenness of our experience only as the meaning we give it.

The phenomenological reduction thus concerns all three dimensions of the intentional correlation, namely, the object, the subject, and experience itself. If we want to study the intentional correlation of our experience with its subject and object, we must refrain from considering the components of this correlation from the point of view of their "real being" in order to stick to the way they manifest themselves in our acts of experience. Only then can we explore the dimension of the intentional correlation and try to discover how its three components relate to each other. This does not mean, however, that we exclude belief from consideration. On the contrary, it is only by ceasing to be interested in the objects of belief that we become able to understand belief as a constitutive element of the intentional correlation. Precisely by "bracketing" our assumptions concerning transcendent being, we are able to address them as assumptions. We must suspend our beliefs if we want to consider them *as* beliefs and inquire how they can gain their validity for us in the course of our experience.[7]

Here we are concerned mainly with the central part of the intentional correlation, which is experience itself. In the following sections, I will address the questions of how the transcendental and the worldly meaning of experience relate to each other and how it is possible that experience is not primarily understood as it is self-given but is endowed with a meaning that transcends its immediate self-givenness. The worldly meaning of experience has two essential features. First, our experience is localized within the objective time of nature (only indirectly within space), and second, it is understood from a third-person perspective as being just one process of experience among other such processes and thereby as being part of the social life of a community. Therefore, I will focus mainly on the temporal and intersubjective structures of experience, although it will also be necessary to take into account at least some of its spatial and bodily characteristics.

3   TRANSCENDENTAL AND OBJECTIVE TEMPORALITY

Experience is not only a temporal process; it is experience of temporality, that is, of duration. This duration is first and foremost the duration of its object, which it presents to us as changing or unchanging. Yet our experience is at the same time experience of its own temporality. In what follows, I will limit my considerations to experience in the most basic sense, that is, to perception.

The temporal sequence we perceive consists in the enduring or changing states of objects that are not temporal processes or their parts. These objects are perceived as persisting from one present to another, and their duration thus consists of a series of successive states. What we perceive is not simply a worldly object but a duration in which the object exists. We can either be directed at the process the object is undergoing or at the object itself. When I am watching a dancer in the theatre, I am primarily directed toward her dancing and not toward her as a person. The dance as a process is extended over a stretch of time, whereas the action of the dancer takes place in a permanent present, whose very permanence, on the other hand, consists in being always different.[8] The successive states of her movement exclude one another, and in this sense her present state is not part of a temporally extended whole, like a tone is part of a melody. She exists always entirely in a passing momentary state. Wherever her dancing body is, it is always there "now;" it never abandons the present. Nevertheless, I perceive her present state as being the limit of a temporal extension that belongs to the immediate past. Moreover, my perception also includes an anticipation of the immediate future. In every moment, I still perceive the part of the dancer's movement that has just occurred; and I am aware of the present phase as continuing the recent past and giving rise to the phases that will follow.

Strictly speaking, our perception always embraces only a small lapse of duration and therefore requires to be supplemented by other forms of awareness. The phases of the more remote past and future do not manifest themselves in an intuitive manner. Nevertheless, they form the horizon of our perception, and our awareness of them is inseparable from the perception itself and must be distinguished from our acts of recollection and expectation. I am still aware of those phases of the dance that have preceded the movements I am seeing; and I am aware in advance of the style of the future phases that do not yet belong to the horizon of my perception. The phases of the past finally become part of the latent and implicit horizon of consciousness, where they remain until I become aware of them again, in a different manner, through associative awakening and recollection.

The perception of the dance consists in the intuitive presence of a continuous multiplicity of successive phases. The just-past phases of the dance are still intuitively given as succeeding each other. They are not merely intended or represented, but they are perceived. If perception is an experiential self-givenness of that which is perceived, the fact that we perceive the dancer's movements seems to be incompatible with the claim that the being of the dancer is not temporally extended but is limited to the present. How can we perceive the previous states of the dancer if these states are given in our perception as having ceased to exist? In order to answer this question, it is important to discern carefully what exactly is given in the perception of duration and in which way the perception of the dance can be understood as a perceptual presence of a worldly process. The previous phases do not appear as being perceived now but as having been perceived before. The just-past phases that are perceptually given and form a stretch of time are not simply the phases of the dancer's movement insofar as they belong to a worldly process that is taking place in the theatre but, rather, these phases are only given insofar as we previously have perceived them. We are aware of them through the previous phases of our perception in which the successive phases of the dance appeared one after the other. The phases that are perceptually self-given in an immediate manner and form the continuity of a duration are the successive phases of our *perception* of the dance and not the successive phases of the dance itself, which exclude each other.

This is what distinguishes the perception of a temporal process from the perception of a spatial object. The latter is accessible through further possible perceptions in which it can be given and is not limited to the way we actually have perceived it. In contrast to this, the access to the phases of a perceived worldly process is restricted to the perception we are having of it when it occurs. I can perceive the just-past phases of the dance only insofar as they have been given in my previous perception. I cannot return to them as phases of a process that just took place publicly in the theatre and perceive them from any of the other possible perspectives. The already-elapsed phases of the dance are not self-present in an immediate manner but appear through my previous perception in which they were given as present.

Since we are not talking about concrete acts of perception but rather about momentary *phases* of a perception in which phases of the object present themselves, it will be better to speak here, as Husserl does, of a "primal presentation" rather than of a perception.[9] Whereas a perception of a spatial object is a direct presence of this object to our consciousness, our temporally extended perception of the just-elapsed duration of a process is a mediated or delayed presence through previous primal presentations. The previous phases of this perception are self-given as phases that have already elapsed, as former primal presentations that are past. For these phases, Husserl uses the term 'retention.'[10]

In other words, the time that is immediately given in time-consciousness is not simply and directly the time of the world around me but the time of my perception of this world, and of the latter only insofar as it is the correlate of my perception. Nevertheless, it must be admitted that our perception is directed toward the duration of the worldly process and not toward the duration of perception itself. This is why the two distinctive features of perception, intuitive presence and intentional directedness, do not entirely refer to the same here. In the sense in which perception is characterized by an immediate intuitive presence, it is first and foremost the duration of perception that is perceived, but to the extent that perception is characterized by an intentional directedness, we must say that we perceive the phases that make up a worldly process, although we only perceive them in a delayed and somewhat "indirect" manner through the retention of their previous presence. We perceive the worldly process through a temporally extended appearance consisting of the successive phases of our perception, which is self-given to us but which is not the *object* of our temporal perception.[11]

The reason the phases of the perception, in contrast to the phases of the dance, are compatible with each other and can form a temporally extended unity is that these phases can be self-given not only as being present but also in a temporally modified manner. When they cease to appear as present, they do not disappear but modify themselves into the past of the following present, which in turn modifies itself together with its past into the past of the next present, and so forth. When a present is modified into the past of the following, its own past is thereby modified into a more remote past. This temporal modification means that the past phases *remain*. Yet they remain in a sense that is different from the usual sense of enduring from one moment to another. To put it differently, the remaining of temporal duration itself is not to be equated to remaining through time. It is not a persisting from present to present, but it is a sinking backward into the past. Whereas "remaining" normally means "remaining unchanged," this kind of remaining consists in a continuous modification. On the other hand, this modification is not a change in the usual sense of being different from one moment to another, and it is not opposed to a remaining but rather is the only possible way temporal phases can remain.

Therefore, we can find several essential differences between the temporal structure of perception and that of a perceived worldly process. *First,* the distinction of simultaneity and succession does not apply to the relation between the phases of perception. Whereas in the temporality of the perceptual world succession and coexistence exclude each other, here we are confronted with a coexistence of different phases *as* succeeding each other. The "succession" that is brought about by the emerging of new phases and the sinking into the past of the others does not exclude the coexistence of the successive phases but presupposes it, since the new phases are added to the previous ones.

This leads us to the *second* difference, which concerns the way the phases of the perceptual process relate to one another. The phases of perception are successive present states that are not substituted by each other but rather are contained within each other. The process of perception cannot be compared to the movement of running along a line but can be compared to a snowball rolling down a hill, to use Bergson's famous metaphor. This is to say that the earlier states are part of the later ones and that the process of perception consists not in an alternation of different phases but in an increasing growth of duration in which each new phase is not an isolated present but a different state of the duration as a whole. When I hear the last tone of a melody, this is a new state of the phenomenon of the melody that is different from its state when I heard the last but one. The emergence of the new tone is part of a modification of the temporally extended phenomenon as a whole; the entire state of its duration, comprising the temporal modes of all its phases, is different from the previous state.

A *third* important difference is that the intuitive presence of the successive phases of our temporal perception is beyond the alternative of static and dynamic temporality. For this reason, one can consider the intuitively given succession neither as being over nor as still going on. The succession we perceive is not merely given as a continuity of past phases that are now conscious in a static manner as being past and more or less past; we also perceive the successive phases in their succeeding each other. The temporality of our perception is truly dynamic in the sense that it is an intuitive givenness of a dynamism or a flow. On the other hand, paradoxically enough, this dynamism, this "becoming," can only be given insofar as it is already there. In our perception of duration, we perceive the very happening of a temporal event, but we perceive it as a happening that has already happened. The succession that is intuitively given is a succession that already has taken place. In this way, the givenness of succession also has a certain *static* side. Consequently, one might say either that the phenomenon of duration is beyond the alternative of being static and dynamic or that the distinction between static and dynamic temporality corresponds to the two different sides of this phenomenon.

The *fourth* difference concerns the sense in which experience of duration can be considered a process. The self-appearance of the time of experience is continuously modified; the duration given in our temporal perception is continuously flowing, and this flow is not a change in the usual sense. The temporal modification, as it appears to us, cannot run faster or slower, since it is only with respect to the passing of time that a conscious process can be considered to be going on fast or slow. This modification can never be said to stop or rest, since any stopping or resting presupposes that the flow of time continues. None of the passing moments of our perception can ever last and extend itself into a duration, and therefore the emergence of new phases and the modification of the previous ones cannot be accelerated or slowed down. The flowing experience of duration that is at the very heart of every experience whatsoever is therefore not a temporal process in the ordinary sense of the word. It does not have the characteristics of such a process but rather has those of time itself, and in this sense Husserl considers it atemporal.[12]

All these differences show that the temporal structure of experience as it presents itself from a transcendental point of view is very different from the temporal structure of a worldly process. The question thus arises how it is possible that we can consider our flowing perceptual experience as a temporal process at the same level as the worldly processes that are objects of our perception. The answer seems to be quite obvious. Since a worldly process consists in a succession of present states, we can understand our perception of such a process as the succession of primal presentations in which these states are perceived. If we consider the worldly process as it is perceived, its phases are strictly simultaneous with the primal presentations in which these phases appear as present.[13] Due to this coincidence, the time of perception, understood as the succession of the primal presentations, can be localized within the time of the perceived world. When I perceive the dancer on the stage, I experience myself as situated at a distance from her. I am seeing the dance from a perspective through which I appear implicitly as localized at a certain place. My perception is thereby apprehended as a process that takes place within the world. The time of my experience of the dance, considered in this way, is the time of my bodily presence in the theatre, which is a temporal process like any other. In this manner, I apprehend my experience as a process that is taking place in the public intersubjective world and is part of a system of intersubjective experiences. The question is therefore how this intersubjective meaning of our "subjective" experience is to be understood and how it is related to the difference between the transcendental and the worldly understanding of experience.

4 EXPERIENCE AND INTERSUBJECTIVITY

This question leads us to consider the structure of the transcendental process of experience in a more concrete manner. All my experience originates in my bodily presence in the world and is interaction with someone or something that I myself am not. In the first place, it is interaction with a spatial and material world that is present in all our bodily and sensory experience as the setting in which our experience takes place. The air I breathe and the earth on which I stand, the heat and cold I feel, daylight and darkness are always affecting me as the states of the world that surrounds me. As long as they fulfill their normal functions as components of the surrounding world, they cannot be that toward which my experience is directed and remain present in a nonthematic manner. Yet in order to be aware of myself as the subject of my experience, it is necessary that I be thematically directed at something that is not merely surrounding me but rather is opposed to me. Experience necessarily has the character of an encounter. I am aware of myself as the identical subject of my experience only insofar as I am directed at an identical unity that is not myself. In an eminent and primary sense, this unity is that of a physical body. What is more, my experience is given as proceeding from the other body as its source, as being that which is in contact with me.

The presence of this body can be experienced as a mere resistance to my activity. At the same time that I am directed toward a bodily unity as an opposed pole of my experience, the sensation in which this pole manifests itself is in its turn directed toward me. This is already the case when this manifestation merely consists in a resistance, which I experience as the counterpart of my activity and as intrinsically related to it. Even a visual presence of something is experienced in relation to its resistance to my looking at it, which of course involves some activity, like eye movement and attention. The resistance affects exclusively the one who is involved in an encounter with the resisting body; it is exclusively directed at the subject who is experiencing that body. By feeling a resistance, the subject experiences itself in its activity, which appears as the other side of the resistance.

However, this merely passive and inertial presence in the way of a resistance is only the minimal mode in which a bodily being can affect me in its otherness. The inertial inactivity of mere resistance, in which a bush or a rock presents itself to me, may be considered the limiting case of the manifestation of an activity that is not my own. The other body is not only able to resist my activity, but it may also manifest itself as active. In this case, my experience of the contact with this body is not given as the result of my own activity or as caused by processes that occur within the surrounding world as, for example, when the branches of a tree are shaken by the wind; rather, it is given as proceeding from that body itself. I am aware of myself as passively experiencing an activity that is not my own. The passivity that is part of my experience is in itself the other side of a foreign activity, namely, the activity of the body I encounter. Its presence is experienced as the presence of an active bodily subject, that is, of a living body, whose moving activity I am suffering. This kind of experience of my contact with another subject whose activity is directed at me and singles me out is what makes the encounter a reciprocal relation. The process of such an encounter is two-sided and consists in the alternation of being affected by the other and affecting her. I respond to the other's activity with my own activity, which in turn is answered by the other. In this reciprocal relation consists the full structure of bodily contact, of which the one-sided experience of an inertial, life*less* body is only a reduced and derivative mode. The one-sidedness of the experiential contact is still an experience of the other's activity, even though this activity is experienced as lacking. To put it differently, we can only experience something as *in*active in relation to the possibility of its becoming active. In this way, the dimension of another body's possible activity belongs intrinsically to the structure of bodily contact. A mere physical body is thus experienced as a derivative mode of a living body, as a body that lacks a dimension other bodies have. This dimension is even present when the contact is actually not experienced as reciprocal. In this case, my experience is still given as being just one side of a potentially two-sided experience.

The other side of the experience of bodily contact is immediately accessible through my experience. In the other's bodily presence to myself, I experience the other in her otherness, and I experience myself in my own bodily presence to her. It is one and the same phenomenal process of bodily contact in which I experience the other and am myself experienced by her. There are not two different processes that occur separately "within different subjects;" there is only one and the same two-sided process, which is given as a whole, but from its two different sides. In the experience of bodily reciprocal contact, I have an immediate experience of the other's lived body, my sensation of the other is identically her sensation of myself, only as given "from the other side." When I experience the other's body as warm, this very same sensation presents itself as being from the other's perspective a sensation of my own body as cold; the sensation of the roughness of the back of her hand is at the same time a sensation of the smoothness of my fingertip that touches it, and so forth.[14] It is true that this other side of the sensation is self-given to me in a different way than it is given to the other in her first-person awareness. Yet this opposite perspective on the sensation is not only necessarily implied in my bodily sensation, but it can also be self-given in the case in which different parts of the same body experience each other. As Husserl points out, the so-called "double-sensations," which arise when one part of my body touches another, can be experienced from two opposite perspectives, depending on which part of my body I apprehend as the touched or the touching one. The two sides of the sensation are given to me at the same time, and therefore I can choose which part I consider as touched or touching and in which one I thereby localize the sensation. By inverting this direction, I can experience the touching hand itself as being touched.[15] Moreover, I can also choose between being directed at the touched hand as it is experienced "from without" or "from within." In any case, I will experience both parts of the body through one and the same sensation "from without" and "from within" at the same time. The peculiarity of double sensations thus consists in the fact that I am aware of one and the same part of my body simultaneously as a touched physical body and as belonging to my own lived body. In this manner, the two sides of an interpersonal experience of bodily contact can be immediately given to me from both perspectives.

In the contact with another subject, I am always present to myself in my being present to the other. Independently of the difference between activity and passivity, there are two different ways of experiencing bodily contact. My sensation can either be apprehended as an experience of the other or as an experience of myself as being experienced by her. Through my tactile sensation, I can be directed at the part of the other's body with which I am in contact either as being touched by me or as touching me. If I apprehend my sensation as an experience of myself as being touched by her, I experience my own body as feeling the touch, and I am aware of myself as being experienced by her in my being-there for her. Something similar holds true for visual contact. When the other and I are looking at each other, I am seeing the other as seeing me. Her gaze is not *behind* what I see but is visible to me. My own gaze is given to me as caught by the other. In the visual contact, I actually experience the other, in her interaction with my own eye movement, as seeing me looking at her; and I thereby experience myself as being seen by the other. This reciprocal experiential contact can also adopt forms that are not purely sensory, such as a conversation. When the other person is talking to me, my listening to her is experienced as the other side of her speaking. The words I hear are given as being individually the very same words that the other utters, although from the perspective of the one who receives them.

If we do not mistake the two different perspectives on the same experience for two different experiences, there is no need for an explanation of how our experience can become experience of another subject, since our experience *is* intersubjective from the very start. It is important not to confuse the intersubjective structure of the encounter, which is essentially dual and second personal, with the kind of intersubjectivity which is characterized by the third-person perspective and essentially excludes any such immediacy. The false identification of intersubjectivity with third-person sociality is one of the main reasons the second-person nature of bodily contact has been commonly overlooked or misinterpreted.

The other's activity, as well as my own, is a flowing temporal process in which each present is unique and coexists with the temporal modifications of the former ones. Since the other's activity is just the other side of my experience of this activity, its temporal structure does not differ from that of my experience. This means that the process of experience has two sides or poles. I experience the other as the "thou-pole" with which I am sharing the process of our encounter. It is only in contrast to her resisting bodily identity throughout the duration of her contact with me that I experience myself as an identical permanent "I-pole." My experience can only be a temporal flow because it is an encounter in which I experience the persistence of an identical pole. It is thus intrinsically a process that—at least potentially—is the other side of another person's experience. Each moment of the shared dual experience of our encounter is unique, and the duration of this process is always perceived from a different temporal perspective. It is exclusively given to the two of us, in an asymmetrical manner, from its two different sides. The bodily intersubjective contact is a process that involves two different subjects as both being part of the life of each other. The experience of this flowing process of sensing each other cannot be shared by anyone else and thus is not part of what is going on in the common natural and social world, which is open to the experience of everyone. But this does not mean that it belongs exclusively to my own subjectivity, since it is shared with another and is the process of our being there for each other, the very process of our being-together. Because of the exclusive and nonpublic nature of the dual experience of the encounter, its unique mode of givenness may be called *intimacy*.

Through the encounter, I am aware of myself as the other experiences me, and in this way my experience of the other situates me in the other's perceptual world. This indirect givenness of myself therefore comes closer to my objectifying self-apprehension than does my self-awareness as the subject of my own experience, since I am not given anymore as the subject for whom the world is there but rather as a subject that appears from the perspective of another subject. Not only my body but also my own perceptual world is thereby indirectly given to myself in the way it would appear to me if I were in the place of the other. My body is given to me as localized with respect to the other's perceiving body, from whose perspective my "here" is a "there," and my perceptual world is thereby oriented not only in relation to my own bodily perspective but also in relation to the other's.[16]

Yet this alienation of my perceptual world still is not a givenness of myself as being part of an objective world that is independent of my experience. My being-situated within the other's perceptual world is still relative to my own bodily perspective, since the perspective of the other is given to me as the perspective of somebody else whom I experience as localized with respect to myself. My "here" is a "there" in relation to a "here" that is related to my own "here." The other's perspective is relative to my own because it is given as the inversion or the mirror image of my first-person perspective; and thereby the other's experience of my perceptual world is correlated to my first-person experience through which the other's perspective is accessible to me.

Only if my awareness of myself as I appear from the perspective of another person is detached from its relativity to my own first-person experience can I be aware of myself as present within the perceptual world of someone else, without this presence being relative to my first-person perspective. Only then does it become possible for the perceptual world to be liberated from its relativity to my first-person perspective. To this end, I must be aware of myself in the way I am present to someone else without his experience being shared by me. In other words, the other who can free my perceptual world from its relativity to my first-person experience must be a "third person," that is, somebody for whom I am present without him being in the very same experience present to me. Precisely for this reason I cannot have an immediate access to my being-experienced in such a way by others. Nevertheless,

I can be indirectly aware of being experienced from a third-person perspective when I notice that somebody is perceiving me without me being in an interpersonal relationship with him. This presupposes, of course, that I know what an experience from this perspective is like. The possibility that I am aware of myself as being experienced in such a way is already contained in the reciprocal second-person experience. I only have to abstract from the fact that I experience the other as experiencing me in order to obtain a third-person mode of givenness of myself. Inversely, I can also abstract from my own being-experienced by the other and thereby adopt myself a third-person perspective on her. This is why the experience of lifeless bodies, that is, of things, corresponds to a third-person perspective, since a thing is experienced, by definition, in a nonreciprocal manner. However, the most natural way to gain access to this third-person mode of givenness is the one indicated by the very term 'third-person perspective,' which refers to the perspective of someone who witnesses an interpersonal encounter without taking part in it. I can gain access to an awareness of this perspective from within when I am myself the "third person."

Since I know what another person's third-person awareness of others is like, I can reproduce it in an indirect manner. This indirect mode of givenness is that of *empathy*, a representational consciousness of the kind of fantasy by which I am aware of something "as if" I were experiencing it from the perspective of the other. It is thus by way of empathy that I access the experience of others who are not involved in a direct interpersonal relation with me. I immediately associate my perception of the other's body with a representation of her experiences. Husserl calls this mode in which the other's experiences are manifest to me through my perception of her bodily movements and facial and verbal expressions that of 'appresentation,' a term that expresses an indirect mode of being present as being associated to something that presents itself.[17] When I perceive another person's body, I apprehend her as the subject of her own experience, and my perception immediately evokes a representation of her experience of the world around her that corresponds to the movements and position of her body. This kind of empathic experience of the other endows my perceptual world with a dimension of givenness that is different from my first-person experience as well as from immediate interpersonal contact.

The reason this mode of givenness is no longer relative to my own experience is that a third person's bodily "here" is not relative to my bodily perspective, because it coincides with a "there" that is common to me and a second person and thereby is given as being independent from each of our different bodily perspectives. From a third-person point of view, the space of my perceptual world thus appears as independent from my perceiving body. When I adopt this perspective, I am aware of myself as existing within my perceptual world like any perceptual object. Because the third person's experience is not reciprocal, the "here" in which the third person is situated can be "anywhere" and the third person can be "anybody." Therefore, the third-person perspective is potentially multiple and is the perspective of others in plural. Whereas the second person is necessarily only *one* and her mode of givenness is intimacy, the third-person givenness corresponds by its very nature to a multiplicity of others and is characterized as *publicity*. As given from a third-person perspective, my being is given to myself in its public accessibility and exposition to the experience of anyone. The third person is characterized by *anonymity*.

It may seem surprising that this rather indirect and derivative third-person point of view is the one from which we normally experience our perceptual world and our own being. Yet it is not difficult to understand why the third-person perspective can be for us a privileged mode of givenness that corresponds to how something "really is." The dimension of the third-person perspective introduces an unlimited multiplicity of possible experiences and consists of a system of infinite possible perspectives that are all instantiations of third-person experience. From the third-person perspective, I gain access to the intersubjective dimension of the identical being of the world that is correlated to the experience of an infinite number of real and possible subjects. This amplification of my access to the perceptual world makes possible a knowledge and appropriation of this world that is incomparably superior to my first-person experience when left on its own. Therefore I am used to understanding the first-person perspective as part of this system of possible perspectives. I apprehend my experience as being just one among all the possible experiences, and this means of course that I consider my first-person experience not as it is given to me but from the point of view of other persons. However, this immense expansion of the reach of our experience and knowledge of the world is not the only reason we understand our being and that of our world of experience as correlated to the third-person perspective. This perspective is also necessarily the predominant mode in which we experience our existence as a social subject, that is, as a member of a community. My social existence mainly consists of my relations to a plurality and even to an anonymous infinity of possible and real others and is therefore predominantly understood from a third-person point of view. After all, as a social subject and as a member of a community, I am "only one among many" and my being is determined by the way I appear to others.

Let me illustrate both of these reasons by our example of watching the dance in the theatre. When seeing the dancer on stage, I am not interested in the way her dance appears to me, but I am taking it as a public event whose experience I share with all the other spectators in the theatre. I experience the dance as a public process that is visible from a multitude of different perspectives, and I understand my experience as a mode of givenness of this process corresponding to the perspective of just one spectator among others. In this manner, I endow my first-person experience of the dance with a third-person meaning. What is more, as a subject of this experience, I am present to myself as "a spectator in a theatre," appropriately dressed, preoccupied with the impression I make on those who accompany me, and judging what I see by the aid of socially established criteria. In a word, I consider myself as I appear to others, as a bodily subject that is part of the natural and social world, and this third-person self-understanding characterizes my whole attitude toward my experience and toward what it shows to me.

The third-person perspective is nevertheless intrinsically relative to a first-person perspective. It is only from my first-person point of view that I can consider another person as a third person, whereas from her own perspective she is of course aware of herself as a "first person." The third-person perspective thus turns out to be a modality of first-person experience in which I am aware of the experience of others. For the very same reason that their experience is not available to me in a first-person manner, its third-person givenness is only possible within a first-person perspective. Because the third-person experience is always relative to first-person subjectivity, our natural understanding of this mode of givenness as the access to the "real being" of everything entails a hidden solipsism. If the being of others is understood in the way it is experienced from the perspective of a different first-person subject, their being is understood as relative to the first-person perspective of this subject. Their own first-person awareness is then interpreted as a subjective appearance of their third-person mode of givenness, which is understood as presenting them "as they really are." To be more precise, third-person intersubjectivity is not simply relative to "a" first-person subjectivity in general but is in each case relative to *my* first-person subjectivity. Far from liberating us from subjectivism, a reduction of the first-person perspective to the third-person mode of givenness is subjectivism in its most extreme form of solipsism. However, this is not noticed because one's own subjectivity is also considered from a third-person perspective and the first-person subject from whose perspective the third-person intersubjectivity is given remains concealed.

On the other hand, if the mode of being of other subjects, as well as that of myself, is understood as it is given in their first-person awareness, this involves a transition from worldly to transcendental intersubjectivity.[18] The access to this first-person intersubjectivity is obviously the universal application of the phenomenological reduction to the first-person perspectives of other subjects. It is extremely curious that this reduction, when applied to intersubjectivity, has an effect opposite to the one it has when it is applied to the natural world. It is not a reduction of transcendence to its being-given to me but rather a recognition of the transcendence of others and a reversal of the third-person perspective's reduction of their being to their being-given to me. Correspondingly, we find that the natural attitude contains precisely such a *reduction* of the first-person existence of others to their third-person givenness. This means that several common ideas concerning the phenomenological reduction and its relation to the natural attitude are mistaken or must be modified.

Transcendental intersubjectivity is a community of first-person subjects. It can only exist in an asymmetrical manner, as a community that is relative to the perspective of each of its members. This community of separated first-person subjects cannot be conceived from an external point of view, and in this sense it cannot form a totality.[19] It exists as a "we" that is inseparable from the first-person perspective of an "I." Yet in each of these first-person perspectives is implied the possibility of all the others and even their reality, to the extent that all subjects are directly or indirectly in real or possible contact with one another through space and time. Transcendental subjectivity and intersubjectivity are thus inseparable. The social and historical community of transcendental first-person subjects exists as a totality only as given from the first-person perspective of one of its members. On the other hand, each of the transcendental subjects and each transcendental process of experience only is possible as part of the historical life of the universal intersubjective community and as part of the concrete communities to which it belongs.

NOTES

1. The classical Kantian definition of the term 'transcendental' runs as follows: "I apply the term transcendental to all knowledge which is not so much occupied with objects as with the mode of our cognition of these objects, so far as this mode of cognition is possible a priori" (Kant 2011, B25).
2. One could just as well say that this kind of knowledge is empirical in a sense that is fundamentally different from the empiricist identification of empirical knowledge with sense experience and induction, that is, with a knowledge limited to facts and causal laws derived from them by inductive inference. It is an intuitive knowledge based upon an immediate givenness of general structures that is part of any particular intuitive experience and can become thematic the moment we turn our interest from the individuals to their general structures, considering them as examples of these structures. It is well known that Husserl always thought of phenomenology as being the true form of empiricism and that he accused classical empiricism of maintaining too narrow a conception of intuition and experience.
3. This unity of the manifestation of the object and of the experience in which it is given is also responsible for the ambiguity of the word 'phenomenon' itself, which can either mean the object that appears or its appearance as such.
4. For Hume's notion of belief, see especially his *A Treatise of Human Nature* (2011), book I, section VII.
5. Husserl finally became aware of this difference when he endowed the transcendental subject with a personality, for example, when he speaks of the transcendental I as a "substrate of habitualities." On the other hand, Sartre in his earlier writings seems to have missed this distinction when interpreting the ego as a transcendent object (cf. especially Sartre 1936).
6. See *Cartesian Meditations* (Hua 1), §31, in which Husserl exposes the threefold structure of the intentional correlation as ego-cogito-cogitatum. However, Husserl normally conceives of the intentional correlation only as twofold, limiting it to the correlation between experience and object (noesis and noema). The reason for this is probably that he focuses more on the permanent presence of an identical I-pole than on its fluctuating self-awareness in which it appears as the concrete subject of its different experiences.

7. It is important to note that we only suspend the attitude of belief as the subject that wants to address experience in a phenomenological manner, whereas the attitude of belief that characterizes the experiencing subject remains intact. In other words, the change of attitude concerns the reflecting subject and not the subject as it is perceived in reflection. This means that we introduce a difference between ourselves as the subject of our experience and as the subject of phenomenological analysis, which is what Husserl calls the "splitting of the I" ('*Ichspaltung*'). See Husserl (Hua 8, 86–97; Fink 1966, 122).

8. This double nature of the present (or the now) was pointed out by Aristotle (*Phys*. IV, 11, 219 b 10–15) and, before him, by Heraclitus in his river simile (DK B 12). Let me stress that I am not considering the temporal structure of worldly processes from an ontological point of view but only insofar as it belongs to the phenomenological structure of the perceptual world and of objects as they appear in perception.

9. Husserl uses this term (*Urpräsentation*) in the *Bernau Manuscripts* (Hua 33), whereas in earlier and later works, he resorts to the term 'primal impression' (*Urimpression*).

10. It should be stressed that the retentions are the self-given past *phases* of perception (as we are aware of them as being past) and not merely modes of a present consciousness *of* the past. (See Hua 10, 69 ff., and 374 ff.) This misunderstanding can easily arise because "being past" in the case of the phases of a worldly process means "being a past present" and also because the retentions are phases of consciousness through which we are aware of the past of a worldly object. Husserl himself usually emphasizes that retentions make something else appear, be it the duration of the object or the succession of the states of the flowing duration of consciousness itself. For a detailed discussion of Husserl's phenomenology of temporal perception, see Obsieger (2006).

11. It can of course become an object in reflection, but thereby its givenness is profoundly altered. This important difference between temporal self-awareness and object-consciousness has been pointed out by Zahavi (see for example 2005, 59 ff.).

12. See Hua 10, 334. See also 63, 66, 113, and 370 ff. Several of the differences by which Husserl characterizes the "atemporal" nature of the stream of consciousness coincide in a striking manner with those Aristotle points out in his distinction between time and change. See *Physics*, IV, 10, 218 b 13–18, and 12, 220 b 3–5.

13. It is well known that the perceived temporal determinations do not fully coincide with the corresponding objective temporal properties as they are studied by the natural sciences, but one must distinguish between the way the world is given in perception and our "objective explanation" of this givenness. (See Hua 10, 61, and 95 ff.) Such an explanation corresponds to a different (third-person) point of view whose relation to the transcendental self-givenness of experience will be addressed in the next section.

14. On this double nature of bodily sensation, see, for instance, Hua 4, 145 f., Hua 5, 119, and Hua 15, 302.

15. The importance of this reversibility for the understanding of intersubjectivity is a central theme of the later Merleau-Ponty (see, for instance, 1964, 185 ff.).

16. This liberation of the perceptual world from its relativity to my bodily orientation has been repeatedly analyzed by Husserl. See, for instance, the *Cartesian Meditations* (Hua 1), §53 and §54.

17. Cf. Hua 1, §52, Hua 13, 224 ff., the texts 28 and 29 from Hua 14, and text 9 from Hua 15.

18. The following remarks describe transcendental intersubjectivity as it was discovered and pointed out by Husserl (cf. especially Hua 13, 14, and 15, and also of course the *V. Cartesian Meditation*). Zahavi has convincingly argued that Husserl's main contribution to the problem of intersubjectivity does not consist in his often-criticized account of our experiential *access* to the other through empathy but in his conception of transcendental intersubjectivity itself. See Zahavi 1996, and 2003, 109–125.
19. This peculiar mode of being of transcendental intersubjectivity (which is different from "being" in its usual sense) is explored in the works of Lévinas. See especially *Totalité et infini* (1961), 24 ff.

REFERENCES

Aristotle. 1936. *Aristotle's Physics: A Revised Text with Introduction and Commentary*. Translated by W. D. Ross. Oxford: Clarendon Press.

Diels, H. and Kranz, W. 1951. Die Fragmente der Vorsokratiker. Griechisch und Deutsch von Hermann Diels. 3 volumes. Hildesheim: Weidmann. (DK)

Fink, E. 1966. *Studien zur Phänomenologie*. The Hague: Martinus Nijhoff.

Hume, D. 2011. *A Treatise of Human Nature*. Oxford: Clarendon Press.

Husserl, E. 1950. *Cartesianische Meditationen und Pariser Vorträge*. Edited by S. Strasser. The Hague: Martinus Nijhoff. (Hua 1). Translation: Husserl, E. 1999. *Cartesian Meditations. An Introduction to Phenomenology*. Translated by D. Cairns. Dordrecht, Boston, London: Kluwer.

———. 1952. *Ideen zur einer reinen Phänomenologie und phänomenologischen Philosophie*. Zweites Buch: Phänomenologische Untersuchungen zur Konstitution. Edited by M. Biemel. The Hague: Martinus Nijhoff. (Hua 4)

———. 1959. *Erste Philosophie (1923/4)*. Zweiter Teil: Theorie der phänomenologischen Reduktion. Edited by R. Boehm. The Hague: Martinus Nijhoff. (Hua 8)

———. 1969. *Zur Phänomenologie des inneren Zeitbewusstseins (1893–1917)*. Edited by R. Boehm. The Hague: Martinus Nijhoff. (Hua 10)

———. 1971. *Ideen zu einer reinen Phänomenologie und phänomenologischen Philosophie*. Drittes Buch: Die Phänomenologie und die Fundamente der Wissenschaften. Edited by M. Biemel. The Hague: Martinus Nijhoff. (Hua 5)

———. 1973a. *Zur Phänomenologie der Intersubjektivität*. Texte aus dem Nachlass. Erster Teil. 1905–1920. Edited by I. Kern. The Hagues: Martinus Nijhoff. (Hua 13)

———. 1973b. *Zur Phänomenologie der Intersubjektivität*. Texte aus dem Nachlass. Zweiter Teil. 1921–1928. Edited by I. Kern. The Hague: Martinus Nijhoff. (Hua 14)

———. 1973c. *Zur Phänomenologie der Intersubjektivität*. Texte aus dem Nachlass. Dritter Teil. 1929–1935. Edited by I. Kern. The Hague: Martinus Nijhoff. (Hua 15)

———. 2001. *Die Bernauer Manuskripte über das Zeitbewußtsein (1917/18)*. Edited by R. Bernet & D. Lohmar. Dordrecht: Kluwer Academic Publishers. (Hua 33)

Kant, I. 2011. *Critique of Pure Reason*. Trans. J. M. D. Meiklejohn, Seattle: Pacific Publishing Studio.

Kern, I. 1966. *Husserl und Kant*. The Hague: Martinus Nijhoff.

Lévinas, E. 1961. *Totalité et infini: Essai sur l'extériorité*. The Hague: Martinus Nijhoff.

Merleau-Ponty, M. 1964. *Le visible et l'invisible*. Paris: Gallimard.

Obsieger, B. 2006. "Die Anschauung des Werdens: Zu Husserls Theorie des Zeitbewußtseins." *Phänomenologische Forschungen* 2006: 159–187.

Sartre, J.-P. 1936. *La transcendance de l'ego*. Paris: Vrin.

Zahavi, D. 1996. *Husserl und die transzendentale Intersubjektivität: Eine Antwort auf die sprachpragmatische Kritik*. Dordrecht: Kluwer. English translation: *Husserl and Transcendental Intersubjectivity*. Translation by E. Behnke. Athens: Ohio University Press, 2001.

———. 2003. *Husserl's Phenomenology*. Stanford, CA: Stanford University Press.

———. 2005. *Subjectivity and Selfhood: Investigating the First-Person Perspective*. Cambridge, MA: MIT Press.

Part II
Subjectivity and Intersubjectivity

4 Transcendental Subjectivity and the Human Being

Hanne Jacobs

In his last, unfinished work, *The Crisis of European Sciences and Transcendental Phenomenology*, Husserl famously speaks of the paradox of human subjectivity: "being a subject for the world and at the same time being an object in the world" (Hua 6, 182). Subjectivity considered as a subject that is for the world is what Husserl calls transcendental subjectivity; and subjectivity considered as an object that is in the world is what he terms the human being (*Mensch*). In his major works, Husserl provides a rather straightforward account of how the subject can be both a transcendental subject for the world and a human being in the world—that is, the transcendental subject that constitutes a world also constitutes itself as a human being in the world (Hua 1, §45; Hua 3/1, §53; Hua 6, §§54, 58). However, considered in the broader context of Husserl's writings, this characterization of the relation between transcendental subjectivity and the human being in terms of self-constitution is puzzling. That is, it is not immediately clear whether and how this account of the relation between transcendental subjectivity and the human being coheres with Husserl's many detailed descriptions of the embodied, personal, and historical character of the transcendental subject that constitutes a world.[1]

In what follows, I propose to take a closer look at Husserl's conception of the human being. On the one hand, my discussion of Husserl's account of the human being shows that the way in which Husserl usually characterizes self-constitution is misleading and, if taken at face value, prevents us from understanding how the subject that is for the world is in the world. On the other hand, however, my discussion also provides the tools to understand why Husserl can characterize self-constitution in the way he does and at the same time describe the subject that constitutes the world as an embodied, personal, and historical subject. Specifically, I argue that we can understand self-constitution in two different ways because Husserl has a dual conception of the human being. On the one hand, and in a way that draws on the natural-scientific conception of the human being of his time, Husserl conceives of the human being as a psycho-physical entity in nature. On the other hand, Husserl also conceives of the human being as an embodied person that acts and engages with others in the socio-historical world of everyday life. In his major works, Husserl usually describes how the transcendental subject constitutes itself as a human being in naturalistic terms—that is, a psycho-physical entity. However, as I aim to show, the constitution of oneself as a psycho-physical entity in nature presupposes a more fundamental and primary constitution of oneself as an embodied person in the world. What is more, it is only when we restore the primacy of this personalistic form of self-constitution that it becomes clear that the subject that is for the world and that Husserl terms transcendental is indeed an embodied, personal, and historical subject in the world.

I begin with a discussion of how, in Husserl's view, the naturalistic approach to the human being as a psycho-physical entity in nature is part of the larger cognitive accomplishment of the constitution of nature by the exact natural sciences. Then I discuss why an exclusively natural-scientific account of reality remains, in Husserl's view, incomplete and show how natural science presupposes the objectivity of the lifeworld in which we live as embodied persons. After developing Husserl's account of the distinction between the human being in the lifeworld and the human being as approached by natural science, I argue for the need for a more developed personalistic account of the embodied person and provide the outlines of such an account on the basis of Husserl's manuscripts.[2] Finally, building on my discussion of Husserl's account of the human being and my elaboration of the personalistic account of the embodied person, I reconsider Husserl's characterization of the relation between transcendental subjectivity and the human being in terms of self-constitution.

1   NATURAL SCIENCE AND THE HUMAN BEING

In Husserl's view, the human being and its body figure in two ways in our natural-scientific understanding of the world. First, the awareness of how the particularities of our human bodies shape the way in which we perceive the world is one of the motives for approaching the world in an exact natural-scientific way. Second, this natural scientific investigation of the world can be extended to include us as embodied perceivers. Thus, the human being that investigates the world in a natural scientific way also becomes the object of this natural scientific investigation. In this section, I first provide Husserl's account of how we posit or constitute the nature of physics and pay special attention to the role of the human body in the coming about of the natural-scientific worldview. Then I consider one of Husserl's arguments for why the natural-scientific worldview cannot be considered complete because this argument can show why Husserl can differentiate between two conceptions of the human being.

According to Husserl, there are at least two ways in which the natural-scientific constitution of nature is motivated. On the one hand, we can come to the realization that how things perceptually appear to us depends on the kinds of bodies we have. This realization can motivate us to strive to overcome this subject-relative experience of the world by approaching the world in a natural-scientific manner—that is, as nature in itself (e.g., Hua 3, §40, §52; Hua 4, §18; Hua 5, 127; HuMa 4, 184–185). On the other hand, the imprecise character of our perceptual knowledge of the causal relations between material things can motivate us to do the same (e.g., Hua 6, §9b and d). I here focus on the first motive because it involves the human being.

Certain irregularities in our individual perceptual experience can make us realize that how the world appears to us in perception is dependent on the particularity or state of our bodily organism. As Husserl's well-known example goes, ingesting santonin will make the world appear yellow, and I apperceive the change as something conditioned by a change in my body and not as a change in the things (Hua 4, 62ff., 73).[3] Not only do such perceptual irregularities show that changes in my body can affect how I perceive the world, they more importantly show that how I perceive the world is always already dependent on my bodily organism (i.e., a normal functioning body). Likewise, encounters with other human beings can evince that the particularity of one's human body always plays a significant role in the way in which the world perceptually appears to us (e.g., I might realize that I am nearsighted). In short, I can become aware of the fact that the way in which I perceive the world varies with and depends on the particularity and state of my bodily organism (e.g., Hua 4, 56, 61ff., 75, 77, 85). Or as Husserl writes in a manuscript, there is a "relativism pertaining to the relation to the lived body, which, intersubjectively speaking, means that the system of appearances pertaining to the univocity of truth can be different for each subject to the extent that each subject can have a different embodiment."[4] The question to which the natural scientific approach to the world is an answer is the following: How can we overcome this relativism inherent in our perceptual awareness of the world?

In Husserl's view, modern natural science attempts to overcome the relativism inherent in our perceptual awareness of the world by trading the intuitive, subject-relative perceptual awareness of the world for an exact mathematical understanding of the world, which purports to be knowledge of true (*wahre*) nature or nature in itself (*an sich*). Husserl certainly acknowledges the validity of this natural-scientific approach to reality. At the same time, however, he also maintains that the natural-scientific worldview is incomplete. As Husserl writes: "Natural-scientific knowledge, understood as physicalistic knowledge, is not a possible ideal of knowledge; this knowledge is by necessity incomplete and necessarily points to a science of appearances."[5]

Of course, one might suggest at this point that we can extend the natural scientific investigation of nature to include the human being and its perceptions of the world, thus also providing an exact natural science of appearances and in this way a complete and exact natural-scientific view of reality. However, Husserl has reservations with regard to extending the exact natural scientific investigation from inanimate nature to the human being. That is, even though Husserl, in line with the developments in experimental physiology, psycho-physics, and psychology of his time, acknowledges that a natural science of the human body and its psychological or mental states is possible, he also thinks that we cannot naturalize or arrive at an *exact* natural science of the human being.

I do not engage here with Husserl's reasons for believing that an exact natural science of the human being is not possible and with whether he is correct in believing that the human being cannot be completely naturalized.[6] I refrain from doing so because Husserl also makes a more fundamental argument against the completeness of an exclusively natural-scientific account of reality (including the human being).[7] That is, a natural-scientific account of reality is incomplete because it presupposes the objectivity of the lifeworld or the world that we perceive in everyday life. I develop this argument only to the limited extent that it allows me to show how, in Husserl's view, the natural scientific account of the human being as an object in nature presupposes the pregivenness and objectivity of the human being that is a subject in the world. I do this by briefly explaining why, in Husserl's view, the natural-scientific investigation of nature presupposes the objectivity of the lifeworld and then by considering one of Husserl's reasons for thinking that a natural scientific account of consciousness cannot guarantee the objectivity of the lifeworld.

I have already stated that in Husserl's view, the natural-scientific approach to reality tries to overcome the subject-relative character of our perceptions by relying on mathematical thought instead of perception in our pursuit of knowledge of reality. In this way, the scientist purports to investigate nature in itself or true nature. Now, according to Husserl's phenomenological account, nature in itself as it is investigated by the natural scientist is only different from the world that we perceive insofar as it refers to the exact determinable features and structure of the extended things that we perceive (HuMa 4, 192). That is, natural science approaches the perceived world in such a way that it only registers what can be understood by means of mathematical concepts and laws. As Husserl writes in a manuscript, "Physics, with its concepts, only draws lines through the unity of the phenomenal thing and its thingly constellations."[8] Or, in the more familiar formulation, the categorial activity of natural scientific understanding throws a "garb of ideas" over the lifeworld (Hua 6, 51–52).

Husserl's characterization of physicalistic nature as the mathematical determinable structure of the natural world that is the object of perception implies that we clearly can and should distinguish between the nature that is the correlate of natural scientific thought and the extended things that we perceive that are the correlate of our perceptions. Nevertheless, this characterization also implies that we should resist the conclusion that we are dealing either with two ontologically distinct natures or with just one physicalistic nature (doing away with perceived nature as mere appearance). On this crucial point, Husserl is quite straightforward and worth citing in full:

> What I aim to determine scientifically is the object of experience and in this sense it is the same object; this object is experienced and is at the same time the subject of logical predicates that have evident grounds in and through the grounding in experience. However, only one object appears and not several; there are also not several objects, only one, though one that is, on the one hand, experienced, and, on the other hand, thought and understood in truth. The physicalistic object is thus nothing new; it only refers to the true concept of the experienced object.[9]

Thus, in Husserl's view, we are dealing with one intuitively experienced or perceived world whose appearance is subject relative and whose mathematizable structure or features are the object of natural science. An exact science of nature is incomplete because it presupposes the pregivenness of the world that is perceived, even if it overcomes the subject-relative appearance of this world by approaching it in an exact natural-scientific manner. What is more, the attempt to overcome this incompleteness by providing a natural-scientific account of our perception of the world is, in Husserl's view, bound to fail because such an account cannot guarantee the objectivity of the world of perception.

One of the reasons Husserl provides for why a natural-scientific account of consciousness cannot guarantee the objectivity of the lifeworld is that a causal account of perception completely subjectivizes this perceived lifeworld. That is, in Husserl's view, a natural-scientific account of consciousness considers nature in itself (the human body included) as the cause of my perceptions. In doing so, however, a causal account of perception would subjectivize both the subjective appearances of things and the perceived things (Hua 3, 114) and would not be able to account for the objectivity of the lifeworld.

Husserl's phenomenological account of natural scientific reason and his argument against an exclusively natural-scientific account of reality are more complex than I can do justice to here.[10] However, the phenomenological argument for the objectivity of the lifeworld that I have presented here suffices to show how Husserl can make room for two distinct approaches to the human being, one from the point of view of the lifeworld or the personalistic point of view and another from the natural-scientific point of view. It is to these two different ways of approaching the human being that I now turn.

2 TWO CONCEPTIONS OF THE HUMAN BEING

Husserl's account of the constitution of physicalistic nature reveals and re-establishes the intuitively given and objectively valid basis of a natural-scientific account of reality—namely, the world that we perceive. Within this world, we also encounter human beings, and we experience ourselves as human beings. When speaking of the human beings that we encounter within the world of everyday life, Husserl often uses the term 'person' (*Person*), which he characterizes as a unity of *Leib* and *Geist* (Hua 4, 236), and he contrasts the person to the human animate organism (*animal*) considered as the unity of *Leibkörper* and *Seele* (Hua 4, 234). Husserl correspondingly distinguishes between two uses of the term 'human being,' which can refer to both the human person as part of the socio-historical world of everyday life and the human animal as part of the natural world as understood by natural science (e.g., Hua 4, 143), even though he also sometimes uses the term 'human being' ambiguously (e.g., Hua 6, 186–187). In order to secure the distinction between these two conceptions of the human being, I first describe how natural science approaches the human being and then turn to a description of the human being as encountered within the world of everyday life—the human being that investigates the world as nature and itself as part of nature. I will not be able to provide a full-fledged account of the person as member of a socio-historical community. Instead, I describe how, according to Husserl, natural science approaches the human being as a psycho-physical entity and how this approach is different from and presupposes the pregivenness and objectivity of the human being in the world of everyday life. Building on this discussion, I then show that there is room within Husserl's phenomenology for a richer and more developed account of our everyday bodily self-awareness than is usually acknowledged, which then provides the tools to rethink Husserl's characterization of self-constitution.

For Husserl, the scientific investigation of the human being is part of the exact natural scientific understanding of material nature insofar as the human body is a material thing like any other (e.g., Hua 4, 143, 170). However, in Husserl's view and in accordance with the experimental physiologists and psychologists of his time, some real features of the human being are not material.[11] That is, when scientifically investigating the body as a material object, there are some residual but real features of this body that make it a lived or living body (*Leib*) and that are not captured by a science of materiality (*Körperlichkeit*)—for example, the sensings (*Empfindnisse*) on the body's surface that occur when it is touched or heated and the kinesthetic sensations (*Empfindungen*) that occur when it moves or is being moved. What is more, sensations (*Empfindungen*) and other mental events occur when certain causal events bring about changes in the sense organs and nervous system.

Correspondingly, Husserl differentiates among three ways in which the human being is natural-scientifically investigated: (1) as a mere material body (*Körper*), the human being is the object of investigation in physics and chemistry; (2) as a lived or living body (*Leib*) whose sense-organs and nervous system give rise to localized and spread out sensings (*Empfindnisse*) and nonlocalized sensations (*Empfindungen*), the human being is the object of a natural-scientific somatology, which includes physiology and psycho-physics;

and (3) insofar as the human being has perceptions and other mental events, it can become the object of an empirical psychology or natural science of the psyche (*Seele*) and its psychological states (e.g., Hua 4, 143; Hua 5, 14).[12]

Husserl's descriptions of the human being naturalistically understood show that the natural scientific investigation of the human being as a psychophysical entity in nature does not only extend the project of natural science beyond mere inanimate nature but also introduces a new way of thinking about the human subject. Specifically, according to Husserl, the human subject comes to be thought of as a kind of "dual entity" or "*Doppelwesen*"[13] (Hua 4, 120) composed of what is the object of the natural scientific investigation of material nature (i.e., the *Körper*) and everything else that is not. According to Husserl, we thus come to think of our psychological life as something like an annex to the living material body (e.g., Hua 4, 177, 190, 209, 211). And the body, being both material object (*Körper*) and sensitive surface and depth (*Leib*), becomes a "turning point" or "*Umschlagspunkt*" (Hua 5, 161) between a material nature and a consciousness that is understood as dependent on the material body insofar as changes in the material body give rise to certain sensations and perceptions.

This natural-scientific understanding of the human being as a psychophysical entity is, as Husserl points out, radically distinct from the way in which our fellow human beings present themselves to us within the world of everyday life. That is, when encountering other human beings within our environing world, we rarely approach them as sensitive material bodies (*Leibkörper*) to which a psyche is annexed. Instead, the human beings we encounter within our daily lives are experienced as original ontological unities (e.g., Hua 4, 234–235, 240, 245). Concretely, when we see another human being move its hand, we do not see a moving hand and infer a psychological state. Instead, the bodily gestures and movements of other human beings are directly expressive (*Ausdruck*) of their personal life (e.g., Hua 4, 192, 204, 236, 325); we directly experience the gesture of another human being as a friendly hand wave, a reluctant smile, or a dismissive shrug.[13]

This of course does not mean that the psycho-physical entity that is investigated by a science of animate nature is ontologically different from the human beings that we encounter within the world. What is the case, however, is that on the account that Husserl presents, the natural scientific investigation of human beings and other animate organisms does more than enable us to scientifically understand what we see. We could say in the language of the *Crisis* that the natural-scientific understanding of the human being also throws a garb of ideas over the human being of the lifeworld. Specifically, even though in everyday life we do not experience others or ourselves as material things with an annexed psyche or mind—that is, as animate or psycho-physical entities—the natural-scientific investigation of the human being introduces an abstractive isolation of the material body from what is not material. This is not any different from how the natural-scientific investigation of the world allows us to isolate a perception of extended things from our rich perception of a practical and socio-historical world (Hua 6, 60–61, 230).

What is more, like the natural-scientific investigation of nature disregards what we in our everyday lives consider to be real and meaningful, many aspects of the human beings we encounter are equally disregarded from the point of view of a science of animate nature. So, with regard to the appearing human body, the only thing that is relevant from a naturalistic point of view is how it reacts to and interacts with the surrounding natural circumstances and how this gives rise to certain sensations or mental events (e.g., Hua 4, 170). Consequently, things that are real and that matter in our everyday lives (e.g., expressive behavior and other forms of incarnated meaning) become irrelevant in this naturalistic perspective. In this sense, the natural-scientific investigation of the human being is not different from the natural scientific investigation of the world.

This is no different with regard to the way in which we experience our bodies from within. That is, our bodily self-awareness amounts to more than having localized and spread-out sensations of touch and warmth or more vaguely localized kinesthetic experiences, which are both forms of bodily self-awareness that can be easily naturalized or understood as being psycho-physically linked to material changes in the body.[14] More generally speaking, and as I aim to develop in the next section, a personalistic account of how we experience our own bodies and our being in the world is quite different from and presupposed by an account of the experience of having a body from the natural-scientific point of view.

3   TOWARD A PERSONALISTIC ACCOUNT OF THE HUMAN BODY

Husserl's phenomenological descriptions of how we experience our own bodies and the fundamental role of this bodily self-awareness for our perceptual awareness of the world are well known and have inspired much discussion within phenomenology. Specifically, Husserl describes how kinesthetic lived-experiences or the awareness of movement play a crucial role in our perception of the world (e.g., Hua 4, 56–58; 151–152). He also points out how sensations of touch are localized, how the body feels itself in touching, and that when I touch my own body, there is a doubling of the localized sensations of touch since sensations are felt in both the touching and the touched hand (Hua 4, 146–147). Finally, Husserl draws attention to the fact that we experience ourselves as the zero-point of orientation (e.g., Hua 4, 56) and that we experience our own body as a volitional organ (*Willensorgan*) with certain practical capabilities (the so-called "I can"; e.g., Hua 4, 152, 258–259).

After having distinguished between the human being naturalistically and personalistically understood, however, one might wonder whether these descriptions of the body do justice to the variety of ways in which we experience our bodies within the personalistic attitude of our daily lives.[15] Whereas the description of the perceiving body in terms of kinesthesia, the zero-point of orientation, and the "I can" suffices when we want to describe the role of the body in the perception of material things, and whereas the description of the localized sensations of touch suffices for the account of the naturalistic constitution of the body as a sensitive material body (*Leibkörper*), a phenomenological account of how I experience my body within the personalistic attitude calls for new and additional phenomenological descriptions. While providing a full-fledged account of the bodily self-awareness of the human subject within the lifeworld falls outside the scope of this chapter, I do outline the different directions such an account can take.[16]

First, whenever I move my body, I never just experience kinesthetic sensations. Rather, my movements are experienced as actualizations of certain movements that are possible within certain kinesthetic systems that I am acquainted with and that inform my implicit awareness of what is within the range of my bodily capabilities (*Vermögen*) and what is not. So, for example, when typing, I do not just feel my fingers moving; instead, I actualize a movement with which I am familiar, that I know that I am capable of, and that is an actualization within a system of possible other movements that together make up the bodily capability of typing. While Husserl does not provide a detailed description of how I acquire my bodily capabilities in the writings published as *Ideas II,* he does provide such descriptions in the D-manuscripts.[17] Specifically, he speaks of the acquisition of familiar kinesthetic systems or organs and the organization (*Organisation*) of different kinesthetic systems or organs into one lived body in and through practice (*Übung*), which results in practical mastery (*Herrschaft*). Such a kinesthetic system is more than the sum of my current kinesthetic awareness (e.g., in my arm, legs, back, etc.). Rather, what Husserl calls a kinesthetic system is the result of what one could call a history of the body in and through repeated and continuously refined actions. Specifically, through repeated and continuously refined actions within the world and in relation to things, my body becomes an organ whose motile capabilities I am familiar with and thus an organ that I can move at will; the acquisition of bodily capabilities in turn informs the way in which I experience and thus relate to my surrounding world.

What Husserl's phenomenological descriptions in these manuscript pages amount to (and what can be read as anticipating Merleau-Ponty's account of the body) is an account of the genesis of the body-subject in and through bodily action into a sophisticated organ of perception and action with acquired systems of familiar movements. In this context, organ should not be understood in the biological sense as referring to a part of the material organism (e.g., the heart, liver, or stomach); rather, 'organ' here refers to the organized and mastered lived body (or part of it) by means of which I can perceptually explore the world and perform actions within it (e.g., the hand, head, and eyes insofar as they refer to specific kinesthetic systems). What is important for the following is that the description of the acquisition of kinesthetic systems or the body as organ of perception and action amounts to an account of the self-constitution of my body over which I hold sway (*Walten*) and can move at will (*Willensorgan*) in and through action in and toward my environing world. That is, by means of the acquisition of habits in and through the performance and mastery of actions within and towards my environing world, I become a certain individual body-subject with specific capabilities with which I am intimately familiar. So, for example, in a manuscript Husserl writes:

> Each I has its own way of behaving, each I has its own habitus in this respect, its changing stock of habits, its innate and acquired capabilities, its way to give itself bodily, its way of walking, dancing, jumping, and of dealing with material things (knives and spoons, cups, etc.) in its daily going-about. (A VI 10/11b; 1913)[18]

The lived body or organ of perception that results from this self-constitution through the acquisition of habit is the lived body that is at the center of the lifeworld and that serves as the basis for any natural-scientific inquiry (either of this lifeworld or of this lived body itself).[19]

Second, a personalistic account of how we experience our bodies within the world of everyday life would also describe how we experience the materiality of our bodies from within. This would amount to more than describing how one, as a lived body, is the bearer of localized sensations (of touch, warmth, etc.) or is able to experience oneself as both touched and touching, as happens in the case in which one of one's organs touches another. So, for example, we experience from within how we have bodily limits (i.e., the "I cannot;" Hua 4, 254), and when reaching those limits, we can be said to become aware of material constraints from within (e.g., I can only turn my eyes and head to a certain extent, and I can only run for a certain amount of time before becoming too tired to continue). In addition, the execution of practical action is always accompanied by a certain feeling of effort (*Anspannung*; D 10/25b, 37a; D 12/15a, 16a, 17b, 19b). Even if a natural-scientific investigation could link these experiences of materiality and effort to underlying material processes, as lived-experiences, they are part and parcel of our experience of embodiment and guide and precede any subsequent natural-scientific investigation of the body.

Third, a personalistic account of our bodily self-experience would also be able to describe the way in which sensings, such as the sensation of touch, are never just an experience of being touched or touching. That is, sensations always arise within a context. For example, there are different ways of being touched (e.g., being touched by a stranger or a friend) and different ways of touching (e.g., handling something gently because it is delicate or because one is disgusted by it). And depending on their context, sensings will have a different significance.[20] On the other hand, in the framework of a naturalistic description, all sensations in my fingertip are considered identical insofar as they are conditioned by a similar or identical change in the material body.

Finally, in addition to opening up new dimensions of description with regard to one's experience of one's body as lived from within, a personalistic account of the body would also describe what it implies for our bodies to be visible to ourselves and others. Specifically, insofar as our bodies are visible, they become the bearers of cultural and socio-historical significations.[21] Consequently, I can be ashamed or proud of the way in which I appear or think I appear in the eyes of others (Hua 4, 382). One could also go further than Husserl in the description of these phenomena and consider to what extent the way in which I move and perceive is influenced by the way in which I am perceived by others (e.g., in response to ongoing or institutionalized humiliating objectification).[22]

All these descriptions, however, are descriptions of the different aspects of my experience of myself as a human embodied person and are descriptions of how I experience myself within the lifeworld or from the personalistic attitude. Even if, within this personalistic perspective, I can differentiate between the body as it appears from the outside and my body as I experience from within, this differentiation is a differentiation within an original unity and does not fall together with the naturalistic distinction between material body and lived body with a psyche annexed to it. This difference between how I experience myself within the lifeworld and how I come to understand myself within a naturalistic perspective allows me, in concluding, to reconsider the paradox of human subjectivity and with it the relation between the transcendental subject and the human being in Husserl's phenomenology.

4   TWO FORMS OF SELF-CONSTITUTION

I began this chapter by calling attention to Husserl's description of what he terms the paradox of subjectivity—that is, being both a subject for the world and an object in the world. Instead of directly dealing with this paradox and the relation between transcendental subjectivity and the human being, I proposed to take a closer look at Husserl's account of the human being. My discussion of Husserl's account of how natural science approaches the world and the human being within it shows in what sense the human being can be considered as an object in the world—that is, as a psycho-physical entity in nature. The account of how we can come to consider ourselves as psycho-physical entities in nature also shows, however, that this natural-scientific conception of the human being presupposes the pregivenness and objectivity of the world of everyday life and ourselves as embodied persons within it.

Now, like Husserl does not differentiate between the world that we perceive and the world that we understand natural-scientifically as two different ontological domains, the human being within the lifeworld is also not ontologically different from the human being as psycho-physical entity. Instead, like nature in itself is the perceived world as approached by natural-scientific thought, the human being as a psycho-physical entity is the human being within the world as looked at through the lens of science. Nevertheless, as my discussion aims to show, the way in which the human being is regarded is quite different in the naturalistic and personalistic attitude, respectively. What is more, and as I aim to develop in this concluding section, this difference is especially pertinent if we aim to understand Husserl's characterization of the relation between transcendental subjectivity and the human being in terms of self-constitution.

In Husserl's account, the transcendental subject that experiences or constitutes a world also constitutes or experiences itself as part of this world. More technically stated, the relation between transcendental subjectivity and the human being is one of self-apperception, self-objectification, or also "enworlding" (*Verweltlichung* or *Mundanisierung*). However, in his major writings, when describing this enworlding, or how transcendental consciousness is aware of itself as a human being within the world, Husserl casts this enworlding in terms of psycho-physical self-apperception (Hua 1, §45; Hua 3/1, §53; Hua 6, §§54, 58).[23] And this accords with Husserl's formulation of the paradox of human subjectivity, in which he only speaks of the transcendental subject for the world and the human being as object in the world (i.e., the psycho-physical human being).

However, merely focusing on Husserl's discussion of the constitution of oneself as a psycho-physical human being will not allow one to fully understand how we, as constituting subjects, constitute ourselves as human beings because this naturalistic self-constitution presupposes that we always already experience ourselves as embodied persons within the world. More importantly, it is only once we realize that, in Husserl's account, the constitution of oneself as a psycho-physical entity in nature presupposes the pregivenness of an objective lifeworld in which we as embodied persons act, live, and interact that we can also start to rethink the way in which transcendental subjectivity or the subject that is for the world is enworlded (i.e., is in the world). Negatively stated, an account of how the subject that constitutes a world constitutes itself as part of the world that is guided by the naturalistic understanding of the human being as a psycho-physical entity unduly limits what being in the world amounts to for a world-constituting subject. That is, in this account, the relation between transcendental consciousness and the human being essentially boils down to a relation between a stream of conscious experience and the body as a material object to which this (now psychologically apperceived) consciousness is annexed. Understood in this way, I as transcendental subject would be enworlded insofar as my intentional lived experiences are apperceived as psychological events and insofar as sensations such as touch sensations are apperceived as psycho-physically conditioned by changes in the material body and localized on my material body, a body that belongs to nature.

Differently stated, when we allow ourselves to be guided solely by Husserl's naturalistic account of the human being, enworlding amounts to a kind of self-objectification of consciousness by consciousness in and through the apperception of oneself as annexed to a material body that is sensitive. Understood in this way, however, the subject that constitutes the world is strictly speaking not *in* the world—even if annexed to and spread out over a worldly *Leibkörper*. This is indeed how Husserl characterizes the relation between transcendental consciousness and the human being in *Ideas I*:

> A peculiar kind of apprehending or experiencing, a peculiar kind of "apperception," effects the production of this so-called "annexation," this reification [*Realisierung*] of consciousness. Regardless of that whereof this apperception consists or of what particular kind of demonstration it may demand, this much is obvious: Consciousness itself, in these apperceptive involvements, or in this psychophysical relationship to something corporeal, loses none of its own essence [. . .] And still it has become something other, a component part of Nature. (Hua 3, 104)

In *Ideas I*, Husserl does not develop what this apperception consists in, and it is not certain that he has the tools there to fully develop what this natural-scientifically understood apperception entails (even though there is no doubt that he does have these tools when he speaks of self-apperception in psycho-physical terms in *Cartesian Meditations* and *Crisis*). However, as I developed in the first two sections, in Husserl's own account of the naturalistic approach to the world, a naturalistic self-apperception can only come about in the framework of the constitution of physicalistic nature. And the constitution of physicalistic nature presupposes the objectivity of the lifeworld and the human person, the constitution of which is described by Husserl's phenomenological account of the personalistic perspective on the world and ourselves.

Now, once one places the naturalistic apperception of oneself as a psycho-physical unity in the broader perspective of Husserl's personalistic account of the human being within the world of everyday life, enworlding appears to amount to much more and something different than a psycho-physical self-apperception as described in the aforementioned passage of *Ideas I*. Specifically, as my discussion of the body from the personalistic perspective in the third section aims to show, being embodied amounts to more than experiencing certain forms of bodily self-awareness. That is, as was indicated in the previous section, according to the personalistic description of our subjective experience, living an embodied life entails, among other things, acquiring specific kinesthetic systems and capabilities in and through actions that one learns to master and that one performs in relation to a meaningful world. What is more, the personalistic description of embodiment also describes what it means to feel and be familiar with the materiality of one's body rather than to understand it natural-scientifically in psycho-physical terms. Now, this personalistic account of the body, even though it certainly can be further elaborated, allows us to understand how transcendental subjectivity as constituting subject is an embodied subject in the world. That is, transcendental subjectivity is not just enworlded in the sense that it apperceives of itself as psycho-physically connected to a sensitive living body. Rather, transcendental subjectivity is also enworlded in the sense that the subject that constitutes a world perceptually explores the world in and through movements with which it is familiar on the basis of acquired bodily habits (an acquisition that occurs in and through performing movements and actions within this world), in the sense that it feels how its movements are more or less effortless, and in the sense that it feels the materiality of its body when confronted with certain bodily constraints from within (e.g., exhaustion).

One could capture the difference between a naturalistically oriented and a personalistically contextualized account of how the subject that is for the world experiences itself within the world by distinguishing two different ways of thinking of self-constitution. That is, a naturalistically oriented understanding of self-constitution will cast this self-constitution in what one could call a vertical sense. More specifically, a solely naturalistically oriented phenomenological description of the relationship between transcendental subjectivity and the human being will describe how transcendental consciousness can become aware of itself as annexed to a material body. This awareness entails a constitution of oneself as psyche (i.e., a consciousness annexed to a material body). Even though this psyche is annexed to a body, it is still radically different from its body, which is a material object (*Körper*). Even if this material body (*Körper*) is also a sensitive organism (*Leib*), the worldly self-constitution of transcendental consciousness as a human being is accomplished from above, so to speak. It is accomplished from above insofar as on this picture, transcendental consciousness becomes aware of itself as localized in a body from which it is nevertheless distinct, even if we acknowledge the way in which sensings are localized and have their own peculiar spatiality (*Ausbreitung*).

If, however, one proceeds from Husserl's descriptions of the personalistic perspective, it becomes clear that the self-constitution of transcendental consciousness as a human being is a lateral or horizontal constitution insofar as the subject that experiences a world has a rich and diversified bodily self-awareness and develops bodily capabilities and kinesthetic systems in and through experiencing and acting in a world. The acquisition of bodily habits in fact amounts to a veritable constitution of the constituting subject because the acquisition of certain bodily habits will shape one's perception of the world. This bodily self-constitution can only occur in and through being practically engaged *in* a world and perceptually exploring this world.

It goes without saying that we as constituting subjects are more than habitual organs of perception. That is, the constituting subject that acquires habits in and through the performance of actions within and in relation to a world also acquires what Husserl calls personal habitualities, which play a fundamental role in how the subject experiences the world (Hua 3, §32). Further, the way in which a constituting subject experiences the world is shaped by a specific socio-historical context or tradition.[24] Thus, Husserl's characterization of self-constitution in terms of psychophysical apperception in his major works is misleading since he does not spell out there everything that is presupposed by such a naturalistic self-apperception. That is, and this is what I hope to have shown, the transcendental subject that is for the world can only apperceive of itself as an object in the world (i.e., a psychophysical entity) because it is an embodied subject in the world. What is more, the constitution of oneself as an embodied person in the world can by no means be characterized as the constitution of an object by a subject; the constituting subject constitutes itself as an embodied subject in and through the way it acts in the world of which it is aware in a way that reflects its history.

NOTES

1. There are many excellent works that deal with these descriptions; see Heinämaa (2007), Steinbock (1995), Taipale (2014), and Zahavi (1994, 1999, 2003).
2. Landgrebe seems to refer to the need for such a personalistic account of the body when he asks, "Was ist dagegen die Natur und was ist unser Leib in der 'personalistischen', der natürlich-lebensweltlichen Einstellung?" (1965, 299). Welton seems to make a similar suggestion when he writes, "if the body as probed by the gloved hand of science arises only in correlation with a specific interest, then we can open the question of how it is related to other entities through other interests" (1999, 41). Melle (1996), Behnke (1996), Zahavi (1999, chapter 9), Reynaert (2000), and Heinämaa (2007, 2010) all distinguish between a personalistic and a naturalistic account of the human being and its body. The personalistic account bodily self-awareness that I develop later (section 3) aims to indicate further avenues of description of our everyday experience of our body. In developing this account, I draw on Husserl's as-yet-unpublished D-manuscripts, which I also use in my discussion of the constitution of nature. Since the D-manuscripts on which I will be relying stem from different periods, I indicate the year of the cited passages in parentheses. I would like to thank the director of the Husserl Archives in Leuven, Prof. Ullrich Melle, for allowing me to cite from these unpublished manuscripts.
3. One could object that, in the example of the santonin, the apperception of the change in color in the appearance of the world as *mere* appearance can only come about when this change is understood to be conditioned by a change in the material body and brain, which seems to presuppose the natural-scientific approach to reality that it is said to motivate. However, this is not the case because the apperception of a change in the appearance of the world as *mere* appearance need not rely on a natural scientific theory of the brain and color-sensations. This is more clear for other examples that Husserl gives—for example, how a blister on the finger changes the way a surface feels, which is something I can ascribe to a change in my bodily organism without having access to any natural-scientific theories pertaining to the sense of touch.
4. The full passage in German goes as follows: "Dann aber der Relativismus der Leibbezogenheit, der intersubjektiv besagt, dass das System der zur Einstimmigkeit der Wahrheit gehörigen Erscheinungen für jedes Subjekt ein anderes

sein kann, sofern jedes eine andere Leiblichkeit haben kann, wobei wieder geschieden wird zwischen dem Normalfall (normaler Menschenleib bei allen) und den Abweichungen" (D 13 I/160b, 1923).

5. The corresponding German passage goes as follows: "Die naturwissenschaftliche Erkenntnis, verstanden als physikalische, ist also kein mögliches Ideal der Erkenntnis: es ist eine notwendig unvollkommene Erkenntnis; sie weist notwendig hin auf eine Wissenschaft von den Erscheinungen" (D 13 I/109a; 1910/1911).

6. Husserl mentions several reasons for thinking that an exact natural science of the human being is not possible. For example, he argues that even if lawful regularities between changes in the material body and sensations can be discovered, mental events are not extended and as such resist a mathematization (Hua 4, 127, 132, 138; Hua 5, 111). Husserl also believes that features that are essential to consciousness being consciousness, such as retention and intentionality, cannot be scientifically accounted for because science does not formulate eidetic laws that concern the essence of consciousness (Hua 4, 293; HuMa 4, 218). Finally, Husserl also suggests that, unlike material events, no psychological event can be repeated because of the temporality and individuality of consciousness and mentions that, unlike natural events, psychological events are historical (Hua 4, 137, 300; Hua 5, 131). The first and second arguments are both challenged by Yoshimi (2007 and 2010, respectively).

7. See also Zahavi (2004) and Trizio (2011).

8. The corresponding German passage goes as follows: "Ja, die Physik mit ihren Begriffen zieht nur Linien durch die Einheit der phänomenalen Dinge und dinglichen Konstellationen" (D 13/107a; 1910/11).

9. The corresponding German passage goes as follows: "Was ich wissenschaftlich bestimmen will, ist ja der Gegenstand der Erfahrung, und so ist er derselbe; er ist gegebenenfalls erfahren und zugleich Subjekt der logischen Prädikate, die in der Begründung in der Erfahrung evidente Gründe haben; erscheinen tun aber nicht mehrere Objekte, sondern nur eines; und es gibt hier auch nicht mehrere, sondern nur eines, aber eines, das einmal bloß erfahren und das andere Mal gedacht und durch Wahrheit begriffen ist. Das physikalische Objekt ist also nichts Neues, sondern besagt nur den wahren Begriff vom Erfahrungsobjekt" (D 13/116a). In another, shorter passage, he states, "In unserer Erfahrung haben wir das wirkliche Objekt, und ein anderes gibt es nicht. Was uns fehlt, ist logische Beherrschung der Erfahrung, die logische Erkenntnis des Erfahrenen" (D 13 I/116b; 1910/11). See also Hua 3/I, §52.

10. For a more complete account, see, for example, Soffer (1990).

11. I do not discuss whether and how the way in which contemporary natural science approaches the human being is different from the way in which physiologists and psychologists of the nineteenth century approached the human being, because this would require an investigation into both the science of Husserl's time and contemporary science. Nevertheless, it seems that Husserl's general claim that a natural-scientific approach to the human being presupposes an everyday experience of the human being does not stand or fall with the accuracy of his account of the natural-scientific understanding of the human being.

12. For a detailed account of Husserl's account of the natural-scientific constitution of the human being, see Trizio (2011) and Bernet (2013).

13. See Heinämaa (2010) for a further discussion of Husserl's account of expressive embodiment.

14. Husserl describes how natural science understands our kinesthetic self-awareness in a manuscript from 1920 in the following way: "Unmittelbar gegeben ist mir das Phänomen des Ich-bewege-meine-Hand, Ich-stoße etc. und

das es manchmal geht und manchmal nicht geht (Widerstand und Widerstandskraft). Dem Sinn solcher Erfahrung nachgehend und sie also zunächst erweiternd, komme ich auf verborgene Zusammenhänge der physischen Leiblichkeit mit dem Ich-bewege. Die innere Struktur des Leibes, die physiologische, die ein subjektives Tun ermöglicht und die in die gewöhnliche Erfahrung nicht eingeht, muss herausgeholt werden" (Hua 13, 451). The natural-scientific apperception of localized sensations (*Empfindnisse*) as caused by material changes in the material body is described by Husserl in section 40 of *Ideas II* (Hua 4, 153–157).

15. This is not to say that a phenomenological description of the body in terms of sensings and kinesthetic sensations is wrong. First, these bodily lived-experiences are part and parcel of the way we experience our bodies within our daily lives (e.g. Hua 4, 212), although they occur in a context of embodied living that consists in more than just having these experiences. Second, a transcendental description of the role of the body in perception that only makes use of these lived-experiences (in addition to pointing out how the body is a zero-point of orientation and organ of perception) is equally correct, but, as the next section aims to show, it does not provide the full picture.

16. Insofar as I develop Husserl's account of bodily self-awareness, my account builds on Zahavi's account of the body in Husserl's phenomenology (e.g. 1994; 1999, 91–109; and 2003, 101–109). See also Taipale (2014, part I).

17. Specifically D 10/21, 31, 42, 43 (1932); D 12/4, 10a, 11b, 16b (1931); and D 13 I/ 8–10 (1921). He does, however, in the so-called *H-Blätter* of 1913, call for such a description when he writes: "Es bedarf hier der Analyse des, Ich kann', und zwar des Ich kann, wie ich je erfahrungsmäßig weiß bzw. was vor aller Reflexion als ‚bekanntliches' ‚das kann ich' charakterisiert ist" (A VI 10/11a). See also Summa (2011, 183ff).

18. The corresponding German passage goes as follows: "Jedes Ich hat seine eigenen Weisen sich zu verhalten, jedes hat darin seinen Habitus, seinen veränderlichen Bestand von Gewohnheiten, seine angeborenen und erworbenen Fähigkeiten, seine Art, sich leiblich zu geben, seine Art zu gehen, zu tanzen, zu springen, in den alltäglichen Betätigungen mit den physischen Dingen (Messer und Gabel, Becher usw.) umzugehen."

19. Husserl does not, to my knowledge, discuss how the acquisition of practical capabilities and habitual systems of familiar movements can be naturalized. However, even if this were possible, this does not change the fact that the bodily self-constitution in and through the acquisition of kinesthetic systems is something that belongs to the personalistic realm or life-world, which is only subsequently natural-scientifically understood.

20. See Al-Saji (2010a), who recently reappraised Husserl's phenomenology of touch from a feminist perspective and argues how sociality structures the sense of touch.

21. Both Alcoff (2006, 179–194) and Al-Saji (2010b) describe how the perception of others can be racialized and how it can become the locus of socio-historical prejudice.

22. See, for example, the descriptions of Fanon (2008) and Young (1990, 141–159).

23. The constitution of oneself as a psycho-physical human being is even more complex than I could account for in this article (see, e.g., Zahavi 1999, 161). That is, this constitution does not only presuppose the constitution of physical nature; it also requires an account of the way in which physical nature and psycho-physical nature are intersubjectively constituted (Hua 4, §43–47). While one's own bodily self-awareness is presupposed for the naturalistic constitution of the *Leibkörper* (Hua 5, 8), it is not sufficient to account for the constitution of myself as a psycho-physical human being, which requires the

constitution of other human beings, which in turn allows one to constitute oneself in their image. This again would require an account of the awareness of others as human beings that can be psycho-physically apperceived and an account of how my own experience of being embodied enables this awareness of other human beings.

24. For an extensive account of these different forms of self-constitution, see Taipale (2014, Part II).

REFERENCES

Alcoff, L. M. 2006. *Visible Identities: Race, Gender, and the Self*. Oxford: Oxford University Press.

Al-Saji, A. 2010a. "Bodies and Sensings: On the Uses of Husserlian Phenomenology for Feminist Theory." *Continental Philosophy Review* 43: 13–37.

———. 2010b. "The Racialization of Muslim Veils: A Philosophical Analysis." *Philosophy Social Criticism* 36 (8): 875–902.

Behnke, E. A. 1996. "Edmund Husserl's Contribution to Phenomenology of the Body in *Ideas II*." In *Issues in Husserl's Ideas II*, edited by T. Nenon and L. Embree, 15–35. Dordrecht/Boston/London: Kluwer Academic Publishers.

Bernet, R. 2013. "The Body as a 'Legitimate Naturalization of Consciousness.'" *Royal Institute of Philosophy Supplement* 72: 43–65.

Fanon, F. 2008. *Black Skin, White Masks*. Translated by R. Philcox. New York: Grove Press.

Heinämaa, S. 2007. "Selfhood, Consciousness, and Embodiment: a Husserlian Approach." In *Consciousness: From Perception to Reflection in the History of Philosophy*, edited by S. Heinämaa, V. Lähteenmäki, and P. Remes, 311–328. Dordrecht: Springer.

———. 2010. "Embodiment and Expressivity in Husserl's Phenomenology: From *Logical Investigations* to *Cartesian Meditations*." *SATS: Northern European Journal of Philosophy* 11 (1): 1–15.

Husserl, E. 1950. *Cartesianische Meditationen und Pariser Vorträge*, ed. S. Strasser, The Hague, Netherlands: Martinus Nijhoff. In English: *Cartesian Meditations*, trans. D. Cairns. Dordrecht, Boston: Martinus Nijhoff, 1960. (Hua 1)

———. 1952. *Ideen zu einer reinen Phänomenologie und phänomenologischen Philosophie, Zweites Buch: Phänomenologische Untersuchungen zur Konstitution*, ed. Marly Biemel. The Hague: Martinus Nijhoff. In English: *Ideas Pertaining to a Pure Phenomenology and to a Phenomenological Philosophy, Second Book: Studies in the Phenomenological Constitution*, trans. R. Rojcewicz and A. Schuwer. Dordrecht, Boston, London: Kluwer Academic Publishers, 1993. (Hua 4)

———. 1954. *Die Krisis der europäischen Wissenschaften und die transzendentale Phänomenologie: Eine Einleitung in die phänomenologischen Philosophie*, ed. W. Biemel. The Hague: Martinus Nijhoff. In English: *The Crisis of European Sciences and Transcendental Phenomenology: An Introduction to Phenomenological Philosophy*, trans. D. Carr. Evanston, IL: Northwestern University, 1988. (Hua 6)

———. 1971. *Ideen zur einer reinen Phänomenologie und phänomenologischen Philosophie. Drittes Buch: Die Phänomenologie und die Fundamente der Wissenschaften*, ed. Marly Biemel. The Hague, Netherlands: Martinus Nijhoff. (Hua 5)

———. 1973. *Zur Phänomenologie der Intersubjektivität. Texte aus dem Nachlass. Erster Teil. 1905–1920*, ed. Iso Kern. The Hague, Netherlands: Martinus Nijhoff, 1973. (Hua 13)

———. 1976. *Ideen zu einer reinen Phänomenologie und phänomenologischen Philosophie I*. Edited by Karl Schuhmann. The Hague: Martinus Nijhoff. Translation:

Husserl, E. 1931. *Ideas. General Introduction to Phenomenology.* Translated by B. Gibson. London: Collier Macmillan Publishers. (Hua 3/1)

———. 2002. *Natur und Geist. Vorlesungen Sommersemester 1919.* Husserliana: Materialienband 4, ed. Michael Weiler. Dordrecht, Netherlands: Kluwer Academic Publishers. (HuMa4)

———. A. *A-Manuscripts* (unpublished).

———. D. *D-Manuscripts* (unpublished).

Ingarden, R. 1965. "Husserls Betrachtungen zur Konstitution des physikalischen Dinges." In *La Phénoménologie et les Sciences de la Nature, Archives de l'Institut International des Sciences Théoriques* 13: 36–87. Brussels: Office International de Librairie.

Landgrebe, L. 1965. "Die Phänomenologie der Leiblichkeit und das Problem der Materie." In *Beispiele. Festschrift für Eugen Fink zum 60. Geburtstag,* edited by Ludwig Landgrebe, 291–305. Den Haag: Martinus Nijhoff.

Melle, U. 1996. "Nature and Spirit." In *Issues in Husserl's Ideas II,* edited by T. Nenon and L. Embree, 15–35. Dordrecht: Kluwer Academic Publishers.

Reynaert, P. 2000. "Husserl's Phenomenology of Animate Being." *Phänomenologische Forschungen* 2: 251–269.

Soffer, Gail. 1990. "Phenomenology and Scientific Realism: Husserl's Critique of Galileo." *The Review of Metaphysics* 44 (1): 67–94.

Steinbock, Anthony. 1995. *Home and Beyond. Generative Phenomenology after Husserl.* Evanston, IL: Northwestern University Press.

Summa, M. 2011. "Das Leibgedächtnis: Ein Beitrag aus der Phänomenologie Husserls." *Husserl Studies* 27 (3): 173–196.

Taipale, J. 2014. *Phenomenology and embodiment. Husserl and the constitution of subjectivity.* Evanston, IL: Northwestern University Press.

Trizio, E. 2008. "Réflexions husserliennes sur la mathématisation de la nature." In *La nature entre science et philosophie,* edited by N. Lechopier and G. Marmasse, 45–64. Paris: Vuibert.

———. 2011. "Husserl and the Mind-Body Problem." *New Yearbook for Phenomenology and Phenomenological Philosophy* 11, 1–15.

Welton, D. 1999. "Soft, Smooth Hands: Husserl's Phenomenology of the Lived-Body." In *The Body: Classic and Contemporary Readings,* edited by D. Welton, 38–56. Oxford: Blackwell Publishers.

Young, I. M. 1990. *Throwing Like a Girl and Other Essays in Feminist Philosophy and Social Theory.* Bloomington and Indianapolis: Indiana University Press.

Yoshimi, J. 2007. "Mathematizing Phenomenology." *Phenomenology and the Cognitive Sciences* 6: 271–291.

———. 2010. "Husserl on Psycho-Physical Laws." *New Yearbook for Phenomenology and Phenomenological Philosophy* 10: 25–42.

Zahavi, D. 1994. "Husserl's Phenomenology of the Body." *Études phénoménologiques* 19: 63–84.

———. 1999. *Self-Awareness and Alterity. A Phenomenological Investigation.* Evanston, IL: Northwestern University Press.

———. 2003. *Husserl's Phenomenology.* Stanford, CA: Stanford University Press.

———. 2004. "Phenomenology and the Project of Naturalization." *Phenomenology and the Cognitive Sciences* 3: 331–347.

5 Husserl on the Factical and Historical Grounds of the Transcendental Subject

Simo Pulkkinen

As is well known, Husserl situated his phenomenological project within the tradition of transcendental philosophy and in his own words aimed at "eidetic study" of "pure transcendental subjectivity." This is often taken to mean that the ultimate goal of his phenomenology was to find universal, atemporal, and unchanging structures of subjectivity and to try to show, much like Kant, how these *a priori* structures determine the way in which things appear to our cognition. In contemporary philosophical debates, Husserl's alleged commitment to the idea of a transcendental subject that constitutes the world through its own unchanging structures makes phenomenology often look like a relic of subjective idealism: both the naturalistically or natural-scientifically oriented philosophy as well as the often explicitly post-phenomenological continental philosophy heavily contest the idea that the form of reality would be determined by some *a priori* structures of subjectivity, the former by asserting the mind-independent, objective being of the reality in itself, the latter by at the very least contesting the idea that the ontological structures of the world would be unchanging and most often also by trying to decentralize the role of subjectivity in the constitution of reality. While it is rather clear that Husserl's project is not straightforwardly compatible with any kind of naturalistic starting point, it is not as self-evident whether his thought is as outdated in respect to contemporary continental philosophy as is often thought. Decisive in this regard is to understand the basic nature and task of the Husserlian version of transcendental philosophy, especially to understand to what extent it actually seeks to clarify the constitution of the world by finding and postulating some unchanging, *a priori* structures of transcendental subjectivity.

Most commentators agree that Husserl was a transcendental philosopher—even a transcendental idealist, as he himself famously claimed. What this transcendental idealism exactly amounts to, how central a trait it is for his project as whole and whether it entails a tenable philosophical position is, however, far from clear or commonly agreed upon.[1] Without going into details of the ongoing debate in this regard, it is crucial to note on a general level that the concept of the transcendental acquires a fundamentally new meaning in Husserl's philosophy. Unlike for Kant, for Husserl the concept of the transcendental is not directly connected to the idea of universal, unchanging *a priori* structures but is primarily motivated by the idea of constitution—that is, by the very broad and formal idea that the world is something that takes its shape and becomes given for us in and through the dynamics of our experiential life.[2] When Husserl speaks about *transcendental* subjectivity, he simply refers to the experiencing subjectivity as a condition of possibility for the appearance of the world, not to some *a priori* structures of subjectivity and experience. Furthermore, this idea of the fundamental constitutive role of subjectivity does not, as such, rely on a predetermined understanding of the exact nature of the subjective world-constitution or the relationship between subjectivity and the world. Rather, to understand the exact manner in which the world is constituted in the experiential life of subjectivity is an open question and task for phenomenology. Thus, Husserl's constant reliance on the notion of "transcendental subjectivity" or the broad idea of "transcendental constitution" does not, by itself, imply any claims about the extent to which, if any, the experiential world-constitution is determined by unchanging essential structures of subjectivity.

In this chapter, I will in fact argue that for Husserl, transcendental subjectivity and its constitutive functioning are from the ground up determined by a radical historicity and facticity. More accurately, I will argue that the transcendental subjectivity is fundamentally drawn into the constitutive process, develops itself in the course of this process, and is thus dynamically entangled with the world that it constitutes. This means that the world-constituting subjectivity cannot be identified with a set of predetermined and universal *a priori* structures; rather, the conditions of possibility for experience are dynamic in the sense that they develop in the very course of experience itself. Eventually, I will argue that it is exactly this experiential dynamics that entails Husserl's much-debated inclusion of such concrete dimensions of human life as intersubjectivity and embodiment to the transcendental field and to the thematic sphere of transcendental philosophy. However, my aim is not to elucidate the richness or the various dimensions of the transcendental field as such, since this is already done in various ways by many others.[3] Instead, I will try to illustrate those structures and fundamental processes of consciousness that make the constitutive subjectivity from its ground up historical, factical, and developing and that thus make this expansion possible in the first place. In short, my aim is to show that the dynamic nature of the constitutive subjectivity is grounded in the reciprocal relationship and interplay of the two basic modes of consciousness, that is activity and passivity. By focusing especially on Husserl's analyses of the passive substratum of conscious life and on the dynamic, reciprocal interplay of passivity with the higher-level conscious activities, I wish to show that transcendental subjectivity is determined by dynamic historicity starting from its most primordial and fundamental levels.

It should be noted from the outset that it is not clear how focusing on the level of passivity could help us understand the dynamic historicity of constitutive subjectivity in Husserlian phenomenology. In the secondary literature, the sphere of passivity is most often seen as an independent substratum of conscious life consisting mainly of internal time consciousness, pure sensibility, and drive-intentionality, that is, as a substratum that in its primal functioning forms a kind of pregiven basis for all other dimensions and developments of consciousness while itself remaining unaffected by them. In fact, it seems that Husserl discovers passivity exactly while searching for the most fundamental and primordial levels of experience and objectivity, or the fundamental substratum or ground of consciousness upon which everything else is, so to speak, built (cf. Hua 11, 291f). Whereas Husserl was in his early works mainly interested in the so-called objectivating acts, or acts of simple object-constitution, as the "foundational level" consciousness upon which additional layers of meaning could be built, by the turn of the 1920s, his focus was redirected by a discovery of an even more fundamental level of experience, the level of passivity or "passive synthesis." Basically, passivity covers the anonymous functioning of consciousness in the background of attention, that is, everything that belongs to consciousness but that exceeds the limits of the specific act that we live through attentionally, the act whose object is in our attentional focus. Husserl described passivity as the most fundamental dimension of consciousness because he came to realize that as all explicit and thematic intentional acts are directed to something, they presuppose by their very structure *a preceding givenness of this something* as a possible object of attention. In Husserl's terms, all conscious acts are thus necessarily founded upon the *underlying sphere of passivity* as the dimension of pregivenness or preconstitution of objectivity in the background of attention.[4] The fundamental and foundational role that Husserl ascribed to passivity within conscious life has been well documented and widely accepted in the secondary literature. And it is exactly in line with this basic characterization of passivity as a pregiven fundament of all conscious activity that passivity is so often conceived of as an independent sphere of primordial constitution (*Urkonstitution*) that is free of all influence of the higher conscious activities of reason and understanding.[5]

In the following, I will, however, argue that this understanding of passivity and passive preconstitution as some kind of a pure and uncontaminated experiential ground is both inadequate and misleading. More accurately, I will demonstrate that this reading is one sided and partial and only captures one aspect of Husserl's argumentation. It accurately emphasizes the structural foundation that passivity provides for all actual conscious acts. But in so doing, it disregards all possible influence that conscious activity may in turn have on the level of passive consciousness. By drawing broadly from Husserl's later works, lectures, and research manuscripts found in *Husserliana,* my aim is to get a richer picture of the field of passive consciousness and preconstitution by clarifying its intimate connection to the sphere of higher conscious activities. The main point that I want to make is rather simple: even though Husserl argues that all *actual* conscious activities are formally and structurally founded upon passivity as a field of pregivenness, he does not think that this would mean that the sphere of passivity would be free of all influence of *previous* conscious activities. By focusing on two fundamental structures of passivity, habituality and association, I will argue that, in terms of their respective constitutive accomplishments, activity and passivity are not separated but bridged in a reciprocal two-way dynamics.[6] My aim is to show that this dynamics has drastic consequences for the makeup of lived consciousness and its constitutive functioning. Most notably, it results in a principal infusion of higher meaningfulness produced in conscious acts into the most elementary structures of passivity and passive preconstitution. That is to say that even the seemingly purely passive sphere of sensibility turns out to be always already "contaminated" by the meaning-products of previous conscious activities of the subject. I will end by arguing that this dynamics of activity and passivity also fundamentally determines the way in which the ground and groundedness of subjectivity should be conceived within Husserlian phenomenology: it reveals that instead of having an independent and self-enclosed ground or foundation on the level of purely passive experience, transcendental subjectivity is as a whole and from its roots up dynamically embedded and grounded in its own facticity, in the preceding dynamics of its own past being. Ultimately, my aim is to show that the reciprocal dynamics of activity and passivity brings transcendental subjectivity into a dynamic process of development and sedimentation and that this entails a fundamental enrichment and broadening of the transcendental field in general.

1 THE ONE-SIDED FORMAL RELATIONSHIP OF ACTIVITY AND PASSIVITY

In his early works, Husserl seems to be moving pretty much in the lines of traditional Kantian transcendental philosophy in that he most often equates the distinction between activity and passivity of consciousness with the distinction between receptivity and spontaneity, that is, equates passivity with the reception of sensible impressions and activity with the spontaneous apprehension and cultivation of these impressions in intellectual activity of the reason. However, from the turn of the 1920s onward, the distinction between activity and passivity undergoes a seemingly minor but fundamental change in Husserl's philosophy. Instead of being a substantial distinction between two basic faculties or functions of consciousness in receptivity and spontaneity, the distinction between activity and passivity becomes purely *formal* and *modal* distinction. This is to say that instead of denoting two different faculties of the mind or correspondingly two different categories of experiences or experienced objectivities, activity and passivity denote two different *forms* or *modes* of carrying out and living through any particular experience or process of consciousness. In Husserl's own terms, 'activity' and 'passivity' name two fundamental "effectuation modes" of intentional consciousness, or two possible ways of being conscious of something (HuaM 8, 203; Hua 31, 4–8; Hua 17, 365).

As we shall see in more detail shortly, activity refers to the subject's conscious and explicit participation in an experiential process, whereas passivity refers to everything that takes place in consciousness without our explicit participation, consent, or even attention. If simply compared to the traditional distinction between spontaneity and receptivity, this move to a purely modal determination of activity and passivity seems, at best, minor: first of all, spontaneity and receptivity are already traditionally distinguished on the lines of active participation and passive being acted upon, and second, Husserl still classifies the reception of sensations as a purely passive occurrence, while all higher acts and functions of reason are still deemed active accomplishments. However, this move still has fundamental consequences as it dismantles the strict correlation of activity and passivity to specific functions of the mind and consequently to certain fundamentally different types or levels of objectivity. In other words, the purely modal and formal determination of activity and passivity allows Husserl to rethink both the functional and the material sides of these modes of consciousness beyond their traditional boundaries. Most importantly for our discussion, Husserl is thus able to see that the scope of passive consciousness and simple givenness needs to be broadened to a sphere of objectivity and meaning that has traditionally been considered a product and correlate of our conscious activity. And as we shall also see, this leads us almost directly to the fundamental historicity of the transcendental subjectivity: Husserl is namely not broadening the scope of passive consciousness by postulating any mysterious passive faculties of mind that would autonomously present us with higher meaningfulness but rather by developing a dynamical understanding of subjectivity in the form of reciprocal interplay and development of activity and passivity. But before we can get to the material determinations of activity and passivity, to their reciprocal, constitutive dynamics, and from there to the historicity of transcendental subjectivity, it is necessary to first clarify the exact nature of activity and passivity as modes of consciousness and the formally one-sided relationship of foundation in which they stand in this respect.

As modes of consciousness, Husserl distinguishes activity and passivity in terms of our participation in their effectuation; more accurately, the line between activity and passivity is drawn at the minimum of participation, the turning of attention. The lowest common denominator and the defining feature of all conscious activity is, thus, the presence of our explicit attention. In Husserl's own words:

> [A]ll study of active functioning of the ego [. . .] moves in the medium of attentional turning to and its derivatives. Attention is, so to speak, the bridge to activity, or it is the beginning that sets the stage for activity. Attention is, furthermore, the constant mode of consciousness in which activity is carried out. All genuine activity takes place within the field of attention. (Hua 31, 4)

This is to say that we cannot be truly active without paying attention; and insofar as we pay attention, we actively participate in the experience in question. According to this definition, the sphere of activity consists of and is limited to a specific type of intentionality: to thematic and explicit intentional acts, that is to various possible forms of attentional and explicit consciousness (cf. Hua 1, 111; Hua 9, 411; Hua 15, 203; EU, 83).[7] These forms range from mere receptivity at the lowest level to various higher conscious activities, those of reason and understanding. According to Husserl, in the lowest form of conscious activity and attention, in receptivity, we are active merely in focusing our attention on some objectivity, for instance on something in the environment, whereas in the higher activities, "the ego functions as creatively constitutive through specific acts of the ego" (Hua 1, 111, cf. EU, 233). In other words, in the higher forms of activity, the ego participates not only by lending its attention to the matter at hand; rather, it also genuinely constitutes new layers of meaning by articulating the environment with the use of attention and the various cognitive capacities, for example, by generalizing states of affairs in propositions, by evaluating things either aesthetically or axiologically, or by instituting practical significance while coming up with new ways of using things.

Seemingly in line with the traditional distinction between spontaneity and receptivity, Husserl often argues that objects of experience can acquire new, higher meaning only through the active use of various cognitive capacities (cf. Hua 37, 307; Hua 9, 112–118; Hua 1, 124; HuaM 4, 123; Hua 39, 266). However, it is important to emphasize again that Husserl defines conscious "activity" neither *functionally* as spontaneous and creative meaning-constution[8] nor *materially* as consciousness that corresponds to a sphere of "higher" meaningfulness and objectivity. Rather, the sphere of activity is defined purely *formally* and *modally* as a specific *form* or *mode* of consciousness: all instances of consciousness in which our attention is operative and directed to the objects in question are active in Husserlian sense, regardless of whether these instances of consciousness constitute new meaning or are directed to higher levels of meaning and objectivity. This is evinced most clearly by the fact that Husserl includes mere "receptivity"[9] in the sphere of activity as "the lowest level of activity" (EU 83), or as "that primordial function of the active ego that merely consists in making patent, regarding and attentively grasping what is constituted in passivity itself as formations of its own intentionality" (Hua 11, 64; cf. Hua 31, 40).

Similarly to activity, Husserl defines the sphere of passivity primarily modally and formally: passivities are "modes of background-consciousness, modes of having something in consciousness without being directed towards it" (Hua 29, 247; cf. Hua 31, 4). In other words, as a mode of consciousness, passivity is the exact opposite of conscious activity: it denotes the silent life of consciousness in the margins of awareness. This marginal, purely passive functioning of consciousness pertains to and constitutes the unthematic background of attention, the halo of consciousness that underlies and surrounds our focal point of attention (cf. HuaM 8, 187, 202). The accomplishments of passivity do not, however, belong to the sphere of complete or utter unconsciousness. Rather, they have a specific mode of givenness and prominence, which Husserl terms 'affectivity' or 'affective pregivenness.' Without being thematically given in our attentional focus, affectively pregiven contents are still part of our consciousness by soliciting our attention in various manners and degrees from the background of attention. In Husserl's terms, this background forms an "affective relief," a field that consists of allures of various intensities or "heights" that in different proportions constantly pull our attention toward themselves without yet entering into our thematic focus (cf. Hua 11, 164, 168). According to Husserl, the attentional focus of conscious activity is always surrounded by this type of inexplicit horizon, background, or margin: as he often points out, even though our attention is always directed at some particular thing or matter, we are never conscious of just one thing but in varying intensities are always also tacitly aware, not only of the thing's immediate surroundings, but ultimately of the whole world that surrounds us and the thing itself. The decisive point here is that the background of attention is by its very nature something passively *pregiven*. In a strict contrast to our active, or at least attentional, participation in the givenness and constitution of the focal object, the background that surrounds and underlies our attention is essentially already there before and independent of any actual conscious participation and even without our explicit attention. In Husserl's words, this passively formed background is part of our consciousness as "*a field of pregivenness, of passive* pregivenness, i.e. as a field that is always already there without any participation, without turning of explicit attention, without any awakening of interest" (EU, 24; cf. Hua 1, 112f; Hua 11, 162).

To summarize, activity and passivity name two fundamentally different possible "effectuation modes" of intentional consciousness. These modes are always operative in the field of living consciousness: "activity" denotes the sphere of attentional consciousness and, possibly, active constitutive participation of the ego, whereas "passivity" denotes the silent and anonymous functioning of the marginal consciousness. As its objective counterpart, activity is correlated to the thematic objectivity in the focal point of attention, whereas passivity is responsible for the formation of the background horizon of attention, the field of affective pregivenness in the margins of awareness. Before entering into a discussion of their material determination and functional entanglement, two things can already be noted concerning the purely formal relationship of activity and passivity as modes of consciousness. *First,* in the field of actual consciousness, passivity and its constitutive accomplishments essentially and structurally exceed and precede the scope of all possible active participation by the ego: passivity is a dimension of *pregivenness* in the sense that the passively formed background-horizon is essentially always already there *before* any conscious activity is directed to it and also regardless of what takes place in the focal point of attention; as our willful participation is by definition limited to the attentional focus, we cannot in any way actively influence the contents of the passively pregiven background. *Second,* all conscious activities are founded upon and presuppose the dimension of passivity. As Husserl quite straightforwardly puts it, "all activity is founded upon passivity" (HuaM 8, 260). This is simply because effectuation of any conscious activity presupposes the passive pregivenness of its possible object: as attentional modes of consciousness, our conscious activities presuppose by their very structure that there is something already passively pregiven, something toward which the attention can be turned. In Husserl's own words: "passivity is something in itself primary because all activity essentially presupposes a foundation of passivity and an objectivity that is already pre-constituted therein" (Hua 31, 3; cf. Hua 1, 112; EU, 74, Hua 9, 209; HuaM 8, 260). In other words, when we study activity and passivity purely formally and modally, we find, according to Husserl, a structural one-way relation of foundation between them: whereas passivity is a sphere of preconstitution and pregivenness that lies beyond the scope of our attention and that cannot be influenced by our current conscious participation, the very possibility of exercising any conscious activity rests on the foundation of having the possible objects of active attention already passively pregiven in the margins of awareness.

2   THE TRACES OF ACTIVITY IN PASSIVITY

As already mentioned at the beginning, it is very usual in contemporary Husserl scholarship to assume that the one-sided formal relation of foundation between activity and passivity also characterizes the constitutive accomplishments as well as the contents of these modes of consciousness. In this vein, all higher formations of meaning, like categorial determinations, values, and goals, are conceived of as correlates of explicit conscious acts, and passivity, on the other hand, is taken to be a self-enclosed sphere, which includes nothing that stems from the various intellectual activities of the reason. Very often the whole sphere of passive pregivenness is, thus, identified with what Husserl calls more accurately "*pure* passivity," or a dimension of consciousness that is both modally as well as materially free of any influence from our active participation.

Husserl never gives a complete list of the elements included in pure passivity, but, in the first place, it seems to comprise (i) sensibility in the form of mere "reception" of sensible impressions, (ii) passive arousal of feelings, and (iii) the blind thrust of drives and instincts.[10] Purely as such, this sphere of pure passivity is structured only by the equally passive functioning of internal time-consciousness and primal association (*Urassoziation*), that is by the primordial associative constitution of sensations, feelings, and drives (as well as all acts and formations of activity) as simple temporal unities within the flow of immanent time (cf. HuaM 8, 122, 295f). This dimension of subjectivity is "purely passive" in two regards: both in regard to its effectuation mode as well as in regard to its content. First of all, our attention is not and cannot be present in this purely passive functioning of consciousness: we cannot, for instance, attentively live through the temporal organization of contents of consciousness or the mere flow of sensible stimuli.[11] Second, and more importantly, taken simply as such, this dimension of pure passivity is completely outside the reach of our willful participation and thus contains no trace of our higher conscious activities. While it is true that we can, at least to a certain extent, freely decide how we react to our sensations, feelings, and drives, we cannot consciously influence the arousal or the content of these sensations, feelings, and drives. According to Husserl, pure passivity is thus a dimension of consciousness that contains no trace of our conscious participation or activities (cf. Hua 11, 342f, Hua 39, 11).

However, the crucial point for us here is that even though there may very well be such a purely passive dimension or stratum to our conscious life, and even though Husserl seems to be most interested precisely in such purely passive elements when studying the differences between activity and passivity, he occasionally emphasizes and makes clear that this type of pure passivity is merely an abstract level of experience, a level that can be reached only through a specific operation of abstraction or purification (cf. Hua 31, 3; Hua 39, 432; EU, 74f). The fact that pure passivity can only be reached through abstractive purification indicates that it is not a separate and independent part of our conscious life but rather a dependent moment of a more concrete whole. Most importantly, the fact that there are such purely passive dimensions to consciousness does not necessarily mean that the full breadth and the full concretion of passivity and passive background-consciousness would have to be restricted to pure passivity, which includes no traces of activity. Rather, as Husserl himself notes, "under the title passivity, [there is] also the second-level passivity, passivity that has issued from activity" (Hua 15, 203; cf. Hua 11, 342f; EU, 336).

In the following, I will argue that the notion of "second-level passivity"[12] refers to a principal inclusion of different kinds of higher, actively constituted meaning into the sphere of passive pregivenness and marginal consciousness.[13] Thus, the concept of second-level passivity denotes a crucial broadening of the scope of passivity over the limits of simple and purely passive sensibility and drive-intentionality. The crucial point is that this broadening is not an artificial construction or a theoretical derivation but, in Husserl's eyes, simply reflects the actual content of our passive background-consciousness in its full, lived concretion. As Husserl quite often points out, the passively pregiven marginal background of our attention cannot be reduced to the achievements of pure passivity, that is, to a mere temporally organized playground of purely passively received sensations, random emotions, and blind drives. If this would be the case, it would mean that the focal point of attention and activity, which is essentially singular and limited in its scope, would be surrounded by an almost chaotic background. But in reality, the horizontal background of our experience is always quite well structured, stable, and at least to some extent always already meaningfully articulated and prefigured. Husserl notes this, for instance, in a lengthy passage in *Experience and Judgment*:

> Our *pregiven* environment is "pregiven" as multifariously prefigured, prefigured according to its regional categories and typified according to various specific types and kinds. This means that everything that affects us in the background [of attention] [. . .] is known to us in a much more detailed sense, it is already in the background passively grasped [. . .] [for example] as a thing, as a human being, as a product of humans and so on in rich detail.
>
> (EU, 35; cf. EU, 34, 299–300; Hua 1, 113)

In other words, we are *de facto* tacitly, passively, and already in the background of attention conscious of an environment that comprises highly structured meaningfulness. The decisive point is that even though this environment is given to us purely passively and in the background of our attention, its meaningfulness cannot be traced back to purely passive functions of sensibility, temporality, and drive-intentionality. Rather, it clearly points to higher meaning-formations of conscious activity and reasoning. In other words, there clearly seem to be traces of conscious activity in the sphere of passive consciousness and pregivenness.

Now the task is, of course, to understand how Husserl thinks that this is possible and how this fits the idea of the one-sided formal relationship between activity and passivity discussed earlier. How and in what way can there be actively formed contents present in the passive background consciousness, that is in the sphere that by its very structure precedes our actual conscious attention and active participation? The key to solving this seeming paradox lies in acknowledging that even though our passively pregiven and marginal background by its very structure precedes and exceeds all possibilities of *actual* active participation, the content of this passive pregivenness can nevertheless still be influenced by our *preceding* conscious activities. As we shall see, in terms of their content and constitutive accomplishments, activity and passivity are not strictly separated but are fundamentally entangled and dynamically interwoven. Through this entanglement, the whole sphere of passivity is thoroughly influenced and internally structured by the results of our previous conscious activity: even the seemingly self-enclosed sphere of pure passivity is, so to speak, encompassed or enveloped by a broader second-level passivity that also includes various higher meaning-formations of preceding conscious activity. In the following, I will try to sketch how, in Husserl's view, this infusion of activity into the sphere of passive consciousness takes place in and through the interplay of two elementary functions of passive consciousness, namely "habituality" and "association." As we shall see, for Husserl, "habituality" denotes a mode of passive pregivenness, a mode that nevertheless is not exactly purely passive but rather draws its content from previous activities of the ego, whereas "association" denotes an overarching infusion of the habitually preserved active accomplishments into the whole of conscious life, including the most elementary structures of passivity.

3   HABITUALITY, ASSOCIATION, AND THE FORMATION OF SECOND-LEVEL PASSIVITY

According to Husserl, habituality forms an essential functional structure of consciousness.[14] In the most basic sense "habituality" refers to the fact that we do not simply live through separate experiences in succession, but these experiences always leave a permanent mark in consciousness, a mark that is present even after the experience itself is over. In this sense, "habituality" does not denote our empirical habits of action and comportment but rather, in a more elementary way, refers to the essential preservation of all results of our meaning-constituting conscious activity. The formation of this type of habituality is, according to Husserl, an essential, purely passive, and all-encompassing functional structure of consciousness: more accurately, it is a necessary part and end result of any active, thematic experience. In Husserl's own words, "every act institutes a persisting (habitual) validity, a lasting position (in the widest sense of the word), which exceeds beyond the flowing act itself" (Hua 39, 47; cf. Hua 1, 112ff; Hua 4, 214, 332; Hua 6, 371–2). In layman's terms, this means that we do not simply *have* singular experiences, but through these experiences we *acquire knowledge of* the environment and *retain* this knowledge as at least a relatively permanent possession. In more technical terms, although all meaning-forming conscious activities are by definition attentional forms of consciousness, their constitutive results do not vanish when the act itself is over and when attention is redirected; rather, these results persist as a "habitual possession" through the changing flow of consciousness (cf. EU, 137–138). Taken in their ever-increasing totality, these habitualities amount to a lasting familiarity with the world. And conversely, because of this habitual preservation of the previous experiences, we are at any given moment always already tacitly aware of a familiar and meaningfully articulated world. As Husserl summarizes it: "[M]y activity of positing and explicating being institutes a habituality of my ego. By virtue of this habituality I permanently appropriate the object in its determinations. These abiding accomplishments make up my current familiar environment" (Hua 1, 102).

The crucial point is that although in terms of content everything habitually familiar is a result of conscious activity and explicit attention, habitual familiarity is, nevertheless, by its very structure a mode of passive background-consciousness and pregivenness: we do not have to, nor can we, actively produce the already familiar meaningfulness of the environment.

Rather, at any moment this meaningfulness is *simply pregiven to us* without any need or possibility of active participation. Similarly, in its entirety, the world is never in our thematic focus; rather, the attention is always limited to a singular theme, and the world surrounds this focus as a marginally pregiven background—and does so in all of its habitually familiar meaningfulness. In short, instead of being present or formed in the thematic focus of conscious activity, the habitually familiar world is passively pregiven in the margins of our awareness. Thus Husserl can state that "everything habitual belongs to passivity, and this includes also all the active that has become habitual" (Hua 11, 342). In other words, habituality denotes a passive givenness of something that was originally instituted in and through our conscious activity. As Husserl puts it, habituality denotes "*a second-level passivity* that essentially points back to its origin in actual spontaneous achieving" (EU, 336).

In essence, this means that habituality broadens the scope of passive experiencing and pregivenness and that the heading "passivity" has to be extended to the givenness of an already familiar and meaningfully articulated lifeworld. So the passively pregiven background of our thematic attention does not consist of any type of primal or formless sensibility but includes a world that is habitually familiar and "multifariously prefigured." As Husserl puts it, passivity is not a mere realm of sensation and blind drives; rather, due to habituality, "passivities [. . .] turn out to be sedimentations of activities (of acquired convictions)" (Hua 15, 367). And correspondingly, as the bearer of these habitualities and as the subject for the habitually familiar world, the constitutive self is, according to Husserl, not an empty pole of identity nor a stable set of predetermined structures (à la Kant) but rather, and already at the level of passive experiencing, a "personal" subjectivity in a constant process of development and change (Hua 1, 100f, 162,163; Hua 9, 414; Hua 15, 55; HuaM 8, 39, Hua 6, 272).[15] That is to say that the constitution of the experientially given world cannot be reduced to a straightforward interplay of sensible receptivity and some *a priori* forms of conceptual spontaneity as two independent sources of consciousness (*Gemüt*), as Kant famously thought.[16] Rather, all activities turn into habitual passivities, their constitutive achievements are retained, and thus the experienced world is a sedimented formation, an accumulative and habitually preserved result of all of our past experience.

As we have seen, habituality quite literally breaches the supposedly one-sided relationship of activity and passivity and denotes a decisive broadening of the sphere of passive, marginal consciousness and pregivenness over the limits of "pure" passivity. Moreover, according to Husserl, habituality is not a mere separate addition to the sphere of passive consciousness but has even broader constitutive significance. Through the constant functioning of another fundamental structure of passivity, namely association, our habitual familiarity with the world takes over the whole landscape of the lived consciousness—starting from and including the seemingly purely passive functions of sensibility, emotions, and drive-intentionality and extending to the active operations of reason and will. As we shall see in more detail, "association" is a general heading for the purely passive formation of connections between various contents of consciousness and for a constant transfer of meaning between these contents. The crucial point here is that, in Husserl's terms, association is not to be understood as a separate operation or a specific type of conscious act but must be conceived of as a universal medium through which all the data of consciousness have to pass in order to affect us in any way. No data of consciousness can affect us, nor even enter the field of our marginal consciousness and passive pregivenness, without being processed by association. In Husserl's words, "without [association] there is no affection, everywhere is association present" (Hua 39, 34; cf. EU, 207).[17]

This all-encompassing associative functioning of consciousness involves two necessary moments: "pairing" (*Paarung*) and "transfer of meaning" (*Sinnesübertragung*). According to Husserl, association is always initiated by a pairing of two or more contents of consciousness on the basis of their similarity. In pairing, these contents are no longer present in separation but as a pair or a group whose each member points to the others. Pairing takes place constantly, purely passively, and without conscious participation. Moreover, pairing is not limited to the present: it takes place within the field of present consciousness, but it also extends from the present to our habitually retained past experiences. The overarching character of association is manifest, for example, in the way in which our present experiences can suddenly awaken and bring to mind past experiences. And even when this type of *explicit* reawakening does not happen, according to Husserl, all of our experiences and experienced contents are, at least potentially, paired with the totality of cotemporal and habitually retained similar experiences (Hua 11, 121, 123, 190; Hua 39, 431–432; EU, 229, 336, 385).

In the first place, such pairing produces an almost all-embracing aura of familiarity in our everyday experience. However, and this is the crucial point here, in Husserl's account, the constitutive function of associative pairing is not restricted to mere acknowledgement of likeness and familiarity. Instead, according to Husserl, it is an "essential fact of association" that pairing is always and necessarily accompanied by what he calls an "apperceptive transfer of meaning" (Hua 39, 450). Apperceptive transfer of meaning means that when the contents of consciousness are paired according to their similarities, be they partial or complete, they acquire from one another also those layers of meaning that exceed the parts that are actually given as similar. For example, in most cases of visual perception, this means that as soon as a new, previously unknown object enters our field of vision, it acquires a richer prefigured meaning from our habitual familiarity with similar things, a meaning that goes beyond what we actually see from the new thing. As Husserl describes it: when a pairing of a new experiential content with a similar old one takes place, "the old data is awakened and the new one acquires the meaning of the old one as assimilation, as apperceptive transfer" (HuaM 8, 253, cf. Hua 1, 143–144; Hua 15, 148, 252; Hua 39, 450, 465; HuaM 8, 269–270). In even more formal terms, Husserl speaks of "an analogizing transfer of meaning-validity [*Soseinsgeltung*] from A to a similar B that for its part is not yet valid in this meaning" (Hua 39, 450; cf. 465). In concretion, this apperceptive transfer of meaning implies that we not only grasp never-before-seen things as resembling some familiar things but also that we instantly and without any active participation conceive of these things as the *same type of things* as the ones with which they are associatively paired. For example, when we see a car that we have never actually seen before approaching us on the street, we effortlessly conceive this approaching thing as a car, that is, as an object that not only looks familiar but participates in the already familiar meaningful relations of traffic and transportation. According to Husserl, association is a purely passive process, and thus all this transfer of meaning happens "passively, instantly and with one stroke" (Hua 15, 252; cf. EU, 210). In other words, because of the constant functioning of association, objects that we have never seen before are instantly given with an already familiar meaningfulness—meaningfulness that is associatively transferred from our previous habitual familiarity with similar things.

The purely passive constitutive functioning of association fundamentally influences the whole landscape of the lived consciousness and brings about an intertwining of even the most elementary structures of consciousness with previous experiences and with the habitual familiarity of things. This is because association and its apperceptive transfer of meaning is operative in the full breadth of consciousness and givenness, including the most elementary structures of pure passivity. As said, according to Husserl, there is no form of marginal awareness or "affectivity" that would not have been already influenced by the overarching functioning of association. This also means that the supposedly "raw data" that the senses provide never *affects us* purely as such. Instead of forming any kind of self-enclosed sphere of purely sensible experiencing, the senses only perform the initiating role of providing material for the play of associative pairings and apperceptive transfers of meaning: insofar as the sensible data enter into our awareness in any way, they are already paired with previous experiences involving similar data and the sedimented results of our previous higher meaning-forming acts. Husserl describes the role of sensations in the dynamics of mature and developed consciousness in the following way: "The sensible stimulus affects an ego that is already a human person, i.e. an ego that in its habituality has the accomplishments of worldly experience. The awakening radiates from the sensible manifold; but what becomes awakened are the [old] constitutive accomplishments and abilities of the ego" (HuaM 8, 100).

This is to say that we never merely "sense" things; rather, perceived things always affect us with a prefigured meaning that stems from our previous conscious life and from the higher acts in which we have originally conceived the meaning of these types of things. As Husserl puts it, because association mediates all affective and marginal givenness "everything that affects us [. . .] has a structure of meaning that stems from activity" (Hua 39, 36). In this sense, the purely passive functions of sensibility and drive-intentionality are only unindependent moments of experience which, in the concrete dynamics of our conscious life, are taken over by the second-level passivity that draws its content from previous conscious activities of meaning-formation. Even though mere reception of sensations and the arousal of drives and feelings are certainly parts of our conscious-life, and even though they may well have an autonomous, purely passive genesis, we are never faced with pure sensations, feelings, or drives; rather, we for instance sense "the appropriate heaviness of a hammer," feel "the joy of scoring a goal," and crave "the unique grill sauce of our favorite restaurant." Following this line of argument, Husserl ends up speaking about our direct passive experience of the environment not as mere sensing but as a "second level sensibility [. . .] that is born out of productive reason" and correlatively as a "reason that has fallen into the sensibility" (Hua 4, 334; cf. Hua 4, 12, 332ff; Hua 9, 408–409; Hua 11, 342; Hua 15, 203, 367; Hua 39, 34–38). In other words, even purely passively born affections are always already, as soon as they affect us, given to us in a broader context of habitual meaningfulness. And it is only afterward that we can, for instance, try to focus on the purely sensible content of a perception. In Husserl's words, "all moments that are constituted passively in the stream of consciousness are always, in their own manner, 'apprehended.' For instance sensible data is apprehended in varying levels of apprehension, so that it is only artificially, only through unraveling of intentional achievement and removal of all layerings of apprehension, that this data comes forth as passively born unit, as pre-existing" (HuaM 8, 187; cf. HuaM 8, 203; Hua 39, 34ff).

This, of course, does not mean that Husserl would want to eliminate passivity from our experience or replace it by a free-floating activity of the creative reason. Nor is the point to claim that the surrounding world would always already be fully and completely articulated. Rather, Husserl's analyses describe a fundamental possibility of reciprocal interplay and entanglement of passive consciousness and marginal awareness with the products of the preceding conscious activity. As said, this interplay fundamentally influences the way in which things are given to us: due to such interplay, the surrounding world is given to us—purely passively and marginally—with vast depths of already prefigured meaningfulness.[18] This prefigured meaningfulness is not an actual conscious accomplishment but stems from the habitually retained totality of our previous conscious accomplishments. Or to put it the other way around, the interplay between the two simple processes of consciousness, habituality and association, explains the structures of higher meanings that, according to Husserl, are *de facto* found throughout the spheres of passive and marginal background-consciousness and simple experiencing. As Husserl himself puts it in *Experience and Judgment*: "The fact that all objects of experience are already from the start experienced as familiar in their type has its grounds in the sedimentation of all apperceptions and in their lasting habitual effect on the basis of associative awakening" (EU, 385; cf. Hua 11, 190; Hua 39, 3ff, 35).

4   CONCLUSION: THE RECIPROCAL DYNAMICS OF ACTIVITY AND PASSIVITY AND THE FUNDAMENTAL HISTORICITY OF TRANSCENDENTAL SUBJECTIVITY

I have argued in this chapter that even though activity and passivity are for Husserl two fundamentally different and separate modes of intentional consciousness, and even though all actual conscious acts are unidirectionally founded upon passivity as the sphere of pregivenness, activity and passivity do not form two materially separate spheres of experience and objectivity. Rather, in terms of their contents and constitutive accomplishments, activity and passivity are fundamentally entangled and intertwined. As we have seen, this is because they enter in reciprocal two-way dynamics through the interplay of habituality and association. This dynamics determines transcendental subjectivity equally in both its active and passive modes of functioning, that is, both in active and explicit meaning constitution and in passive pregivenness and marginal awareness. First, this dynamics results in a passive and marginal pregivenness of a lifeworld that is already at first sight laden with various layers and levels of habitually familiar meanings stemming from previous active meaning-constitution. Second, our conscious and meaning-forming activities are themselves grounded upon this dynamics and also incorporated into it: they must not be conceived as free-floating acts of meaning-formation that would start from a chaotic stream of formless sensations. Rather, besides the beginning of the stream of consciousness as an ideal limit-case, all our active meaning-articulation starts from second-level passivity, that is from the passive and marginal pregivenness of an already meaningful world and, at best, articulates this pregiven world a little further. Ultimately, this means that our experience is never, nor on any level, pure or uncontaminated. Rather, it is as a whole, in all its modalities and, most importantly, by its very structure, grounded in and determined by the factical totality of past experience. In more technical terms, this means that Husserl's analyses of passivity do not demarcate an independent and purely passive substratum of conscious life but thematize a dynamic interconnection between passivity and activity and thus disclose transcendental subjectivity as a fundamentally developing being—as a being that is in its constitutive functioning dynamically grounded upon its own past experiential life and, correlatively, situated in the world that it has already, at any given moment, learned to know by this past experience.

While Husserl never articulates this in a concise manner, I believe that his analyses on the constitutive dynamics of activity and passivity fundamentally alter the way in which we should understand the whole of his transcendental nomenclature. Even though Husserl at times speaks in seemingly traditional terms of a "structure of transcendental subjectivity that expresses itself in the invariable form of the world of realities" (HuaM 8, 434), the analyses on the constitutive interplay of activity and passivity seem to uncover a radical historicity and facticity of constitution and of the constituting transcendental subjectivity. This is because the reciprocal dynamics of activity and passivity means a fundamental relativization of the roles of "the constituted" and "the constituting," the constitutive functioning of everything previously constituted in the formation of new meaning.[19] Instead of simply constituting the world unidirectionally through some stable set of *a priori* structures or rules, world-constituting subjectivity is itself conditioned by and rooted in an already constituted, habitually familiar world. As a result, we have a dynamic development of what could be called "the conditions of the possibility for experience." This is to say that the way in which we now experience and conceive of the world is influenced and conditioned by our previous experiences, and, in turn, influences and conditions the way in which we will conceive the world in future. In short, through the interplay of habituality and association, world-constitution is from its roots up dynamically determined by the factical history of previous constitutions. Thus the transcendental field, the conditions of possibility for experience and objectivity, cannot in any way be reduced to a predetermined or stable set of *a priori* structures or rules but must rather be understood as fundamentally historical, factical, and dynamic. In this regard, it is not surprising that Husserl's lecture course on passive synthesis, on the most fundamental and grounding levels of experience, culminates in the idea of world-constitution as a "continuous progression of levels [. . .]," as "a never-ending history of [. . .] constitution of ever higher formations of meaning" (Hua 11, 219). To recapitulate, world-constitution is grounded neither on a stable set of *a priori* structures of subjectivity nor on an independent ground of pure passivity but is rather dynamically grounded on its own facticity and development. In Husserl's own words, constitution has to be seen "as a structure of different levels of constitutive accomplishments, in which ever new objectivities, objectivities of ever new kinds are constituted in ever new levels or layers" (Hua 11, 218, cf. Hua 1, 111–114, 156–159; Hua 4, 186ff; Hua 6, 170, 176, 371–272; Hua 11, 216–222; Hua 17, 252, 257; Hua 37, 292; HuaM 8, 395).

Most importantly, this dynamism of the transcendental field also entails its fundamental broadening: the constitutive conditions of objectivity do not have to be limited to what can be considered universal, endogenous, and *a priori* characteristics of whatever consciousness in general. Rather, these conditions are something that develop through the actual course and progress of experience, something into which we grow instead of being born. In my view, it is exactly this dynamics of experience that permits Husserl's most interesting and most debated expansion of the transcendental field, that is the "intersubjective transformation of transcendental philosophy," as Dan Zahavi calls it (cf. Zahavi 1996). Even though Husserl famously thematizes the so-called "open intersubjectivity" or "*a priori* intersubjectivity," the open plurality of possible viewpoints, as something that results already from the structural horizontality of all worldly experience, it is in the end only the dynamic development of constitutive subjectivity that allows us to understand the constitutive significance of intersubjectivity in its full breadth. When we acknowledge that experiences are not isolated occurrences but that their constitutive results can become an integral and effective part of the experiencing subjectivity through their inclusion in the constitutive interplay of habituality and association, it becomes easy to see, at least in principle, that we not only experience individual others, but rather through these experiences we can gradually grow into various social and cultural frameworks that, for their part, function constitutively in our experience. As these experiences and this process of integration into a community with others has played a fundamental role in our lives starting from earliest childhood, it also has a fundamental "transcendental significance" in the way in which we constitute the world as something not only possibly shared by anonymous others but as something that we tacitly and purely passively know to harbor within itself almost inexhaustible depths of culturally, historically, and intersubjectively determined meaningfulness (cf. Hua 15, 391; Hua 39, 201f). In other words, what I think takes place in Husserl's later thought is not an artificial expansion of the transcendental field with features that would strictly speaking go beyond the experiential life of singular subjectivity. Rather, Husserl develops an enriched and dynamic understanding of the experiencing subjectivity, which in turn allows for a fundamental broadening of the transcendental field from within.

Consequently, even the ideas of transcendental philosophy and transcendental idealism would seem to become more tenable. For transcendental idealism, world-constitution is strictly a personal matter, something that takes place in and through the experiential life of (in at least some fundamental sense) a singular subjectivity. But as a personal being, the human subjectivity is for Husserl fundamentally developing and, consequently, something that in its constitutive functioning can become thoroughly and fundamentally integrated into an intersubjective community and its various historical and cultural frameworks. Thus the Husserlian version of transcendental idealism does not point to solitary subjectivity imposing its *a priori* structures on the world but rather conceives of world-constitution as a complex, multileveled, and multifaceted experiential dynamics that takes place in communion with other people and that corresponds to the rich meaningfulness of the experienced world.

Of course, this idea of the historical and factical dynamism of the transcendental field would seem to come at the cost of risking irreversible historical relativism and consequently of giving up any hope of clinging on to the eidetic side of Husserl's project, or of finding universally valid, scientifically interesting results from the thoroughly factical conscious life. However, it is to be noted that even though our worldly experience is, according to Husserl, changing and factically determined, it is in no way chaotic or form-less. Rather, it is determined exactly by formation of habitualities as at least relatively stable structures of generality that, furthermore, are developed not in isolation but in constant communication and reciprocal influence with others. Thus, it would seem possible to find both "morphological-static" general structures of experiencing as well as "historical-genetic" conditions of possibility for the development of these particular structures of experiencing that would have general, scientific significance in understanding the factical makeup of the experientially given lifeworld. And it could be argued that these are the only forms of generality that Husserl's eidetic method was after in the first place.[20] After all, by its very definition, this method is only about finding invariable generalities from those experiences that we *de facto* have; and the possibility of finding general or even essential features of some factical experiences does not presuppose that it would be necessary to have exactly these types of experiences, that there would have to be some kind of *a priori* universal structure of subjectivity that would essentially prede-termine what kind of experiences we have and can have. But even if the possibility or the limits of such an eidetic research of factical consciousness would be put into question, it would at least seem necessary to contest the common reading of Husserl as a relic of subjective idealism. Rather, Hus-serlian phenomenology would seem to have something to offer even for the contemporary "continental" philosophical discussion as it points towards the possibility of finding and studying some of its central themes right within our own subjectivity.

NOTES

1. This debate goes back to the time of publication of the first book of *Ideas* (Hua 3/1), in which Husserl for the first time relied heavily on the transcen-dental nomenclature and advocated many of the basic ideas that later on led him to claim that phenomenology is to be understood as "transcendental ide-alism" (cf. Hua 1, 118f., Hua 8, 181). In recent years, several prominent schol-ars, among others Dermot Moran (2005), have argued that this idealism was a fundamental mistake and something that one should try to dismiss in order to focus on the more positive contributions of Husserl's thinking. Neverthe-less, for instance, Dan Zahavi (2010) and Rudolf Bernett (2010) have recently argued that transcendental idealism is not only a central trait in Husserl's phe-nomenology but, correctly understood, it provides a fruitful, even necessary, starting point for phenomenological research in general.
2. The meaning that Husserl gives for the term 'transcendental' is that it desig-nates the experiencing subjectivity as that which is constitutive of the tran-scendence, that is, in the first place of the world (cf. Hua 1, 65; Hua 17, 257f.; Hua 3/1 106f., 198). In this sense I think that Dan Zahavi is accurate in pointing out that the defining feature of *transcendental* subjectivity "is that it is constituting, that is meaning-bestowing and world-disclosing" (Zahavi 2002, 104; cf. Zahavi 2003, 72ff.).

3. For example, Anthony Steinbock (1996) and Dan Zahavi (1996) have written extensively on intersubjectivity as a central dimension of the transcendental field, while for instance Sara Heinämaa (2012) and Joona Taipale (2014) argue for the central transcendental significance of embodiment in Husserlian phenomenology.

4. In other words, whereas objectivating consciousness was in the early works conceived of as the most fundamental level of conscious acts, the sphere of passivity was from the 1920s onward discovered as a necessary foundation for the whole realm of intentional activity.

5. Thus Anthony Steinbock, for example, suggests that "we only gain this level of experience of passivity for reflection when we abstract from the accomplishments of activity" (Steinbock 2004, 23). This tendency to approach passivity primarily in abstraction from any and all influence of higher conscious activities is very prominent in the literature and is also present in some of the most prominent commentators (cf. Sokolowski 1964, 138f., 197; Steinbock 2001, xxxviii–xliii; 2004, 22f.; Zahavi 2003, 73). It is to be noted that, in studying passivity, Husserl himself was mostly but not exclusively interested in so-called pure passivity and thus himself often calls for this type of abstraction (cf. Hua 31, 3; Hua 39, 432; EU, 74f.).

6. Dieter Lohmar (2012) is pointing in the same direction as he speaks of both *upward* and *downward* dynamics of experience, the former denoting the effect that lower levels of consciousness have on higher ones and the latter denoting the effects that the higher levels of consciousness can have on the lower levels.

7. For Husserl, 'attentional consciousness' does not mean reflective attention that would be directed to the act itself but rather points to attention that is present in the act insofar as attention is directed to the object of this act. In this sense, a simple act of thematic perception directed to any worldly entity is an instance of attentional consciousness and thus belongs to the sphere of conscious activity and attention, whereas in this type of simple act there is no trace of reflective attention directed to the act itself. According to Husserl, it is in fact only through phenomenological reduction and analysis that we direct the attention from the objects of consciousness to the subjective process of being conscious of something (cf. Hua 29, 74; Hua 1, 83f.; Hua 9, 147; Hua 3/1, 211f.; Hua 38, 68ff.; 406).

8. Instead of equating conscious activity with creative, meaning-constituting spontaneity, Husserl defines creative spontaneity as one specific type of conscious activity, as a higher level of activity (cf. EU, 63, 233; Hua 11, 64).

9. By 'receptivity' (*Rezeptivität*), Husserl does not mean mere reception of something to the field of consciousness, for example, the functioning of sensibility, but rather receptivity denotes a specific attentional mode of being conscious of something, that is being receptive in the sense of being explicitly aware of something and attentively directed to it (cf. Hua 11, 64, 358; Hua 31, 4, 40.)

10. Ulrich Melle classifies these three classes of primal passivities respectively as a presupposed ground for three fundamental categories of acts: sensibility as the ground for acts of theoretical reason, feelings as the ground for acts of valuation and axiological reason, and drives and instincts as the ground for acts of practical reason and will (Melle 2007, 4). A similar classification is done by Husserl himself at least in a manuscript from year 1914 (Hua 28, 422ff.; cf. also EU 73–74).

11. As such, this is not to say that it would be impossible to turn *reflective* attention to these matters. However, even if I would manage to abstract from everything else and to reflect for instance the mere temporal flow sensations, this would not mean that I would attentively live through this flow itself; rather, in Husserl's terms, I would be attentively reflecting at this purely passive flow from the outside from the point of view of an uninvolved observer (*Unbeteiligte Zuschauer*).

12. Husserl's expression '*sekundäre Passivität*' is usually translated as 'secondary passivity.' In order not to cover up the fundamental and primary role of this type of passivity in experience and in order to indicate its composition as a higher-level process, I have decided to deviate from this convention here and to translate '*sekundäre Passivität*' as 'second-level passivity.' The fundamental significance of second-level passivity is emphasized recently also in Biceaga (2010) and Smith (2010), but not in this thematic context. I have recently explored the centrality of Husserl's analyses on the second-level passivity in relation to the question of pregivenness of higher-level cultural meaningfulness (Pulkkinen 2014).

13. Husserl defines second-level passivity as passive pregivenness of various kinds of actively formed meaning (Cf. Hua 15, 203; EU, 336).

14. For a detailed account of Husserl's phenomenology of habituality and its relationship with the broader philosophical discourse on habits and habituality, see Moran (2011).

15. According to Husserl, transcendental subjectivity is "personal" exactly insofar it is not an empty pole of identity or a stable structure of experience but rather a bearer of various habitualities and the habitually familiar world. Or conversely, as the bearer of habitualities, the subject is something that, in the course of its experience, develops a unique and "personal" constitutive character. (cf. Hua 1, 100f., 162f.; Hua 39, 274.) Heinämaa (2007) offers a more detailed reading on Husserl's notion of the person and on its central position among Husserl's various conceptions of the self.

16. Cf. Kant, KrV, A 50/B 74.

17. In essence, this is because some kind of primitive associative structuring of experiential content, that is the constitution of various types of contrasts, is required for things to even stand out as separate in the field of consciousness (cf. Hua 39, 34f.; HuaM 8, 251, 295f.; EU, 74–79, 386, Hua 11, 153, 159f). For this reason, Husserl even at times terms association 'the general title for unity-formation [*Einheitsbildung*]' (HuaM 8, 298; cf. Hua 11, 153, EU, 386). Although Husserl most often discusses association in this primitive sense in the context of pure sensibility, he in no way restricts the functioning of association to sensibility.

18. I would like to thank Professor Dermot Moran for pointing out that this cannot mean that we would experience the environing world as fully prefigured and completely familiar. However, I think that it is equally important to note that, according to Husserl, this is a quantitative restriction, not a qualitative one: although the marginally given world is for a large part unknown and only partially determined, this partial determination can in principle involve any type or level of meaning.

19. Following this line of argument, Husserl at times speaks of the relativization of the "hyletic sphere," that is, the functioning of the previously constituted as the pregiven "material" for new constitutive accomplishments (cf. Hua 39, 8; HuaM 8, 70, 100).

20. For instance, Steven Crowell (2003) and J. N. Mohanty (1985, 191–246, esp. 219) have argued in this vein.

REFERENCES

Biceaga, V. 2010. *The Concept of Passivity in Husserl's Phenomenology—Contributions to Phenomenology, Vol. 60*. Dordrecht, Heidelberg, London, New York: Springer.

Bernet, R. 2010. "Transzendentale Phänomenologie?" In *Philosophy, Phenomenology, Sciences,* edited by C. Ierna, H. Jacobs and F. Mattens, 41–70. Dortrecht, Heidelberg, London, New York: Springer.

Crowell, S. 2003. "Facticity and Transcendental Philosophy." In *From Kant to Davidson—Philosophy and the Idea of the Transcendental,* edited by J. Malpas, 100–121. London and New York: Routledge.

Heinämaa, S. 2007. "Selfhood, Consciousness, and Embodiment: A Husserlian Approach." In *Consciousness: From Perception to Reflection in the History of Philosophy,* edited by S. Heinämaa, P. Remes, and V. Lähteenmäki, 311–328. Dordrecht: Springer.

———. 2012. "The Body." In *The Routledge Companion to Phenomenology,* edited by Søren Overgaard and Sebastian Luft, 222–232. London and New York: Routledge.

Husserl, Edmund. 1948. (EU) *Erfahrung und Urteil. Untersuchungen zur Genealogie der Logik,* edited by Ludwig Landgrebe. Hamburg: Claassen Verlag.

———. 1952. (Hua 4) *Ideen zu einer reinen Phänomenologie und Phänomenologischen Philosophie, Zweites Buch: Phänomenologische Untersuchungen zur Konstitution, Husserliana Band IV,* edited by Marly Biemel. Haag: Martinus Nijhoff.

———. 1959. (Hua 8) *Erste Philosophie. Zweiter Teil: Theorie der phänomenologischen Reduktion,* ed. Rudolf Boehm. Haag: Martinus Nijhoff.

———. 1962. (Hua 9) *Phänomenologische Psychologie. Vorlesungen Sommersemester 1925, Husserliana Band IX,* edited by Walter Biemel. Haag: Martinus Nijhoff.

———. 1966. (Hua 11) *Analysen zur passiven Synthesis. Aus Vorlesungs- und Forschungsmanuskripten 1918–1926, Husserliana Band XI,* edited by Margot Fleischer, Haag: Martinus Nijhoff.

———. 1973. (Hua 15) *Zur Phänomenologie der Intersubjektivität. Texte aus dem Nachlass. Dritter Teil: 1929–1935, Husserliana Band XV,* edited by Iso Kern. Haag: Martinus Nijhoff.

———. 1973. (Hua 1) *Cartesianische Meditationen und Pariser Vorträge, Husserliana Band I,* edited by Stephan Strasser. Haag: Martinus Nijhoff.

———. 1974. (Hua 17) *Formale and transzendentale Logik. Versuch einer Kritik der logischen Vernunft, Husserliana Band XVII,* edited by Paul Janssen. Haag: Martinus Nijhoff.

———. 1976. (Hua 3/1) *Ideen zu einer reinen Phänomenologie und phänomenologischen Philosophie. Erstes Buch: Allgemeine Einführung in die reine Phänomenologie. Husserliana Band III, 1. Halbband,* edited by Karl Schuhmann. Haag: Martinus Nijhoff.

———. 1976. (Hua 6) *Die Krisis der europäischen Wissenschaften und die transzendentale Phänomenologie: Eine Einleitung in die phänomenologische Philosophie, Husserliana Band VI,* edited by Walter Biemel. Haag: Martinus Nijhoff.

———. 1988. (Hua 28) *Vorlesungen über Ethik und Wertlehre (1908-1914), Husserliana Band XXVIII,* edited by Ullrich Melle. Dortrecht/Boston/London: Kluwer Academic Publishers.

———. 1992. (Hua 29) *Die Krisis der europäischen Wissenschaften und die transzendentale Phänomenologie. Ergänzungsband. Texte aus dem Nachlass 1934–1937, Husserliana Band XXIX,* edited by Reinhold N. Smid. Dortrecht/Boston/London: Kluwer Academic Publishers.

———. 2000. (Hua 31) *Aktive Synthesen. Aus der Vorlesung "Transzendentale Logik" 1920/21. Ergänzungsband zu "Analysen zur passiven Synthesis", Husserliana Band XXXI,* edited by Roland Breeur, Dortrecht/Boston/London: Kluwer Academic Publishers.

———. 2002. (HuaM 4) *Natur und Geist – Vorlesungen Sommersemester 1919, Husserliana Materialen Band IV,* edited by Michael Weiler, Dortrecht/Boston/London: Kluwer Academic Publishers.

———. 2004. (Hua 37) *Einleitung in die Ethik. Vorlesungen Sommersemester 1920 und 1924, Husserliana Band XXXVII*, edited by Henning Peucker, Dordrecht: Kluwer Academic Publishers.

———. 2004. (Hua 38) *Wahrnehmung und Aufmerksamkeit. Texte aus dem Nachlass (1893–1912), Husserliana Band XXXVIII*, edited by Thomas Vongehr und Regula Giuliani. Dorthrecht: Springer.

———. 2006. (HuaM 8) *Späte Texte über Zeitkonstitution (1929–1934) (Die C-Manuskripte), Husserliana Materialen Band VIII*, edited by Dieter Lohmar. Dortrecht: Springer.

———. 2008. (Hua 39) *Die Lebenswelt. Auslegungen der vorgegebenen Welt und ihrer Konstitution. Texte aus dem Nachlass (1916–1937), Husserliana Band XXXIX*, edited by Rochus Sowa. Dorthrecht: Springer.

Kant, I. 1904. (KrV) *Kritik der reinen Vernunft,* First Edition ("A"): Academy Edition, Vol. IV. Berlin: G. Reimer, 1911; Second Edition ("B"): Academy Edition, Vol. III. Berlin: G. Reimer.Lohmar, D. 2012. "Genetic Phenomenology." In *The Routledge Companion to Phenomenology,* edited by S. Luft and S. Overgaard, 266–275. London and New York: Routledge.

Melle, U. 2007. "Husserl's Personalist Ethics." *Husserl Studies* 23: 1–15.

Mohanty, J. N. 1985. *The Possibility of Transcendental Philosophy*. Dortrecht: Martinus Nijhoff.

Moran, D. 2005. *Edmund Husserl: Founder of Phenomenology*. Cambridge: Polity Press.

———. 2011. "Edmund Husserl's Phenomenology of Habituality and Habitus." *Journal of British Society for Phenomenology* 42 (1): 53–77.

Pulkkinen, S. 2014 (forthcoming). "Lifeworld as an Embodiment of Spiritual Meaning: The Constitutive Dynamics of Activity and Passivity in Husserl." In *The Phenomenology of Embodied Subjectivity,* edited by R. Jensen and D. Moran.

Smith, N. 2010. *Towards a Phenomenology of Repression—A Husserlian Reply to the Freudian Challenge*. Stockholm Studies in Philosophy 34. Stockholm: Stockholm University.

Sokolowski, R. 1964. *The Formation of Husserl's Concept of Constitution*. The Hague: Martinus Nijhoff.

Steinbock, A. 1996. *Home and Beyond—Generative Phenomenology after Husserl*. Evanston, IL: Northwestern University Press.

———. 2001. "Translator's Introduction." In Edmund Husserl: *Analyses Concerning Passive and Active Synthesis*. Translated by A. J. Steinbock, xv–lxv. Dordrecht, Boston, London: Kluwer Academic Publishers.

———. 2004. "Affection and Attention: On the Phenomenology of Becoming Aware." *Continental Philosophy Review* 37: 21–43.

Taipale, J. 2014. *Phenomenology and Embodiment. Husserl and the Constitution of Subjectivity*. Evanston, IL: Northwestern University Press.

Zahavi, D. 1996. *Husserl und die transzendentale Intersubjektivität: Eine Antwort auf die sprachpragmatische Kritik*. Phaenomenologica 135. Dordrecht: Kluwer Academic Publishers.

———. 2002. "Transcendental Subjectivity and Metaphysics—A Discussion of David Carr's Paradox of Subjectivity." *Human Studies* 25: 103–116.

———. 2003. *Husserl's Phenomenology*. Stanford, CA: Stanford University Press.

———. 2010. "Husserl and the 'absolute.'" In *Philosophy, Phenomenology, Sciences,* edited by C. Ierna, H. Jacobs and F. Mattens, 71–92. Dortrecht, Heidelberg, London, New York: Springer.

6 The Animal and the Infant
From Embodiment and Empathy to Generativity

Sara Heinämaa

It seems to me that the human-animal contrast serves at least two different functions in Husserl's philosophy of other selves and intersubjectivity. One of these functions is related to the constitution of the natural world and the other related to the constitution of the cultural-historical world. In my reading, the fifth Cartesian Meditation involves both of these ideas, but it only explicates the former, the one that concerns the constitution of the natural world. The other idea remains implicit and can only be illuminated with other Husserlian sources: we must turn to the Intersubjectivity volumes to see more clearly how the human-animal contrast serves Husserl's account of the constitution of the cultural world.

The aim of this chapter is to offer explications of both lines of thought and a rational reconstruction of their interconnection. I will proceed by first explicating the analysis that we find in the fifth Cartesian Meditation. Here we encounter Husserl's technical concept of empathy and need to clarify its role in his account of the constitution of the senses of *own lived bodiliness* and *alien lived bodiliness (Leiblichkeit)* and the dependent sense of the intersubjective nature of perception. This is the task of the first part of the chapter (sections 1 and 2). The second part turns to the third Intersubjectivity volume and studies how the human-animal contrast functions in Husserl's account of the constitution of the sense of the true world, that is the cultural-historical world (sections 3 and 4). At the end I hope to be able to put forward some claims about the relation between these two discourses and thereby clarify the nature-culture divide in Husserl's transcendental phenomenology.

1 THE CONSTITUTION OF LIVED BODIES AND PERCEPTUAL NATURE

The fifth Cartesian Meditation begins with an analysis of the sense of the *alien lived body*[1] (*Leib*) and with an account of the constitution of this sense. In order to understand the different ways in which bodies can appear to us as animated, that is, as belonging to conscious subjects or selves, Husserl suggests that we perform a special methodological operation of sense isolation. He proposes that we abstract all sense of alien conscious life from our experience and all sense that depends on such life and that we start by studying first how our own living bodiliness is constituted for us in artificial abstractive isolation (Hua 1, 124–130/92–99, 140–143/110–113; Hua 4, 81–82/86–87; cf. Hua 6, 109–110/107–108, 220–221/216–217; Hua 14, 7). Only after this preparatory step we can study the conditions under which other bodies, that is, bodies environing our own body, appear as experiencing and living to us. Husserl calls this move "the reduction to the sphere of ownness" (Hua 1, 124–125/92–93; cf. Hua 4, 77–78/82–83).

The point is not to derive the sense of another living body from the sense of my living body nor to superimpose some subjective idea on objective being. The point of the abstractive isolation is to get clear about the multiple senses of alienness and otherness involved in our experience of the world and to inquire into their mutual relations of dependency and independency.[2]

Within the solipsistic "universe," I do not experience any living things as long as I refrain from touching myself. All thinghood belongs to external objects and all life belongs to me as the sole living, operating subject that explores the objects (Hua 1, 128/97; cf. Hua 4, 144–152/152–160, 164–166/172–174). But when I touch myself, for example, when I scratch my itching nose with my right-hand fingers, then from the "point of view" of my operating organ, the scratching fingers, the pleasurable sensation belongs to the object touched, the nose. Thus my fingers are able to perceive a very peculiar kind of material object, an object that does not just appear with thingly qualities, such as smoothness and warmness, but is also furnished with sensations of its own, in this case sensations of being touched and sensations of pleasure. Husserl summarizes: "If I speak of the physical thing (. . .), then I am abstracting from these sensations (. . .). If I do include them, then it is not that the physical thing is now richer, but instead it becomes living body [*Leib*], it senses" (Hua 4, 145/152, cf. 151–153/158–159; Hua 11, 13–14/50–51; Hua 14, 75).

The description given here delivers an important point about the necessary role of self-touching in the constitution of one's own living body. However, it is somewhat misleading since it suggests a temporal dependency. This is not the case, so it must be emphasized that the relation is transcendental and not temporal: the capacity to touch oneself is a necessary condition for the constitution of the organs of one's own lived body. Husserl argues:

> *A subject whose only sense was the sense of vision could not at all have an appearing living body* [*Leib*]; in the play of kinesthetic motivations (which he would not apprehend lively [*leiblich*] this subject would have appearances of things, he would see real things. (Hua 4, 150/158)

This means that the phenomenon of double sensation, in which a perceiving body touches itself, is crucial to the constitution of the primary sense of living bodiliness: the living body is a material thing that entertains a system of sensations and sensory appearances. The constitution of such a thing requires kinesthetic sensations and touch sensations (as the constitution of any thing), but in addition to these, it also involves a double way of apprehending sensations. Some sensations have to be grasped as thingly qualities, while others must at the same time remain subjective sensings:

> The living body [*Leib*] constitutes itself originally in a double way: first it is a physical thing, *matter;* it has its extension, in which are included its real properties, its color, smoothness, hardness, warmth (. . .). Secondly, I find on it, and I *sense* "on" it and "in" it: warmth on the back of the hand, coldness in the feet, sensations of touch in the fingertips. (Hua 4, 145/153, translation modified; cf. Hua 1, 128/97; Hua 14, 75; Merleau-Ponty [1945] 1993, 108–109/92–93, 465–468/406–409, 1964, 170/133, 185–195/140–149, 307–310/254–257)

Husserl's solution to the problem of other experiencing, living bodies rests on two grounds: the primary constitution of my own living body and the idea of transfer of sense. He argues that the experience of localized sensations and the primitive sense of living as sensing is transferred over from one's own body to other bodies in the environing space (Hua 1, 142–143/112–113; Hua 4, 164–166/172–174; Hua 14, 97). The transfer is motivated by the similarity of perceived movements. Some things that I detect and observe in space resemble my own living body and its organs in their perceived movements (Hua 1, 141–144/112–114; Hua 14, 3–4; Hua 15, 183). A body over there reacts to external stimulation, to the cold wind or the freezing rain, for example, in the same way as my own arms and hands: it shivers (cf. Hua 14, 118). And when it bumps into another thing, it does not halt or bounce back but restores its balance and circumvents the obstacle. Moreover, without any detectable causal influence by other material elements or things, it spontaneously turns to this or that direction. And finally: it also manifests the types of reflexive movements that are familiar to me from my own case.

Such behavioral similarities motivate a complex of synthetizing experiences that terminates in an act in which the sense of sensing is transferred over to a body perceived at a distance. As a result, that body over there appears as a material thing with its own systems of sensations and appearance systems, sensations that I cannot have or live through but that are expressed and indicated to me by the thing's movements and behaviors. This is not an inferential step that gives us a new proposition but a perceptual switch based on passive associations.

The living thing does not appear in perception as an amalgam or compound of two separate realities, one psychic and the other physical, nor as a two-layered psycho-physical reality. Such conceptualizations belong to the psychological and life sciences, not to straightforward perception, and they depend on the goals, the methods, and the techniques of these sciences. Instead of manifesting itself as a compounded or layered structure, in which physical realities indicate hidden psychic units, the living being appears as a *uniform whole* saturated with governed movements, meaningful gestures, and significant behaviors. The fifth Meditation states: "If we stick to the factical, i.e. to the experience of someone else as it comes to pass at any time, we find that actually the sensuously seen body [*Körper*] is experienced forthwith as the body of someone else and not as merely an indication of someone else [*für den Andered*] (. . .) What I actually see is not a sign (. . .); on the contrary, it is someone else" (Hua 1, 150–153/121–124; cf. Hua 4, 234–241/245–253).

2   PAIRING OF BODIES AND PERCEPTUAL ANOMALIES

Husserl argues repeatedly that the empathetic transfer of sense that he studies is not any sort of reasoning or interpretation (e.g., Hua 1, 141/111). The sense *living* is not derived, deduced, or induced in any manner from the perceived behavior. My perception does not serve as a basis for an inference but motivates in me a new type of apprehension, one that I already master in my own case but that I now can perform also in another case similar to mine.

For example, when I clean the swimming pool by removing fallen leaves from the water surface with a pool net, I suddenly detect a "quivering" movement among the yellow and beige leaves that have fallen from the oak tree nearby. The quivering stands out immediately in my perceptual field, and I switch from perception of mere matter to perception of a living thing: a grasshopper or a noctuid moth. The shape and the color of the insect merges with those of the leaves, and all these buoyant entities are in motion on the rippling surface of the water. However, some of these little brownish things move differently than others and in ways that resemble my own movements, and as such they attract my attention in a particular way. A contrary switch happens, for example, when I study angleworms contained in a bucket in order to remove dead individuals (cf. Hua 14, 126). I can distinguish lifeless animals from living ones simply by their motions: in a small bucket, all bodies move, but the dead ones move in a different way than the living.

In addition to mere sensings, we transfer also other types of consciousness to perceivable bodies, depending on the complexity of their behaviors (*Gebaren*) and their relations to the environment. Thus the class of living things is not identical with that of sensing things but also includes feeling things as well as desiring and willing things (Hua 4, 164/172, 235/246–247, cf. 166/174–175). What is transferred is not any mental or psychic unit (such as a mental state, event, process) or a series of such units, nor any mental substance, but the sense *lived body* or *conscious embodiment*. This transfer is supported by a passive associative synthesis that links, pairs, or couples, two (or several) bodies on the basis of resemblance or similarity and thus allows the transfer to happen between them. The validity of the sense is verified by the experience of harmony in the behavior of the body or bodies perceived. Husserl writes:

> The lived body [*Leib*] of another continues to prove itself as actually a lived body, solely in its changing but incessantly *harmonious behavior* [*einstimmig Gebaren*]. Such *harmonious* behavior (. . .) must present itself fulfillingly in original experience and do so throughout the continuous change in behavior from phase to phase. The organism becomes experienced as a pseudo-organism precisely if there is something discordant about its behavior. (Hua 1, 144/114, translation modified)

Husserl's *Logical Investigations* (1900–1901) offers an illuminating example of how the anticipations implicated by such experiences can be disappointed. Husserl reports an experience of meeting a unknown woman on the stairs when entering the Panopticum Waxworks in Berlin. When the person first enters the gallery, he notices a woman standing on the stairs; he approaches the woman and prepares to greet her while passing, but when he comes closer to the figure, he realizes that he has been tricked by a wax sculpture. As long as he is tricked, Husserl argues, he experiences a perfectly good percept: a person momentarily resting on the stairs. When the illusion vanishes, he sees a statue that only represents a human person, a woman (Husserl [1901] 1984, 458–459/137–138; cf. Hua 11, 33/72, 350–351/431–432; Hua 14, 124).[3]

The experience proceeds in stages and in accordance with the bodily movements of the perceiving subject: when he approaches the figure, new sensory materials "come in" and are "typified." He associates the perceived object with other similar ones and ultimately with his own living body. Its visual shape and posture remind him of the gestalt that is familiar to him from his own case. The association generates anticipations that the percept will move and comport itself toward the environment in certain ways. When he comes closer to the figure, however, his anticipations are disappointed, as new sensory material does not confirm the association but, on the contrary, conflicts with it. The figure stays motionless; more particularly, what remains absent are the vital movements that characterize living beings and the spontaneity, responsiveness, and reflexivity that belongs to human and animal bodies. He sees now that the object resembles humans only in visual form but not in movement or comportment, and so the associative synthesis fails, and he sees a dummy.

Two points must be emphasized concerning the associative passive synthesis and the pairing of the two percepts central to this synthesis.

First, Husserl argues that the pairing that makes possible the transfer of sense needed for the experience of another conscious living being does not only involve the body over there perceived by me and my own body in its double form of givenness sensing-sensed. The transfer of sense *living* from my own body to the body perceived is mediated by a spatial variant of my own body.[4] He writes:

> I do not apperceive him as having (. . .) the spatial modes of appearance that are mine from here; rather, as we find in closer examination, I apperceive him as having the spatial modes of appearance like those I should have if I should go over there and be where he is. (Hua 1, 120/117, cf. 148–149/117–119; Hua 14, 9, 83, 96–97)

So the transfer of sense necessary for the experience of another bodily subject or conscious body happens between my own body as I live it here and the other's body as I see it over there, but it is, as it were, "assisted" by a imaginative and counterfactual variant of my own body: my body as I would experience it if I stood where it stands and would orient myself as it orients itself.

The second thing to emphasize is that the resemblance between the two bodies does not have to be total or comprehensive but can be partial and focused. We do not just experience fellow humans as conscious living beings but also as different types of animals, even biologically very simple creatures, and animals that have a limited repertoire of operative sensory organs in comparison to us (Hua 14, 115–118).[5] We can of course think and conceive of such beings as complicated machines, and Descartes's famous descriptions introduced them as such to modern natural philosophy, but perceptually all these beings differ from falling stones, flying pieces of paper, and floating plastic bottles by manifesting a distinctive way of responsive, spontaneous, and reflexive movement. Even animals that hide and protect themselves by imitating vegetable shapes and ways of movement, such as the seahorse, the leaf fish, or the praying mantis, stand out in the spatial-thingly environment. What betrays their conscious living-sensing character are, for example, their operating eyes, their tentacles, or their fins. The possibility of experiencing such beings as living depends on the stratified or layered character of our own embodiment. We are able to remove complete components from our synesthetic experiencing—locomotion, vision, or audition—and transfer the remaining partial sense of experiencing to alien bodies. Husserl calls such removal "dismantling" (*Abbau*), and thus we can say that our possibilities of extending our empathetic approach to nonhuman animals depends on our capacity to dismantle our own experiencing (e.g., Hua 14, 115–119).

The subjects that in empathetic apprehension intend one another as perceiving, experiencing beings with sensory-motor bodies constitute together the natural world (Hua 1, 149–153/120–125; Hua 4, 86/91, 197/207, 201/211; Hua 14, 101–103, 129). Animals belong here as subjects for whom this world is given with its multiple objects and thus also as members of the community of co-constituters (e.g., Hua 15, 625–626; cf. Hua 14, 99–103, 115–119, 126). This is not the nature of the mathematized natural sciences composed of neurons, molecules, atoms, and black holes but is the perceivable nature that includes perceptive elements and substances and their qualities and types as well as the living beings that intend such entities (cf. Hua 1, 157–158/129–130; Hua 4, 164–164/172–173, 191–197/201–207, 217–218/228–229; Hua 6, 142–143/138–140, 461–462/381–383; Hua 14, 97–98).

Subjects deprived of sense capacities, for example the blind and the deaf, take part in the constitution of the perceptual nature in so as far they do not operate from within their deprivation (Hua 1, 154/125–126; Hua 15, 178). On the other hand, such subjects also broaden or deepen our grasp on this world by their unaffected sense organs that compensate for their deprivations and may manifest intensified and over-developed performance (Hua 14, 133).[6] Analogously, animals with "superpower" senses, such as the shark and the microbat, add to our sensory-perceptive grasp upon nature (cf. Hua 15, 167). Also sensorily anomalous animals, for example the starnosed mole, may reveal to us aspects of things that we cannot grasp directly (Hua 14, 133–134, cf. 126). However, all such anomalous subjects, human and animal, take part in the constitution of perceptual nature thanks to their fundamental sensory-motor similarity with us (Hua 1, 154/125; cf. Hua 14, 7, 112–114, 126).

3   MORTAL SUBJECTS AND THE CONSTITUTION OF THE CULTURAL-HISTORICAL WORLD

Husserl discusses sensory deprivations explicitly in the fifth Cartesian Meditation.[7] He introduces the topic under the headings "anomalous others" and "abnormal others" by writing:

> It is implicit in the sense of successful apperception of others that their world, the world of their appearance-systems, must be experienced forthwith as the world of my appearance-system; and this involves the identity of the appearance-systems. But we know very well that there is something that is called *abnormalities,* blind, deaf etc., and thus that the appearance-systems are by no means always absolutely identical and that whole strata can differ (though not all strata). (Hua 1, 154/125)[8]

The main point here is that the transfer of sense, necessary for the experience of other experiencing subjects, does not imply a complete identity of the sensory-motor capacities of the subjects at issue but allows variance. In other words, I do not have to transfer the whole sense of my lived bodiliness with all sensory capacities involved but can transfer just parts of this sense, like the auditory part, the tactile part, or just parts of the kinesthetic system (cf. Hua 14, 115). However, the transfer must result in a partial identity of appearance systems at a minimum and cannot establish completely different systems. In other words, another lived body with "completely different" sensory-motor capacities is a conceptual construction and not an experiential reality.

In order to highlight the variance of alien bodiliness in the fifth Meditation, Husserl brings in the case of the animals:

> Among the problems of abnormality the *problem of animality* and that of the levels of *higher and lower* animals are included. Relative to the animal, man is, constitutionally speaking, the normal case—just as I myself am the primal norm [*Urnorm*] constitutionally for all men; animals are essentially constituted for me as anomalous *variants* [*Abwandlungen*] of my humanness, even though among them in turn normality and abnormality may be differentiated. (Hua 1, 154/126)

The parallel between sensory deprivation and animality suggests that the animal is abnormal in the very same sense as the blind or deaf fellow human: by differing partially from us by their appearance-systems. This reading is supported by many sections that discuss animals as abnormalities in the Intersubjectivity volumes.

However, in the third Intersubjectivity volume, Husserl also develops another discourse on animals, one in which the animal is not paralleled with the deaf and the blind, that is, with humans suffering sensory deprivations, but is paralleled with the infant.

I believe that this part of Husserl's discourse on animality leads us away from the natural world that is constituted in perception and empathetic apperception and allows us to pose a series of questions concerning the constitution of the cultural-historical world. For Husserl, the cultural-historical world is the world in the true or genuine sense. This is the world that functions as the horizon for our scientific, religious, artistic, and economic practices. It depends on the natural world in a specific sense, but it also includes completely new types of objectivities and is characterized by a new temporal openness or endlessness that is absent from the natural world. Moreover, engaging in cultural-historical practices changes one's relation to nature since cultural practices are precisely practices of inspecting, manipulating, and developing nature within the openness-horizon of the cultural. For example, a human being who plants trees that will outlive not just him but also his offspring looks at saplings and stems in a different way than an agent that merely seeks wood for timber.

We will see that, on Husserl's analysis, taking part in the constitution of the cultural world requires a particular kind of self-awareness from the subject. In other words, not all subjects that participate in the co-constitution of the natural world of perception are able to take part in the constitution of the cultural world. In order to get to the philosophical core of Husserl's discourse, I will compare his characterizations of animal with his comments on infants and study the grounds on which he excludes both from the community that collectively constitutes the sense of the cultural-historical world.

3.1   A Question Concerning Constitution

At the end of the second part of *The Crisis,* in paragraph §55, Husserl puts forward a series of questions concerning the constitution of the world and the kinds of subjects involved in this collective undertaking. He writes:

> But then new questions impose themselves in regard to this mankind: are the insane also objectifications of the subjects being discussed in connection with the accomplishment of world-constitution? And what about children, even those who already have a certain amount of world-consciousness? After all, it is only from the mature and normal human beings who bring them up that they first become acquainted with the world in *the full sense of world-for-all,* that is, the world of culture. And what about animals? (Hua 6, 191/187, emphasis added)

In the third Intersubjectivity volume, Husserl develops an important argument according to which both animals and infants do not belong to the community that constitutes this full sense of the world. In secondary literature, this argument has not been given the attention that it deserves; Husserl's statements about animals and infants as anomalous others, along with his whole discourse on anomality, is usually rejected as an outdated or prejudiced approach with only marginal, if any, philosophical value.[9] I believe that this is a mistake: even if Husserl's discourse on anomalous others may prove problematic, the analyses that he provides are crucial to us insofar as we want to understand the difference between the natural and the historical-cultural order.

Husserl argues that both animals and infants are ego-subjects with egoic states (Hua 15, 177) and both have a world in some sense of the term. At the same time, he insists that neither of these subjects can partake in the constitution of the true or genuine sense of the world. The grounds on which he argues for this position are paramount to us because they reveal what Husserl takes to be the core of the world in the full sense of the term and because they correlatively indicate what kind of consciousness is needed for having this world. Both aspects of the correlation concern time. We will see that the world in the true sense is distinguished from lesser senses on the basis of the world's temporal structure and, correspondingly, that the type of consciousness that is able to participate in the constitution of this sense must relate to its own life in a particular way.

3.2   Non-Mortal Subjects: The Animal and the Infant

Both the animal and the infant are excluded by Husserl from the collective of co-constitutors on the same grounds: neither experiences itself as a member of a generation that is connected to other generations and to an open chain of generations by the means of language. In this respect, both the animal and the infant differ from subjects with sensory deprivations who, despite their deprivation, consciously belong to generational chains of human subjects and to generations of subjects with identical deprivations (Hua 14, 133; cf. Hua 14, 127–129; Hua 15, 140, 167–169, 171, 184, 626–627).[10]

Husserl contends that both the animal and the infant consciously participate in many different types of communities of contemporaries and even in communities that use signs for practical purposes. However, what he considers crucial is that neither the animal nor the infant experiences itself as a being who is born and who will die. This implies that neither can grasp itself as a being who shares a communal past and future with other similar beings that are not present and cannot become present in flesh and blood.

The others that in our mature human experience are separated from us by our birth and death are not just contingently absent for us but are absent in their very essence: some will live after our demise and others have lived before we were born. Neither can be intended by animal and infant subjects in so far as these subjects lack the sense of themselves as natal and mortal beings, that is, beings who are born and who will die (Husserl Hua 15, 140, 168, 171, 184–185; Merleau-Ponty [1945] 1993, 415–417/361–364, 489–492/427–430).

In my reading, the crucial positive claim that Husserl makes while discussing animals and infants as anomalous others is that we mature adults are constantly consciously related to past and future others and to whole chains of generations of such others and that language is our means of intending perceptually absent subjects. These absent others are of course not constantly in the thematic focus of our attention, but their existence is implied by the cultural-historical practices in which we engage in our everyday and professional lives. We can bring these others in the thematic focus of our intention and this can happen in several ways. For example, we may hear or read stories about our ancestors and we may address such others in prayer or orison. Moreover, we can capture their very words as repeated by our older contemporaries and we can also read their writing without any mediation by third persons. Analogously, we can address our successors by our own writing and we can rehearse our younger contemporaries to repeat our words in the view of not being present forever. All these activities are senseless for the animal and for the infant in so far as these subjects do not understand themselves as mortal and natal beings who have generations of others behind and ahead of them in time. Husserl explains:

> An animal (. . .) does not have a *unity of time which spans over generations* as historical time nor a unity of the world which continues through time, it does not "have" this *consciously.* (. . .) *The animal itself has no generative world in which it would live consciously, no conscious existence in an open endlessness of generations* and correlatively no existence in a genuine environing world, which we humans, anthropomorphizing, attribute to it. (Hua 15, 181, emphasis added)

Several deprivations or lacks are implied by the fundamental lack of generative time and trans-generational communication. In so far as the animal and the infant have no conscious membership in chains of generations, they cannot participate in transgenerational practices as transgenerational and cannot share the accomplishments of such practices. This deprives them of culture and tradition as a whole: cultural-historical goals that are shared with countless subjects in an endless openness of generations; cultural-historical tools and utensils that are retained, maintained, and repaired in view of a chain of successors; and ultimately the cultural-historical world that contains all this openness. This world includes all the products of our cultural practices, from the most basic ones, such as cooking, farming, raising cattle, building, and mining, to the most advanced spiritual activities, essential to our religious, artistic, and scientific lives.

> Only human striving (. . .) has endless horizons; only a human being strives, handles, acts by creating enduring products which satisfy enduring goals (. . .) An enduring product is not a product for a momentary need; but is meant for an endless repetition of similar needs of the same person or other persons in the same social circle. Its goal is an open endlessness of similar goals which are synthetically united in its idea. Each tool, each utensil, a house, a garden, a statue, a sacrificial altar, a religious symbol etc.—all these are examples [of this]. The goal of such a cultural object is to fulfill an infinite endlessness of goals, which refers to an endlessness of persons and real possible circumstances. And this holds for each cultural object in general. (Hua 27, 97–98)

Many familiar animals can of course use tools. We all have seen films and video clips in which primates use instruments, like sticks and stones, for capturing food. Even some mollusks are known to manifest practical intelligence: while detecting an edible object in a glass jar, an octopus is disposed to unscrew the cap. In Husserl's analysis, such instruments are given, and can be given, to nonverbal animals only in a way that is temporally restricted compared to us, and thus their givenness is crucially different from the givenness of human tools. Animal and infantile tools are used merely, or at best, for present purposes and they are only shared with contemporaries (Hua 27, 97–98; cf. Hua 1, 141/111). They are not, and cannot be, experienced by animals and infants as objects inherited from predecessors nor as objects shared with successors, since the experience of permanently absent others—others that cannot be empathetically apperceived—is not articulated for these subjects. In other words, animal and infantile tools do not, in their practical sense, imply asynchronous others who share goals with present users despite the fundamental separation in time.

Thus, Husserl argues that the senses of culture, tradition, and history go hand in hand and that all these senses depend on the senses of death, birth, and generations (e.g., Hua 15, 141, 168–189, 177–181, 280; cf. Hua 1,

169/142; Hua 6, 191/188). For him, no subject who lacks these fundamental senses can intend cultural-historical objectivities as such. He makes this point by describing his own experiential condition as an infant:

> I had no notion of death and birth, even if I already had the words for these. I knew nothing about literature, science, art, nothing about historical culture in general, even if I already had an environing world with pictures,[11] with utensils etc. The ontic sense *world* that I had was under constant reconstruction of sense, and *not by mere extension of sense* through possessed horizons. The world-horizon had no determinate delineation [*Einzeihnung*], at least *no openly, endlessly continuing determinate delineation,* even if it already had a certain openness. (Hua 15, 140, emphasis added)

The open endlessness of generations is necessary for the constitution of the sense of the world as an infinitely open whole. More limited senses of world, for example, the world as an environment and the world as a perceptual or experiential field (e.g., Hua 15, 168, 626), are possible for non-generative subjects, but the *full sense* of world as an open infinity requires for its constitution subjects who consciously connect to other subjects in an endless and endlessly branching chain of generations. Thus, the world in the sense of an infinite "metahorizon" of all horizons[12] is the constitutive correlate of *historical* self-conscious intersubjectivity. We read:

> We, the subjects of world experience, have the endlessly open world completely according to its known realities and unknown possibilities, we each have it completely starting from us, each starting from him or herself through the mediation of others and finally through their participation. (Hua 15, 220)

So we can say that for Husserl, the most important and fundamental difference between mature human subjects, on the one hand, and infantile and animal subjects, on the other hand, is that the latter lack the experience of generations and the linguistic mediation that is implied in this experience. These lacks are mutually implicating since language is the means of intending others in multiple generations and in an infinite openness. Husserl discusses this under the heading "The function of language in the chain of generations" (Hua 15, 224, cf. 169, 181) and writes:

> A communal life of humans becomes possible as life of a linguistic community which is of a completely different kind than the communal life of animals. *The homeworld of humans,* which is the fundamental element [*Grundstück*] for the structure of the objective world for <them> (. . .) *is essentially determined by language.* Only through [language] is established, not merely a sensible common world, a concrete world of

presence (in an extended sense which also includes the horizons of co-presence and past, and in one part the living future), but a practical human homeworld with an incomparably extensive circle of experience which encompasses as operative also the linguistically mediated experiences of the comrades [*Genossen*], and not only [experiences] which are really fully intuitively understood according to others (. . .), but also linguistic knowledge-structures which are not understood intuitively at all. (Hua 15, 224–225, cf. 181; see also Hua 6, 307/328)

As pointed out above, animals use many sorts of signals and indicative signs. They leave traces and they mark their territories, their orientations, and their states, and they are able to grasp the marks produced and used by other animals. Thus they consciously live social lives not just in the immediacy of perceptual bodily exposure but also in the mediation of signs and signals (Hua 15, 180). However, they lack the linguistic system of expressive signs that makes possible a peculiar way of sharing not by producing indications that point to intentions but by objectifying meanings themselves. This involves two inseparable aspects. On the one hand, linguistic meanings are special sorts of objects shared, known, and managed by all speakers of the language. On the other hand, these objects can be materialized in multiple ways; the very same sentence can, for example, be recited, sung, and signed; it can be printed on paper and inscribed an a sheet of papyrus, it can burned into wood, hammered in stone, and drawn in sand. Transgenerational communication of linguistic signs requires some material means but is not dependent on any particular means. Moreover, all human languages are able to express these meanings and, by the practice of translation, human subjects are able to understand speakers of other languages, contemporary and past.

4 GENERATIVITY, LANGUAGE, AND THE HOMEWORLD

We have seen that in Husserl's analysis, the experience of generativity is necessary for the constitution of sense of the cultural-historical world, the world for all in the extended sense of chaining and branching generations. However, this alone is not enough to establish the most pregnant sense of us all and the related sense of the true objective world. Generativity only gives us a unified community that temporally opens onto two directions, the past and the future. For the universal sense *all*, more is needed. Husserl explains:

Enchained communication would not give any tradition which would be a tradition for all, not any community of spiritual acquisitions which would be accessible for all, not "the real world" already horizontally outlined for all. What is missing is: *Homeworld*—alien homeworld, which is valid, not for us, but for them. From there a path to the relativization, but also the problem of the new world for all—all "humanities." (Hua 15, 169n1; cf. Hua 1, 159–162/131–135)

In effect, Husserl argues that a plurality of generative communities is implied in the pregnant sense of us all. A mere temporal historical openness to past and future is not enough; what is needed is also an open plurality of alien communities with alien practices, goals, and means and their temporal horizons. In order to account for this other type of openness, one that connects us to alien cultures and peoples, Husserl introduces the concepts of homeworld (*Heimwelt*) and alienworld (*Fremdenwelt*).[13]

He argues that our world of experience is disclosed to us as a limited field of culturally specific, habituated, and inherited practices and interests only when it is exposing to us a set of alien practices and interests and to an alien practical community. In this disclosure, our world loses its absoluteness as the totality of all things and the horizon of all individual-personal horizons, and we realize and rearticulate it as one particular horizon among other horizons in a more encompassing horizon that also includes the communal experiences of alien others. Moreover, this is the only way in which our world of experience can lose its absoluteness and gain a more specific sense as a homeworld, such as by being compared to subjects and objects of alien practices. Husserl explains:

> My homeworld, my people. The universe in the first form as homeworld only *stands out* [as such] when other homeworlds, other peoples are already in the horizon along with the homeworld. The lived environment [*Lebensumwelt*] in the horizon of alien lived environments, my people surrounded by alien people. (Hua15: 176n1)

> There is constituted an alien humankind, an alien humanity, as alien people for instance. Precisely thereby there is constituted for me and for us "our own" home fellowship, fellowship of our people in relation to our cultural environing world [*Kulturumwelt*] as the world of our human validities, our particular ones. So I have a change [*Änderung*] (. . .) of my world-experience and our world-experience and [a change of] the world itself. In "the" world are we, my people, and the other people, and each has its environing world of people (with its non-practical horizon). Environing world is distinguished from world. (Hua 15, 214; cf. Hua 27, 186–188; Hua 39, 336–337)

This means that three different senses of world are constitutively stratified one upon the other, but in such a manner that each new layer of sense relativizes the prior one, encompasses it in a new, more inclusive, and more complex whole and thus shows its limits. Thus we proceed from (a) the natural world as the totality of all perceptual things to (b) the world as the horizon of the temporally continuous and developing community and finally to (c) the world as the horizon of all such communal horizons.

The natural world includes all subjects of perception, and they all are included in this world both as subjects of perception and as objects of perception. This world is thus given to all perceivers, both human and animal, and it is constituted collectively by them in relations of empathetic apperception. The cultural-historical world, on the other hand, only includes subjects who are conscious of their own natality and mortality and of similar subjects in the past and in the future. This world is the intentional correlate of the plurality of generative communities in mutual implication; it is organized in structures of generations and generative homeworlds and alienworld. Thus the sense of the world as the common ground and infinite field for different historical peoples is not a correlate of any conscious activities whatsoever, individual or communal, but is a complicated constitutional achievement that includes mutual recognition of communal subjects who are conscious of the temporal limits of their own lives (Hua 15, 430).

NOTES

1. The German word "*Leib*" that Husserl uses to refer to the living bodies of both animals and human beings is translated in several different ways. In Cairns's translation of *Cartesiaischen Meditationionen* (Hua 1) from 1970, "*Leib*" is rendered into "animate organism." In the English version of the second volume of *Ideen* (Hua 4), the translators Richard Rojcewicz and André Schuwer use the term 'Body' with a capital "B."

   In contemporary phenomenology, these technical terms are often replaced by the term 'lived body' in order to emphasize the fact that a living thing experiences its own body in a special way: the animal does not grasp its body as a perceptual thing among other things but as a means of manipulating perceivable objects and as the zero-point of orientation and action in space.

   Here I will use both 'lived body' and 'living body' interchangeably for Husserl's concept of *Leib*. I choose to do so in order to keep in mind the essentially double character of the body as sensing and sensed, experiencing and experienced, accentuated by the phenomenon of double sensation.

2. Several commentators have interpreted this sense-isolating operation as a fundamental ontological resolution and have argued that it severely weakens or perverts Husserl's discourse on other selves and their bodily being. The most well known of such commentators are of course Emmanuel Lévinas and Jean-Paul Sartre, but the notion is widely accepted. On such interpretations, Husserl would start from a solipsistic universe and would aim at construing the existence of other subjects on a hopelessly narrow ground. Husserl's point, however, is not ontological or metaphysical but transcendental. It concerns the order of sense constitution and the dependences between different senses, and the method that he proposes is not constructive but analytical.

3. For the gendered aspects of this exemplary phenomenon, see Heinämaa (2011).

4. Several commentators argue that Husserl's account is dominated by a model of visual perception and distorted by the limitations of this model. One complaint is that his idea of the transfer of sense from one percept to another presupposes that the two percepts are separated by a spatial distance, one standing "here" and the other over "there," and that this implies that the two percepts must be captured visually since only vision, or some other distance

sense (e.g. audition), can connect spatially distant objects. It seems to me that this is type of critique is based on a misunderstanding of the sense in which my own lived body is "here" and any other lived body is "there": the two bodies can of course be in constant contact, can continually touch one another, and still be distinguished by the sensory chasm between "my here" and "its there."

5. Husserl's examples include insects, mammals, and primates.

6. See Jorge Louis Borges's "Blindness" in *Ficciones* (1962, original 1944); cf. to fictional stories, for example, "The country of the blind" (1904) by G. H. Wells and *Das Parfum* (1985) by Patrick Süskind.

7. For explications of Husserl's concepts of normality, abnormality, and anomality, see Folter (1983), Römpp (1992, 89–91), Steinbock (1995), and Zahavi ([1996] 2001, 86–97).

8. The assumption here is that the reader belongs among sighted individuals. From the point of view of the blind person, the situation of course is the opposite: the sighted individuals are the abnormal ones.

   Husserl operates with two different concepts of normality; on the one hand, he defines normality by harmony and concordance and, on the other hand, he defines normality by optimacy. An experience is normal in the first sense if it concords with other experiences; an experience is normal in the second sense if it adds to the richness, differentiation, and completeness of experiencing. By using these concepts, we can say two things about sensory deprivations, for example, blindness. In terms of harmony and concordance, blindness is just another norm of experiencing, parallel to sight; in terms of optimacy, blindness is an abnormality since it restricts the spatial richness and distinction of experiencing (cf. Hua 14, 133–134). For more detailed explications, see Steinbock (1995, 138–166).

9. The commentary literature is largely influenced by Derrida's (1962) critique that rejects Husserl's concepts of normality as an unhappy mixture of empirical and transcendental concerns (Derrida 1962, 74–78/79–83; cf. Lawlor 2002, 112–113). More recent contributions divert from this general approach; see Steinbock (1995).

10. A seriously demented person ignorant of himself as part of a generation would in Husserl's analyses be analogous to the infant and the animal; but a person who attacks windmills, a person who searches Satan in Moscow, and a person who serves human brains at dinner all suffer from a different type of deprivation. Thus, the category of the mentally ill is not uniform in respect to the task of sense constitution but includes many different kinds of cases.

11. For Husserl's concept of pictorial presentation, see his *Phäntasie, Bildbewusstsein, Erinnerung: Zur Phänomenologie der anschaulichen Vergegenwärtigungen* (Hua 23).

12. Or "the style of all styles," in Merleau-Ponty's terms ([1945] 1993, 381/330).

13. Husserl's concept of homeworld is wide since it is defined by shared activities and practices; it refers to ethnographically and religiously shared worlds but also to professional and literary worlds. For a comprehensive explication and discussion of these concepts, see Steinbock (1995).

REFERENCES

Borges, J. L. [1944] 1962. "Blindness." In *Ficciones*. Ed. A. Kerrigan. New York: Grove Press.

Derrida, J. 1962. "Introduction." In Husserl: *L'origine de la géométrie*. Paris: PUF. In English: *Origin of Geometry: An Introduction*. Trans. J.P. Leavet. Lincoln: University of Nebraska Press.

Descartes, R. AT. [1964–1976] 1996. *Œuvres de Descartes,* eds. Charles Adam and Paul Tannery. Revised edition. Paris: Vrin/C.N.R.S. In English: *The Philosophical Writings of Descartes,* trans. J. Cottingham, R. Stoothoff, and D. Murdoch. Cambridge, MA: Cambridge University Press, 1984–1991.

Folter, R. J. de. 1983. "Reziprozität der Perspektiven und Normalität bei Husserl und Schütz." In *Sozialität und Intersubjektivität: Phänomenologische Perspektiven der Sozialwissenschaften in Umkreis von Aron Gurwitsch und Alfred Schütz,* eds. R. Grathoff and B. Waldenfels, 157–181. München: Wilhelm Fink.

Heinämaa, S. 2011. "A Phenomenology of Sexual Difference: Types, Styles, and Persons." In *Feminist Metaphysics: Explorations in the Ontology of Sex, Gender and Identity,* ed. C. Witt, 131–155. Dordrecht: Springer.

Husserl, E. 1950. Hua 1. *Cartesianische Meditationen und Pariser Vorträge,* ed. S. Strasser, The Hague, Netherlands: Martinus Nijhoff. In English: *Cartesian Meditations,* trans. D. Cairns. Dordrecht, Boston: Martinus Nijhoff, 1960.

———. 1952. Hua 4. *Ideen zu einer reinen Phänomenologie und phänomenologischen Philosophie, Zweites Buch: Phänomenologische Untersuchungen zur Konstitution,* ed. M. Biemel. The Hague: Martinus Nijhoff. In English: *Ideas Pertaining to a Pure Phenomenology and to a Phenomenological Philosophy, Second Book: Studies in the Phenomenological Constitution,* trans. R. Rojcewicz and A. Schuwer. Dordrecht, Boston, London: Kluwer Academic Publishers, 1993.

———. 1954. Hua 6. *Die Krisis der europäischen Wissenschaften und die transzendentale Phänomenologie: Eine Einleitung in die phänomenologischen Philosophie,* ed. W. Biemel. The Hague: Martinus Nijhoff. In English: *The Crisis of European Sciences and Transcendental Phenomenology: An Introduction to Phenomenological Philosophy,* trans. D. Carr. Evanston, IL: Northwestern University, 1988.

———. 1966. Hua 11. *Analysen zur passiven Synthesis. Aus Vorlesungs- und Forschungsmanuskripten, 1918–1926,* ed. M. Fleischer. The Hague: Martinus Nijhoff. In English: *Analyses Concerning Passive and Active Synthesis: Lectures on Transcendental Logic,* trans. A. J. Steinbock. Dordrecht: Kluwer, 2001.

———. 1973. Hua 14. *Zur Phänomenologie der Intersubjektivität. Texte aus dem Nachlass. Zweiter Teil. 1921–28,* ed. I. Kern. The Hague: Martinus Nijhoff.

———. 1973. Hua 15. *Zur Phänomenologie der Intersubjektivität. Texte aus dem Nachlass, Dritter Teil (1929–1935),* ed. I. Kern. The Hague: Martinus Nijhoff.

———. 1980. Hua 23. *Phäntasie, Bildbewusstsein, Erinnerung. Zur Phänomenologie der anschaulichen Vergegenwartigungen, Texte aus dem Nachlass (1898–1925),* ed. E. Marbach. The Hague: Martinus Nijhoff.

———. 1988. Hua 27. *Aufsätze und Vorträge. 1922–1937,* eds. T. Nenon and H. R. Sepp. The Hague: Kluwer Academic Publishers.

———. 2008. Hua 39. *Die Lebenswelt: Auslegungen der vorgegebenen Welt und ihrer Konstitution. Texte aus dem Nachlass (1916–1937),* ed. R. Sowa. Dordrecht: Springer.

———. [1901] 1984. *Logische Untersuchungen, Zweiter Teil. Untersuchungen zur Phänomenologie und Theorie der Erkenntnis,* ed. U. Panzer. The Hague, Netherlands: Martinus Nijhoff. In English: *Logical Investigations. Volume II,* ed. D. Moran, trans. J. N. Findley. London and New York: Routledge, 2001.

Lawlor, L. 2002. *Derrida and Husserl: The Basic Problems of Phenomenology.* Bloomington: Indiana University Press.

Merleau-Ponty, M. [1945] 1993. *Phénoménologie de la Perception.* Paris: Gallimard. In English: *Phenomenology of Perception,* trans. C. Smith. New York: Routledge & Kegan Paul.

Römpp, G. 1992. *Husserls Phänomenologie der Intersubjektivität und ihre Bedeutung für eine Theorie intersubjektiven Objektivität und die Konzeption einer phänomenologischen Philosophie.* Dordrecht: Kluwer.

Steinbock, A. J. 1995. *Home and Beyond: Generative Phenomenology After Husserl.* Evanston, IL: Northwestern University Press.

Süskind, P. 1985. *Das Parfum: Die Geschichte eines Mörders.* Diogenes Verlag. In English: *Perfume: The Story of a Murder,* trans. J. E. Woods. New York: Alfred A. Knopf, 1986.

Wells, G. H. 1904. The country of the blind. In *The Country of the Blind, and Other Stories* by G. H. Wells. www.gutenberg.org/ebooks/11870

Zahavi, D. [1996] 2001. *Husserl and Transcendental Intersubjectivity,* trans. E. A. Behnke. Athens: Ohio University Press.

7 Transcendental Social Ontology

Timo Miettinen

INTRODUCTION

It is one of the peculiarities of contemporary social and political philosophy that it has had practically no use for the notion of "transcendental." Despite the immense variation in the approaches of contemporary social or political thinkers—such as Michel Foucault, Jürgen Habermas, or John Searle—it seems that all of them, at least in some stage of their work, have situated themselves in critical relation to philosophical currents labeled as transcendental. And as is often the case, this criticism has been linked to the general dissatisfaction with phenomenology, which, by turning its gaze to the constitutive functions of transcendental subjectivity, seems to look away from phenomena of the social sphere—discourses, societal practices, and political institutions. As Foucault once put it in his critique of Husserlian subjectivism: "One has to dispense with the constituent subject, to get rid of the subject itself, that is to say, to arrive at an analysis which can account for the constitution of the subject within a historical framework" (Foucault 1984, 59). And while Searle has developed his own social ontology around the notion of intentionality, he has spent considerable effort in arguing that this notion has basically nothing to do with the phenomenological, antinaturalistic understanding of this notion: "I am confident that collective intentionality is a genuine biological phenomenon, and though it is complex, it is not mysterious or inexplicable" (Searle 2006, 16).[1]

In this chapter, I would like to engage in a discussion on the possibility of reinstituting the relevance of transcendental philosophy for social ontology. With social ontology, I denote a field of study examining the different modes and types of human cooperation that characterize different kinds of associations, communities, societal practices, and institutions. I claim that Husserl's philosophy of intersubjectivity provides us with a rich dynamic of communal existence, one that is able to afford communities a certain transcendental status.[2] This means that the question of intersubjectivity cannot be returned to shared mental states or interpersonal experience, but it entails a fundamental relation to *transcendence*, that is, to the constitution of a common world. Thus intersubjectivity, according to the phenomenological position, must be approached from the idea of *transcendental correlation,* that is, the relation between constituting subjectivity and constituted accomplishments.

As I argue, while Husserl emphasized the role of empathy (*Einfühlung*) in intersubjective relations, he nevertheless maintained that this experience of the other has its foundation in the primordial constitution of the objective world. This idea of a "transcendental we" (*transzendentale Wir*) formed the fundamental starting point for the constitution of individual communities and their particular lifeworlds. By doing so, Husserl began to discuss the idea of community with regard to specific constitutive capabilities that cannot be simply returned to the individual ego; instead, communities themselves were to be understood as personal subjects. It is my claim that Husserl's insistence on seeing communities as conscious entities can only be appreciated fully if we take into account the transition from static to genetic phenomenology—that is, to the temporal constitution and sedimentation of meaning—which significantly broadened the scope of transcendental subjectivity and consciousness. This makes it possible to approach the problem of community from the perspective of what Husserl called the full sense of self-consciousness, that is, the idea of a self-guiding community of will, the "personality of a higher order."

1   PHENOMENOLOGY OF INTERSUBJECTIVITY

Husserl's earliest texts that deal with the problem of intersubjectivity date back to 1905.[3] These early analyses took their starting point from the role of other subjects within individual experience, more precisely, from the observation that others are not merely there in one's field of perception as objects, but they appear as containing a unique inner horizon. Other living beings carry within themselves a specific depth, a personal world of experience into which I have no direct access. Despite its unattainability, this "world" is by no means without significance. It plays a crucial role in my personal experience and makes possible a wide variety of intentional relations and attitudes.

With regard to Husserl's early analyses, we can distinguish between two different approaches to the problem of intersubjectivity: the individualistic and the social (or reciprocal). First of all, since the manner of givenness that characterizes other subjects differs radically from that of natural and cultural objects, Husserl wanted to find a suitable conceptual approach in order to account for this givenness. Around 1908, this problem was first answered under the title of "empathy" (*Einfühlung*) and "alien experience" (*Fremderfahrung*): even though I have no direct access to the experience of the other, I relate to it in several ways (Hua 13, 3, 8–9, 17ff).[4] By taking his point of departure from the idea of empathy—and, for instance, not from Hegelian recognition (*Anerkennung*)—Husserl wanted to distinguish himself from the neo-Kantian tradition that approached the topic of intersubjectivity primarily from a normative point of view, for instance, as a question of just ethical behavior or a righteous political community. As Husserl insisted, the problem of intersubjectivity was to be located in the very heart of theoretical reason and was to be discussed and analyzed in connection with the constitution of a common world, which provides the basic conditions for practical cooperation.[5]

Second, since the early 1910s, the analyses of empathy were complemented by what Husserl called a phenomenological "social ontology" (*soziale Ontologie*), an investigation of those forms of intentionality or "givenness" that characterize our sense of belonging to a community (Hua 13, 98–104). This line of investigation—what Husserl also denoted as the phenomenology of "socialities" (*Sozialitäten*)[6]—was based on the idea of the fundamentally *two-sided* character of social relations: unlike other forms of intentionality, social relations embody within themselves a specific sense of reciprocity on the basis of which social phenomena (e.g., institutions, collectives) acquire their unique objectivity or reality. Thus, besides containing elements that are characteristic of all experience (e.g., seeing and listening), social relations are characterized by unique forms of intentionality such as envy, love, and persuasion—but also the use of power and violence. This approach was developed into a theory on specific social "functions" entailing an intrinsic practical relevance: my relation to others is fundamentally characterized by different kinds of responsibilities and anticipations that are unique to interpersonal experience (Hua 13, 104).

There is, however, a possibility of analyzing yet another perspective on the problem of communality, the point of view of the *collective*. Although Husserl's phenomenology was committed to a certain methodological primacy of the individual—that is, the idea that all objectivity and sense presuppose a sense-bestowing consciousness—he nevertheless insisted on the possibility of approaching the idea of community also as a personal, self-regulating whole. Especially in the context of *Ideas II*, Husserl began to consider human communities as *"personal unities of a higher order,"* which, as he proclaimed, *"have their own lives*, preserve themselves by lasting through time *despite the joining or leaving of individuals"* (Hua 4, 182).[7] Instead of mere correlates of individual consciousness, communities were to be understood as unique subjectivities that can be understood on their own, with regard to a personal history (genesis) and a teleological structure. Although this idea of a "group mind" can already be traced to Plato's theory of the state, Husserl was influenced here particularly by Max Scheler's theory of the "collective person" (*Gesamtperson*) and its different modes of consciousness (Scheler 1980, 512).[8] This idea, however, was never really discussed in Husserl's published works; it remained a marginal theme only to be discussed in the manuscripts.

This did not mean, however, that the idea of a collective *person* would have been a mere thought experiment or a meaningless bypath. Already in *Ideas II*, Husserl presented the relation between the theory of person and the theory of community as one of the fundamental questions of our entire worldview (Hua 4, 172). This emphasis was highlighted through the gradual replacement of social ontology with a phenomenological account of *social ethics,* which Husserl began to develop especially in the context of the so-called *Kaizo* essays of the early 1920s.[9] This line of approach—whose origin Husserl located in Plato (Hua 7, 14ff, cf. Hua 27, 88)—referred evidently to the close alliance of the descriptive and normative aspects of social theory. Affected especially by the devastating experience of World War I, Husserl was disappointed with the powerlessness of contemporary social theory as well as modern liberalism, which had avoided the possibility of collective renewal.[10] Thus, social ethics was not to "be attained by subjecting the practical relations towards one's companions (*Nebenmenschen*) to individual-ethical investigation" (Hua 27, 21)[11]—instead, the communal perspective was indispensable for the sake of a genuinely interpersonal ethics and cultural renewal.

Let us, however, first consider the question of "transcendental" sociality from a theoretical point of view—an idea that can perhaps be best approached by considering the distinction between subjective and collective accomplishments.[12] Beginning with the simple static analysis of intentional experiences, most of the things we constitute appear as having their objectivity through my personal experience. As I see an object such as a bottle of water, its reality and meaningfulness derive their legitimacy from my constitutive capabilities; as I utter a phrase, I intend a certain meaning for which I am responsible. However, in our daily lives, we encounter a whole set of things, expressions, and accomplishments that cannot be attributed to any particular subject. A piece by a symphonic orchestra, a novel theory created by a scientific research group, or even a "collective" declaration of independence are all examples of interpersonal accomplishments that cannot really be attributed to any particular agent. They are created and shared together based on a common resolution or a common goal.

Thus it is understandable that our contemporary philosophical theories of the social sphere—often discussed under the rubric of social ontology—have often taken their point of departure from the phenomenon of "social interaction," that is, the active and reciprocal cooperation between individual agents. Such activity characterizes not only groups and associations but also more complex forms of cooperation like digital networks, political parties, or states. In contemporary debates, this idea has been discussed especially through the notion of "collective intentionality"—a shared directedness characteristic of social bodies—that John Searle has considered the basic psychological presupposition of social reality. According to this account, collective intentionality is that function of consciousness that affords the things of the world their intersubjective functionality, for instance, as a piece of paper functions as money and is considered to represent value (a "status function"). In *The Construction of Social Reality* (1995), Searle distinguished "social" and "institutional" facts that belong to collective intentionality from the "brute facts" of nature on the grounds of voluntary acceptance: according to his "realist" definition, whereas the facts of nature exist mind-independently, the social and institutional facts presuppose human agreement (Searle 1995, 46).[13] If these conditions are not fulfilled, social facts cease to exist: they need to be confirmed and corroborated by others.

This stance, however, has its own weaknesses. First and foremost, it has had difficulties in dealing with those forms of collective experience that do not presuppose any kind of initiative on behalf of the collective comprising individual subjects. Alongside of the active forms of social cooperation, there is a wide variety of social phenomena that rely on involuntary adaptation, or, to put it in John Dewey's terms, on "social conditioning" (Dewey 1984, 35)—phenomena that are by no means "natural" in the biological sense of the term.[14] Modern consumerism, political apathy, or the fear of alien immigrants are examples of collective behavior that do not rely, at least explicitly, on active acceptance or common agreement. Still, these beliefs define and structure our common life in various ways. Moreover, although most of the people actively accept the fact that without certain substantial changes in our way of life, the planet will eventually become uninhabitable, we do not collectively "live" according to this belief—it does not translate to any kind of social cooperation.

In the context of modern philosophy, this idea of collective adaptation as the basic form of political and social cooperation has been articulated, above all, by the ideology-critical current of Marxist philosophy. According to the dominant idea of this tradition, it is an inherent feature of all ideologies to regulate our beliefs and practices in a manner that fundamentally distorts our shared perception of the real world. By offering a skewed view of the existing societal conditions—by concealing the history of suppression that founds the existing relations of power—the dominating ideologies aim at presenting the existing societal divisions and relations as natural, as if they had always existed (e.g., Marx and Engels 1970, 47). By promoting a form of collective "false consciousness"—a notion that is absent from Marx's own writings—ideologies hinder the formation of a true class consciousness. Instead, they suppress the revolutionary potential of the oppressed. This *experiential dimension of ideologies* is also known from the works of a few psychoanalytically oriented social theorists, but it has also been discussed by Fredric Jameson's well-known theory of "the political unconscious" (Jameson 1983)—a hermeneutic-narratological study of the production of ideological subjectivity.[15]

Speaking from a Husserlian perspective, however, even these conceptions can be said to suffer from certain inadequacies. First of all, because the Marxist critique of ideology has focused on analyses of the capitalist mode of production as well as its respective accomplishments, it has had little use for the idea of phenomenological correlation, that is, the division between the *acts* and *accomplishments* of a collective. Jameson, for one, defines his project in terms of an "unmasking of cultural artifacts as socially symbolic acts," (Jameson 1983, 5) and thus evades the distinction between the community as a set of interpersonal relations and its common accomplishments.[16] Second, in order to present themselves as efficacious, these reflections have usually promoted some form of historicism with regard to the socio-symbolic structures they wish to criticize. "The only effective liberation from the constraint [of the political unconscious]," argues Jameson, "begins with the recognition that there is nothing that is not social and historical—indeed, that 'in the last analysis', everything is political" (Jameson 1983, 5). Thus it is not surprising to find Jameson describing his project under the title of *hermeneutics*: rather than relying on a transcendental theory of subjective or collective experience, this investigation starts from the "fact" of the irreconcilability of different socio-cultural frameworks and seeks to demonstrate their historically constructed character. According to this account, there is no need for a *transcendental* theory of ideological subjectivity; all critique remains solely on the level of generalizations derived from historical evidence.

What seems to me to be the critical potential of Husserl's phenomenology of intersubjectivity in this respect is that it is quite possible to promote a theory of social ontology that does not begin with the phenomenon of interaction but seeks to address its unconsciously constituted basis in different forms of passivity (what Husserl calls "passive genesis"). These forms, I argue, extend from the very basic level of intersubjective experience to higher-order normative presuppositions, including all kinds of collective habitualities, styles, and convictions. What I consider to be the key feature of this Husserlian approach is that the recognition of the seemingly constructed (or "top-down") character of collective beliefs and desires does not result in neglecting the transcendental approach. Rather, it is precisely on the basis of a "rigorous social philosophy" (Hua 27, 57)—a *transcendental social ontology*—that one is able to do justice to the "constructed" and political character of socio-ideological commitments.

2   INTERPASSIVITY AND THE TRANSCENDENTAL WE

Instead of active cooperation, Husserl based his social ontology on an involuntary and nonreflexive relation to others—an approach we might designate by the term 'interpassivity'.[17] Before any concrete encounter with other subjects, others are embedded in my experience through the horizontal structure of experience, though not as concrete subjects but as someone who participates in the constitution of the common world. Further, as we engage with each other in different kinds of social relations, not only do we create all sorts of common accomplishments, but we also build for ourselves a common history, which constitutes a kind of implicit background for further orientations. In this regard, the scope of the Husserlian idea of *interpassivity* can be divided into two domains: (i) the passively constituted basis of social interaction, which is both doxic-theoretical as well as practical, and (ii) all kinds of collective beliefs or "social habitualities" (Hua 15, 208) that originate from an active institution of meaning but do not presuppose any kind of active confirmation on behalf of the agents themselves.

For those who have been accustomed to discuss passivity primarily in terms of affectivity and receptivity, Husserl's notion of passivity may strike one as odd. It also seems that Husserl himself understood passivity in several regards, beginning from prepredicative (or prelinguistic) perceptual experience to all sorts of involuntary affects that lie beyond our active attentiveness.[18] What we can say without hesitation, however, is that Husserl wanted to overcome the modern division between the domain of passivity as purely subjective receptivity and the sphere of activity as synthetic and communicative engaging:

> My passivity stands in connection with the passivity of all others. One and the same thing-world is constituted for us as well as the one and the same time as objective time so that my "now" and the "now" of others [. . .] are objectively simultaneous. [. . .] My life and the life of another do not merely exist, each for themselves; rather, one is "directed" toward the other. (Hua 11, 343)[19]

By arguing that "my passivity extends to the passivity of all others," Husserl was by no means suggesting any kind of telepathy or parapsychism. My experience, my stream of consciousness is given to me only, and I have no direct access to those of others (Hua 13, 111n1). What he was suggesting, however, was that already in my passive experience of the objective world, there is an internal reference to other possible subjects not as objects of experience but as someone who constitutes this world with me. This claim, however, requires further clarification.

In a manuscript written at the time of the *Cartesian Meditations,* Husserl put forward the claim according to which "everything worldly is intersubjectively constituted" (Hua 15, 45). Evidently, for those who have become accustomed to proceed to intersubjectivity from the phenomenon of empathy, this claim appears problematic. If I do perceive others as being in the world with me—as someone whose body I perceive as analogical to mine—but at the same time, this very perception presupposes the existence of others, the problem of intersubjectivity appears to be a *circulus vitiosus.*[20] How can others be both the *precondition* as well as the *object* of empathy? Now, according to Husserl, the vicious circle is evaded as soon as we pay attention to the fact that others are indeed there already at the elementary level of world-experience, though not as objects to be constituted or bodies to identify with but as the *manifold of possible perspectives.* This idea is what Husserl sometimes calls "open intersubjectivity" (*offene Intersubjektivität*), which constitutes the primary form of Husserlian "interpassivity":

> In the normal experience of the world, which has the character of an objective (intersubjective) experience of the world from the start, myself and everything objectively experienced has the character of an apperceptive

conception in relation to the open intersubjectivity. Even when I do not possess an explicit representation of the others, their presence is in constant co-validity and in an apperceptive function. (Hua 9, 394)[21]

Others are there in my structure of perception not as actual others but as potential others that make possible the idea of several horizons. "The intrinsically first other (the first non-ego)," Husserl writes, "*is the other ego*" (Hua 1, 137)—and here we should be careful—not as an "object" of empathy but as the anonymous other devoid of any spatio-temporal or personal existence.[22] Without this coconstitutive function, there could be no idea of objectivity, reality, or the world; simply because I would not be able to imagine several coexisting points of observation. In other words, I could not imagine an object as being perceived from two distinct but equally valid perspectives (or "horizons") at the same time. Thus unlike Hegel, who could attribute the constitution of thinghood to a presocial (i.e., perceptual) consciousness, Husserl's idea of object-constitution pointed toward "the necessity of transcendental co-existence" (Hua 15, 370)[23]—the others, so to speak, secure the validity of my object-consciousness, and they do so exactly by verifying the multiplicity of possible perspectives to the world.

Thus, what we gain with the constitution of the objective world is nothing less than *the primal form of a community*, that is, the ascending, though unarticulated, sense of a "we" (Hua 1, 137; Hua 29, 80; HuaM 8, 126). Against the prevalent usage of the first-person plural, this primordial form of "we" or "we-community" (*Wir-Gemeinschaft*) does not yet delimit itself with regard to a "they." Instead of referring to those forms of collectivity that we encounter in mutual recognition or agency, this idea of a "primal we" refers solely to the copresence of horizons through which the objective world retrieves its validity. In other words, this primal form of community is devoid of any norm that would separate the different perspectives from each other: it is constituted in a formal, *universal* coexistence of anonymous others. Respectively, its intentional correlate is what Husserl calls the *one identical world* ("*Die*" *Welt* or *Die eine Welt*) as the static foundation of all particular objectivity—a world that still lacks all socio-cultural meaning (Hua 13, 399; Hua 14, 202; Hua 15, 358).

Does this mean that after the introduction of transcendental "we," Husserl was inclined to split the sphere of transcendental experience into two separate dimensions—the personal and the communal? This is not the case. As Husserl put it in the *Kaizo* essays, the individual and the community should be understood as an "a priori undistinguishable pair of ideas" (Hua 27, 6), which, from the viewpoint of objective world-constitution, necessarily presuppose each other. I can never completely renounce the personality or individuality of my experience, even if we are dealing with very high forms of meaning-constitution. The point, rather, is to clarify the different ways in which this personal constitution acquires for itself novel dimensions through its associations with other subjects in the life of the community.

Therefore, instead of conceiving of the individual and the community in terms of two distinct spheres of constitution—as two absolutes—Husserl articulated their difference in terms of *two modalities of the same phenomeno-logical absolute.* As Husserl put it in the *Cartesian Meditations*, the transcendental ego is indeed the final absolute without which any sense of givenness could not be thought of (Hua 1, 97, 117). However, this ego *does not enclose the absolute as such.* Or, to be more precise, the transcendental ego is not the sole modality of the phenomenological absolute but rather a particular aspect of what Husserl called the "concrete absolute" (*konkrete Absolute*) that is constituted within the manifold of subjects (Hua 14, 272ff).[24] By focusing on the constitutive activity of the individual ego, we literally *abstract* from that concrete foundation that gives transcendence its sense and validity: the "transcendental we." Interestingly, in a manuscript from the beginning of the 1930s, Husserl asked whether the ego attained by the transcendental reduction was actually an "equivocation" (i.e., a confusion concerning the true scope of a term), albeit an "absolutely necessary one" (Hua 15, 586; cf. Hart 1992a, 165ff). While paying attention to the transcendental ego as the absolutely necessary dative of manifestation, it abstracts from the genuine subject *of objective reality itself,* the transcendental "community of monads."

This controversial point was also confirmed by Husserl in his seemingly paradoxical formulation that "in their absolute being, the monads *are depen-dent*" (Hua 14, 268).[25] The apparent paradox of this statement is done away with as soon as we grasp the constitutive role of intersubjectivity in its necessary function. In normal experience, the objectivity of my accomplishments is constantly confirmed by others not only in their validity—as happens with regard to dreams and hallucinations—but in their very objectivity and reality *per se*: the very idea of objectivity derives its sense from the multiplicity of subjects. Dependence (on one another) and not independence is what endows monads with their constitutive capability. For this reason, it is precisely transcendental intersubjectivity that can be called *the concrete absolute.*

However, in order to fully appreciate Husserl's idea of constitutive inter-subjectivity, we need a more *concrete* understanding of social activity. More precisely, it must be asked how this activity is able to produce lasting accomplishments and pass them forward in the course of tradition. For this purpose, we need to move forward from the problem of *passive genesis* to *active genesis*, that is, into that dimension where others are not solely anonymous others but concrete worldly subjects with whom one can engage in different ways: in communication, understanding, common striving, love, hate, sexuality, and so on.

3   EMPATHY AND THE COMMON WORLD

In the existing Husserl scholarship, it is somewhat common to introduce the higher forms of social interaction through the problem of empathy (*Einfüh-lung*).[26] Accordingly, Husserl himself stressed the central role of empathy with regard to the higher-level problems of human sociality, including the problem of cross-cultural experience (Hua 1, 161; Hua 14, 165–166; Hua 6, 320; see also Hua 1, 35; Hua 15, 26).

The concept of empathy, however, was not to be understood in the everyday sense of the word, as a compassionate identification with another person and with her emotions (Hua 37, 194). As Husserl put it, the problem of empathy was to be understood primarily as a problem of a "fictive genesis" that concerns the first (though hypothetical) identification with the other subject not only as an object of perception but as one who shares a common world with me (Hua 14, 477). As Husserl emphasized, this experience was to be understood as a specific form of association or "pairing" (*Paarung*), in which I relate my experiential abilities to those of the other person: I see the other "as if I were there" (Hua 15, 427). Husserl insisted, however, that empathy was not to be conceived as a projection to the mental states of the other; on the contrary, empathy could only be understood on the basis of the specific inaccessibility that characterizes the other as a concrete, worldly being.

In a parenthesis to the Fifth Meditation, Husserl presented the radical claim that not only does the other gain his or her subjectivity through empathy, but this goes also for the "mineness" of the self as such. Although the other is experienced phenomenologically as a "modification of myself, I receive this character of being 'my' self by virtue of the contrastive pairing that necessarily takes place" (Hua 1, 144).[27] Thus the ego, Husserl wrote, "cannot be thought without the non-ego to which it is intentionally related" (Hua 14, 244 cf. Hua 4, 96). Here, perhaps the most obvious reading is of course the Fichtean-Hegelian one: the ego, by distinguishing itself from the other ego, gains itself the idea of complete self-consciousness: it realizes itself as a personal subject among other subjects. Self-consciousness, accordingly, does not emerge merely as an apperceptive unity of experience, but it entails a necessary relation to others, which makes the self-consciousness something that Kant never saw it to be: an intrinsically *social phenomenon*.[28]

Despite this similarity, it would be misleading to identify Husserl's idea of empathy with Hegelian recognition. Whereas for Hegel the process of recognition entailed a transition from the "perceptual" (*wahrnehmende*) or "understanding" (*verstehende*) modes of experience—modes that Husserl would have considered as belonging to the domain of theoretical reason—to that of practical reason, Husserl's notion of empathy did not entail such a transition. Empathy did not "explain" the emergence of conflict of individual wills—what Hegel called the dialectic of Master and Slave—or the accomplishments of objective spirit (cultural objectivity), but it came to define the very existence of a common world. Since the relation between the self and other is characterized by an inevitable discrepancy (*Widerstreit*) between two personal "worlds" of experience, even empathy must have its foundation in something that is shared: the experience of a common nature (Hua 1, 149; Hua 14, 141). It is exactly this commonness that serves as the necessary platform for the experiences of concordance and discordance, which, through the mediation of individual situations, give the surrounding world its normatively (i.e., culturally, historically) specific character:

> We are in a relation to a common surrounding world—we are in a personal association: these belong together. We could not be persons for others if a common surrounding world did not stand there for us in a community, in an intentional linkage of our lives. Correlatively spoken, the one is constituted essentially with the other. (Hua 14, 191)[29]

Empathy, as it gives rise to what Husserl calls a "unity of similarity," is able to give the latent sense of transcendental "we" its concrete form (Hua 1, 142). However, this step necessitates that this unity is able to proceed to the "definite contents belonging to the higher psychic sphere," especially to the domain of communication (*Mitteilung*; Hua 1, 149). The emergence of communication simply means that the sense and reality of the world can be confirmed or disputed through joint agreement; it is thus through communication that the objective reality is able to acquire for itself a specific permanence (Hua 14, 202).

This idea of an intersubjectively shared correlate was articulated by Husserl especially through his concept of the "lifeworld" (*Lebenswelt*). Especially in the context of Husserl's later works—most notably, the *Crisis*—the problematic of the lifeworld was introduced as a novel "path" to transcendental phenomenology, which, by "questioning back" (*rückfragen*) to the objective accomplishments of transcendental subjectivity, was able to fully appreciate the essentially *intersubjective* as well as *dynamic* character of meaning constitution.

It is perhaps instructive to note briefly that within Husserl's overall philosophy, the notion of lifeworld served several purposes and it acquired several functions. Despite the long period of development, these tensions are evident even within the *Crisis,* where Husserl speaks of the lifeworld, for instance, both as the "realm of original self-evidences" (*Reich ursprünglicher Evidenzen*) as well as the world of cultural and spiritual accomplishments, including the objective accomplishments of modern natural sciences (Hua 6, 130ff, 294–313). Lifeworld denotes the *a priori,* universal ground of all meaning, but Husserl speaks of it in essentially historical terms, as a world of human values, practices, norms, and interests. Although Husserl most often employs this notion in singular form—as the correlate of transcendental intersubjectivity that encloses within itself all possible forms of objectivity, those of nature as well as culture—we sometimes find this notion also in the plural, for instance, in the sense of cultural lifeworlds, for example, "Indian" or that of "Chinese peasants" (Hua 6, 141; cf. Hua 29, 313). It is actually possible to speak of different levels of lifeworld, beginning from the practical sphere of a certain profession or a social role ("the world of a musician") to very broad concepts of lifeworld, as in the case of cultural identities.

For Husserl, however, this discrepancy was not a sheer misunderstanding of the natural attitude. Instead, it was originally introduced by the philosophical enterprise as such, which brought within itself "a *necessary* and at the same time *dangerous* double meaning of world" as the universal, *a priori* foundation of sense (*Sinnesfundament*) and its individual realizations, or "particular worlds" (*Sonderwelte*; Hua 6, 460). Husserl, however, did not interpret this division in terms of a split into two distinct domains, for instance, those of universal nature and particular culture or sensibility and reason. Although Husserl treated the world-constitution as proceeding from the lower levels of intentionality—peculiar to the constitution of material nature—to the more complex forms of animal nature and spiritual accomplishments, this did not entail a transition from the "absolute" to a "relative" sense of the world. On the contrary, the lifeworld was to be conceived, from the start, as a correlate of transcendental intersubjectivity—its sense and validity, however, are constantly shaped by our encounters with other people. As Husserl maintained, the intersubjective world is permanently "on the march," that is, it is constantly defined and demarcated through concrete others (Hua 15, 45).

In order to avoid the scattering of the lifeworld into two distinct objects of experience, Husserl invoked the notion of *horizon* (*Horizont*) to explain its essentially "pregiven" (*vorgegeben*) nature.[30] This notion can be understood in two regards. In its "horizontal character" (*Horizonthaftigkeit*), the lifeworld does not denote a specific intentional correlate of consciousness; rather, it functions as the *necessary background of sense* through which individual things acquire their meaningful character. As such, the lifeworld is "constantly pre-given and constantly valid in advance" (Hua 6, 461)— it structures our experiential field by offering a comprehensive *preview* of the surrounding world. It is against this background that individual things, objects, events, and practices have their "default value": they are always projected with regard to a certain idea of expectancy and normality, *of familiarity* (*Bekanntheit*) and *routine* (*Gewohnheit*; Hua 14, 623–624; see also Hua 14, 228; Hua 15, 214). As this normality is specified through intersubjective confirmation in its social, historical, and cultural specificities, a particular lifeworld becomes understandable as the "delimitation" (Gr. *horizein*) of the world as the universal ground of experience—what Husserl sometimes called the "universal horizon" of all experience, or what Merleau-Ponty calls the "horizon of all horizons" (Hua 6, 147; Merleau-Ponty 1962, 381).

Accordingly, the idea of lifeworld points toward a crucial feature in the constitution of human communities. With the help of this concept, Husserl wanted to refute the idea according to which the existence of communities would reside merely in collective mental states, or the acceptance or construction of a common narrative. Although stories and myths may have a special role in strengthening the sense of unity within different social bodies, these narratives have their foundation in the idea of the lifeworld that functions as the indispensable horizon of communal activity.

Transcendental intersubjectivity entails a necessary relation to *transcendence*, to a common world.

But this insight also entails that the problem of communities cannot be resolved into a question of cultural accomplishments, political institutions, or even relations of production. Instead, understanding this question in phenomenological-transcendental terms necessitates that we take our point of departure from the idea of *correlation* that prevails between the transcendental we and its common accomplishments. To put it differently, the question of culture does not resolve itself into a question of ideas, values, products, and institutions—it also refers to an idea of constituting "we" with its unique temporal form, a style and a habitus. Communities do not merely manifest themselves in cultural objects but constantly transform, renew, and justify them in various ways. To understand how these processes manifest themselves in interpersonal cooperation, we need to consider more carefully Husserl's argument concerning communities as personal wholes.

4 PERSONALITIES OF A HIGHER ORDER

One of the most puzzling features in Husserl's theory of human sociality is his idea of communities as *subjective* or *personal* totalities. This idea, as developed by Husserl from the end of the 1910s onward, was formulated with the help of several different concepts, for instance, those of "we-subjectivity" (*Wir-Subjektivität*), "suprapersonal consciousnesses" (*überpersonale Bewusstsein*), and "personalities of a higher order" (*Personalität der höherer Ordnung*). Although we might be tempted to read these notions primarily as metaphors or analogies, Husserl was quite insistent in rejecting this interpretation. As he put it very clearly, the analogy of the individual and the community was not to be understood as merely heuristic but "real" (*wirklich*; Hua 27, 21). Communities were also to be understood as personal totalities that can be characterized through such attributes as "personal act," "style," "memory," and a "collective will" (Hua 6, 326; Hua 14, 205; Hua 27, 53). They constitute for themselves a life that cannot be simply reduced to individual consciousnesses.

These notions, however, have not been easily accepted. Alfred Schütz, for one, acknowledged the significance of Husserl's analyses of intersubjectivity for his own phenomenology of the social world; however, he conceived the idea of a "personality of a higher order" as being completely unfounded. Phenomenology was to remain a philosophy from the first-person perspective, and even with regard to the problematic of intersubjectivity, its strength relied essentially on its capability to understand personal cooperation from the point of view of the individual. Thus, as Schütz put it: "The attempts of Simmel, Max Weber, [and] Scheler to reduce social collectivities to the social interaction of individuals is, so it seems, much closer to the spirit of phenomenology than the pertinent statements of its founder" (Schütz 1975, 39).

Paul Ricoeur shares this idea, although he relates it to Husserl: "The decisive advantage of Husserl over Hegel appears to me to lie in his uncompromising refusal to hypostatize collective entities and in his tenacious will to reduce them in every instance to a network of interactions" (Ricoeur 1991, 244). Following David Carr (who is more sympathetic toward this idea), it may thus seem that the idea of suprapersonal consciousness appears at first glance as "something *prima facie* unphenomenological" (Carr 1987, 268). Since the notions of consciousness, subjectivity, and act seem to imply a form of givenness that can only be realized within the conscious life of the individual, their extension to the life of the community may appear to be an unfounded hypostatization. What kind of givenness characterizes the suprapersonal consciousness, or to whom is it given?

It is perhaps instructive to note here that for Husserl, the notions of consciousness, subjectivity, and person were not static notions that could be identified with the "Cartesian" idea of undisturbed self-reflexivity. Especially by broadening his methodological scope to genetic reflections on temporal forms and relations of constitution, Husserl began to discuss the ideas of consciousness and subjectivity as developing unities of acts that are manifested in abiding forms of personal life. Accordingly, Husserl began to understand the phenomenon of subjectivity essentially in terms of *temporal development*—a genesis—for the sake of which individual affects and acts are conjoined with each other. Subjectivity, according to this account, was to be understood in terms of constant *habituation* through which these affects and acts unify themselves into the form of permanent personal characters. As Husserl put it in *Ideas II,* although this process realizes itself originally within the genetic development of the individual ego, it does not restrict itself merely to this—instead, as we consider the interpersonal modes of affectivity and activity, we discover an analogical process of habituation:

> In the course of these temporal ego-events, the person is constituted originally as person, i.e., as substrate of personal characters, as, in its temporal being, substrate-unity. [. . .] If one studies the person in his unity, which manifests itself in his acts and affections, then one studies how he "affects" other persons and likewise how he spiritually undergoes effects from them, and furthermore one studies how personalities of a higher order are constituted, how individual persons and collective personalities of a higher level perform, how as correlates of their spiritual performances cultural objectivities and cultural arrangements are constituted, how individual persons, communal personalities, and cultural formations develop, in which forms they do so, in what typicality, etc. (Hua 4, 357–358)[31]

To speak of collective persons as "higher-order" phenomena refers precisely to this idea: communities as personal wholes are inextricably *founded* on the acts of individual egos. However, as the acts of individual subjects associate with each other, they are also able to constitute lasting unities that have their unique style and habitus. An orchestra, for instance, acquires for itself a personal form through the association of individual acts (e.g., different musicians playing different patterns) and affects (feelings, moods, etc.)— its unique style is due to its common history constituted in the group activity. This entails that the performed musical piece is to be conceived not only as an end product of distinct individuals but as something whose uniqueness originates from the personal style of the community itself. Thus, on the basis of this specific conjoining of individual acts, we are able to acknowledge a conscious life of a higher order:

> Consciousness unites with consciousness, overlapping time in the form of simultaneity as well as in chronological order. Personal consciousness becomes one with others [. . .] and constitutes a unity of a suprapersonal consciousness. (Hua 14, 199)[32]

Although Husserl's earlier manuscripts occasionally refer to the Hegelian notions of "objective spirit" (*objektiver Geist*; Hua 13, 65n2; Hua 15, 559) and "collective spirit" (*Gemeingeist*; Hua 14, 165, 192, 200; Hua 27, 53), his theory of community differed from that of Hegel's in one crucial respect. Husserl insisted that in order to arrive at an accurate transcendental account of human communities, one should insist on the conceptual difference between the intrapersonal collective and its accomplishments, that is, the difference between community (*Gemeinschaft*) as a habituated form of individual activities and culture (*Kultur*) as the objective accomplishments of this community.[33] Whereas Hegel's notion of objective spirit seemed to conflate these two aspects under the title of objective spirit, Husserl insisted on the essential difference between the two sides of the correlation. A particular social whole cannot be simply reduced to its own accomplishments—language, religion, science, or even the relations of production—for this would entail that we fail to appreciate the differences that prevail in their formation. A community has its habitual character only within the life of individuals and the unity of their social acts, but culture has its permanent duration in objective accomplishments (e.g., accomplishments that are materialized in writing). These aspects, of course, belong inherently together, for the sense of cultural accomplishments is constantly vivified by the personal community. However, as in the case of the Rosetta Stone, the extinction of a particular community does not necessarily do away with the possibility of understanding its accomplishments or the process of sedimentation that is characteristic to these.

This contrast to Hegel can also be elucidated from a socio-ethical point of view. Hegel conceived world history in terms of a dialectical development, in which particular formations of culture—styles of artistic representations, forms of political institutions—are superseded by new ones. Although Hegel's notion of spirit allowed for a teleological reading of this development—old culture is not merely replaced but also preserved in temporal genesis—he seemed to place the capability of renewal primarily in the hands of individual subjects. "Objective spirit," as it acquires for itself a lasting form in the spirit of a time, is constantly prone to the loss of meaning through cultural alienation; however, it is only through great "world-historical individuals" who transcend their own spirit of time that history realizes its reformatory potential. Thus for Hegel, cultural renewal takes place essentially through individual human subjects, "who appear to draw the impulse of their life from themselves," but who secretly follow the demands of the world-spirit (Hegel 1899, 30). Against this account of cultural development through individual action, through hidden motives (the "cunning of reason") and often violent outbursts, Husserl wanted to develop an idea of communal renewal that would take its point of departure from the demands of inter-subjective cooperation and the complete transparency of means and goals:

> A particular humanity can and must be viewed truly as a "human at large," and also in its possibility for self-definition in communal-ethical regard. Hence, it must be thought as being expected to define itself ethically. This possibility, however, must be examined in its principal possibility, and it must be made univocally demanding, so that it allows practical definition in disclosed eidetic possibilities and normative necessities that can be discovered through investigation. (Hua 27, 22)[34]

Hence, individual ethics was to be supplemented with *social ethics*—"the ethics of communities *as* communities" (Hua 27, 22)—clarifying the modes of self-inspection, self-critique, and renewal characteristic of personalities of a higher order. Communities, like individual subjects, were to be conceived of as being able to understand themselves as subjective totalities and as embodying a personal history through habituation and sedimentation of meaning. Moreover, they were to be treated as being able to reflect their total history in mutual understanding, as potentially capable of renewing their way of being through social cooperation.

However, in order to describe the kind of cooperation that makes possible the emergence of lasting cultural accomplishments, Husserl introduced the idea of *social and communicative acts*. These are acts through which individual subjects are able to communicate with each other in a way that makes possible the emergence of permanent ideas and meanings, or objective ideality. As Husserl puts it in *Ideas II*:

> Sociality is constituted by specifically *social, communicative acts*, acts in which the ego turns to others and in which the ego is conscious of these others as ones toward which it is turning, and ones which, furthermore, understand this turning, perhaps adjust their behavior to it and recipro-cate by turning toward that ego in acts of agreement or disagreement, etc. It is these acts, between persons who already "know" each other,

which foster a higher unity of consciousness and which include in this unity the surrounding world of things as the surrounding world common to the persons who take a position in regard to it. (Hua 4, 194)[35]

As Aristotle put it, whereas animals are capable of "communicating" (*hermeneuein*) with each other on the basis of natural indications of pain, joy, longing, and so forth, it is only through "symbolic" communication based on "mutual agreement" (*kata synthēken*) that this cooperation is able to produce for itself lasting objectivities—human language—which makes possible the idea of common striving through shared goals, values, and beliefs. This was exactly what Husserl meant with suprapersonal consciousness: a unity of coexisting or successive acts leading to the constitution of a shared belief, decision, or telos. In this reciprocal activity, writes Husserl, "my act and his activity at the same time are a complex act that not only in part is immediately from him and only in part immediately done by me or to be done by me."

> In a higher founded sense the total action and achievement is mine and also his, even though each acts for himself immediately "in his share" of the matter and achieves a primary action which belongs exclusively to him; but this is also part of the secondary action which is founded and which has its completeness from both of us. So it is with all communal works. (Hua 14, 193)[36]

Of course, not all communities function in such a conciliatory manner. We know that in the contexts of science, politics, and religion, it is exactly dissent, rather than consensus, that constitutes the prevalent mode of cooperation (Zahavi 2001, 85ff). As it is often the case, different interest groups may even express this conflict as a battle of language, which "fails" to execute its function as a common cultural objectivity. As Husserl insisted, these discrepancies should not prevent us from considering the possibility of rational cooperation, in which all parties are acknowledged as equal contributors to the emergence of shared accomplishments.

This idea was articulated by Husserl with the notion of "community of will" (*Willesgemeinschaft*), which not only lives according to shared cultural constraints—common language, law, morality—but which is able to reflect these accomplishments through common deliberation. In other words, a community of will is such that it can acknowledge its accomplishments as a product of common cooperation, and is able to take a reflexive stance toward its own personal history:

> The most important issue is that the community is not a mere collective of individuals, and the communal life and its communal accomplishments are not a mere collective of individual lives and individual accomplishments [. . .] but a community as a community has a consciousness. As a

community it can, however, have in the full sense a self-consciousness: It can have an appreciation of itself and a will to direct itself, a will to self-formation. (Hua 27, 48–49)[37]

Especially in the context of the *Kaizo* essays, this is what Husserl meant with the idea of a "personality of a higher order," which has the possibility of "carrying out communal accomplishments that are not mere collections of individual accomplishments, but that are in a genuine sense personal accomplishments of the community, its striving and will" (Hua 27, 22).[38] Let us note immediately that Husserl is not referring to the idea of the complete and undisturbed consensus of individual wills. The idea of a personality of a higher order entails a critical and reflexive stance towards the habituated form of communal cooperation and not a single, "totalitarian" model of life permeating the lives of individuals. Ethical life, as already accentuated, was to be understood as a practical idea based on an active-reflexive stance toward passively habituated objectivities, styles, and convictions.

As Husserl seems to suggest on several occasions, it is exactly through the diverging views—and not despite them—that a community realizes its "common will." The unity of a community does not rest upon the "similarity of manners, forms of personal dealings, ways of thinking, opinions, scientific activity etc." but, as he emphatically put it, on "persons who stand within a unity of a spiritual communion of action" (Hua 14, 183).[39] It is sometimes precisely critique of others that makes possible a lasting communal cooperation—a communal life that does not do away with personal self-responsibility but that can elevate it and make it work for the common good.

CONCLUSION

As I have argued, the scope of Husserl's transcendental phenomenology was not restricted merely to the domain of individual consciousness, but it was able to account for those forms of meaning-constitution that take place within interpersonal cooperation: in communities, associations, and societies. Even more importantly, Husserl understood the whole idea of transcendence as essentially dependent on the domain of transcendental intersubjectivity—on the idea of the transcendental "we," which functions as the "concrete absolute" of objective world constitution. Without the idea of other subjects, accordingly, I could not constitute for myself the idea of an objective world, which goes beyond my perceptual givenness and allows itself to be called transcendence in the pregnant sense of the term.

In this regard, the question of empathy did not arise simply as the basic starting point for intersubjectivity *per se* but as a transitional phenomenon that makes possible the emergence of culturally and socially specific objectivities and accomplishments. This process of specification, I showed, constituted the basic point of departure for Husserl's ambiguous concept of the lifeworld, conceived as both the fundamental correlate of transcendental intersubjectivity as well as its normatively specific instances, and cultural and historical lifeworlds in the plural. The problem of culture, accordingly, was to be understood on the basis of the transcendental-phenomenological correlation of community and its accomplishments, both of which have their unique form of existence.

Lastly, this insight enabled us to approach Husserl's controversial analysis of communities as "personalities of a higher order," that is, as conscious, self-regulating subjectivities. This distention of the individualistically oriented vocabulary of transcendental phenomenology—of consciousness, subjectivity and person—was not based on the dismissal of the "robust" sense of self-consciousness as phenomenal givenness. Instead, it was based on the significant shift of perspective that commenced in the transition from static to genetic phenomenology. The implications of this idea, however, were not restricted to the domains of ontology or epistemology—of theoretical reason—but most importantly, they made possible a novel understanding of communal cooperation and social ethics. As Husserl insisted, the ongoing crisis of European humanity could only be overcome by showing the possibility of a genuinely intersubjective idea of responsibility and renewal—something that the individualistically oriented liberal tradition had neglected.

Indeed, while Husserl's transcendental vocabulary may be thought odd to those working in the social sciences, I believe it points toward an important insight into the two-sided task of social theory. While it is completely true that without focusing on the concrete structures and institutions of the social and political sphere, all talk about "collective intentions" and "we-subjectivities" may appear to be abstract, it is likewise true that without a theory of collective cooperation, the normative analysis of societal and political institutions remains essentially powerless: it becomes, so to speak, mere critique. Is it not the case that many of the central problems of today's world—climate change, the growing gap between the rich and the poor—necessitate also the recognition of an active, "revolutionary" subjectivity, a subjectivity that is essentially a collective one? Following Arendt, does not the whole philosophical problematic of the political depend on the two-sided relation between human communality and the common world, a world which is both the condition as well as the genuine object of political deliberation?

NOTES

1. On Habermas's critique of Husserl's transcendental intersubjectivity, see Habermas (2001, 41–43).
2. With the notion of transcendental, I am basically following the most general definition that Husserl gives to this term, that is, as denoting the sphere of constitution that allows *transcendence*—world, objectivity and its sense and meaning—to come about (Hua 1, 65).

3. On the early development of intersubjectivity, see Iso Kern's introduction in Hua 13, xxiv–xliii.

4. Here, Husserl's work was influenced especially by the so-called Munich phenomenologists—a group of students assembled around the neo-Kantian philosopher Theodor Lipps who had made significant contributions to the theory of empathy. Husserl's aim, however, was to show why Lipps's position fell short in explaining the true character of emphatic encounter. Already in the *Logical Investigations,* Husserl had been critical of what he considered to be the psychologistic position of Lipps, and toward the turn of 1910s, almost every piece written on empathy took its point of departure from the criticism of Lipps. See, for example, Hua 13, 21ff, 70ff; Hua 14, 236ff.

5. As Husserl puts it in an appendix to *Crisis:* "We already have a certain 'community' in being mutually 'there' for one another in the surrounding world (the other in my surrounding world)—and this always means being physically, bodily there." (Hua 6, 307).

6. As Husserl put it in the C-manuscripts, for the constitution of "socialities," the community of empathy is like "the spatial form is for reduced nature," or the "social space" that allows the temporal simultaneity and succession of individual subjects (HuaM 8, 317).

7. "die Personen sind vielmehr Glieder von Gemeinschaften, von personalen Einheiten höherer Ordnung, die als Ganze ihr Leben führen, sich bei Zutritt oder Abgang von einzelnen in der Zeit fortdauernd erhalten [. . .]."

8. Here, Scheler ascribes the collective person a unique form of intentional consciousness ("*Bewusstsein-von*"), which cannot be reduced to individual subjects.

9. It is exactly in these essays that we encounter the topic of Europe in connection to the problematic of rational development of culture. Especially in the essay *Formale Typen der Kultur in der Menschheitsentwicklung,* Husserl addresses the birth of Greek philosophy in terms of a transition from the religious-mythical to the scientific worldview, resulting in the "philosophical form of culture" characteristic of medieval and modern times.

10. For instance, as Max Weber put it in his *Economy and Society,* "collectivities must be treated as solely the resultants and modes of organization of the particular acts of individual persons, since these alone can be treated as agents in a course of subjectively understandable action" (Weber 1968, 13).

11. "Letztere ist nicht etwa damit schon gegeben, daß das praktische Verhalten des Einzelmenschen zu seinen „Nebenmenschen," das ist zu seinen Genossen in der Einheit der Gemeinschaft, individualethischer Forschung unterzogen wird. Es gibt notwendig auch eine Ethik der Gemeinschaften als Gemeinschaften."

12. Also, Husserl follows this procedure in many of his manuscripts (cf. Hua 14, 192. Cf. Donohoe 2004, 105ff).

13. This stance is also common to other leading theorists of social ontology, for instance, Raimo Tuomela. In his analysis of what he calls the "we-mode of collective intentionality," Tuomela considers two conditions that need to be fulfilled in order for the shared directedness to come about: "(i) the shared 'for-groupness' based on collective acceptance and (ii) collective commitment to the shared content" (Tuomela 2008, 3).

14. Thus Dewey contrasts his idea of social conditioning with the "myth" of the natural capabilities of the individual. See Dewey (1988, 299).

15. Following Freud's later insights on the "collective unconscious" (*Kultur-Über-Ich*), theorists such as Erich Fromm and Herbert Marcuse have analyzed the suppressive character of modern (capitalist) ideologies and their relation to the unconscious dimension of human existence (see Fromm 1961; Marcuse 1987).

16. On this division, see Hart (1992b, 643ff).

17. In his intriguing work *Die Illusionen der Anderen,* Robert Pfaller has coined the term 'interpassivity' to describe the common tendency of human beings to realize their beliefs, acts, and desires with regard to an unconscious relation to other subjects (2002, 25ff). Echoing Heidegger's analyses on the anonymous others (*das Man*), as well as the Lacanian idea of the symbolic father, Pfaller has paid attention to different modes of self-transposition that take place not only on the level of beliefs—like when I say that "People are envious," when I actually mean "I am envious"—but also with regard to emotions, desires, and drives. It is an inherent feature of especially the modern era that it works toward the transposition of our passive reactions. This happens in the case of canned laughter on TV, by which we engage in a TV show by letting the object do the laughing for us.

18. With respect to the first category, Husserl spoke of the sphere of "pure passivity" (*reine/pure Passivität*)—which we could read as synonymous to transcendental aesthetics—that investigates the associative structures of conscious life that constitute the foundation for abiding forms of intentionality (see Hua 15, 75–82). In its most general form, however, Husserl conceived passivity to be "the realm of associated nexuses (*Verbindungen*) and affiliations (*Verschmelzungen*), where all meaning that emerges is put together passively" (Hua 6, 372). In this regard, it also encompasses the realm of acquired convictions, or what Husserl sometimes calls by the name 'secondary passivity (*sekundare Passivität*; see Hua 27, 110).

19. "Meine Passivität steht in Konnex mit der Passivität aller anderen: Es konstituiert sich eine und dieselbe Dingwelt für uns, ein und dieselbe Zeit als objektive Zeit derart, daß durch diese mein Jetzt und jedes anderen Jetzt und so seine Lebensgegenwart [. . .] und meine Lebensgegenwart objektiv „gleichzeitig" sind. [. . .] mein Leben und das eines anderen existieren nicht nur überhaupt beide, sondern eines „richtet" sich nach dem anderen." See also Hua 28, 68.

20. Indeed, the genetic problem of first empathy was something that Husserl tackled from the beginning of the 1920s onward (see, e.g., Hua 14, 112–120).

21. "In der normalen Welterfahrung, die von vornherein den Sinn einer objektiven (intersubjektiven) Welterfahrung hat, hat jedes als Objekt Erfahrene und so auch ich selbst eine apperzeptive Auffassung in bezug auf die offene Intersubjektivität. Auch wenn ich keine explizite Vorstellung von Anderen habe, ist doch das Dasein von Anderen in kontinuierlicher Mitgeltung und in apperzeptiver Funktion." On the idea of open intersubjectivity, see also Hua 14, 289 (cf. Zahavi 2001, 39ff).

22. In a manuscript pointed out by Ichiro Yamaguchi, Husserl interestingly makes a reference to what he calls an "anonymous" empathy, "suspended from its function" (Yamaguchi 1982, 103; cf. Zahavi 2001, 73).

23. "Die intentionale Beschlossenheit ist Notwendigkeit der transzendentalen Koexistenz."

24. See esp. Hua 14, 274: "Und konkret genommen ist absolut: diese Vielheit als eine Vielheit von Subjektpolen, Polen für ein jedem solchen Pol gesondert zugehöriges konkretes Leben, konkretes Meinen, Erfahren, einstimmig Erfahren, richtig oder unrichtig Denken, darunter auch wissenschaftlich rechtmässig Denken."

25. "Die Monaden in ihrem absoluten Sein bedingen sich."

26. See, for example, Theunissen (1984, 70ff).

27. "Notwendig tritt es vermöge seiner Sinneskonstitution als intentionale Modifikation meines erst objektivierten Ich, meiner primordinalen Welt auf: der Andere phänomenologisch als Modifikation mezhes Selbst (das diesen Charakter mein seinerseits durch die nun notwendig eintretende und kontrastierende Paarung erhält)."

28. What this process of empathy implied was a transition from the anonymous functioning of self-awareness to its thematic or "indexical" sense ("I" as distinguished from "you," "he/she," etc.) from "latent" to "patent" self-consciousness. See Zahavi (2001, 56).

29. "Wir sind in Beziehung auf eine gemeinsame Umwelt—wir sind in einem personalen Verband: das gehört zusammen. Wir könnten für Andere nicht Personen sein, wenn uns nicht in einer Gemeinsamkeit, einer intentionalen Verbundenheit unseres Lebens eine gemeinsame Umwelt gegenüber stünde; korrelativ gesprochen: eins konstituiert sich wesensmäßig mit dem anderen."

30. For the lifeworld as a pregiven horizon, see Hua 6, 141–146; Hua 39, 99–105. See also Husserl (E&U, 24ff; cf. Yamaguchi 1982, 19; Steinbock 1995, 104ff).

31. "Im Gang dieser zeitlichen Ich-Vorkommnisse konstituiert sie sich ursprünglich als Person, d.i. als Substrat personaler Charaktere, in ihrem zeitlichen Sein als Substrateinheit. [. . .] Studiert man die einheitliche Persönlichkeit, die sich in ihren Akten und Affektionen bekundet, so studiert man, wie sie auf andere Persönlichkeiten 'wirkt' und ebenso geistig von ihnen Wirkungen erfährt, wie Personalitäten höherer Ordnung sich konstituieren, wie Einzelpersönlichkeiten und höherstufig kollektive Persönlichkeiten Leistungen vollziehen, wie als Korrelat ihres geistigen Leistens Kulturgegenständlichkeiten, Kulturordnungen usw. sich konstituieren, wie Einzelpersönlichkeiten und Gemeinschaftspersönlichkeiten, wie Kulturgebilde sich entwickeln, in welchen Formen, in welcher Typik und was dergleichen mehr."

32. "Bewusstsein vereinigt sich so mit Bewusstsein, alle Zeit übergreifend, übergreifend die Zeit in Form der Gleichzeitigkeit wie in Form der Zeitfolge. Personales Bewusstsein wird eins mit anderem, individuell von ihm notwendig getrennten Bewusstsein, und so wird Einheit eines überpersonalen Bewusstseins."

33. On the definition of culture in Husserl, see Orth (1987, 116ff) and Hart (1992b). For a more detailed analysis, see Miettinen (2013).

34. "Eine Menschheit kann wirklich, und muß, als „Mensch im großen" betrachtet und dann gemeinschaftsethisch als sich möglicherweise selbstbestimmende, somit auch als sich ethisch bestimmen-sollende gedacht werden. Dieser Gedanke aber muß in seiner prinzipiellen Möglichkeit geklärt, zwingend einsichtig gemacht und nach Erforschung der in ihm beschlossenen Wesensmöglichkeiten und normativen Notwendigkeiten praktisch bestimmend werden."

35. "Die Sozialität konstituiert sich durch die spezifisch *sozialen, kommunikativen Akte,* Akte in denen sich das Ich an Andere wendet, und dem Ich diese Anderen auch bewußt sind als die, an welche es sich wendet, und welche ferner diese Wendung verstehen, sich ev. in ihrem Verhalten danach richten, sich zurückwenden in gleichstimmigen oder gegenstimmigen Akten usw. Diese Akte sind es, die zwischen Personen, die schon voneinander „wissen", eine höhere Bewußtseinseinheit herstellen, in diese die umgebende Dingwelt als gemeinsame Umwelt der stellungnehmenden Personen einbeziehen."

36. "Speziell was die Handlung anbelangt, so kann mein Wille darauf gehen, dass der Andere will, mag ich ihm es befohlen haben und ihn als unter meinem Befehl stehend ansehen, mag ich ihn willentlich auf andere Weise dazu bestimmt haben, dass er etwas tue, was für mich praktisch Gewolltes ist. Seine Tat ist dann mittelbar auch meine Tat, und ist das Verhältnis ein wechselseitiges, so ist meine Tat und seine Tätigkeit zugleich für mich eine komplexe Tat, die nur zu einem Teil von ihm und zu einem von mir unmittelbar getan und zu tuende war. Die gesamte Handlung und Leistung ist meine Handlung und ist auch seine Handlung im höheren, fundierten Sinn, während jeder für sich an „seinem Teil" unmittelbar an der Sache handelt und eine primäre Handlung vollzieht, die ausschliesslich die ihm eigene ist, die aber Teil der

sekundären, fundierten ist, die die volle eines jeden von uns ist. So bei allen Gemeinschaftswerken."

37. "Die bedeutsamste Tatsache ist aber die, daß die Gemeinschaft nicht ein bloßes Kollektiv der einzelnen und das Gemeinschaftsleben und die Gemeinschaftsleistung nicht ein bloßes Kollektiv der Einzelleben und der Einzelleistungen sind [. . .] eine Gemeinschaft als Gemeinschaft hat ein Bewußtsein, als Gemeinschaft kann sie aber auch ein Selbstbewußtsein im prägnanten Sinn haben, sie kann eine Selbstwertung haben und auf sie sich richtenden Willen, Willen der Selbstgestaltung."

38. "Personalität höherer Ordnung werden und als solche Gemeinschaftsleistungen vollziehen nicht bloße Zusammenbildungen von einzelpersonalen Leistungen sind, sondern im wahren Sinne persönliche Leistungen der Gemeinschaft als solcher, in ihrem Streben und Wollen realisierte." On the notion of personality of a higher order, see Miettinen (2013).

39. "Gemeinschaft besagt nicht Gleichheit von Arten, Formen personaler Handlungen, von Denkweisen, Meinungen, wissenschaftlichen Betätigungen etc., sondern in Gemeinschaft stehen Personen, die in solcher Hinsicht in der Einheit eines geistigen Wirkungszusammenhanges stehen, mag im einzelnen die Wirkung überall sichtlich werden oder nicht."

REFERENCES

Carr, D. 1987. *Interpreting Husserl: Critical and Comparative Studies*. Dordrecht: Martinus Nijhoff.

Dewey, J. 1984. *The Later Works of John Dewey 1925–1953*. Volume 5. Collected Works of John Dewey (1925–1953 Essays). Carbondale: Southern University of Illinois Press.

———. 1988. *The Later Works of John Dewey 1925–1953*. Volume 2. Collected Works of John Dewey. Carbondale: Southern University of Illinois Press.

Donohoe, J. 2004. *Husserl on Ethics and Intersubjectivity: From Static to Genetic Phenomenology*. Amherst, NY: Humanity Books.

Foucault, M. 1984. *"Truth and Power."* In *The Foucault Reader:* Edited by Paul Rabinow, 51–75. New York: Pantheon Books.

Fromm, E. 1961. *Marx's Concept of Man*. New York: Frederick Ungar.

Habermas, J. 2001. *On the Pragmatics of Social Interaction: Preliminary Studies in the Theory of Communicative Action*. Translated by B. Fultner. Cambridge: MIT Press.

Hart, J. G. 1992a. *The Person and the Common Life: Studies in a Husserlian Social Ethics*. Dordrecht: Kluwer.

———. 1992b. "The Rationality of Culture and the Culture of Rationality." *Philosophy East and West* 42/4: 643–664.

Hegel, G. W. F. 1899. *The Philosophy of History*. Translated by J. Sibree. Revised Edition. New York: Colonial Press.

Husserl, E. 1952. *Ideen zur einer reinen Phänomenologie und phänomenologischen Philosophie. Zweites Buch: Phänomenologische Untersuchungen zur Konstitution*. Edited by Marly Biemel. The Hague, Netherlands: Martinus Nijhoff (Hua 4).

———. 1956. *Erste Philosophie (1923/4). Erste Teil: Kritische Ideengeschichte*. Edited by Rudolf Böhm. The Hague, Netherlands: Martinus Nijhoff (Hua 7).

———. 1966. *Analysen zur passiven Synthesis. Aus Vorlesungs- und Forschungsmanuskripten, 1918–1926*. Edited by Margot Fleischer. The Hague, Netherlands: Martinus Nijhoff (Hua 11).

————. 1968. *Phänomenologische Psychologie. Vorlesungen Sommersemester 1925.* Edited by Walter Biemel. The Hague, Netherlands: Martinus Nijhoff (Hua 9).

————. 1973. *Cartesianische Meditationen und Pariser Vorträge.* Edited by S. Strasser. The Hague, Netherlands: Martinus Nijhoff (Hua 1).

————. 1973. *Zur Phänomenologie der Intersubjektivität. Texte aus dem Nachlass. Erster Teil. 1905–1920.* Edited by Iso Kern. The Hague, Netherlands: Martinus Nijhoff (Hua 13).

————. 1973. *Zur Phänomenologie der Intersubjektivität. Texte aus dem Nachlass. Zweiter Teil. 1921–28.* Edited by Iso Kern. The Hague, Netherlands: Martinus Nijhoff (Hua 14).

————. 1973. *Zur Phänomenologie der Intersubjektivität. Texte aus dem Nachlass. Dritter Teil. 1929–35.* Edited by Iso Kern. The Hague, Netherlands: Martinus Nijhoff (Hua 15).

————. 1976. *Die Krisis der europäischen Wissenschaften und die transzendentale Phänomenologie. Eine Einleitung in die phänomenologische Philosophie.* Edited by Walter Biemel. The Hague, Netherlands: Martinus Nijhoff (Hua 6).

————. 1984. *Erfahrung und Urteil.* Hamburg: Felix Meiner Verlag (E&U).

————. 1988. *Aufsätze und Vorträge. 1922–1937.* Edited by T. Nenon H. R. Sepp. The Hague, Netherlands: Kluwer Academic Publishers (Hua 27).

————. 1988. *Vorlesungen über Ethik und Wertlehre. 1908–1914.* Edited by Ullrich Melle. The Hague, Netherlands: Kluwer Academic Publishers (Hua 28).

————. 1992. *Die Krisis der europaischen Wissenschaften und die transzendentale Phänomenologie. Ergänzungsband. Texte aus dem Nachlass 1934–1937.* Edited by Reinhold N. Smid. The Hague, Netherlands: Kluwer Academic Publishers (Hua 29).

————. 2004. *Einleitung in die Ethik. Vorlesungen Sommersemester 1920 und 1924.* Edited by Henning Peucker. Dordrecht, Netherlands: Kluwer Academic Publishers (Hua 37).

————. 2006. *Späte Texte über Zeitkonstitution (1929-1934). Die C-Manuskripte.* Husserliana Materialenband VIII. Edited by Dieter Lohmar. New York: Springer (HuaM 8).

————. 2008. *Die Lebenswelt: Auslegungen der vorgegebenen Welt und ihrer Konstitution. Texte aus dem Nachlass (1916–1937),* ed. R. Sowa. Dordrecht: Springer (Hua 39).

Jameson, F. 1983. *The Political Unconscious: Narrative as a Socially Symbolic Act.* New York and London: Routledge.

Marcuse, H. 1987. *Eros and Civilization.* London: Routledge.

Marx, K. and Engels, F. 1970. *The German Ideology.* Edited by C. J. Arthur. New York: International Publishers.

Merleau-Ponty, M. 1962. *Phenomenology of Perception.* Translated by Colin Smith. London: Routledge & Degan.

Miettinen, T. 2013. *The Idea of Europe in Husserl's Phenomenology: A Study in Generativity and Historicity.* Philosophical Studies from the University of Helsinki 36. Helsinki: Multiprint.

Orth, E. W. 1987. "*Kulturphilosophie* und Kulturanthropologie als Transzendentalphänomenologie." *Husserl Studies* 4: 103–141.

Pfaller, R. 2002. *Die Illusionen der anderen. Über das Lustprinzip in der Kultur.* Frankfurt am Main: Suhrkamp.

Ricoeur, P. 1991. *From Text to Action: Essays in Hermeneutics II.* Translated by Kathleen Blamey and John B. Thompson. Evanston, IL: Northwestern University Press.

Scheler, M. 1980. *Der Formalismus in der Ethik und die materiale Wertethik: neuer Versuch der Grundlegung eines ethischen Personalismus.* Bern: Francke Verlag.

Schütz, A. 1975. *Collected Papers III: Studies in Phenomenological Philosophy*. The Hague: Martinus Nijhoff.

Searle, J. 1995. *The Construction of Social Reality*. New York: The Free Press.

———. 2006. "Social Ontology–Some Basic Principles." *Anthropological Theory*, vol. 6, no. 1, 12–29.

Steinbock, A. 1995. *Home and Beyond. Generative Phenomenology after Husserl*. Northwestern University Studies in Phenomenology and Existential Philosophy. Evanston, IL: Northwestern University Press.

Theunissen, M. 1984. *The Other: Studies in the Social Ontology of Husserl, Heidegger, Sartre, and Buber*. Translated by Christopher Macann. Cambridge: MIT Press.

Tuomela, R. 2008. "Collective Intentionality and Group Reasons." In Schmid, Schulte–Ostermann, and Psarros (eds.), *Concepts of Sharedness*, 3–20. Frankfurt: Ontos Verlag.

Weber, M. 1968. *Economy and Society*. Ed. Guenther Roth and Claus Wittich. Berkeley: University of California Press.

Yamaguchi, I. 1982. *Passive Synthesis und Intersubjektivität bei Edmund Husserl*. The Hague: Martinus Martinus Nijhoff.

Zahavi, D. 2001. *Husserl and Transcendental Intersubjectivity: A Response to the Linguistic-Pragmatic Critique*. Athens: Ohio University Press.

Part III
Mind and the World

8   The Emergence and Transformation of Husserl's Concept of World

David Carr

A central component of Husserl's turn to transcendental phenomenology in the period leading up to the publication of *Ideen I* was the emergence of his concept of *world*. This concept occupies an increasingly important position in Husserl's work and in the whole phenomenological tradition he founded; yet it had hardly been present at all, and even the term was rarely used, in the *Logische Untersuchungen* (1901) and in the lectures of the ensuing decade. When he turned his attention from his concrete investigations—concerned with such topics as perception, thing and space, fantasy, picture-consciousness, and time-consciousness—to the development of phenomenology as a distinctive philosophical method, Husserl first put the emphasis on the *eidetic character* of his investigations and did not characterize phenomenology in terms of a transformation in the attitude toward the world. Even in his famous *Logos* essay of 1911, eidetic reflection was the key to achieving through phenomenology the goal of "Philosophy as Rigorous Science."

But already in the lecture course "*Grundprobleme der Phänomenologie*," in the winter semester of 1910 to 1911, a new element entered the picture, which would become prominent in *Ideen I*, namely that of the "natural attitude" and of the "world of the natural attitude." While there are hints of this in the lectures of 1907 (*Die Idee der Phänomenologie* [Hua 2, 17] and *Ding und Raum* [Hua 16, passim]), they are not developed as they are in 1910. The general idea here is that the life of consciousness, with its acts and their meaningful or intentional objects, also involves certain attitudes (*Einstellungen*), which are not themselves acts but somehow underlie those acts. The most basic of these attitudes is called "the natural attitude" and is directly linked to the life of experience (*Erfahrung*) in general and perception (*Wahrnehmung*) in particular. The intentional correlate of the natural attitude is the *world*. The idea of intentionality is that we cannot think of experience without intentional objects. Now we learn that, thanks to the natural attitude, experience is related essentially not just to objects but also to the world to which they belong. The world is not itself just another intentional object, nor is it the collection of all such objects, but somehow constitutes the background and horizon of all objects.

Once the concept of world moves into a central position in Husserl's formulation of the phenomenological method, it undergoes a series of transformations in the ensuing years, culminating in the concept of the life-world in the 1930s. In this chapter, I want to trace the emergence and the subsequent transformations of this important concept. Especially in their early stages, these transformations contain some ambiguities and even confusions that turn out to be decisive for the development of Husserl's full-fledged transcendental phenomenology. The clarification of these confusions helps us better understand Husserl's phenomenological method and the kinds of transcendental inquiries that it makes possible.

1   THE EARLY EMERGENCE OF THE CONCEPT OF WORLD

The *Grundprobleme* lectures begin with the natural attitude, but Husserl informs us right away that we turn to this attitude only in order to depart from it in the direction of a "completely different attitude," the phenomenological. This foreshadows the strategy of *Ideen I* (Hua 3, 57ff.), where Husserl speaks of "The Thesis of the Natural Attitude and its Suspension," and there are many parallels between the two texts, suggesting that the later draws on the earlier. After discussing the natural attitude, Husserl informs us in both texts that while it is an extremely important project to describe this attitude in greater detail, he has more important things to do (Husserl 2006, 15; Hua 3, 62), namely to suspend the natural attitude and to introduce the phenomenological attitude. But in both cases the description of the natural attitude, though short, is extraordinarily rich and full of elements that hitherto had not been part of Husserl's conceptual repertoire. The emergence of a certain concept of the world is the most important of these.

The first thing to be noted about the 1910 lecture course is that the natural attitude is linked from the outset with what Husserl calls the "natural concept of the world"—*der natürliche Weltbegriff*. This is an expression borrowed from the first section of Richard Avenarius's 1891 book *Der menschliche Weltbegriff* (Avenarius 1891, 4ff). In the lectures, Husserl introduces the expression in quotation marks, and he explicitly links it to Avenarius's name; moreover, he discusses Avenarius briefly and critically in a couple of places. In *Ideen I,* by contrast, neither this expression nor Avenarius's name appears. And even in the 1910 lectures, he does not refer explicitly to Avenarius's text. One gets the impression that the term "*natürlicher Weltbegriff*" was such a compelling one that it had separated itself from its originator and entered the language, at least the language of philosophers.[1]

What is the significance of Husserl's appropriation of Avenarius's term, and how much does he actually retain from Avenarius's approach? The first thing to be noted, which in my view is of enormous significance, is the adoption of a first-person singular discourse. In parallel passages in the lectures (Husserl 2006, 8) and in *Ideen I* (Hua 3, 57), Husserl says that to describe the natural attitude, "it is best" to speak in the first-person singular or "*Ichrede.*" Avenarius too had adopted this discourse ("Ich mit all meinen Gedanken und Gefühlen fand mich inmitten einer Umgebung" (Avenarius 1891, 4); compare to Husserl's almost identical wording: "Each of us [. . .] as an I [. . .] finds himself at all times as a center of a surrounding [*Umgebung*]" (Husserl 2006, 2)). Admittedly Husserl is rather offhanded in saying this—it is "best," but perhaps not necessary, to adopt this mode of discourse—and is also inconsistent in carrying it out in the pages that follow, often reverting to the usual authorial "we." He does not accord this shift in discourse the importance that I think it deserves. But with this Husserl clearly signals, among other things, that the *world* is to be considered, not just in general, but from my personal—individual, subjective—point of view. This point of view may have been implicit in certain earlier investigations, especially those concerned with perception of thing and space, but it was not made as prominent as it is here. I would go so far as to say that the first-person point of view is not only employed here systematically for the first time but also emerges, at this point, as a *theme,* indeed perhaps the central theme of transcendental phenomenology. Phenomenology is henceforth not only carried out in the first person, it is also *about* the first-person point of view. As he says later, transcendental phenomenology can be described as universal, systematic "egology" (Hua 1, 69). It is at this point, too, that *Descartes* appears as a major point of reference in Husserl's presentations of phenomenology, directly and indirectly. Not only does he discuss Descartes explicitly in this section of *Ideen I,* he also describes his first-person investigations as "meditations" (Hua 3, 57).

A second feature of both Husserl texts is the introduction of the term '*natürliche Einstellung*' or 'natural attitude.' '*Einstellung*' differs from '*Begriff*' in important ways, as we shall see, but Husserl's term still echoes Avenarius's '*natürlicher Weltbegriff.*' Certainly one of the important features of Husserl's natural attitude is that it is directed toward the world, and what Husserl sets out to describe in the first section of this chapter of *Ideen I* is not just the attitude itself but the "world" of the natural attitude. His treatment of the natural attitude now leads very quickly, however, at least in the *Ideen* text, to the striking proposal to suspend (*ausschalten*) or bracket (*einklammern*) what he calls the "natural thesis" (Hua 3 III, 63). This "thesis" is not found in Avenarius. But it should be noted that a key element has been introduced here that is decisive for this proposal: the natural attitude, says Husserl, has a "general thesis." This thesis does not manifest itself as an articulated, predicative judgment "*about* existence;" rather, it "somehow lies unthematic, unthought, unpredicated in original experience" (Hua 3, 64) as long as the attitude—"natural, waking life [*Dahinleben*]"—endures or is in effect. Once it has been fully articulated, as it now is by Husserl, it amounts to the claim: "'*Die' Welt ist als Wirklichkeit immer da.*" It affirms "*die [. . .] immer daseiende Welt*" (Hua 3, 53).

The importance of this "general thesis" for Husserl's method, of course, is his claim that, once articulated, this "thesis" can be treated exactly as if it were any other thesis: namely, we can bracket it or put it out of action. Critical questions can easily be raised about this procedure. It may seem that Husserl is here making a series of rather debatable claims without much description or justification, namely: first, that there is such an implicit thesis, underlying or hidden, unarticulated, within our experience; second, that this thesis can be dredged up and articulated as a judgment "about existence"— in particular, about the existence of the world; and third, that this supposed judgment can then be treated as can any other judgment, even though its referent and content are so vastly different from those of any other judgment. Since this move is crucial to Husserl's presentation of his epoche and transcendental reduction, its questionableness may explain the misgivings many of Husserl's readers have had about this (for Husserl) decisive feature of his method.

In any case, Husserl is here making a claim about what he later (in *Ideen I*) calls *Urglaube* or *Urdoxa* (Hua 3, 259), the belief-character of experience (*Erfahrung*) that posits existence. Belief is not itself judgment, but it can be expressed in a judgment. The belief in question here, however, is different from all other beliefs because its object is the world as such or as a whole. It underlies or encompasses all other experiential beliefs, because what we take to exist in particular we take to be part of the world, in whose existence we believe at the most fundamental level. My beliefs about what exists in particular may change and be subject to correction, as he says here (Hua 3, 63), but my belief in the existence of the world is unshakable even if, as Husserl now proposes, I "make no use" of this belief for purposes of phenomenology. "*Die Thesis ist Erlebnis*," he says here (Hua 3, 65): I am still "living" the judgment, and the underlying belief it expresses, even when I put it out of action. I am not at liberty to transform judgments or beliefs into denials, conjectures, or doubts; for these I must have motives or reasons. But bracketing, because it does not really touch the underlying *commitment* of my belief, lies within my "perfect freedom" (ibid.).

The relation between particular beliefs and our underlying belief in the world is an important part of what Husserl is trying to express here. In a manuscript from 1928, he puts it this way: "'*Die' Welt ist uns vorgegeben. Richten wir den aktiven Blick geradehin auf irgendetwas, so war es schon da [. . .]*" (Hua 39, 26). The scare-quotes around "die" echo those of the passage from *Ideen I* that I quoted above, and emphasize, I believe, the *singularity* of the world in its role as object of this underlying belief. That the particular object of my intention was "already there" indicates the "*Vorgegebenheit*" of the world as a whole. Indeed, the pregivenness of the world, in relation to any particular objects, is one of its most important features. But can we say more about it? So far we know precious little: it is '*immer da*,' '*immer daseiende Welt*,' '*da*,' '*vorhanden*.' These terms are rather empty, in the sense that they seem to point solely to the *existence* of the world. *Vorgegebenheit* tells us how it is given. But *what is it* that is given, and *what is it* that exists? How to describe the world of the natural attitude?

2   NATURAL ATTITUDE, NATURAL WORLD

The answer to this question will lead us to the transformations I spoke of at the outset. The sense or character of the world of the natural attitude, as articulated in *Ideen I* and the 1910 lectures, is gradually supplanted by a different concept, as we shall see. And the key to the original formulation, and the source of its inadequacy, are tied up with a key term that we have not discussed so far: *natürlich*. Husserl sets out to describe the *natural* attitude, and Avenarius speaks of the *natural* concept of the world. What does "natural" mean here? In both English and German, we can distinguish two different senses of 'natural.' On the one hand, it refers to the naïve, the unreflective, the unsophisticated. On the other hand, it refers to "nature," as it might be contrasted with the mental, the spiritual, or the cultural. I believe that Husserl, at this stage, either conflates these two senses or perhaps sincerely believes, without explicitly articulating it, that they belong together. This is something he takes from, or at least shares with, Avenarius. And the development and transformation of Husserl's concept of world, as I seek to describe it here, can be seen as Husserl's eventual recognition of and his attempt to unravel this conflation.

'Natural' in the first sense, when combined with 'attitude,' recalls a standard philosophical trope. Sometimes called "common sense," the view of the "man in the street" (before the advent of gender consciousness), or what the Germans call "healthy" human understanding (*gesunder Menschenverstand*), 'natural' in this sense suggests a kind of wholesome innocence. Here naiveté is a virtue, sophistication a vice, because it leads to the errors of one's philosophical opponents. One returns to innocence in order to overcome those errors once and for all. Volumes could be written about the quest for this elusive, prelapsarian figure and about its dangers and pitfalls. A similarly precarious position is occupied in philosophy by the notions of "everyday experience" and even "ordinary language." This is, in any case, what Husserl and Avenarius are after. In Husserl's case, since 'natural' modifies 'attitude' here, we are speaking of what is "natural" to that attitude, what belongs to its nature. *Natürliches, waches Dahinleben* is another expression he uses (Hua 3, 63), where '*dahin*' means as much as unthinking or unreflective or unaffected. In this sense it can be contrasted with any specialized intentions directed at particular aspects of the world, any theoretical formulations or abstractions, in particular any scientific endeavors aimed at controlling or predicting the world's events. These are the sciences of the natural attitude, as Husserl calls them (ibid.), which remain within the natural attitude, are founded upon it, but which are not identical with it. As in any founding relation, the natural attitude can exist without developing into science, but these sciences cannot exist without the natural attitude. The latter can also be contrasted with the phenomenological attitude, which is Husserl's main purpose here, in which the thesis of the natural attitude is suspended. In *Ideen II,* Husserl describes the phenomenological attitude as "artificial" (*künstlich*; Hua 4, 180), and indeed in ordinary speech the "natural" is often contrasted precisely with the "artificial." If 'artificial' comes from 'artifice' or the 'man-made,' then the point here would be that the philosopher, or perhaps the scientist, steps in and alters or modifies, for special purposes, what would otherwise be left in its "natural" state.

The link to the "natural" in the *second* sense is to be found in the description of the *world* of the natural attitude as "*die eine raum-zeitliche Wirklichkeit*" (Hua 3, 63). Fundamental to the whole attitude and its beliefs is experience (*Erfahrung*), and, in particular, perception (*Wahrnehmung*). "*Körperliche Dinge,*" bodily things, are available to me through my senses, are spread out around me in space, and make up my surroundings (*Umgebung*) or surrounding world (*Umwelt*; Hua 3, 57). At one point in the lectures, Husserl describes my awareness of space as the "knowledge" that my immediate surroundings make up merely a piece of the world "and that things continue on in endless (Euclidian) space" (Husserl 2006, 3). Notice the scare quotes around 'knows;' in a parallel passage in *Ideen I* he says explicitly that this is a "knowledge [*Wissen*] that has nothing of conceptual thought" (Hua 3, 58). Nevertheless, it is significant that *what* one knows is linked here with Euclidian space. In the lectures, the natural attitude is directly linked to the *a priori,* material ontology of nature (Husserl 2006, 21). As he puts it there, "*The 'ontology' of nature presents in its various disciplines the pure, formal-general sense of the natural thesis*" (Husserl 2006, 25). In sum, at this stage it seems to be the case that the thesis of the natural attitude asserts the existence not just of the world but of the *natural* world in the sense of the material ontology of nature. The sciences of the natural attitude are referred to as "the so-called 'positive' sciences" (Hua 3, 63), a term usually reserved for the natural sciences. Thus we could say that, in Avenarius's language, *the natural concept of the world is really the concept of the natural world.* It is true that Husserl avoids the term *Begriff* and has denied that our awareness of the world amounts to conceptual knowledge, at least at this stage. But it is directly linked, at least implicitly, to *a priori* material ontology, which in turn underlies the empirical sciences of nature.

This point is the occasion for a dispute with Avenarius in the lectures. Husserl denies that the natural world-concept could be a "legacy of the animal evolution over millions of years" or the result of a progressive "adjustment to the conditions of nature on the part of animals and, finally, man" (Husserl 2006, 26). According to Husserl, any such empirical account would presuppose, and thus could never explain, the natural attitude, which thus remains "*valid in an absolute and a priori sense*" (ibid.). By the same token, Husserl denies the view, which he attributes to Avenarius, that we could ever "relinquish" the natural attitude by engaging in natural science. He notes that the natural world concept in his sense is "not that concept which humans have formed for themselves prior to science; rather, it is the world-concept that comprises the sense of the natural attitude both before and after science" (Husserl 2006, 27 n.43).

Thus it seems clear that Husserl's earliest concept of world, as it emerges around 1910 to 1913, partly as a result of his interaction with Avenarius, is that of the natural world. The "natural attitude" consists primarily in a deep, doxic commitment to the existence of the "natural" world, the very same world that becomes the theme of the natural sciences. It is true that, in *Ideen I*, Husserl says that the world of the natural attitude is not just a fact-world but also a world of values and goods, a practical world, and that these features of the world are grasped with the same immediacy as its spatio-temporal features (Hua 3, 59). He also mentions other subjects, both human and animal, and has a few words to say about the social descriptions (friend and foe, servants and superiors, relatives and strangers) under which such subjects are experienced (Hua 3, 60). But his main point in introducing these is to say that others are cosubjects who, from different points of view, experience spatio-temporal reality and posit it as the surrounding world that exists for all of us and to which we ourselves also belong (Hua 3, 62).

Ideen I also contains some very different observations on the natural attitude and its world at the very beginning of the book. Under the heading "natural knowledge and experience" (*natürliche Erkenntnis und Erfahrung*), he begins with the very Kantian statement "natural knowledge begins with experience and remains within experience" (Hua 3, 10). He then goes on to describe the "natural" attitude as a "theoretical" attitude and the "world" as the total horizon of possible research (*Forschung*). World is also called "the totality [*Gesamtinbegriff*] of objects of possible experience and experiential knowledge, of objects that on the basis of actual experiences can be known in correct theoretical thinking" (Hua 3, 11). These passages, taken together with those in the later section on the natural attitude and its suspension, raise certain questions. Is the natural attitude a "theoretical" attitude or is it somehow pretheoretical, a "knowledge" (*Wissen*) that has no conceptual thought in it? Does it have some role prior to and independent of the natural sciences, or is it just an incipient science, providing us with access to the world and the objects that will be covered by scientific theory?

In manuscripts of the 1920s, Husserl begins to reflect more deeply on the world of the natural attitude. In a manuscript from 1926, he begins his reflection with the relation of the "perceptual field," which is at the heart of our direct acquaintance with the world, to the hidden but still intended horizons extending indefinitely beyond it. Here Husserl uses the term 'unconscious' (*"Horizont des 'Unbewussten'"*), but says this horizon is nevertheless intentional: somewhat paradoxically, he writes that "in it too we are conscious of something in a broader sense. [...] More is always meant than is actually grasped" (Hua 39, 27). So far this is still part of Husserl's account of perception, thing, and space. At the same time, it is as if he is opening the door to a broader sense of experience, as it might relate to the direct and naïve grasp of the world. He begins to speak of the cultural world as something somehow built up genetically on top of the perceptual, "natural" world. "Any world that is pregiven as cultural refers back genetically to a world that is cultureless and free of objective spirit" (Hua 39, 28). "The universe of objects which are given to me directly in immediate experience [. . .] is *nature*" (Hua 39, 30). What is built upon that, starting with other persons, is mediated, no longer immediate. He sees his task here as that of tracing this genesis.

3   THE BEGINNING OF THE TRANSFORMATION

At the same time, a counter-consideration begins to intrude. Every human being is born into a chain of generations and thus into a communal world. Each such world emerges out of a similar world before it. "In this chain of generative life, then, we find no cultureless world . . . Whether a historical zero-world is even thinkable, [i.e.] a world that is naked, so to speak, or free of all spiritual meaning [*geistige Bedeutung*] [. . .] is questionable from the start" (Hua 39, 29). The whole idea of a direct and unmediated grasp of nature, prior to and innocent of all cultural features, as our access to the world of the natural attitude, is beginning to look like an abstraction. We are all immersed in the realm of cultural objectivities (*das Reich der Kulturgegenständlichkeiten*) that have only a relative objectivity. So far Husserl has treated nature as the hard "kernel of necessary objectivity" at the heart of all this cultural relativity. "But basically the same is true of nature [i.e. it too belongs to the cultural sphere], which for us cultured Europeans has a fixed objectivity only because we share the norm of natural science, in which we have been educated historically" (Hua 39, 33).

This leads, in another manuscript of this period, to a very different view of "nature" as it relates to the natural attitude. Husserl returns to Avenarius's expression "*natürlicher Weltbegriff*" (Hua 39, 259). But if nature is still described as a "*Kernschicht*" or nuclear stratum of the world, it is now considered abstract, not concrete, and attaining this stratum is possible only by means of a "dismantling" procedure (*Abbau*), starting from the concrete world of experience (*Erfahrungswelt*) (Hua 39, 265). Nature in this sense, which is the object of both the empirical sciences of nature and the eidetic ontology of nature, is considered no longer as something that is given directly to us in experience but as something arrived at by a complex procedure. To attain it, we must subtract from our experienced world everything that is "intentionally spiritual" ("*intentional Geistigen*") and merely subjective. In the concrete world of experience, there are no "mere things;" things are endowed everywhere with "predicates of spiritual significance, related to subjects" (Hua 39, 266). The term 'natural' in 'natural attitude' begins to lose its association with "nature" and to revert to its other sense, that of naïve, direct, unsophisticated. Husserl now puts 'natural' in scare-quotes and substitutes 'necessary' as modifying '*Weltvorstellung*,' which refers to "the world as it is experienced [*erfahren*] in human experience, indeed purely as experienced, in '*pure experience*.' We contrast experience with theoretical determination, and we ask after the experiential world which *precedes* all theorizing, interpreting, conceiving as [*Auffassen als*] this or that" (Hua 39, 260).

Continuing to treat "nature" as a "thematic abstraction," Husserl considers the notion of *die Allnatur,* that is, the universe of all natural things. Then he asks if there is a corresponding notion of *der Allgeist,* a corresponding universe of things spiritual. The answer is no (Hua 39, 272), but why? Nature is strictly circumscribed, and it is "the great accomplishment of modern natural science, which has secured its sense, to have constructed these thematic walls" that separate it from all else (Hua 39, 273). Once we scale these walls to find what is outside them, once we ask what makes humans human and animals animal, we find something very different from the "universe" we have left behind. The spiritual world does not organize itself into "things" that make up a totality. Here we enter the intentional subjective sphere of human experience, where human bodies (*Leiber*) are not merely natural objects.

In these manuscripts from the late 1920s, Husserl is becoming convinced that the idea of nature that has been dominant in the discussion of the natural attitude, starting with Avenarius but also including his own earlier work, is in fact a powerful abstraction with historical origins. To this abstraction he now contrasts "*die konkrete Erfahrungswelt*" in which "the non-natural, the spiritual [*die Geistigkeit*], is everywhere predominant, attaches itself to everything, but in different ways." Eventually the idea of space-time reappears, but no longer in the objective, scientific sense. This is now the space-time of the *Umwelt,* of a generative tradition, the historicity of a "homeland" with a "historical temporality" (Hua 39, 344).

In this context, it is interesting to recall Husserl's dispute with Avenarius on the "evolutionary" development of the natural concept of the world. In the 1910 lectures, Husserl had insisted that the natural concept of the world corresponded to the *a priori* ontology of nature. Now he seems ready to admit that this concept of nature is the product of a certain development. To be sure, his account of its development is not a biological-evolutionary explanation, in the positivist manner, but a historical one. Still, he is moving toward the theory of idealization and mathematization that reaches its full expression in the *Crisis.*

But these changes in Husserl's views found their expression long before the period of the *Crisis.* Their best-known formulation is found in the third part of *Ideen II.* There the context is the three-part theory of constitution, which begins with "material nature" and then moves on to "animal nature." The third part, devoted to the "*Konstitution der geistigen Welt,*" seems to date from the same period as some of the texts we have been quoting, that is, the mid- to late 1920s (Hua 4, xviii). It begins with an extended reflection on the concept of "attitude." Constitution always presupposes an attitude toward the world and the objects in it, and the attitude tacitly presupposed in the discussion of the constitution of nature has been that of the natural sciences. Even the discussion of "animal nature" had been oriented toward the idea of a scientific psychology. Animals and humans are perceived as objects in the natural world, but when we take them as "ensouled" beings, we are aware of sensitive and psychic properties and capacities that constitute a "*Realitätsüberschuß,*" a surplus over the physical (Hua 4, 176). Here Husserl uses the word *Introjektion,*' a term that harks back to Avenarius and his discussion of the natural concept of the world—though Husserl also notes that this term can be "easily misunderstood."

In his transition to the "*geistige Welt,*" Husserl notes that one great merit of the phenomenological reduction is that it can free us from the limitations imposed by "the natural attitude or any relative attitude," limitations that are not noticed by "natural man, [*natürlicher Mensch*] and in particular the scientist of nature [*Naturforscher*]" (Hua 4, 179). Terminologically, Husserl in this passage is still identifying the "natural attitude" with that of the natural scientist. But then he suggests a distinction between "*natürlich*" and "*naturalistisch,*" reserving the latter for the attitude of the natural scientist and pointing out that the attitude toward persons, communities, and the social world is "*sehr natürlich.*" (Hua 4, 180) What he now calls the "personalistic attitude, which we are always in when we live together, speak to one another," and so on, is "a thoroughly natural, and not an artificial attitude that has to be attained and maintained by special means" (Hua 4, 183). Finally, Husserl is implicitly recognizing the distinction between the two senses of 'natural' we noted above and reserving the term 'natural attitude' for what is opposed to the "artificial."

Having articulated the differences between the naturalistic and the personalistic attitudes, Husserl describes how the scientist, like everyone else, lives in the personalistic attitude but, for purposes of scientific inquiry, assumes the naturalistic attitude. He now arrives at the following, rather striking conclusion:

> Looked at more closely, it will even become clear that we are not at all dealing with two attitudes, possessing equal rights and equal status, two equal and mutually interpenetrating apperceptions, but rather that the naturalistic attitude is subordinate to the personalistic and has acquired a certain independence through a kind of abstraction, or rather through a sort of self-forgetfulness of the personal ego, at the same time unjustifiably absolutizing its world, [i.e.] nature. (Hua 4, 183–184)

We can now see that the "world of the natural attitude," sought by Husserl in the early pages of *Ideen I,* has been completely transformed. Although in some sense, in that text, Husserl wanted to capture the naïve and unsophisticated view of the world, in fact the natural attitude was correlated with the scientific view of nature and represented the view of the natural scientist, or at the very least the incipient or aspiring natural scientist. Now the natural attitude is that of the nonscientist, or even the scientist in his or her off-hours, and the *world* of the natural attitude is the world of persons, of motivations, of social relations, of communities and of "spiritual" entities and predicates. Here natural science is construed as a social enterprise, and nature makes a return appearance not as something absolute but as "something constituted in the intersubjective band of persons" that make up the scientific community (Hua 4, 210).

4   THE COMPLETION OF THE TRANSFORMATION

While Husserl seems here to be asserting the priority of the spiritual over the natural world, he nevertheless ends this section of *Ideen II* wondering if we are left with a "two-worlds" theory, or a theory of "fundamentally different 'regions.' Is it really a matter of two different worlds, 'nature' on one side, the world of the spirit on the other, separated by cardinal ontological distinctions?" (Hua 4, 210). The two worlds need not be unrelated: the spiritual from the naturalistic standpoint can be seen as an "annex" of the physical body; and the natural, as we have seen, has its place within the spiritual world. But Husserl seems dissatisfied with this outcome, for two reasons: first, the seeming equality of the two sides, and second, the fact that the *world* seems to have lost its unity, sundering itself into the kind of metaphysical dualism that resembles that of Descartes. At the end of *Ideen II*, Husserl seems to conclude that the one side of this dualism swallows the other up: the third chapter bears the title "The Ontological Priority of the Spiritual World over the Naturalistic" and concludes with the section called "Relativity of nature, absoluteness of spirit." This, in my view would be to replace a metaphysical dualism with a metaphysical monism—actually a metaphysical or ontological idealism.

But this solution to the unity of the world seems to operate at a level different from that of the "world of the natural attitude." The "phenomenological investigations on constitution" that make up the three parts of *Ideen II* are very much geared to the emergence of the sciences: the natural and psychological sciences in the first two parts and the *Geisteswissenschaften* in the third. Each of these corresponds to a different "region of reality" addressed by each of these sciences. Husserl seems to presuppose these regions as fully developed scientifically when he raises the issue of their equality or nonequality and then proposes that one swallows up the others.

But in the lectures on phenomenological psychology of 1925, Husserl looks elsewhere for the unity of the world and the relation among the regions. In this text, in which Husserl also returns to Avenarius's expression *der natürliche Weltbegriff*, he writes the following:

As scientific themes, nature and mind do not exist beforehand; rather, they are formed only within a theoretical interest and in the theoretical work directed by it, upon the underlying stratum of a natural, prescientific experience [*Erfahrung*]. Here they appear in an originally intuitable intermingling and togetherness; it is necessary to begin with this concretely intuitable unity of the prescientific experiential world and then to elucidate what theoretical interests and directions of thought it predeliniates, as well as how nature and mind can become unitary universal themes, always inseparably related to each other, in it. (Hua 9, 55)

Thus the unity of the three regions is to be found not at the scientific level but in the prescientific world of the natural attitude, a conception that presages that of the lifeworld in the *Crisis*. In other words, the world is unified prior to and independently of its being theoretically divided into regions, not after it has been so divided.

The view expressed in this passage from *Phenomenological Psychology*, as further developed in the *Crisis*, completes the transformation of Husserl's concept of world and goes beyond even the important changes found in *Ideen II*. There the attitude underlying the human sciences is found to be more "natural" than that of the natural sciences, and Husserl expresses the view that the spiritual world in a sense encompasses the natural world and renders it secondary and dependent. But the lifeworld of the *Crisis* and the natural attitude (or natural world-life, as Husserl sometimes calls it) that corresponds to it is prior to all regions, prior to all scientific or even protoscientific attitudes, prior even to all practical attitudes that divide up the world for some purpose or other. As Husserl says in the *Crisis*, the life-world is

that which is *taken for granted*, which is presupposed by all thinking, all activity of life with all its ends and accomplishments. [. . .] Before all such accomplishments there has always already been a universal accomplishment, presupposed by all human practice and all scientific and prescientific life. The latter have the spiritual acquisitions of this universal accomplishment as their constant substratum, and all their own acquisitions are destined to flow into it. (Hua 4, 115)

And in one of the *Beilagen*, he writes:

The life-world is that world that is constantly pregiven, valid constantly and in advance as existing, but not valid because of some purpose of investigation, according to some universal end. Every end presupposes it; even the universal end of knowing it in scientific truth presupposes it. [. . .] Now though we must [further] make evident the fact that the life-world itself is a "structure" [*Gebilde*], it is nevertheless not a "purposeful structure" [. . .]. (Hua 6, 461–462)

5   SELF AND WORLD

In conclusion, I want to say something about the role of the self or subject in Husserl's developing concept of world. One of the most fascinating aspects of Husserl's early presentation of the world of the natural attitude is found in the following passages from *Ideen I:* The world "is ever 'present' for me, and I am a member of it [*(die Welt) ist immerfort für mich 'vorhanden,' und ich selbst bin ihr Mitglied*]" (Hua 3, 59). "I find constantly present, as over against me, the one spatial-temporal reality, to which I myself belong [*Ich finde beständig vorhanden als mein Gegenüber die eine räumlich-zeitliche Wirklichkeit, der ich selbst zugehöre*]" (Hua 3, 63). Similar passages can be found elsewhere. According to this conception, I am part of the world that is present, that stands over against me. That is, I am present to myself, I am "over against" myself.

This kind of self-presence, especially when described as "over against," suggests reflective self-awareness, but that is clearly not what Husserl has in mind, not when he is describing "*natürliches Dahinleben.*" My own self is at best something always hovering on the horizon of my ordinary experience, and as such it is a potential but only occasionally actual object of my experience. But in either case, we can ask the question of how or as what the self appears in the "natural" attitude. And it turns out, not surprisingly, that this conception of self undergoes the same transformation as the conception of the world. Prior to the late 1920s, the self is either the transcendental ego, or, as empirical self, it is embedded in the spatiotemporal world and conceived as a "psychophysical" entity. In other words, it is experienced—I experience myself—as a potential object of natural science, for example, physiology or some kind of empirical psychology. To some extent, this conception is undermined by the recognition of the subjective body, or *Leib,* in the second part of *Ideen II.*

But in an interesting manuscript in the *Lebenswelt* volume, dated 1928, Husserl speaks of physical reality, "bound in the unity of nature as a whole [*Allnatur*], in which the real relational form of external causality [. . .] rules." Then he goes on to describe the view that "to this externality [*Außereinander*] [. . .] belongs also the externality in man, as the co-existence of corporeal body and 'soul.'" The "spiritual side" of man is thought to be spatiotemporally located there where the body is and grounded in it.

This conception of man becomes the traditional naturalistic one of the whole modern age, when it pretends to be the whole truth, that is, when it believes itself capable of expressing fully and exclusively the experiential sense of man. Any other conception seems totally out of the question (Hua 39, 685f.).

In other words, the conception of the natural world, and of man within it, which Husserl himself largely shared, is now seen as a historically relative, modern appearance. If we are not "naturalistically blinkered" (*naturalistisch verblendet*), he goes on to say, and rely on "original experience itself" and its own "indwelling experiential sense," then we will gain a better idea of the spiritual than that which places it within the natural world and learn about the spiritual world to which it rightly belongs (Hua 39, 687). This ties in with the third section of *Ideen II* in which Husserl describes the "spiritual I and its comportment to the surrounding world" (Hua 4, 215).

6 CONCLUSION

The transformation of Husserl's concept of the world, as I have described it in this chapter, is at the same time a transformation of his assessment of natural science and its place in phenomenology. Like the educated European that he is, and as a former mathematician with a certain familiarity with natural science, he inherits the general admiration of science and shares the belief that it tells us how the world really is. And if this is the way the world is, then this must be the way the world is given to us. Thus he absolutizes this world and even phenomenologizes it, initially describing our consciousness of the world as that of an incipient natural scientist.

His gradual arrival at a conception of the natural attitude as something more "natural" than the attitude of the scientist is at the same time the gradual beginning of a historical relativization of the sciences of nature and of the concept of nature they have developed. This in turn leads Husserl to inquire into the historical origins of this concept of nature, which he famously traces to Galileo in the *Crisis*. This allows him to understand modern natural science in a new way and thus transforms the phenomenology of natural science.

But as Husserl also points out in the *Crisis*, the concept of the lifeworld, as he calls it there, has an importance extending beyond its role in relation to the sciences. Liberated from its close ties with the scientific worldview, it now becomes a "universal problem for philosophy" (Hua 4, 135), one whose "magnitude and difficulty take on enormous proportions." When we reach this point, science as a problem "loses its self-sufficiency and becomes a mere partial problem" within that of understanding the life-world as a whole (Hua 4, 137f).

NOTE

1. The term does not go away. It turns up again in Heidegger's *Sein und Zeit* in the title and the text of his §11, wearing the sort of scare-quotes that designate a commonplace or cliché. But Heidegger does not reject the notion, merely tells us that capturing it is "difficult." (See Heidegger 1957, 50ff.) And the term is passed along in the first pages of the famous preface to Merleau-Ponty's *Phénoménologie de la perception* (1945, 7f.), where it is implicitly attributed to Husserl, equated with "*Lebenswelt*," and identified as the source of "*tout Sein und Zeit*"! In neither Heidegger's nor Merleau-Ponty's text is Avenarius even mentioned, though Heidegger quotes Avenarius in another context. See his *Prolegomena zur Geschichte des Zeitbegriffs* (1979, 225).

REFERENCES

Avenarius, R. 1891. *Der menschliche Weltbegriff*. Leipzig: O. R. Reisland.
Heidegger, M. 1957. *Sein und Zeit*. Tübingen: Max Niemeyer Verlag.
———. 1979. *Prolegomena zur Geschichte des Zeitbegriffs*. Frankfurt: Klostermann.

Husserl, E. 1950. Hua 1. *Cartesianische Meditationen und Pariser Vorträge*, ed. S. Strasser, The Hague, Netherlands: Martinus Nijhoff. In English: *Cartesian Meditations*, trans. D. Cairns. Dordrecht, Boston: Martinus Nijhoff, 1960.

———. 1950. Hua 3. *Ideen zu einer reinen Phänomenologie und phänomenologischen Philosophie I*. Edited by Karl Schuhmann. The Hague: Martinus Nijhoff. Translation: Husserl, E. 1931. *Ideas. General Introduction to Phenomenology*. Translated by B. Gibson. London: Collier Macmillan Publishers.

———. 1952. Hua 4. *Ideen zu einer reinen Phänomenologie und phänomenologischen Philosophie, Zweites Buch: Phänomenologische Untersuchungen zur Konstitution*, ed. Marly Bimel. The Hague: Martinus Nijhoff. In English: *Ideas Pertaining to a Pure Phenomenology and to a Phenomenological Philosophy, Second Book: Studies in the Phenomenological Constitution*, trans. R. Rojcewicz and A. Schuwer. Dordrecht, Boston, London: Kluwer Academic Publishers, 1993.

———. 1954. Hua 6. *Die Krisis der europäischen Wissenschaften und die transzendentale Phänomenologie: Eine Einleitung in die phänomenologischen Philosophie*, ed. W. Biemel. The Hague: Martinus Nijhoff. In English: *The Crisis of European Sciences and Transcendental Phenomenology: An Introduction to Phenomenological Philosophy*, trans. D. Carr. Evanston, IL: Northwestern University, 1988.

———. 1968. Hua 9. *Phänomenologische Psychologie. Vorlesungen Sommersemester 1925*, ed. W. Biemel. The Hague: Martinus Nijhoff.

———. 2006. *The Basic Problems of Phenomenology*. Translated by I. Farin and J. Hart. Dordrecht: Springer.

———. 2008. Hua 39. *Die Lebenswelt: Auslegungen der vorgegebenen Welt und ihrer Konstitution. Texte aus dem Nachlass (1916–1937)*, ed. R. Sowa. Dordrecht: Springer.

Merleau-Ponty, M. 1945. *Phénoménologie de la perception*. Paris: Gallimard.

9 Phenomenological Sources, Kantian Borders

An Outline of Transcendental Philosophy as Object-Guided Philosophy

Sophie Loidolt

INTRODUCTION

Transcendental philosophy, according to Kant, deals with the necessary conditions for the possibility of objects of experience. Since its very beginnings, this question is tied to the relation of mind and world and to the subjective part that is implied in the givenness and intelligibility of objectivity. This means that transcendental reflection is not exhausted by a formal inquiry into *y*s that are necessary conditions for the possibility of *x*s. Its task is to elucidate the old medieval question of the identity of Being and thinking that has deep roots in ancient philosophy. For Kant, *experience* is at the same time the ground of this identity and the only legitimate departing point for an investigation into real conditions of objectivity. Experience is not only the process of friction between mind and world but their common root, in the sense that it is our access to what "mind" and, correlatively, having a coherent world amount to. The important thought is thus that transcendental structures are conditioning forces on both sides: they confine which experiences are possible by confining which worlds are possible, or *coherently conceivable*—which implies a vice versa process. Or, in Kantian language: the condition for the possibility of experience of objects is the condition for the possibility for the objects of experience (Kant 1974, A159/B198). This is to say that the possibility of objectivity coincides with the structure of subjectivity and that a transcendental investigation of experience directly correlates with an investigation of the structure of the objects of experience themselves. Beyond that, the transcendental approach involves the idea that this common root of subjectivity and objectivity in experiencing has a processual character. Transcendental philosophy is thus methodical work and reflection on occurrent experience and the objectivity of its objects, by which it must ascertain their conditions.

In this chapter, I would like to defend these Kantian claims by elaborating them in a phenomenological way. I believe that this kernel of Kant's transcendental thought still offers a convincing way to philosophically conceive of the reality of the objective world without falling into a metaphysical realism that naïvely forgets or consciously neglects that the world is given to us in the first place—and that this subjective givenness has to be taken into account as fundamental or irreducible. The interesting point about transcendental philosophy is that it offers a way to *maintain or sustain the narrow coupling of subjectivity and objectivity as well as the tension between them*—a crucial and indissoluble tension that I am going to take as a positive term for transcendental philosophy in the following. It is a tension that necessarily arises from the antagonistic meanings of subjectivity as making objectivity possible and objectivity as being the manifestation of independence of subjectivity. In Zahavi's rephrasing of Putnam's words: the tension that we don't create the world but don't just mirror it either (cf. Putnam 1978, 1; cf. Zahavi 2003, 72). Transcendental philosophy has to establish its theoretical elements, its methods, and its contents as means to productively preserve this tension and to avoid its dissolution into a subjective idealism on the one or a metaphysical realism on the other hand. Therefore, I conceive of transcendental philosophy as a theory that philosophically elaborates on the subjective accomplishments that are involved in the experience of objectivity, while, at the same time, it holds on to the simplicity of our experience of a world of objects and of the world as objective (i.e., not subjectively created by my experience)—this is what I will call "object-guided" in the following.

This last feature is extremely important for my outline and for my understanding of "the transcendental." I want to argue that Kant's core-thought of simple and basic objectivity linked to subjective conditions of experience is deepened and reinforced in the *phenomenological approach*, even if—or rather because—the transcendental setting is fundamentally transformed. But just as much as there are problems in the Kantian outline (that I will address in the next section) that seriously endanger and compromise his very core-thought of a vice-versa coupling of subjectivity and objectivity in experience, there are also problems in the phenomenological conception of the transcendental (which will be addressed in section 3) that threaten the transcendental tension field: both have to do with *losing touch with* (a) *the simplicity and reality of the object in its very givenness in experience and* (b) *the categoriality of objectivity as first-order transcendentality* (this will be elucidated at the end of section 3 and in section 4). By the word 'simplicity,' I refer to the term '*Schlichtheit*' or '*schlicht*' (simple, plain) that both Husserl and Heidegger use to phenomenologically confirm our everyday experience that every act of perception grasps its object directly or grasps this object itself (cf. Husserl 1970b, 282). "An act of perception grasps *A* as a whole, at one 'blow' and in straightforward fashion" (Husserl 1970b, 287). Or: "In *sense*-perception, the 'external' thing appears 'in one blow,' as soon as our glance falls upon it. The manner in which it makes the thing appear present is *straightforward*: it requires no apparatus of founding or founded acts." And Husserl adds another sentence whose importance will become clear in the course of this chapter: "To what complex mental processes it may trace back its genetic[1] origin, and in what manner, is of course irrelevant here" (Husserl 1970b, 283). According to Husserl, "sensuous objects are present in perception at a *single act level,*" which means that "the object is an *immediately given object* in the sense that, as *this object perceived with this definite objective content*, it is not *constituted* in relational, connective, or otherwise articulated acts, *acts founded on other acts which bring other objects to perception*" (LI II, 282). It is directly apprehended "*in a straight-forward (schlichter) manner*" (LI II, 282). In other words: It is *not experienced to be constructed* in any way. In his lecture-course *History of the Concept of Time,* Heidegger adds to this explanation that the simplicity in the plein perceptual givenness of the object even endures when the object has before been explicated in its features by more complex acts (which Husserl and Heidegger call "categorial acts" or "founded acts"). (Imagine, e.g., that you have analyzed the colored dots of the teacup in front of you thoroughly in their features and arrangement and still see it standing there.) This, says Heidegger, allows us to understand "the objectivity both of simple perception and of founded acts as a unified objectivity." He continues:

> It permits us to see how even simple perception, which is usually called sense perception, is already intrinsically pervaded by categorial intuition. The intentionality of perceptual apprehension is in fact simple and straightforward, but this in itself does not rule out a high degree of complexity in its act-structure" (Heidegger 1985, 60).

And in a passage shortly afterward, he again repeats:

> *Simplicity means the absence of multi-level acts, which institute their unity only subsequently.* This feature of the "simple" therefore refers to a way of apprehending and that means a *feature of intentionality.* As a way of apprehending, such a feature does not rule out the highest degree of complexity in the structure of this perception (as we have already said). Simplicity of perception also does not mean simplicity of the act-structure as such. Conversely, the multi-level character of categorial acts does not exclude the simplicity of these acts. (Heidegger 1985, 61)

This straightforward or simple presence of the object that equals the experience of its nonconstructedness by the mind is a decisive phenomenological feature of its experienced *reality.*[2] Husserl and Heidegger are perceptual realists in this sense, just like Kant is an "empirical realist."

It is important to hold on to this crucial phenomenological feature of realism when pursuing transcendental reflection, as otherwise the tension that narrowly couples subjectivity and objectivity breaks down. Also, it is important to stress that I want to hold on to this realist moment *within* a phenomenological correlative analysis that precisely seeks to grasp the common root of subjectivity and objectivity in the noetic and noematic moments of experiencing. To emphasize the orientation of my proposal, which seeks to revive the Kantian focus on objectivity for transcendental phenomenology, I will call this outline *phenomenological transcendental philosophy as object-guided philosophy (Transzendentalphilosophie vom Gegenstand her)*. By the term 'object-guided,' I mean a *constant orientation along the character of givenness of objectivity and the objective world that is simple and straightforward, even if the analysis of its constitution brings to light a complex structure.* To keep the analysis "object guided" means to attend and do justice—in spite of all the complexity that might show up in the analysis of intentional and genetic structures—to the *phenomenologically given feature* of simplicity and straightforwardness, which, to a large part, accounts for the reality and nonconstructedness of objectivity. If phenomenologists want to hold on to the important claim that the object *as* it appears is the same as the object *that* appears, its direct and immediate givenness as an object (and not as a "mere appearance") that stands in a transcendentally relevant tension with constituting (inter-) subjectivity must remain a guidepost and boundary for their transcendental reflection.

The way I have formulated this first outline of an object-guided transcendental philosophy is already a decidedly phenomenological way that operates with phenomenological terminology and a phenomenological conception of the transcendental (which I will explain in the following, especially in how it differs from the Kantian conception). In the case of Kant's philosophy, simplicity and object guidedness are guaranteed by the two features of *critical limitation* and *objective validity*.[3] Both features will be elaborated and clarified in the coming section as well. They are closely linked to what I have presented as the Kantian transcendental core-thought at the beginning. This core-thought, to repeat it, is the Kantian idea of a common actualization of mind and world in experience that implies necessary transcendental structures that are the "forms" that hold together and open up the intelligibility of mind and world.[4] To go beyond them means to go beyond legitimate claims about objectivity and subjectivity.

In the following, I want to further elucidate this core-thought by taking a look at how it has been pursued but also violated, both in Kant and in phenomenology.[5] My aim is to retrieve this thought for phenomenology and combine it as a complementary principle with the straightforward givenness of objectivity. Thus, I think that a phenomenological elaboration and reformulation of the transcendental approach with this Kantian element is especially promising. As a first step in a larger project, this chapter aims at sketching out a rough methodological outline on the main departing points and prerequisites needed for a phenomenological interpretation of transcendental philosophy as an "object-guided" investigation. I will try to achieve this mainly by an interpretation and critique of Husserl, taking Heidegger's early readings of Husserl into account as complementary comments but also as a second source of phenomenological reflection of the topic. Three main trains of thought will be developed in the text that shall also function as methodic guiding lines for my proposal: first, a comparison between Kant's and Husserl's transcendental approaches with the aim of capturing the main Kantian ideas for an object-guided transcendental philosophy and relocating these ideas in a phenomenological framework (sections 1 and 2). Second, a critique of genetic phenomenology in the light of the tension between subjectivity and objectivity that is to be sustained as an essential element of a transcendental account of mind and world (section 3). Third, a concept of transcendental philosophy as object-guided philosophy that will be established along the lines of an explorative reading of Husserl, Heidegger, and Kant (section 4). My approach will thus simultaneously affirm phenomenology and criticize some of its tendencies in order to defend it as a strong transcendental project and to point out further steps for its development.

1   KANT AND THE SPACE OF VALIDITY

Kant first developed and elaborated the transcendental approach systematically. As a preliminary consideration, I will briefly point to some of the crucial features in Kant's structural composition of his transcendental philosophy, which, partly and rightfully, have been criticized by phenomenologists. In a parallel move, I will try to elaborate what nevertheless constitutes the "object-guided" element and transcendental core-thought in Kant's outline that phenomenology should keep as a guiding line. Both aspects will be elaborated through Heidegger's comments on Kant (and also the neo-Kantians in contrast to Husserl) in the lecture *History of the Concept of Time* from 1925. This shall give us a first orientation of how a phenomenological approach treats these problems before turning to the work of Husserl himself.

Transcendental philosophy can take different forms that correspond to the respective philosophical and methodological framework. This also creates respective problems that are specific for each version of transcendental philosophy. In the case of Kant, one of these problems is the figure of the "thing in itself," which purports that the subject deals with appearances as opposed to the "more real" noumena,[6] which are, somehow, responsible for the sensible affection. By locating it in this setting, the initial idea of the foundation of objectivity and its validity gets corrupted: Kant's actual accomplishment, which is spelled out in the transcendental deduction, is to answer the question concerning the *objective validity* of categorial forms with an investigation on the necessary conditions for objectivity. Categorial forms consequently coincide with the objectivity of the object. Now, this move to link subjectivity to the necessary and only possible form of objectivity (and thus to *real* objectivity) by means of validity is considerably weakened by a thing in itself that still looms behind or beyond this relation, suggesting another inscrutable and transcendent form of objectivity. Phenomenologists, for different reasons, have strongly criticized this double-standard notion of objectivity implied in the idea of a "thing in itself" (cf. Hua 3/1, §43; Heidegger 1977/GA 25, §6b, 99 f). It is a violation to Kant's own transcendental core-thought and his realist intentions, even if there are good reasons for him to introduce it in his system.

Let us therefore not dwell on the thing in itself but focus on the tight connection between subjectivity and objectivity that characterizes Kant's argument on objective validity. Although I consider this to be Kant's main strength, the way he conceptualizes this coupled intersection is also not devoid of difficulties. To point them out, I would like to draw attention to Kant's *structural composition* of the coupling: as I indicated, it is the categorial forms that coincide with the objectivity of the object and thereby establish their validity. These forms, however, that should guarantee for objectivity stem from subjectivity. This creates the picture of a swarm of appearances and a chaotic multitude of affecting stuff (Kant speaks of a "swarm of appearances," "*Gewühl von Erscheinungen*"; Kant 1998/1974, A 111), which is formed into objects only by subjective forms and processes of synthesis—aesthetically, categorially, and schematically. This amounts to another violation of the transcendental core-thought: the autonomy of objectivity is lost as soon as its validity and reality are gained in this way (just like it is lost or weakened by the thing in itself). The problem lurking behind this picture is explicitly named and criticized by Heidegger in *History of the Concept of Time*:

> Sensuousness is characterized as receptivity and understanding as spontaneity (Kant), the sensory as matter and the categorial as form. Accordingly, the spontaneity of understanding becomes the formative principle of a receptive matter, and in one stroke we have the old mythology of an intellect which glues and rigs together the world's matter with its own forms. (Heidegger 1985, 70)

Thus, according to Heidegger, in Kant's transcendental philosophy, the old concept pair of form and matter/stuff is not employed in an ontological/phenomenological context (as it should be), that is, directly located in the object/phenomenon itself. Rather, it has been incorrectly and misleadingly split according to the modern concept pair of the internal realm of subjectivity and the external world of objectivity. Since the internal and external realms are considered to be essentially separate spheres (the spheres of *res cogitans* and *res extensa*), the dominant question of classical epistemology arises how mind and world can get together, respectively how the mind attains to the real world, the true reality. In contradistinction to this outline, Heidegger defines his own position, inspired by Husserl's phenomenology, more precisely:

> The categorial "forms" are not constructs of acts but objects which manifest themselves in these acts. They are not something made by the subject and even less something added to the real objects, such that the

real entity is itself modified by this forming. Rather, they actually present the entity more truly in its "being-in-itself." (Heidegger 1985, 70)

In the next sections, I will explain in detail how phenomenologists establish and defend Heidegger's claim that categorial forms are correlated to categorial intuitions and can thereby be viewed again as belonging to the object, even if their disclosure is dependent on subjective acts (cf. especially section 4). Heidegger's respective talk of "manifestation" already indicates how a phenomenological approach means to dissolve or deconstruct the problem of how mind and world can get together. Phenomenology intends to declare it a pseudo-problem of modernity by means of the concept of *intentionality*. By this concept, as I will show, we can understand that and how we are always already "out there," in the world. Objects are thus not something immanent "in" consciousness but something transcendent. A theory of *internal representation (Bildertheorie)*, as it is not only common in modern-age epistemology but also sometimes falsely assigned to Husserl, is therefore contradictory to the concept of intentionality as well as "counter-sensical" (Husserl 1982, 92; *widersinnig*; Hua 3/1, §43): (1) first, because we would have to step "out" of our minds to find out if the representation of x indeed pictures x. This, of course, is impossible according to the presuppositions: since I can only have x as an internal representation, the real x is out of reach. (2) Second, because representations are not something one is simply bestowed with like sense data. For something to be a conscious representation (a representation I am aware of), *someone has to take it as* a representation, since representations, as any contents or structures of active consciousness, imply an attentive ego; mere "objective" similarity or causal-functional dependency is never enough. And (3) third (this follows from (2)), representation simply is a very different mode than direct presentation: I can only take something as representing something if I am "presented" with anything in the first place (cf. Hua 19/1, 436–440). However, in arguing this way, we have already changed into different, or phenomenological, registers and it is exactly this register change from Kantian to phenomenological transcendental philosophy that I would like to focus on the next section.

Meanwhile, Kant's case could be taken in two directions: on the one hand, one could claim that he is the ultimate internal representationalist, as he explicitly speaks of "representations" (*Vorstellungen*) of the mind and sees representations of objects as objective nature itself. On the other hand—and this, in my opinion, is the correct interpretation—this radical resolution amounts to the dissolution of the mind-world problem and therefore also arrives at the same view as the phenomenologists: namely to take it as a pseudo-problem. Why? Because (composed) experience (*zusammengesetzte Erfahrung*)[7] plainly gives the objectivity of the object, beyond which there is nothing to know and nothing to ask—with respect to knowledge and theoretical philosophy. I hold this thought to be a strength in Kantian philosophy. Because in giving the foundational *critical* impetus the sharpest expression, it upholds most clearly the necessary tension-relation of transcendental thinking: it remains true to the simplicity of experience and neither lets it slip into idealist nor metaphysical realist nor genetic accounts that dissolve the object into subjective activities and passivities. *Critical limitation* and *objective validity* are therefore the two features that stand out against Kant's own violation of the transcendental core-thought. It is true that the "need of reason" (*Bedürfnis der Vernunft*) wants to go beyond experience and its objects—but this is exactly what these two features intend to inhibit.

Heidegger's critique that the Kantian project entails a highly problematic subjectivistic distortion of the ontological matter-form principle (he speaks of "misinterpretation," "traditional exhaustion and impoverished meaning;" Heidegger 1985, 71) arguably hits the structure of the transcendental-philosophical framework but not Kant's transcendental-philosophical core-thought. It does not weaken the thought that the space that is constituted by composed experience is the ultimate *context of validity*—behind, above, beyond, beneath, and below which all further thought-exercise lacks the real ground/basis, namely its basis and grounding in experience. This critical core-thought concerning the *border* of the meaningful[8] I would like to uphold in the following. The task will be to reformulate it in a phenomenological framework.

2   HUSSERL AND THE DEPTH-DIMENSION OF GIVENNESS

I would like to go back now to the change of registers I mentioned earlier and make this more explicit. What does this change of registers amount to in the phenomenological version of transcendental philosophy? What is fundamentally different, what can thereby be accomplished and what not?

Husserl's central concept, and this is made unmistakably clear also by Heidegger in *History of the Concept of Time*, is *intentionality*. By asking the question what givenness and appearing amount to, Husserl fundamentally changes the way in which the question about the condition of the possibility of objects of experience is asked. Intentionality is the structure of givenness itself: a twofold structure of givenness *of* X and givenness *for* S, designating the conscious "thereness" of something for someone. In Heidegger's words: "*a reciprocal belonging together of intentio and intentum*" (Heidegger 1985, 46), which "is a structure of lived experiences as such and not a coordination relative to other realities, something added to the experiences taken as psychic states" (Heidegger 1985, 29). Intentionality is thus an *intrinsic* feature of consciousness (i.e., of *lived experiences*). It does not indicate a relation between two entities (consciousness and object) but designates the special structure of "aboutness" of conscious acts themselves. Through this new insight and departing point, transcendental reflection, which before had to be thought along the lines of a theoretical grasp on the composition of experience, shifts to a totally new picture of a "lived" relation of the correlation of experiencing and the experienced. Or, to put it differently: Kant establishes the transcendental sphere by conceiving the content of experience as a composition of affecting sensible matter (intuitions) and universal categorial form (concepts). Husserl establishes the transcendental sphere by conceiving experience in its intrinsic *intentional* character: this means that experience has the structure of being an experience *of* something (the experienced) *for* someone, which is consciously lived through in the act of experienc*ing*. The content, the experienc*ed*, is thus necessarily correlated to a subjective side of experiencing. By the insight into this structure, Husserl uncovers that the experienced is always given by the "depth dimension" (cf. Hua 6, §32; cf. also Kern 1964, 49, 230) of experienc*ing* (consciousness); that is, this "depth dimension" is disclosed as a condition of the possibility of the experienced. This is why Husserl always stresses that by means of the phenomenological reduction, nothing in experience gets lost; that the reduction is thus not a reductive undertaking but a tracing/leading back to X (*re-ducere*).

By the shifting of this initial transcendental situation, not only do the tasks of a transcendental philosophy change dramatically, but also its methodical evaluation and setup receive thoroughly new traits: the *correlation* now occupies center stage. This is to say that it is the correlation that sustains the strong coupling between subjectivity and objectivity and that builds its joint nucleus. Now, in order for this constellation to be able to be a transcendental philosophy, it has first (1) to be ensured that this undertaking does not just amount to psychology (in the sense of empirical psychology). This can solely be achieved by the eidetic method (by speaking of "givenness of x as such/*überhaupt*," which correlates the "act structure y *überhaupt*") in order to determine *general and necessary* conditions and structures of experience. In a second step (2), it has to be secured that the result is not only eidetic psychology but indeed transcendental phenomenology. Here the notion of *constitution* comes into play.

(1) To begin with, I would like to throw light on the first step and its implications. Husserl regards the "*a priori* of correlation" (*Korrelationsapriori*) as his most shattering and forceful (*erschütternd*) discovery.[9] It shows that intentional correlation is a correlation of eidetic necessity: each object qua object-type is correlated to its mode of consciousness (*Bewusstseinsweise*) qua type of consciousness. For example: a tone is given in a different invariant essential mode of consciousness than a spatio-temporal object or a mathematical insight/formula—would a tone be given in the form of a mathematical insight, it simply would not be a tone anymore. This makes conceivable a completely new sense of "*a priori*" that is not formal but is gained by an intuition into correlative structures of givenness of object-types in experience-types. Also,

this changes how the *a priori* structuring of experience is conceived: while in Kant, experience is always already taken up by the forms of an anonymous subject-structure, in Husserl, experience is always already structured by *a prioris* of correlation through which each object-type is necessarily correlated with its very own mode of consciousness. (Another shift in Husserl is that the realm of objectivity becomes much wider, since experience qua givenness is a much broader conception than just empirical experience: it can be experiences of categorial and logical structures, like in the *Logical Investigations* or experiences of values, like in Husserl's ethics.) Like Kant, Husserl assigns a necessity and generality to the transcendental structures of experience—however, not a purely formal one but an eidetic-correlative one. This new transcendental access via the *a priori* of correlation does not underlie the single experience with a structuring form (in order to found its validity) but transforms the single experience into a type: like we conceive a type when we perceive a single triangle drawn on paper as the geometrical figure. It's not the form "on the one side," which puts the matter/stuff "on the other side" into universal and necessary structures; instead, we have form and matter, as it were, on both sides, doubled in the correlation of act and object (noesis and noema). Necessity now is the necessity of a type-like correlation, not that of a structuring form, directly accessing the swarm-like given matter.

For this new account, a new method is needed that can exhibit and prove (*ausweisen*) this—also—new form of validity. It is new, because the universality and necessity of the forming does now not lie *in itself* qua universal and necessary form, but the universality and necessity of the *eidos* of a certain *a priori* of correlation lies in the *insight* into this relation. Intuitiveness (*Anschaulichkeit*)—that is, living, present (*leibhaftig*) intuitiveness—replaces the core-thought of *formal* justification. One could also say: justification is now turned toward the first-personal aspect, the actual accomplishment of realizing the validity of the valid, instead of precisely relying on the non-subjective third-personal validity of the formal justification—and thus only on one side of the correlation (cf. Hua 17, §8, §§56–61). Here the decisive difference between phenomenologists and logicists breaks open, as Husserl would continue to argue that the nonsubjective formally valid justification can of course *only be given, accessed and actualized subjectively*, that is, in a correlative structure of a certain kind (which is the structure of *evidence*), while philosophers like the early Wittgenstein would consider this to be the transgression beyond the borders of validity. Wittgenstein can only see "psychology" on the subjective side and thus regards it as a "danger" for his own method (Wittgenstein 1984, 4.1121). In contrast, evidence, for Husserl, is "logical origin" (*logischer Ursprung*; Hua 36, 10). By this he insists on the forgotten subjective side of logic that is not a contingent psychological feeling but a necessary transcendental structure of givenness: givenness of the evident (Hua 17, §56, §82 ff., §82 ff). This is what his whole transcendental logic, which primarily intends to be "noetic validity theory" (*noetische Rechtslehre*), revolves around.

It has often been noted and criticized that to speak of insight, evidence, or intuition as the "last source of validity" (*letzte Rechtsquelle*; cf. Hua 3/1, §24; Hua 17, §59–61) reminds of the Platonic terminology of intuition or "vision" (*Schau*). However, instead of a real return to Plato,[10] I would rather regard this terminology as the consequence of understanding the transcendental on the grounds of givenness and thus relocating the transcendental center in the correlation: How, for example, the givenness of a melody correlates with a certain time-structure of consciousness cannot be found out by formal or logical reasoning on generality and necessity alone but has to rely on a certain "insight" into this conditional structure determined by *content* and not only form. This neither means that this insight is infallible nor that intersubjectivity doesn't play a decisive role in validating it. It only claims that intuition of or insight into eidetic structures is needed as much in philosophy as it is needed, for example, in geometry (nobody ever empirically sees "the triangle" and its geometric relations).

Another question that could be raised is whether Husserl doesn't also emphasize one side too strongly, namely the subjective side of the correlation. Does the demonstration of validity (*Geltungsausweisung*) thereby become "too" subjective, that is arbitrary, contingent, psychological? Phenomenology's and especially Husserl's answer is a definite "no." Since evidence only correlates to the evident, both elements are strictly bound together without losing the transcendental tension. The strictness of Husserl's method demands that it must always be an *actualized* evidence, an evidence in the course of its original accomplishment (not a remembered, retained one). Only in the actual sustaining of evidence there is the evident. Evidence is thus not a feeling that adds to anything but is plain givenness of the evident (Hua 3/1, 46; Hua 17, 286, 289 f; Hua 18, 183–185).[11]

Yet there is a tendency for the subjective element of insight to be to the fore and there is also a reason. It concerns Husserl's conception of a transcendental-phenomenological idealism that leads us to a transition to the second step (2) mentioned above. The intentional manifests itself only "in" consciousness that, correctly speaking, does not have an "outside" any more and is, in this sense, the absolute sphere (Hua 3/1, §44; Hua 36). Or, to put it differently: *the intentional only manifests itself as an awareness of x.* The actually accomplished being-true and being-valid have to be related to this depth dimension of consciousness; but they should not be conceived as immersed in it. Otherwise, the correlation would not be kept up and the objective side would indeed be merged into the subjective side. This, however, is a position Husserl always opposed: the objectively present *is* the real world and cannot be dissolved into elements of consciousness like sensations. Very much to the contrary, Husserl sees a "true gap" between the two kinds of being: being as consciousness and being as reality. Reality appears and *presents itself* as a certain form of consciousness, but as radical transcendence[12] it is not dissolvable in(to) consciousness (Hua 3/1, §42, §49; Hua 36, 28 f, 106). This presence of the real as transcendence and nondissolvability is given to us *as meaning/sense (Sinn)*. Its presence is a *meaningful presence that manifests itself as a certain structure of consciousness (als Bewusstseinszusammenhang)*. Consequently, justification (*Ausweisung*) of the evident as evident, as intended and itself present, is also only possible through and as meaning. Only through intending and positing consciousness (*meinendes Bewusstsein*) is validity attained as a fulfilled intuitive consciousness of this positing. On a wider scale, this implies that the *correlation is thus nothing else but the opening-up or disclosedness of meaning*. This "space of meaning" (Crowell 2001) has often been regarded as the actual achievement of phenomenology (and enjoys a much more lively continuation by the following generations of phenomenologists than, e.g., Husserl's eidetic project). What is decisive about it is that givenness that is not only conceived of as correlation but as the transcendental *Urboden* and methodological starting point opens up a space of meaning from the very beginning—and doesn't have to be constructed but only understood in the right way (cf. Hua 6, 193).

Thus, the theoretical picture employed is not a subject (or subject-structure) that judges as opposite an entirely unintelligible, blind compilation of matter (or sense-data) and thereby "makes" the latter intelligible. Rather, it is a subject that has a world (or is in a world), which is *an intelligible world from the very beginning,* which is a or *the* horizon of meaning.[13] In principle, Kant precisely recognized the necessity of this *Ur*-intelligibility of the world and has given it expression in his outline that the world (qua nature) is only accessible as conceptually interwoven experience. (This, certainly, is also the point that John McDowell stresses in his reading of Kant in *Mind and World*, 1996.) But here also lies the big difference: what Kant wants to attain by "conceptual interwovenness," originating in the subject, acquires a completely new articulation and setup in phenomenology through the concept of intentionality—a setup that radicalizes some of Kant's ideas and avoids the pitfalls of the epistemological paradigms of the modern age (like the subject-object divide). As Heidegger makes clear, it is by this concept of intentionality that it has become possible to meaningfully unite and ground *Kant's transcendental philosophy and ontology as phenomenology* (Heidegger 1985, 71).[14] The phenomenological approach can thus be regarded as a strongly modified but successful continuation of the Kantian core-thought of object-guided transcendental philosophy, which does not fall prey to the Kantian violations that weakened the transcendental tension. First, because the objective side keeps its dignity: this side is not merely being constructed by subjective forms as the shift to the paradigm of "correlation" has made clear; the subjective side merely enables the object to appear and be recognized *as itself* (in the sense of correlatively manifesting itself in consciousness as such and such).[15] Second, because the transcendental approach is not abandoned, or the idea that the condition of the possibility of objectivity lies in subjectivity. This rightfully creates a field of tension in the sense that subject-relative objective (i.e., subject-independent) givenness does not flip into a naïve ontology that would go without the dimension of givenness. By pointing out these two antagonist elements, I want to emphasize that in this initial situation of a phenomenological approach to transcendental philosophy, both sides of conditioning subjectivity and objectivity are conceptualized strong enough to sustain the necessary tension needed in a transcendental outline. My idea to reintroduce an object-guided element, that is, attention to the straightforwardness of objective givenness, within this setup, reacts to tendencies in phenomenology that have weakened this initial conception.

(2) In the last paragraphs, I have already been moving deep into the transcendental realm. In fact, I have made the step from eidetic psychology to transcendental phenomenology from the very beginning. According to Husserl, this step is just a change of perspective anyway, a "decisive nuance" (Hua 24, 211). It makes explicit what it means that "givenness" is taken as "the condition for the possibility." Consciousness is no longer regarded as an object in the world but as the place of the appearance of the world. This, in short, can be described as the "transcendental reduction." One concept that is paradigmatic for this change of perspective but still and repeatedly causes problems is the concept of *constitution*. This is so because it can mislead into regarding the objective again as quasi "subjectively produced" and thus relinquishes the object-side of the tension. What I have in mind here is not any stark misinterpretation of Husserl's notion of constitution but the kernel of truth that lies in them (after all, even Eugen Fink has associated the notion of constitution explicitly and with Husserl's approval to the notion of "production;" cf. Fink 1959, 227 f; 1966, 143; Strasser 1976, 170).

This leads me to my critique of some tendencies in phenomenology that ease the transcendental coupling force I would like to emphasize. It is not meant as a critique of the concept of constitution as such, as "constitution" can also be conceived as the explicitly disclosing moment in the correlation. Heidegger does this very aptly in his interpretation of Husserl's phenomenology: "'*Constituting*' does not mean producing in the sense of making and fabricating; it means *letting the entity be seen in its objectivity*" (Heidegger 1985, 71). Constitution, if rightly conceived, is thus not the problematic point for an object-guided transcendental philosophy. Rather, the related and quite necessary idea of "layers of constitution" (time-consciousness, basic association, and affection as prerequisite accomplishments in order to constitute the objectivity of objects) tempts one to *leave the realm of simple and straightforward objective experience* (like, e.g., just perceiving a table with a lamp on it in front of me). Instead of taking the latter as a departing *and aiming* point of a genetic reflection (which is a reflection precisely on "layers of constitution"), it can develop a momentum of its own that dissolves the "objective" into the "genetic." Here lies a danger that is located on the very opposite side of Kant's problematic thought of a thing in itself and thus a "more real" object outside the correlation. But the danger on the phenomenological side just as much relinquishes the transcendental tension.

This happens by suggesting a "more real" origin of the simply experienced in the diversification into its historicity down to the deepest levels of constitution: from passive meaning-sedimentations through time-consciousness up to whole cultural processes of meaning-production and-sedimentation in history.

Both the Kantian and the phenomenological conception thus have their tempting intuitions and also good reasons for them—but both pose a problem for the transcendental core-thought. To at least see this problem is a first step toward an object-guided transcendental philosophy. Although it is clear that the correlative structure is not a simple "mirroring" (to recall the Putnam quotation I gave at the beginning) and that consciousness has to be investigated with regard to its basic systems of constitution and, again, their constitution, it is important not to lose sight of what sort of experience allowed for such an inquiry from the very beginning. Even if we can concede that some systems of constitution (like time-consciousness) are indeed generated or "created" by consciousness and even if there indeed is a historicity of systems of constitution, it will never be possible to create a coherent world-experience if nothing coherently correlates to these systems (which is, somehow, also the condition for the possibility of historicity). Thus, it is crucial not to *substitute* the genetic investigation for the stable experience that allowed for it from the outset. In the next paragraph, I would like to show that this tendency holds both for strongly "idealist" positions like Husserl's as well as for his followers who rejected the idea that consciousness has a sort of "supremacy" with regard to constitution.[16]

3   SOME CRITICAL REMARKS ON GENETIC PHENOMENOLOGY IN THE LIGHT OF AN OBJECT-GUIDED TRANSCENDENTAL PHILOSOPHY

Many phenomenologists like Heidegger, the later Merleau-Ponty, Patočka, Lévinas, and others have refused to accept Husserl's steadfast thesis that meaning is autonomously produced by a meaning-giving consciousness (*Sinn setzt sinngebendes Bewusstsein voraus*).[17] One could understand this refusal in the context of the transcendental-philosophical core-thought of "tension" I mentioned at the beginning. Meaning, one could argue, is not given (in the sense of sovereignly bestowed upon), meaning is *experienced, it happens*, and sometimes it even *befalls* us (*erfahren und widerfahren*). However, Husserl's successors who have followed this way of critique share one crucial theoretical trait or philosophical conviction with him, which, like him, and in spite of it all, continuously leads them out of the tension between the subjective and the objective—a tension that can only consist and persist in the ongoing experience of the objective: they all dissolve this tension into a genesis or a genetic account of the one or the other side. In the notion of constitution, the notion of its own archaeology constantly seems to call for an elaboration, be it understood as "production" or as "befallenness" (*Widerfahrnis*): as "I constitute" or as "I am constituted" or as "it constitutes."

This is also due to the following setting: the transcendental in Husserl is the *productive*. It is the creating and accomplishing life (*schöpfendes und leistendes Leben*). In contrast to Kant, for whom the necessary stability of objective experience is at stake and who thus looks for a stable subject-*structure*, Husserl, from the very beginning, conceives of a version of transcendental philosophy that suggests a much more productive and dynamic picture. This tendency increases the more he dedicates himself to his genetic investigations. What Husserl shares with his followers like Maurice Merleau-Ponty or Marc Richir is this version of the productive, dynamic, and genetic, out of which forms emerge, as it were, like out of the fluid, out of the anonymously stream-like. Instead of forms that are always already there to make our thinking and perceiving possible, we can "watch" and describe these forms emerging as if we could watch the "primordial soup" ("watching" in quotation marks here means that this is not a real lived experience but rather something like an inner theater of the mind when engaging in constructive genetic analyses that Husserl also calls *Aufbau- und Abbauanalyse*).

My point of critique on behalf of an object-guided transcendental philosophy thus does not lie on the often and heavily criticized "egologic" of constitution, which ultimately, and in spite of all transcendental and historistic intersubjectivity, for Husserl does take place in the realm of an "*Ur-Ich*" (I believe that, correctly understood, this causes no contradiction). Viewed from the transcendental-philosophical perspective I would like to establish, I regard it as much more crucial that in both, in the egologic and the non-egologic[18] version of a transcendental philosophy, which regards the transcendental as the productive, the objectivity of the object is in danger of getting lost or simply of getting out of sight. Why, or how? Just like Husserl genetically traces back transcendental subjectivity to the very basic structures like *Urzeitigung, Urpassivität, Urassoziation*, vice versa the objective space of meaning is dissolved into "savage meaning" (Merleau-Ponty)[19] or the "Apeiron" (Richir)[20]—beyond subjectivity and objectivity.

Far from designating this move or its theoretical figures in any way as "wrong," in my opinion it seems to disregard and undermine the rigor of the transcendental core-thought and the *border* it reveals: If structures are transcendental, then they constitute the condition of the possibility of how we can think about them and what we can say about them, too. We can make these structures visible and conceivable by transcendental reflection but cannot transgress them—otherwise they would not be transcendental anymore. That is: we *can* transgress them in speculative reflection that is reason's desire all the time, but we lose our legitimate grounds when doing so. In this sense, transcendental reflection is always reflection on sources *and* borders: the sources of subjective accomplishments in the givenness of objectivity and the borders that come into sight when the structures enabling objectivity are discovered. Everything beyond these structures loses its grip on objectivity and leaves the common root of lived experience that alone guarantees for a common actualization of subjectivity and objectivity, of mind and world. In the introduction and the section on Kant I underlined his critical core-thought concerning the border of the meaningful and pointed to the argument on objective validity, by which Kant links subjectivity and objectivity (on the criticizable basis of universal forms originated in the subject) and at the same time shows that these transcendental structures are conditions for a subject's objective experience. Kant's idea is to inquire into the conditions of how it is possible that we conceive a coherent world by asking what are the conditions of coherency and objectivity as such. Thus, the discovered transcendental structures are structures of *validity* of and warrant for *real* objectivity. At the same time they are structures of legitimacy concerning theoretical reflection on the mind-world-relation, since subjectivity and objectivity are held together in the actualization of these structures.

To retrieve this thought of a border of the meaningful implied in transcendental reflection for phenomenology, one would have to appeal to the phenomenological dedication to the *things themselves*. It is the lifeworld to which our actual experience (with all its spontaneity) is bound to as a ground. A reflection on its dynamic sources is useful for making genetic layers visible to the extent that they still correspond to this lifeworldly experience. Such a reflection on dynamic sources must not forget, however, that its outcomes are dependent on and themselves do not lack a certain regularity without which experience would simply dissolve into some confusing awareness. I am not against genetic inquiries *tout court*. I just think they should remain oriented along the main features of the "outcome" of these processes, because this is what they actually *have to* start with—it is the very lifeworldly transcendental condition of genetic reflections. When they become standalone, or rather free-floating theories, they lose this narrow coupling with the world and, from a phenomenological point of view (referring to "originary intuition" as its principle of all principles), also confer certain methodological problems upon themselves.

It seems that genetic approaches have been regarded as much more "interesting" in the last decades than investigations into categorial forms, as the former seem to reveal a fluid and vibrant source of the latter. The price that is paid for this disregard or conscious neglect is that newer and contemporary phenomenology has a lot to say about the event, about creative processes, about surplus, befallenness, and ruptures, but less about that which is ruptured: the *constantly experienced simple objectivity and intelligibility of objects*, the—regarding the genetic accounts—astonishing stability of the world and the possibility of its categorial and scientific ascertainment. (Since many phenomenologists reject Husserl's eidetic project that includes an *a priori* of the lifeworld, I am not sure this problem is considered to have already been "solved" by Husserl's own investigations.) The desire or need to descend to the deepest depths of a *sense se faisant* (a self-building meaning), as interesting and exciting it can be, at times leads far beyond actual and everyday experience—and in this sense is a phenomenological parallel to transgressing and violating the transcendental border of validity and meaning Kant has established.

Husserl's genetic phenomenology never became a free-floating project and its problem is also not that his genetic phenomenology becomes completely detached from static phenomenology (this is a more technical way of expressing how the transcendental border is transgressed and the tension between subjectivity and objectivity is lost).[21] But Husserl has another problem with transgressing the features of direct givenness (and thus the transcendental border), which, apart from losing grip on straightforward and everyday experience, is also characteristic for genetic approaches, namely when confronted with the categorial (I dubbed this feature (b) in the introduction): the price Husserl had to pay—ironically and tragically for someone who cared so much about logic—is that he cannot explain anything other with his "genesis of logic" in *Experience and Judgment* than that which Heidegger already appraisingly highlights about the "categorial acts" in the *Logical Investigations*:

> Categorial acts are founded acts; in other words, everything categorial ultimately rests upon sense intuition. [. . .] It does not say that the categories ultimately can be interpreted as sensory. Rather, 'resting' here means that they are founded. (Heidegger 1985, 69)

Husserl cannot elucidate anything *more* with his genetic model in 1935 than with the *Logical Investigations* in 1900, since the decisive work of transforming the prepredicative into ideal, universal, repeatable forms is still done by *spontaneity*—and this work of spontaneity still remains an enigma (i.e., spontaneity is not explained any better or clearer than in Kant). The categorial is thus still *founded* on something (which is carefully explained in its origin in experience), but the leap between the sensory and the categorial, taking place in the very unity of the experienced object, still is of the same quality. Instead, and with bad consequences, the identity of the prepredicative and the predicative gets split up through the genetic account, because the given is not categorial from the outset, but its categoriality is explained as a process. The ideal, therefore, seems likely to have been created in a psychological process—certainly contrary to Husserl's own intentions. What, according to Heidegger, in *Logical Investigations* is merely "accentuated" or "drawn out" (*gehoben wird*) *from the experienced object itself* as the categorial (Heidegger 1985, 63) in *Experiment and Judgment* seems to be the *subjectively accomplished product* of a complicated *process*—which, in the end, does not hold anything much surprising, since it only *reconstructs* the logical forms in a sensible way. So, if we accuse Kant of *constructing* experience (an accusation often made by phenomenologists), I would say that Husserl's genesis of logic is no less constructed, or better, *reconstructive,* especially as everything runs toward an already fixed outcome: the logical forms and forms of predication. Equally, the simplicity of perception, which Heidegger also praises in *History of the Concept of Time* as one of the achievements of Husserl's phenomenology, gets lost in the genetic account. In simple perception, the object is just there all at once (*mit einem Schlag*)—and not in its genetic layers.

Thus, on the one hand, in genetic phenomenology this simplicity, which is in fact the driving force of the transcendental tension, is neglected (feature (a) in the introduction); on the other hand, ideality and categoriality do not become any clearer by having a "transcendental history" or a structure in layers (feature (b) in the introduction). It seems puzzling, but what in fact happens when constituting structures (i.e., transcendental structures) are again questioned with respect to their transcendental conditions, which is the goal of a genetic phenomenological reflection, then original straight-forwardness and categoriality get softened. The reason for this seems to be the transgression of a transcendental border that genetic phenomenology ignores in its transcendental hyperreflexivity on the structural genesis of structures of constitution (cf. footnote 21). To avoid any misunderstandings, it has to be noted that genetic phenomenology is always a transcendental and not an empirical or psychological project. It seems that the differences between such outlines become easily blurred and ambivalent, precisely when straightforwardness and categoriality lose their first-order transcendentality.

It is therefore not astonishing that subsequent phenomenological outlines do not continue this project of a *genesis of the categorial* but instead focus on that which *interrupts* these tendencies toward concordance or harmony (*Einstimmigkeitstendenzen*).[22] Certainly, this is an interesting question to ask. However, it still cannot explain the categorial and its "surplus"[23] with regard to a mere tendency to concordance—just like the surplus of rigorous universality cannot be explained by comparative universality. Thus, be the focus on an accomplishing, constituting consciousness or on a self-constituting meaning, for a transcendental-philosophical project it seems crucial to me to remain with the *simplicity of experience in all its intelligibility* (point (a) and (b) together).

It should be clear that a phenomenological account of these questions does not simply "leave everything as it is," to paraphrase Wittgenstein, but seeks explication in the description and clarification of intentional structures of how the world is given to us. Since Heidegger elaborates on these topics convincingly with Husserl in *History of the Concept of Time* (in the course of following his ontological project), I will now shortly turn toward Heidegger's interpretation in the last section of this chapter. His considerations will help us sketch out a first draft of what are the important guidelines for a phenomenology conceived of as object-guided transcendental philosophy. Additionally, we can identify the strands in phenomenology which are already there to be further elaborated in this direction.

4 HEIDEGGER READS HUSSERL: CATEGORIAL INTUITION

In his illuminating analysis of categorial intuition (1985, 47–72), Heidegger speaks of the "full objectivity of the simply experienced entity" (Heidegger 1985, 66; "*volle Objektivität des schlicht erfahrenen Seienden;*" GA 20, 89). By "full objectivity" he means that even relations of states of affairs are comprised in objectivity. Heidegger takes the examples of simple perceptions of a yellow (upholstered) chair and "two platelets of different hues" (Heidegger 1985, 65), a and b (this is what the following predications "is yellow" and "being brighter" refer to). I will quote a longer passage in order to make Heidegger's style of analysis accessible:

> In the simple perception of an entity, the perceived entity itself is first there simply [in "onefold," as it were] without complication. This simplicity means that the real parts and moments included in it do not stand out in relief. But inasmuch as they are present in the unity of the whole object which is apprehended simply, they can also be brought out explicitly. This bringing into relief takes place in new and special acts of explication. Consider, for example, the simple accentuation of the q, of the "yellow" in the perceived chair, in the S, that is, in the whole of the subject matter perceived as a unity. Simply drawing out the color as a specific property in the chair first makes the q, the "yellow," present as a moment, [that is, in a form] which was not present before in the simple perception of the thing. Accentuating q as something which is in S however also involves accentuating S as a whole containing the q within itself. [. . .] In other words, the being-yellow of the chair, the previously unarticulated subject matter, now becomes visible through the articulation, through the arrangement which we call the state of affairs. However, even though this accentuation of the state of affairs is grounded in the perceived subject matter, it cannot be said that the state of affairs itself, the composition brought out in the subject matter, is a real part or portion of this matter. The being-yellow of the chair, this state of affairs as such, is not a real moment in the chair like the arms or the upholstery. This state of affairs is [. . .] of an ideal nature. The chair does not contain its being-yellow as a real property. What is real is the yellow, and in the state of affairs only the quality is accentuated as something real, objective. (Heidegger 1985, 63).

Equally, relations of states of affairs are *ideal* relations. For example, they accentuate the "being brighter" of one object in relation to another in a predication. This "being brighter" is not to be found in one chair or between the two chairs that are compared, thus it is not a real feature that would be individuated by its location in time and space, but an ideal feature that can be individuated by several real entities (like the "being-yellow"). What is crucial now (this is also what Heidegger emphasizes) is that the ideality of the relation of states of affairs in no way implies that it would therefore be "not objective or even the least bit less objective than what is given as real" (Heidegger 1985, 66). This means that the ideality of the state of affairs that has been drawn from the simply experienced object belongs to the "full objectivity" of the simply experienced entity. Thus, objectivity does not exhaust itself in reality. It is not reducible to real features like the yellow of the chair but also includes its being-yellow and its being-brighter than the other chair. The ideal or categorial is therefore not added to the real from outside like a new structure—for example, by a subject that possesses language—but intrinsically belongs to its objectivity. The question is only how these deeper dimensions of objectivity that go beyond real features are present. "Brighter-than is already there at the ground level of perception as a content of the real subject matter [. . .]. Being-brighter-than, however, is accessible only in a new act, namely, in the first founded act of predicative relating" (Heidegger 1985, 66).

I regard this insight as extremely important for a phenomenologically object-guided transcendental philosophy and would like to build on it in the following. This is exactly why, however, I would like to point out a certain *oscillating* of Heidegger's account between the object as "given" (*gegeben*) and the object as "thought" (*gedacht*; as this also happens in Kant).[24] After all, the crucial point lies in the question what "accentuating" (*heben*) and "being comprised in" (*beschlossen sein in*) *really means*. If Heidegger says, "In this accentuation, we have a form of more authentic objectification of the given matter" (Heidegger 1985, 63; "*Wir haben in der Hebung der Sachverhalts-Beziehung eine Weise eigentlicherer* [!] *Vergegenständlichung der vorgegebenen Sache*" GA 20, 86), then one can ask oneself which kind of "object" we had before. Because, at bottom, to speak of a "full objectivity of the simply experienced entity" (Heidegger 1985, 66) contains a sort of contradiction. In the simply experienced entity, everything is indeed somehow there, but the full objectivity is not yet "*gehoben*" (accentuated, disclosed). Nevertheless, everything is "already there": "Drawing out the state of affairs thus transforms nothing in the given matter; nothing happens to the chair and its simply given reality" (Heidegger 1985, 63). But what does this exactly mean that "brighter-than" is already there and "being-brighter-than" is not? The solution of this difficulty seems to lie in the idea of "expression": the object "becomes expressly visible precisely in what it is [. . .] through this new objectivity of the accentuated state of affairs" (Heidegger 1985, 63).

What, then, is the nonexplicitness (*Unausdrücklichkeit*) in pregivenness (*Vorgegebenheit*)? Is it just mute? Can one not, instead of expressing it as a state of affairs, address it in a transcendental reflection, precisely *as an inexplicit transcendental form* (nota bene: what I want to address here is the objectivity of objects, not something specific like "brighter than")? What I want to defend is a basic and crucial intelligibility of the object that is there in its very simple appearance and that—admittedly—can only be addressed after the fact in a transcendental reflection. All of this is anticipated in Husserl and Heidegger. However, there are two constricting tendencies or issues:

(1) First: Although the early Heidegger seems to be interested in such an object-oriented (object-guided) categorial work, his interest decreases on his way to *Being and Time*. The focus is "existentialia" (*Existenzialien*), which are supposed to be categories for a being like "*Dasein*" in contrast to "*Vorhandensein*." However, for the later Heidegger, these existentialia again seem to be too subject oriented. He turns away from the "subjective side" of *Dasein*. Yet what he focuses on in his later work is rather the opening or disclosedness of the space of meaning as such (and how thinking can be "aware" of it and "respond" to it) and not the appearing objects and their intelligibility. Certainly, this is a possible and important direction to take. It does not, however, justify the denigration of epistemological questions Heidegger's approach openly entails. The intelligibility of objects has to remain object oriented, as neither a hermeneutic account of existence nor a history of Being can explain what objectivity in its meaning as being independent from subjectivity is about and how our constitution of objects can be a valid constitution of reality.

(2) Second: It seems more appropriate to me to address transcendental forms, which are equal to the intelligibility of the objectivity of objects, in their nonobjectifiability and nonexpressivity/nonexpressiveness. Transcendental reflection is not supposed to lead to predication (S *is* p) but to highlight the necessarily employed forms *for* predication; it is also not supposed to lead to expression as its end. Of course, it *is* an expression in a certain sense, but it should make sure that that which is expressed by it points back to its originary nonobjectivity (*Nicht-Gegenständlichkeit*). Closely following Husserl, Heidegger writes that "'Allness,' 'and,' 'but' . . . [are nothing like consciousness, nothing psychic, but] a special kind of objectivity" (Heidegger 1985, 59). This is what they are *in predication* and/or in categorial intuition that makes them explicit. *Yet as transcendental forms, they are originarily not objects but make objects intelligible.* Thus, in the form of an object or "in expression," as a predication, and the like, transcendental forms are somehow deformed. With this thought, I go back to Kant's conception of transcendental forms being always already in play in an unarticulated way, but without the component of locating their origin in the subject: form is not equal to that which originates in the subject; instead, it is the transcendental root that *is* the intelligibility of the object, *its givenness as being intelligible.*

With this outline, I do not mean to follow the theoretical approach against which Heidegger forcefully argues and that is his real opponent in the quoted lectures: a Rickert-like, neo-Kantian scaffolding of validity (*Geltungsgerüst*) lacking in content, and determining, quasi-"clinically," what objectivity (and its validity) would amount to. If this structure is, "in the worst of all cases," understood as originated in subjectivity to form a formless, swarm-like matter (*Gewühl*) and thus "a picture of the world"

(Heidegger 1985, 71), we arrive, according to Heidegger, at the utter misapprehension of modernity. This, however, is not my intention when trying to develop and restrengthen a phenomenological version of an object-guided transcendental philosophy. What I would like to argue for in turn is that one cannot speak about '*Sachhaltigkeit*' ("the content of a subject matter;" Heidegger 1985, 71)—the term by which Heidegger wants to replace the term 'matter'—without being untrue to the transcendental claim that demands that we can only speak about "things themselves," "Sachhaltigkeit," "sensible intuitions" (*sinnliche Anschauungen*), "simple givenness" (*schlichte Gegebenheiten*), and so forth, *if certain structures are at work that make objects intelligible in the first place by showing themselves in the correlation.*

Toward a "phenomenological object-guided transcendental philosophy," I would thus first (i) link the dimensions of being given and being thought (*Gegebenheits- und Gedachtheitsdimension*) closer and more unambiguously to one another than is the case in Heidegger, who still oscillates between them. In the dimension of being given, being thought has to be implied in a way that resists a reification of the forms that make objects and the world intelligible to us. The "always already" has to be captured as the common root of the coherence of objectivity/world and consciousness/Dasein.

Second (ii), I would like to link the dimensions of givenness and validity (*Gegebenheits- und Geltungsdimension*). The crucial difference in the understanding of the transcendental dimension between Kant and phenomenology is that for Kant it is primarily the (objective-)*validity-founding dimension* (in the scheme of affecting matter, swarm-like affections, and subject-originated form) and for Husserl, it is primarily the *dimension of givenness*. (Heidegger develops this further as the dimension of openness and disclosedness he interprets as the structure or *Seinsweise* of Dasein). Both of these dimensions, *validity and givenness*, have to be closely reconnected in order to arrive at a new object-guided, phenomenological transcendental philosophy. As I have emphasized, many of the components and prerequisites are already there in Husserl's and Heidegger's phenomenological outlines from which this object-guided orientation must be revived. On the one hand, this will involve a careful critique of genetic phenomenology that must show its borders and inherent problems. On the other hand, it will also be important to hold onto Husserl's vital "subjective" element. Given all the deconstruction of the "ego" and the "subject," Husserl's insight should not be forgotten, that is, the insight that there is only a "space of meaning" if there is some dimension of "awareness"—one does not have to accept the stronger formulation given in terms of meaning-bestowing consciousness (*ein Gewahrendes statt ein sinngebendes Bewusstsein*). This core character of "awareness" (*Gewahren*), be it ego-like or anonymous, eventually *is* the crucial feature of what Husserl calls "consciousness." It is not only the essential (*wesentlich*) but the founding (*wesensbildend*) element of phenomenology.

Therefore, the Kantian transcendental-phenomenological core-thought of *borders* of meaning (or "bounds of sense") must be reintegrated in the form of *tension fields* within a phenomenological outline that, at the same time, remains faithful to its depth dimension of "awareness/consciousness." This could be successfully achieved in the following way: despite Husserl's idealism, which regards consciousness as the "source of the world,"[25] there are three strong tensions that keep phenomenology not only "realist"[26] but also dedicated to the strong coupling of consciousness and world/subjectivity and objectivity. The first and strongest tension I have already mentioned at the beginning is that the meaning of objectivity, which manifests itself in consciousness alone, designates nothing else but *to be independent of consciousness*. Another strong tension (on another level) is the irreducible plurality of constituters that can manifest itself again only in an *Ur-Ich*. Finally, the third tension is that between transcendental, constituting subjectivity and empirical, constituted subjectivity (cf. Hua 6, §§53–55). These tensions are to be *sustained* in experience without resolving them into a genetic historicity. Thereby, the project of an "object-guided transcendental philosophy" wishes to hold on to the openness of reality, including its contingency; but also to its stability and simplicity that is defended against its genetic dissolution.

NOTES

1. Translation modified at this point. In German Husserl says, "Aus welchen und aus wie komplizierten psychischen Prozessen sie genetisch entstanden sein mag, ist hierfür natürlich ohne Belang" (Hua 19/2, 676).
2. "This characteristic manner of apprehension in sense perception and its single-level character also permit a definition of the *real* object. This definition, which certainly has its limits, is first derived strictly within this analysis of perception and its object. For Husserl, this sense of the 'real' signifies the most original sense of reality: a real object is by definition a possible object of a simple perception" (Heidegger 1985, 61). In Husserl's own words: "If we may presume to have cleared up the sense of the concept of a *straightforward* percept, or, what we take for the same, of sense-perception, then we have also cleared up the concept of a *sensible* or *real object* (in the most basic sense of 'real'). We define a real object as the possible object of a straightforward percept" (Husserl 1970b, 285).
3. I also take it that the transcendental core-thought I want to restrengthen for phenomenology has inspired philosophers across different philosophical approaches and has therefore received different articulations (examples would be the early Wittgenstein and Strawson, whose approaches I won't pursue here).
4. Employing this wide definition intends to capture the transcendental trait in very different philosophical approaches: transcendental structures that enable objectivity can be pure concepts like in Kant (1998) or logical forms like in the early Wittgenstein (1984), or language like in Strawson (2007) or McDowell (1996). Concerning my specific outline of transcendentality, my use of the concept of "subjectivity" (e.g., in the sentence "the possibility of objectivity coincides with the structure of subjectivity") implies "*intersubjectivity*" since for a Husserlian outline this understanding is crucial for transcendental structures (cf. Zahavi 2003, 109–125).

5. I am not pursuing the reasons for these violations in this chapter, but one central one might be the difficulty to hold on to the tension-relation and the "desire of reason" to overcome the tension.

6. Certainly, Kant emphasizes that appearances are not mere appearances in the sense of "mere illusions" (Kant 1998, B 70). But as soon as he opposes them to things in themselves, this impression is again fortified: "In fact, if we view the objects of the senses as mere appearances, as is fitting [!], then we thereby admit at the very same time that a thing in itself underlies them, although we are not acquainted with this thing as it may be constituted in itself, but only with its appearance, i.e., with the way in which our senses are affected by this unknown something" (Kant 1997, §32, 66).

7. I do not want to oppose Kant's concept of composed experience to what I have elaborated on above as the simplicity and straightforwardness of objective experience in phenomenology. Composed experience is something else than founded acts and something else than genetic transcendental structures, and both methodological conceptions of transcendental philosophy are so different that it would be wrong to see a direct opposition here (cf. section 2). Rather, I would argue that Kant manages to analogously uphold what phenomenologists grasp as simplicity by his critical limitation. Moreover, conceptually interwoven experience involves a certain simplicity of intelligibility, as I will point out later. The problem is therefore not the composedness of experience as such but how this can still guarantee for an autonomous and nonconstructed objective side.

8. Peter Strawson (2007) has articulated this thought within the frame of language philosophy in *The Bounds of Sense* from 1966. Apart from this inspiration, it is also one main idea from Wittgenstein's *Tractatus* (1984) that serves as a guiding line for an object-guided transcendental philosophy: Wittgenstein's "fundamental idea" that "logical constants do not represent" (4.0312) amounts to the same thesis expressed in section four of this chapter: that transcendental forms are originarily not objects but make objects intelligible in a pre-expressive way.

9. Husserl writes in a footnote in the *Crisis* (Hua 6): "The first breakthrough of this universal a priori of correlation between experienced object and manners of givenness (which occurred during work on my Logical Investigations around 1898) affected me so deeply that my whole subsequent life-work has been dominated by the task of systematically elaborating on this a priori of correlation" (Husserl 1970a, 166; Hua 6, 169).

10. I do and can certainly not want to give an account of the interesting but quite complicated relation of Husserl to Plato with this short remark. The only thing I want to emphasize here is the idea that for Husserl, our grasping of eidetic objects or essences (e.g., in geometrical thinking) is a specific type of correlation and that he therefore chooses the term 'intuition' to characterize it (as in 'eidetic intuition').

11. For a very informative paper on the notion of "evidence" and its development in Husserl, see Heffernan (2009). Generally spoken, evidence as the intentional accomplishment of self-givenness has to be considered as a main function of intentional life and makes up an intrinsic part of intentionality itself (givenness implies self-givenness; Hua 17, §§59–60).

12. For Husserl, the transcendence of reality is always a transcendence given, at least potentially, to an actual consciousness. To conceptualize radical transcendence as a "thing in itself" is "countersensical" (*widersinnig*) for Husserl, as he explains in §48 of the *Ideas I*: "The hypothetical assumption of something real outside this world is, of course, 'logically' possible [. . .]. But when we ask about the essential conditions on which its validity would depend, about the

mode of demonstration [. . .] we recognize that something transcendent necessarily must be experienceable not merely by an Ego conceived as an empty logical possibility but by any *actual* Ego as a demonstrable unity relative to its concatenations of experience. [. . .] If there are any worlds, any real physical things whatever, then the experienced motivations constituting them must be *able* to extend into my experience and into that of each Ego [. . .]. Obviously there are physical things and worlds of physical things which do not admit of being definitely demonstrated in any *human* experience; but that has purely factual grounds which lie within the factual limits of such experience" (Husserl 1982, 109).

13. This does not make the transcendental project as such superfluous because even if the world is intelligible to us naturally, our world-*relation* must and can be illuminated by self-reflective investigations.

14. "There is no ontology *alongside* a phenomenology. Rather, *scientific ontology is nothing but phenomenology*" (Heidegger 1985, 72). Heidegger thereby announces a revival of ancient ontology with the help of the method of phenomenology that asks for the how of givenness of modes of being.

15. By this, I want to argue and emphasize that Husserl's conception of consciousness (also after his "transcendental turn") *allows* for autonomous objectivity in the sense that objectivity is given *as autonomous within the correlation*. This mode of givenness is *not overruled* by Husserl's distinction between the absolute nature of immanent consciousness and the relative nature of transcendent reality: relativity here is a relativity to givenness in consciousness that does not exclude that this givenness in consciousness presents itself as independent of consciousness, as *real*. After all, this is the transcendental tension I am trying to promote as an indispensible element in these reflections. To put it differently: Even if the nature of consciousness is all encompassing in terms of sense, this does not mean that the object *as* it appears (as sense) *creates* the object *that* appears. To understand Husserl's idea of absolute consciousness in this way is a widespread misunderstanding that wrongly conceives it as an all-encompassing governor of senses and sense-production. For Husserl, however, absolute consciousness is not an autonomous or self-regulating producer of sense (God-like) but a foundation or source of the sense of individuality (cf. Hua 4, §64). Moreover, Husserl in his later work returns to the question of the *Urfaktum*, which entails the factual necessity of the existence of a consciousness (having a world) for eidetic phenomenological reflections (László Tengelyi has elaborated on this question in this volume). This again throws a different, metaphysical light on the issues of reality and the absoluteness of consciousness.

16. In a programmatic text on "What Phenomenology can mean today," Rudolf Bernet (2010) has pointedly portrayed the transition from Husserl to his successors and their partial misunderstanding of his conception of a "transcendentally constituting consciousness" as well as their focus on the borders of transcendental constitution in the sense of *Sinnbildung* ("sovereign constitution").

17. Husserl formulated this utterly clearly in the *Ideas I* (Hua 3/1): "*All real unities are 'unities of sense'* which presuppose [. . .] a sense-bestowing consciousness, which, for its part, exists absolutely and not by virtue of another sense-bestowal" (Husserl 1982, §55, 128 f).

18. While an egologic phenomenology refers to a subject of experience in the description of intentional consciousness (an intentional awareness not only of an object but also that it is experienced by me), nonegological accounts in phenomenology (e.g., by Sartre, Gurwitsch, and the early Husserl of the *Logical Investigations*) omit such a reference.

19. In his later work, Merleau-Ponty searches for an access to the realm of the not-yet-expressed or the to-be-expressed, especially in the context of creative acts—he calls this a "savage" dimension or "savage meaning" (*sens sauvage*), which is not yet conceptually determined and which demonstrates a cohesion without concepts (*cohesion sans concept*; Merleau-Ponty 1964, 199). Savage meaning calls for creative expression and new articulation as it stands against experiences along the lines of familiar categories. (Merleau-Ponty 1964, 149; 199)

20. Marc Richir develops a phenomenology of spontaneous self-building meaning in continuing Merleau-Ponty's project of a "*sens se faisant.*" For Richir, the "given" is the place where the phenomenological and the symbolical dimension of experience meet: this entails that symbolic meaning-endowments actually deform the given, which always—as in Merleau-Ponty—calls for an "adventure of meaning." It is that which yet has to be said or expressed. Richir is thus not interested in types of objects or objectivity (which are always already a product of symbolic meaning endowment) but rather in the flowing indeterminateness/indeterminableness and ambiguity of meaning building and dissolving processes beyond intentional consciousness or institutions of symbolic meaning like culture or language. This field of the wholly undeterminable, indefinite, and unbounded as the source of all meaning is called the "*Apeiron*" by Richir (Richir 1983, vol. II, 38–40). For a very informative short introduction, Gondek/Tengelyi (2011), 41–114.

21. Very briefly, one could characterize static phenomenology as elaborating on systems of constitution (i.e., transcendental conditions) and genetic phenomenology on the genesis of these systems (i.e., transcendental conditions of transcendental conditions of objectivity). The hypertranscendentality I have indicated with the formulations in brackets, on the one hand, is the only way not to fall back into psychologist or empirical versions of genesis; on the other hand, it creates the danger of losing grip on the original objectivity of world-experience. This is the problem I want to address.

22. For a very rich study dealing with the interruption of tendencies to accordance, see Tengelyi (2007). With the background of Merleau-Ponty's and Richir's genetic phenomenologies, Tengelyi develops the concept of "experientials" as opposed to "categories": while the latter stand for fixed meanings, the former represent the forms of "savage meaning" in the flow of experience.

23. The notion of "surplus" is typically used for designating meaning that transcends the categorial. But it seems obvious that "universality" and "necessity" just as well are meanings that exceed empirical tendencies to concordance. While one aspect gives testimony to experiential content that exceeds our categories, the other gives testimony of sheer spontaneity.

24. This is an oscillation we can actually find in Kant himself: at the beginning of the transcendental deduction (*Critique of Pure Reason*, §13), Kant considers that "appearances could after all be so constituted that the understanding would not find them in accord with the conditions of its unity, and everything would then lie in such confusion that, e.g., in the succession of appearances nothing would offer itself that would furnish a rule of synthesis" and that certain "concepts would therefore be entirely empty, nugatory, and without significance." Somehow surprisingly, he continues, "Appearances would nonetheless offer objects to our intuition, for intuition by no means requires the functions of thinking" (Kant 1998, 223, A90 f). This sounds as if we could have intuitions without thoughts (although Kant famously states that "intuitions without concepts are blind" [Kant 1998, 194, A51]) or as if we would *first* intuit and *then* think (or—in the other case—not be able to think the intuited/the given).

25. "Consciousness, Being in the radical sense, *is* in the radical sense of the word. It is the root and—in a different picture—the source of all that which is called and can be called 'Being'" (Hua 36, 70).
26. "No ordinary 'realist' has ever been so realistic and so concrete as I, the phenomenological 'idealist'" (Husserl 1994, 16).

REFERENCES

Bernet, R. 2010. "Was kann Phänomenologie heute bedeuten?" *Information Philosophie* 4: 7–21.

Crowell, S. G. 2001. *Husserl, Heidegger, and the Space of Meaning: Paths Toward Transcendental Phenomenology.* Evanston, IL: Northwestern University Press.

Fink, E. 1959. "Les concepts opératoires dans la phénomenologie de Husserl," *Husserl – Cahiers de Royaumont, Philosophie III.* Paris, 214–241.

———. 1966. *Studien zur Phänomenologie (1930–1939).* The Hague: Martinus Nijhoff.

Gondek, H.-D. and L. Tengelyi, 2011: *Neue Phänomenologie in Frankreich.* Frankfurt am Main: Suhrkamp.

Heffernan, G. 2009. "On Husserl's Remark that '[s]elbst eine sich als apodiktisch ausgebende Evidenz kann sich als Täuschung enthüllen . . .' (XVII 164:32–33): Does the Phenomenological Method Yield Any Epistemic Infallibility?" *Husserl Studies* 25: 15–43.

Heidegger, M. 1977. *Phänomenologische Interpretation von Kants Kritik der reinen Vernunft.* Gesamtausgabe Band 25. Edited by Ingtraud Görland. Frankfurt am Main: Vittorio Klostermann. (GA 25)

———. 1979. *Prolegomena zur Geschichte des Zeitbegriffs.* Gesamtausgabe 20, edited by Petra Jaeger. Frankfurt am Main: Klostermann. (GA 20)

———. 1985. *History of the Concept of Time, Prolegomena* (translation). Bloomington: Indiana University Press.

Husserl, E. 1952. *Ideen zu einer reinen Phänomenologie und phänomenologischen Philosophie. Zweites Buch. Phänomenologische Untersuchungen zur Konstitution.* Edited by Marly Biemel. The Hague: Martinus Nijhoff. (Hua 4)

———. [1954] 1962. *Die Krisis der europäischen Wissenschaften und die transzendentale Phänomenologie: Eine Einleitung in die phänomenologische Philosophie,* Husserliana 6. Edited by Walter Biemel. The Hague: Martinus Nijhoff. (Hua 6) Translation: Husserl, E. 1970a. *The Crisis of European Sciences and Transcendental Phenomenology: An Introduction to Phenomenological Philosophy.* Translated by D. Carr. Evanston, IL: Northwestern University Press.

———. 1970. *Logische Untersuchungen. Erster Band: Prolegomena zur reinen Logik,* Husserliana 18. Edited by Elmar Holenstein. The Hague: Martinus Nijhoff. (Hua 18)

———. 1974. *Formale und transzendentale Logik. Versuch einer Kritik der logischen Vernunft,* Husserliana 17. Edited by Paul Janssen. The Hague: Martinus Nijhoff. (Hua 17)

———. 1975. *Logische Untersuchungen. Erster Band: Prolegomena zur reinen Logik,* Husserliana 19/1. Edited by Elmar Holenstein. The Hague: Martinus Nijhoff. (Hua 19/1) Translation: Husserl, E. 1970b. *Logical Investigations.* 2 vols. Translated by J. N. Findlay. London: Routledge & Kegan Paul, 41–247.

———. 1976. *Ideen zu einer reinen Phänomenologie und phänomenologischen Philosophie I,* Husserliana 3/1. Edited by Karl Schuhmann. The Hague: Martinus Nijhoff. (Hua 3/1) Translation: Husserl, E. 1982. *Ideas Pertaining to a Pure Phenomenology and to a Phenomenological Philosophy, First Book: General*

Introduction to a Pure Phenomenology. Translated by Fred Kersten. The Hague: Martinus Nijhoff.

———. 1984a. *Logische Untersuchungen. Zweiter Band. Untersuchungen zur Phänomenologie und Theorie der Erkenntnis,* Husserliana 19/2. Edited by Ursula Panzer. The Hague: Martinus Nijhoff. (Hua 19/2) Translation: Husserl, E. 1970b. *Logical Investigations.* 2 vols., 248–869. Translated by J. N. Findlay. London: Routledge & Kegan Paul.

———. 1984b. *Einleitung in die Logik und Erkenntnistheorie. Vorlesungen 1906/07,* Husserliana 24. Edited by Ullrich Melle. The Hague: Martinus Nijhoff. (Hua 24)

———. 1994. *Briefwechsel,* Husserliana Dokumente III/1–10. Edited by Karl Schuhmann and Elisabeth Schuhmann. Dordrecht: Kluwer.

———. 2003. *Transzendentaler Idealismus. Texte aus dem Nachlass (1908–1921),* Husserliana 36. Edited by Robin Rollinger. Dordrecht: Kluwer. (Hua 36)

Kant, I. 1974. *Kritik der reinen Vernunft.* Edited by Wilhem Weischedel. Frankfurt am Main: Suhrkamp.

———. 1997. *Prolegomena to Any Future Metaphysics.* Translated by Gary Hatfield. Cambridge: Cambridge University Press.

———. 1998. *Critique of Pure Reason.* Translated and edited by Paul Guyer and Allen W. Wood. Cambridge: Cambridge University Press.

———. 1964. *Husserl und Kant. Eine Untersuchung über Husserls Verhältnis zu Kant und zum Neukantianismus.* The Hague: Martinus Nijhoff.

Loidolt, S. 2009. *Anspruch und Rechtfertigung: Eine Theorie des rechtlichen Denkens im Anschluss an die Phänomenologie Edmund Husserls.* Dordrecht: Springer.

McDowell, J. 1996. *Mind and World.* Cambridge, MA: Harvard University Press.

Merleau-Ponty, M. 1964. *Le visible et l'invisible.* Paris: Gallimard.

Putnam, H. 1978. *Meaning and the Moral Sciences.* Oxford: Routledge & Kegan Paul.

Richir, M. [1981] 1983. *Recherches phénoménologiques,* 2nd vol. Brussels: Ousia.

Strasser, S. 1976. "Der Begriff der Welt in der phänomenologischen Philosophie." *Phänomenologische Forschungen* 3: 151–179.

Strawson, P. 2007. *The Bounds of Sense: An Essay on Kant's Critique of Pure Reason.* London and New York: Routledge.

Tengelyi, L. 2007. *Erfahrung und Ausdruck: Phänomenologie im Umbruch bei Husserl und seinen Nachfolgern.* Dordrecht: Springer.

Wittgenstein, L. 1984. *Tractatus logico-philosophicus. Tagebücher 1914–1916. Philosophische Untersuchungen.* Frankfurt am Main: Suhrkamp.

Zahavi, D. 2003. *Husserl's Phenomenology.* Stanford, CA: Stanford University Press.

10 The Bodily Feeling of Existence in Phenomenology and Psychoanalysis[1]

Joona Taipale

INTRODUCTION

In recent decades, the psychoanalytic concept of the *mind* has gained a lot of interest among philosophers and especially among phenomenologists. Much less emphasis has been given to the psychoanalytic concept of the *body*. The generally accepted view in philosophy is that when psychoanalytic scholars discuss the body, they interpret it as a mere natural scientific object—a matter of physiology, biology, and neuroscience with no special philosophical relevance. To be sure, psychoanalysis is indeed (and, from a phenomenological point of view, rightly) trying to avoid *reducing* experiential life to current neurophysiological circumstances—a move that largely characterizes contemporary psychiatry. However, thus holds the received view, in lacking a proper philosophical framework, psychoanalysis simply falls victim to mystifying descriptions of the foundations of the mind, ending up endorsing a view reminiscent of the Cartesian dichotomy between a disembodied mind (the subject matter of the human sciences) and the material body (the subject matter of the natural sciences).

The psychoanalytic concept of the body is thus mostly considered to be worlds apart from what phenomenologists call the lived-body. As to Freud, such an interpretation is hardly surprising, given his background in medicine and neurology—and it is in fact indisputable that Freud sometimes, especially in his early work, identifies the body with a subject matter of the natural sciences exclusively. What is generally neglected, however, is that Freud and his followers also introduce an experiential concept of the body and describe the bodily foundations of the mind in a manner that comes relatively close to the phenomenological analyses of Husserl and Merleau-Ponty. In this chapter, I will focus on what Freud, together with his successors, calls the *body-ego* (*Körper-Ich*). I will argue that this notion comes quite close to what Husserl terms the 'lived-body.' My purpose, of course, is not to claim that their conceptualizations are identical. Rather, by bringing forth certain fundamental affinities between them, my aim is to make way for a dialogue between the two disciplines. By discussing the bodily foundations of experiential life as they are interpreted in phenomenology and psychoanalysis,

I will illustrate how psychoanalysis, a particular nontranscendental discipline, may challenge and complement phenomenology.

1 PHENOMENOLOGY AND BODILY SELF-AWARENESS

I will begin with Husserl's concept of the lived-body, illustrating how he interprets the relationship between body and self. As is well known, Husserl distinguishes between the lived-body (*Leib*) and the body as a material thing (*Körper*), and he provides elaborate and detailed descriptions on how our own lived-body stands out from all other things in our perceptual field. In the following, I will briefly recapitulate some of the main features of Husserl's analysis.

First of all, our own body is distinguished from all other things in that it is the only thing that we can move immediately: all other things can be moved only in a mediated manner, namely by moving our own body. This entails that whereas any other external thing (whether animate or inanimate) may always perceptually appear from a different angle and perspective, in the case of our own body, our possibilities are remarkably limited. In this sense, unlike all other perceivable things, our own body is a "remarkably imperfectly constituted thing" (*ein merkwürdig unvollkommen konstituiertes Ding*; Hua 4, 159): we cannot walk around our own body, we cannot take distance to our face in order to see it from further away, and so on. Moreover, all other things are located at some direction with respect to our body (they are "over there," "on the left," "right," "in front of us," "behind us," "above," "below," "near," "far," and so on) whereas our own body, instead, is always "here." As Husserl puts it, our body serves as the "zero-point of orientation" (*Nullpunkt der Orientierung*), as an experiential *origo*.

The metaphor of a zero-point or *origo* is illuminating. Like a mathematical *origo* cannot be simply taken to be included in the (*n*-dimensional) coordinates *for which* it serves as the point of reference (and, in this sense, a condition of possibility), our own body cannot be experientially included in the spatial realm for which it serves as the point of reference. That is to say, our own lived-body is not *in* space in the same sense as any other thing that is introduced in our sense perception. To be sure, this by no means entails that the lived-body is not spatial, to say nothing of it being somehow excluded from the spatial environment. Rather, the point is that traditional philosophical dichotomies, such as "subject/object" or "inner/outer," prove problematic when it comes to our own lived-body.

Our own body further distinguishes itself from all other things insofar as it is the only "thing" that we *sense* immediately. This links to what I just said about movement: whereas other things (and other bodies too) are accessible to our sense perception only through our bodily sensing, our own body is sensed immediately. While turning around, we already kinesthetically "know" that it is precisely our perceiving body that moves, and not the perceived environment—and this "knowledge" precedes deliberation and reflection. In order to proprioceptively "know" where our hands are, we do not first have to think about this. And, more generally, to "know" that we exist bodily *here and now,* we do not normally first have to take look at our body or touch it.

This brings us to yet another distinctive feature of our own body. Our sensations (or "sensings," as Husserl also calls them) are localized in and on our body (see Hua 4, 146–153). We incessantly feel not only our posture and movement (and our being-still), but we also constantly sense our bodily surfaces as well as some of its visceral areas (see Leder 1990). Touching accordingly yields not only an experience of sensuous qualities of the thing that is touched but also a sensation of the bodily surface that touches the external thing. For example, if I explore the surface of a table with my hand, coolness is experienced as the property of the table, but the sensation of coolness is localized on my hand that is sliding over it. That is to say, I experience the coolness of the table precisely *with my hand,* and I "know" this because the sense of coolness is localized on it. The localized sensation endures for a short while after I raise my hand from the table. Yet it should be noted that localization is not something that takes place once in a while and only in respect to experiences that reach our thematic consciousness but that it rather characterizes our experience all the time: before (and while) actively exploring objects like the table, with other parts of our body we still tacitly sense the temperature of the room, the chair on which we sit, our clothes, and so on. That is to say, whereas all other things count as something merely *sensed* but not *sensing,* our own body originally stands out as a "thing" that senses.

Thanks to localization, we are all the time aware of our material boundaries. These boundaries are questioned, however, as soon as the object of touch is our own body. In this case, namely, not only the touching hand but also the touched area provides sensations that are localized and thus organized as part of one's own self. As Husserl puts it, our lived-body is the only thing the touching of which yields "double sensations" (Hua 4, 145). I will not here go into this complex issue (e.g., the problems of "reversibility") in more detail—the issue has already been sufficiently discussed and highlighted in the previous literature. It is worth noting, however, that one particular issue has almost been neglected in this literature. Namely, it should be emphasized that such "double sensations" are not something that occur only sporadically or contingently—say, while we applaud or scratch our head. Rather, there are several areas in and on our body where such "self-palpating" is taking place all the time: with our tongue, for instance, we constantly feel our oral cavity, gums, mouth, and so on, whereas we also constantly feel our tongue with the mucosa of our mouth. I will come back to this issue later on.

Due to the mentioned peculiarities, traditional dichotomies become blurred in the case of our own body. Husserl insists that should traditional terms be employed while investigating embodiment (which, as I see it, is always necessary at least to a certain extent), the lived-body ought to be recognized as both subject and object, as a being experienced both internally and externally (Hua 4, 195; cf. Merleau-Ponty 1945, 111). Instead of unambiguously fitting into either side of the subject/object or inner/outer dichotomies, our own body rather precedes and predates these distinctions and serves as their condition of possibility; it is not exclusively either something subjective or objective, either something internally or externally felt, but the original "point of intersection" (*Umschlagspunkt, Umschlagstelle*) between these realms, as Husserl also puts it (see Hua 4, 160, 286).

The mentioned ambiguity of the lived-body manifests itself in the relationship between body and self. Namely, Husserl seems to be rather irresolute about the question whether the self and the lived-body should be identified with one another.[2] He claims, on the one hand, that "I am not in space like things are in space, and not [even] in the manner that my lived-body is in space"; "the ego exists as *having* a spatial 'here' and 'there,' but [it] is not itself *in* space and time, [it is] not itself *in* the world" (Hua 15, 283, 644). On the other hand, Husserl often emphasizes that the self is "embodied" (*verkörpert, verleiblicht*), and he explains that this means not only that I myself and my lived-body "belong together inseparably" (*unabtrennbar einig*) but moreover that "I am one with my lived-body, I am embodied" (HuaM 8, 380; Hua 15, 283). In such connections, Husserl also uses expressions like 'bodily swaying ego' (*leiblich waltendes ego*), 'bodily ego' (*leibliche Ichlichkeit*), and even 'ego-body' (*Ichleib*), which interestingly resonate with the mentioned psychoanalytic concept of the "body-ego" (*Körper-Ich*; see Hua 39, 623, 632–634; Hua 15, 19; Hua 6, 110; Hua 14, 331; Hua 16, 161).

This chopping and changing—the dithering and wavering in saying both that the self is and is not identical with the lived-body—can be made intelligible in reference to the mentioned duality of the lived-body. Husserl develops this theme further especially in his manuscripts on intersubjectivity. He stresses, first of all, that the distinction between the physiological body and the lived-body is not an exhaustive phenomenological description of the body; the lived-body is also in itself a "twofold unity" (*doppelsichtige Einheit*): "my lived-body is accordingly conceivable in two senses: [1] immediately in self-perception and self-manifestation, and [2] in a mediated fashion by way of external manifestation that refers back to self-manifestation" (Hua 13, 263, 48). What Husserl means by claiming that external manifestation of one's own body refers back to immediate bodily self-manifestation is that we can experience and recognize one externally perceived body as our own only insofar as we can sense it not merely through external perception but also immediately—from within, so to speak. If we wake up having slept on our own hand so that the hand is completely numb, senseless, and immovable, the hand is not simply constituted as part of our own functional body or organized as part of our experiential bodily self. More generally, if our body were not accompanied by immediate kinesthetic-sensuous self-manifestation at all, it could not, while being experienced externally, appear as our own body (see Hua 4, 150)—this is what experientially distinguishes our own body not only from all other things but also from someone else's body.

Husserl further explicates the two dimensions of the body by writing that "the spatiotemporal experience *of* the lived-body (. . .) refers back to the lived-body as functioning," and that, in this sense, "the lived-body presents the difficulty that an experience *of* it always already presupposes it" (Hua 15, 326–327). In some of his later manuscripts, Husserl characterizes the peculiar two-foldness of the lived-body by distinguishing between "lived-bodily interiority" (*Innenleiblichkeit*) and "lived-bodily exteriority" (*Aussenleiblichkeit*; e.g., Hua 14, 327–329, 336–337). Many later phenomenologists, such as Sartre, Merleau-Ponty, and Henry, develop Husserl's insights further by distinguishing between "being a body" and "having a body" (*je suis mon corps, j'ai un corps*; see, e.g., Merleau-Ponty 1945, 173–175, 194–195). Also Heidegger, who doesn't have that much to say about the body—according to his own words, this has to do with the immense difficulty of the subject matter—employs this distinction and writes the following: "It is not that we 'have' [*haben*] a body; rather, we 'are' in a bodily manner" (*wir 'sind' leiblich*) (Heidegger 1961, 99; 1987, 292).

This distinction, I believe, explains Husserl's wavering. That is to say, the self cannot simply be identified with the lived-body without further specifications, but it can be identified with what Husserl calls lived-bodily interiority (*Innenleiblichkeit*), which essentially pertains to the notion of the lived-body. As Husserl explains, this notion refers to a perpetual and incessant kinesthetic-sensuous self-manifestation, self-affection, or, to put it in less technical terms, to a constant bodily "feel." Unlike "lived-bodily exteriority," this fundamental bodily "feel" is not something that could become an object of sense perception. It is the purely subjective dimension of the lived-body, what constitutes its "livedness," and as such it is not something palpable or visible. To be sure, it is not altogether invisible either, as it can be perceived in *expression* (*Ausdruck*): as the term literally suggests, "ex-pression" is an event in which something immediately felt is "pressed" or "squeezed" out, thereby gaining a perceivable exteriority. Yet, instead of being something possibly seen or touched, lived-bodily interiority as such is rather a condition of possibility of all experience whatsoever, touching and seeing included. It may therefore be associated with what Henry and other later phenomenologists have termed 'transcendental body' (Henry 1975, 73; cf. Melle 1983, 114–115).

In other words, in Husserl's phenomenology selfhood and the lived-body are not simply and unambiguously synonymous. On the one hand, the self *has* a perceivable exteriority in the sense that it is expressed in the externally perceivable movements, but the self is neither exhausted by nor reducible to this exteriority. On the other hand, the self is what makes up the "livedness" or subjectivity of the lived-body; it *is* this interiority, and hence something that is expressed *in* the externally perceivable movements. In this sense, self-hood fundamentally amounts to *a bodily feeling of existence.*

The feeling of existence, the sense of enduring, the feeling of going through—or, simply: *life*—not only essentially pertains to the phenomeno-logical concept of the body; the feeling of existence, moreover, is in itself essentially a bodily matter. In this light, it hardly comes as a surprise that embodiment has such a comprehensive role in Husserlian phenomenology. This centrality can be witnessed not only in Husserl's numerous thematic analyses of the lived-body but also in the manner in which he introduces other fundamental concepts of phenomenology—such as "time-consciousness" and "constitution" (see, e.g., HuaM 8, 112). Husserl explicitly considers sens-ing as the original consciousness of time (*Das Empfinden sehen wir an als das ursprüngliche Zeitbewusstsein*; Hua 10, 107); he treats the lived-body as the bearer not only of the "here" but also of the "now" (*Träger des Hier und Jetzt*; Hua 4, 56); and he claims that subjectivity and selfhood, everything subjective and mental, is founded on the lived-body (Hua 4, 282–283). In this sense, as Husserl also puts it, *"a human being's total consciousness is* (. . .) *bound to the lived-body,* though, to be sure, the intentional lived experiences themselves are *no longer* directly and properly *localized* (Hua 4, 153).[3]

2   PSYCHOANALYSIS AND THE BODILY ROOTS OF THE EGO

In the Husserlian phenomenology, bodily experiencing, selfhood, and the feeling of existence intertwine in a manner that proves interesting from the point of view of psychoanalysis—and, as we shall see later on, this also holds *vice versa*. In a manner reminiscent of Husserl, Freud too assumes that the self originates at the junction point of inner and outer (Freud 1923, 252/24).[4] Freud likewise locates this intersection in bodily experience and argues that the self is first and foremost a bodily ego (*körperliches Ich*) or "body-ego" (*Körper-Ich*; Freud 1923, 253–254/25–26). This view has been generally embraced and multifariously developed further by Freud's succes-sors. Let us take a closer look at Freud's train of thought.

The psychoanalytic tradition differs from phenomenology by its strong developmental emphasis. Margaret Mahler argues: "The biological birth and the psychological birth of the individual are not coincident in time. The former is a dramatic, observable, and well-circumscribed event; the latter a slowly unfolding intrapsychic process" (Mahler et al. 1975, 3). Accord-ingly, whereas Husserl claims that already the unborn fetus must have an elementary experiential "primordiality" (see, e.g., Hua 14, 604–605), a "pre-reflective self-awareness," Freud assumes that the contrast between the sub-jective and the objective is not there from the outset (Freud 1925, 13/236) and that even the most primal self or ego is not something original but rather something unfolding in the course of time: "we are bound to suppose that a unity comparable to the ego cannot exist in the individual from the start; the ego has to be developed" (Freud 1914, 141–142/76). In one of his latest writings, Freud distils his view into the following words:

> Normally, there is nothing of which we are more certain than *the feeling of our self, of our own ego* [*Gefühl unseres Selbst, unseres eigenen Ichs*]. This ego appears to us as something autonomous and unitary, marked off distinctly from everything else. (. . .) Further reflection tells us that the adult's ego-feeling [*Ichgefühl*] cannot have been the same from the beginning. (. . .) An infant does not as yet distinguish his ego from the external world as the source of the sensations flowing in upon him. He gradually learns to do so (. . .) . In this way, then, the ego detaches itself from the external world. Or, to put it more correctly, originally the ego includes everything, later it separates off an external world from itself. (Freud 1930, 424/65–66)

Against this background, Freud furthermore claims that the adult's "ego-feeling" or "sense of self," as Daniel Stern has called it (Stern 1985), is but a "shrunken residue" of the infant's rather "oceanic" feeling (Freud 1930, 425/67).[5]

How does the primal, infantile sense of self unfold and become structured, then? Here Freud turns to embodiment. He emphasizes the role of so-called surface sensations, and he writes: "the ego is ultimately derived from bodily sensations, chiefly from those springing from the surface of the body. It may thus be regarded as a mental projection of bodily surfaces" (Freud 1923, 253/25; cf. Freud 1938, 72/150).[6] This emphasis is, first of all, owing to developmental reasons. As René Spitz later on explicates: at the "earliest stage of life *distance* perception is not operative but only *contact* perception" (Spitz 1955, 223). In other words, "the early sensory world of the infant is poorly differentiated and it has a coaenesthetic nature with a dominance of the somato-sensory modality" (Lehtonen 2006, 202). Besides developmental ones, the emphasis on bodily surfaces also has ontological, purely philosophical reasons. This is due to the fact that perceptual superficies comprise an "area whose frontiers belong both to the outer world and to the ego" (Freud [1938] in Jones 1957, 494). Like Husserl, Freud accordingly thinks that the experiential borderline between inner and outer originally unfolds in the body—and Freud too outlines the role of kinestheses and "double sensations" in the differentiation between these basic realms (Freud 1915a, 212, 227/118, 133; Freud 1923, 252/24).

Freud himself does not explicitly elaborate the notions of "ego-feeling" and "body-ego," nor does he explain what he actually means by characterizing the latter as "a mental projection of bodily surfaces." Freud's contemporary, Paul Federn, instead discusses these notions at length and in detail—and Freud also refers to Federn's work while mentioning the concept of *Ichgefühl.* In an article titled "Some Variations in Ego-Feeling" (1926), Federn interestingly identifies ego-feeling with a *feeling of existence* (Federn 1952, 25ff.). He distinguishes between mental and bodily ego-feeling and claims that Descartes's phrase *cogito ergo sum* may be interpreted as a rational formulation of the mental ego-feeling (Federn 1952, 26). Instead, Federn explicitly identifies the "bodily ego-feeling" with what Freud terms as 'body-ego.' Federn goes on to clarify that even though the body-ego or "bodily ego-feeling" is an experiential formation, it ought not be considered simply identical with "body image" or even with "body schema" that had been discussed by Henry Head, Gordon Holmes, and Paul Schilder before Federn's writings (Federn 1952, 27; cf. Head and Holmes 1911/1912; Schilder 1923).[7] However, what is especially interesting is that having generally distinguished the body-ego from the two mentioned notions, Federn surprisingly states that the *adult's* body-ego can indeed be identified with body schema (Federn 1952, 30). In the case of infants, the "body-ego" and the "body schema" *are not identical,* whereas in the case of adults they *are identical.* How should we understand this?

The bodily experience of the infant is not organized in the way that it is organized in adult life, but neither is it chaotic. Some sort of organization can be found already from the infant's experience—and as is well known, this view today enjoys strong empirical support.[8] However, we tend to think that in the organization of the bodily experience of the infant on the one hand and of the adult on the other, there is but a difference *in degree,* as if bodily self-awareness would be formed *linearly* in time, continuously gaining a greater extent of precision and hence following the same logic throughout. This might not be true, or at least not the whole truth. The concept of body schema is a very complex one and there are several interpretations to it, but what is common to most (if not all) conceptions is that they unfold under what Freud calls the "reality principle." As Head, Holmes, and Schilder have determined it, the body schema refers to a unitary bodily feel established from the basis of facts (actually experienced distinctions between self and other, actually experienced sensations, feelings, emotions, etc.). It is something that is built in the course of time, gradually, as the child learns to familiarize herself with the factual bodily capacities and limitations.

Now, if the infant's experiences are somehow organized very early on, already before the fact-based and intersubjectively validated environment has experientially emerged, then the environment has to first be arranged from the basis of a different logic (see Taipale 2013). In clarifying this idea, psychoanalysis has offered something that no other discipline has contributed. In the psychoanalytic tradition, it is emphasized that in the psychic reality of the infant, facts do not originally have a supremacy over fantasies, needs, and desires. Freud discusses this idea by introducing—besides "reality principle"—a "pleasure principle," meaning that psychic reality (i.e., the experiential dimension, including bodily self-experience) is at first organized not according to facts, to correctly ordered sensations of one's own body, but according to the affective quality of the experience in question. Freud writes:

> A tendency arises [in the infant] to separate from the ego everything that can become a source of unpleasure, to cast it outside and to create a pure pleasure-ego which is confronted by an alien and threatening "outside." The boundaries of this primitive pleasure-ego cannot escape rectification through experience. Some of the things that one is unwilling to give up, because they give pleasure, are nevertheless not [part of the] ego but [of the] object; and some sufferings that one seeks to expel turn out to be inseparable from the ego in virtue of their internal origin. One comes to learn a procedure by which, through a deliberate direction of one's sensory activities and through suitable muscular action, one can differentiate between what is internal—what belongs to the ego—and what is external—what emanates from the outer world. In this way one makes the first step towards the introduction of the reality principle which is to dominate future development. (Freud 1930, 423–424/65–66)

> The original pleasure-ego wants to introject into itself everything that is good and to eject from itself everything that is bad. What is bad, what is alien to the ego and what is external are, to begin with, identical. (Freud 1925, 12/236)

Everything pleasant (that which is wanted or wished for) is incorporated and organized as part of oneself, whereas everything unpleasant (that which is wanted to go way) is initially cast off, shut off from the self, and organized as part of what is external to the self—this logic is not always that alien to adults either, in the case of quarrelling with someone, for instance.

We can accordingly think that the infant's bodily sense of self is not initially organized against the background of the *factual* actualities and potentialities of the body. The child is not at first familiar with her factual limits and boundaries: these are arranged in her psychic reality into experiential and functional norms only subsequently and gradually. Before this, the organization of the experiential realm follows a different logic, so to speak—the logic of pleasure. Therefore many such things that, objectively speaking, are not part of the infant's body may be experientially organized as obvious parts of the infant herself. Johannes Lehtonen has argued that in the case of breast-feeding, for instance, the immediate sensuous content of the infant's experience is provided by the pleasure-filled "fusion" or "confluence" of the infant's mouth and mother's nipple, of the skins of the infant and the mother, and not of these two elements as clearly demarcated from one another. Insofar as the very core of the infant's bodily selfhood, body-ego, or bodily feeling of existence is developed in and through such experiences, we can furthermore think that central elements of the original bodily egoity of the infant initially involve ingredients from both the infant and the mother (Lehtonen 1991, 30–32; see also Freud 1923, 257/28).

3   THE TEMPORAL UNFOLDING OF BODILY EXPERIENCE

The bodily feeling of existence is not just something fleeting, a feeling coming and going along with particular sensations, perceptions, and experiences, but something that transcends them as temporal formation. It is not just a structural, purely formal and "synchronic" self-reference, pertaining to each experience, but also a "diachronic" sense of enduring. In the psychoanalytic tradition, it is generally thought the feeling of existence is solidified through a coherent recurrence of nursing and interaction. Insofar as nursing is "good enough," meaning that the infant's basic needs are fulfilled in a sufficiently coherent and continuous manner, the infant's sense of existence will be gradually stabilized, and it is precisely this solidification that designates the inception of the infant's primitive sense of existence, her psychological birth (Lehtonen 1991, 31). As we already saw above, Freud addresses this issue in terms of the birth of a "pure pleasure ego."

While discussing the emergence of a rudimentary bodily sense of self, psychoanalysis moves beyond phenomenology. Both disciplines are in fact well in line with the tradition of philosophy, which, at least since Aristotle, has endowed a constitutive primacy to the tactile sense. The difference is that whereas phenomenology has not introduced any further elaboration of primacy within the tactile sense, the whole psychoanalytic theory in its classical form is basically founded on the idea of such developmental hierarchies. In the phenomenological concept of the lived-body, a primacy is given to the tactile field on the whole; in the psychoanalytic concept of the body-ego, in contrast, the primacy is given to certain tactile areas of the body. The tactile areas of the body have a different status in different phases of development. Particular areas of the body are experientially organized as part of one's own functional body from the start, whereas other areas are "incorporated" only gradually, and this has consequences to the structure of the self. Not only must the infant gradually discover her own body, but moreover, while doing so, she must also learn to distinguish herself from her mother (this is one important aspect of the process of adopting the reality principle). As already said, some areas that are, thanks to their recurrent functional presence, originally fused as part of the bodily self may gradually be differentiated from the self and become constituted as pertaining to other persons (a paradigmatic example of this is, of course, the mother's breast in respect to which the infant manifests the gestures of an owner). The process of "separation and differentiation," in other words, is always very concretely also a bodily experience.

In psychoanalysis, the developmental primacy is accordingly given not to the tactile body on the whole but to certain areas of the latter—and here psychoanalysis and phenomenology stand out from one another. In this light, the psychoanalytic emphasis on "orality" becomes intelligible. The mouth and the oral cavity initially have an important role to play given their central role in fulfilling the infant's primal needs. During breast-feeding, the infant senses her own tongue, the mother's nipple, and milk through the mucosa of her mouth; with her tongue, she senses the mucosa of her mouth, the milk, and the breast; and all this time the muscles of the mouth actively execute the movement of sucking. The fact that this perpetually repeating event is accompanied by "double sensations" (provided by the infant's mucosa, tongue, and lips) makes the situation even more blurred and makes it convincing to say that it is hardly clear for the infant where the self "ends" and the (m)other begins.

Due to its primal centrality in the need-fulfillment of the infant, the mouth accordingly has a special status. As Spitz puts it: "the mouth (. . .) is the bridge between inner reception and outer perception; it is the cradle of all external perception and its basic model; it is the place of transition for the development of intentional activity, for the emergence of volition from passivity" (Spitz 1955, 238). With her colleagues, Margaret Mahler even argues that, in this sense, *hands*, for instance, are but a subsequent "extension of the growing body-self" (Mahler and McDevitt 1982, 837). Some commentators even go so far as to speak of a "mouth-ego" that gradually becomes extended into a body-ego (Hoffer 1950, 160).[9]

To this extent, at least, the psychoanalytic view seems to move beyond the phenomenological view that claims that the foundation of selfhood rests on kinesthetic-sensuous bodily experience in general but recognizes no hierarchies within the former. At the same time, it may serve to challenge phenomenologists into specifications. According to the psychoanalytic view, our bodily experience unfolds from the basis of bodily experience that is not primarily outlined by our factual sensations alone but also by our fantasies, needs, and desires—both conscious and unconscious ones. If this possibility is neglected—say, by making too strong a contrast between ontological and developmental structures or by tacitly considering (neutral) facts experientially more fundamental than (emotionally flavored) fantasies, both options of which are not rare in philosophy—the account of selfhood easily remains too abstract.

4   BODILY EXPERIENCE, FALLING ASLEEP, AND REGRESSION

In the framework that I have just presented, the "body schema" and the "body image" are developed gradually in time, from the basis of the infantile body-ego that was determined as a bodily feeling of existence. It should also be clear by now that although the bodily feeling of existence is a layered (or sedimented) sensuous-affective bodily "feel," it is not identical with the content of bodily self-experience at any given moment. The body-ego rather refers to the charged (or, as psychoanalysts put it, "cathected") condition of the bodily organs and members that we, in the register of facts, constantly sense (Federn 1952, 27). In this light, it is also understandable why the body-ego of the infant and of the adult cannot be identical. To rephrase Freud, it is precisely as reality oriented that the adult's ego-feeling is "narrower and more sharply demarcated," a shrunken residue, in comparison to the infant's "oceanic" ego-feeling the unfolding of which was not yet throughout governed by facts.

It should be emphasized here, moreover, that as the body schema is gradually developed in the course of time, the infantile body-ego is by no means substituted for it—the body schema is developed from the basis of body-ego, but this does not mean that the body-ego is developed into a body schema. Instead, the infantile body-ego is retained, and it continues to have a life of its own at the foundations of the more clearly demarcated bodily sense of self of the adult. It serves as a basic tone of experiential life that determines our existence. As such, it usually remains tacit, in the background of our conscious experiences, but once in a while it may surface in our consciousness (Lehtonen 2011, 44–45). The coexistence of the infantile body-ego and the adult bodily self-awareness has been illustrated, for instance, by discussing experiential anomalies related to the process of falling asleep. Psychoanalysts have argued that while we fall asleep, our psychic interests and cathexes are "withdrawn" from the sensory environment: they stream into our bodily ego, whereby the latter becomes "hypercathected" (e.g., Isakower 1938, 336–337; Spitz 1955, 236–237). As a consequence, we gradually sink into a state that mainly characterizes the experiential life of newborn infants (see Freud 1915b, 432/416; Lehtonen 1997, 47). When we sleep or are about to fall asleep a loud sound is most likely to wake us up, which is another way of saying that the withdrawal of cathexes by no means suggests that we no longer register external stimuli at all, as if we were to become deaf, for instance. Neither does it mean that the body or bodily self thereby becomes a thematic object of our conscious attention. The environment is rather pushed to the background in the sense that we psychically so to speak "let go" of it and thus "snuggle" into ourselves—into the "warmth and intimacy" of our immediate bodily self-awareness, to rephrase William James (e.g., James 2007, 331).

As we thus "snuggle" into ourselves while falling asleep, the boundaries between our own body and the environment may become blurred. Federn illustrates how in different phases of falling asleep, our body (or parts of it) may come to appear in a bizarre manner: certain parts of our body—mostly mouth, face, head, or chest—may still be present in a relatively clear manner, but the rest of our body may gradually become obscure, so that (actually) symmetrical parts of our body, such as hands or legs, may appear in unequal length, their location might seem undetermined, or our whole body might present itself as an "amorphous" or "vague mass" (Federn 1952, 30). As we all know from experience, even the smallest body movement during falling asleep "dispels the illusion" and restores our relatively clearly outlined adult body-ego. At the same time, this prevents us from falling asleep.[10] Falling asleep accordingly requires a certain childlike surrender: a "disentangle-ment" from or a "suspension" of the reality principle.

Many psychoanalysts, like Federn, Spitz, Isakower, and Lehtonen, have argued that such synesthetic and amorphous experiences ought to be inter-preted as traces of our earliest bodily sense of existence. Besides the anoma-lous experiences reported by Federn, also the "hypnagogic hallucinations," studied extensively by Otto Isakower, and the idea of a "dream screen," introduced by Bertram Lewin, have been interpreted as exemplifying how in the process of falling asleep we regress to developmentally more primal bodily experiences, ultimately to earliest body-ego experiences, solidified through recurrent need-fulfillment (experiences during nursing, breast-feeding, etc.; see Isakower 1938; Lehtonen 2011, 77ff; Lewin 1946). The regres-sion seems to run to the opposite direction in the course of development through which our body schema has gradually been structured, proceeding toward a primitive and indeterminate (although normally soothing) bodily self-presence (Federn 1952, 30). This basic experience not only underlies and founds our bodily schema and body image, but it also serves as the soil of our personality on the whole. If structured normally, the body-ego may thus serve "as a reservoir of a primitive, reassuring sense of existence" (Lehtonen 1997, 47).

CONCLUDING REMARKS

I have here elaborated some affinities and differences between the phenom-enological and the psychoanalytic account of embodiment. Many interesting points of resemblance have been introduced: both disciplines consider self-hood fundamentally a bodily matter, both interpret the body as a junction point between inner and outer, both discuss the body as an experiential being, both conceive the feeling of existence in terms of bodily experience, and both regard the self as a layered or sedimented being that is structured in time. Already in the light of these points of intersection, I believe that a dialogue between phenomenology and psychoanalysis would be extremely fruitful.

The psychoanalytic view may also challenge and thereby also comple-ment and improve phenomenology. As an example of this, I have empha-sized two particular aspects in how these disciplines consider the formation of the bodily self. On the one hand, both consider the tactile sense as the fundamental one, but psychoanalysis develops this idea further. It suggests that there are constitutional hierarchies also *within* the tactile field, and argues, moreover, that these hierarchies are reflected in the structure of the bodily self. To neglect this possibility threatens to lead to an abstract and too neutral view of the bodily self. It might be interesting to investigate and analyze the implications of the psychoanalytic view to what Husserl termed "genetic phenomenology." On the other hand, unlike phenomenology, psychoanalysis puts into question the assumption that bodily awareness is fundamentally and primarily organized by *factually registered sensations*. And by questioning this, it also challenges the claim that there is always already an experiential boundary between self and the (m)other, which Husserl considers to be essential.

According to the psychoanalytic view, it is not in bodily experiences of just any kind that the infant comes to gain and stabilize a fundamental sense of existing, self-awareness, and hence a minimal selfhood but precisely in those bodily experiences that involve need-fulfillment—and hence in bodily experiences in which other people play an essential role. In the phenomenological view, by contrast, kinesthetic-sensuous experience is considered a sufficient ground for the constitution of the self/nonself distinction, and hence there is a danger that the self in its most fundamental form is taken to emerge and exist independently of others. That is to say, in phenomenology, the emerging self is "not conceivable without the *non-self,* to which it is intentionally related" (Hua 14, 244; *my italics*), whereas in psychoanalysis the emerging self is neither conceivable without the *other,* the caregiver, that constitutionally serves as an "auxiliary ego" nor as the "mothering side of symbiotic self" (Mahler et al. 1975, 52; Spitz 1965, 114, 263). The challenging question that may accordingly be addressed to phenomenology is the following: What kind of role does the dimension of needs, desires, and fantasies play in the organization of bodily experiences and in the early formation of the self-other relationship, and has this role been sufficiently taken into account in phenomenological scholarship?

NOTES

1. I want to thank Rudolf Bernet, Henrik Enckell, and Johannes Lehtonen for their comments on an earlier version of this article.
2. I have elsewhere argued in detail that this hesitance unfolds into what Husserl later calls the "paradox of subjectivity;" see Taipale (2014); cf. Husserl Hua 6, 182ff.
3. This has remarkable consequences for our experience of others. For an elaboration of some of these consequences, see Taipale (2012).
4. While referring to Freud, the former page number(s) refer(s) to the German original text, whereas the latter number(s) refer(s) to the English translation used.
5. In a situation in which self-awareness truly is "all-inclusive," there would difference between saying that there *is a self* on the one hand or that there *is no self* on the other. This might explain certain disagreements of different psychoanalytic schools.
6. This footnote first appeared in the English translation (1927), in which it was described as having been authorized by Freud.
7. Head and Holmes (1911/1912), who originally coined the term 'body schema,' defined it as a complex system of motor movement coordination,

which consists of an *interoceptive sense of posture* (a "postural schema") and an *exteroceptive sense of localized tactile sensations* (a "superficial schema") that serves to provide information about the interface between body surface and external objects.

8. For example, the received view today is that infants begin to differentiate between themselves, the environment, and other people already from birth and that they are social beings from the start (see Hobson 2002; Reddy 2008; Stern 1985; Trevarthen 1977, 1979).

9. Interestingly, William James, coming from very different tradition, likewise observes that we are most distinctly aware of our "cephalic motions" (James 2007, 301).

10. Let me note in this connection that a detailed phenomenological analysis of the experience of falling asleep might accordingly be helpful while investigating the structure and origin of certain experiential disorders related to falling asleep.

REFERENCES

Federn, P. 1952. *Ego Psychology and the Psychoses.* New York: Basic Books.

Freud, S. 1914. "Zur Einführung des Narzissmus." *Gesammelte Werke* 10, 137–170. London: Imago Publishing Co., Ltd. Translation: Freud, Sigmund. (GW 10). "On Narcissism," *The Standard Edition of the Complete Psychological Works of Sigmund Freud* (SE), Volume 14 (1914–1916): On the History of the Psycho-Analytic Movement, Papers on Metapsychology and Other Works, 67–102. Translated by James Strachey. London: Hogarth Press.

———. 1915a. "Triebe und Triebschicksale." *Gesammelte Werke* 10, 210–232. London: Imago Publishing Co., Ltd. Translation: Freud, S. (GW 10). "Instincts and their Vicissitudes." *The Standard Edition of the Complete Psychological Works of Sigmund Freud* (SE), Volume 14 (1914–1916): On the History of the Psycho-Analytic Movement, Papers on Metapsychology and Other Works, 109–140. Translated by James Strachey. London: Hogarth Press.

———. 1915b. *Vorlesungen zur Einführung in die Psychoanalyse. Gesammelte Werke* 11, 3–484. London: Imago Publishing Co., Ltd. Translation: Freud, S. 1917. Introductory Lectures on Psycho-Analysis. *The Standard Edition of the Complete Psychological Works of Sigmund Freud,* (SE), Volume 16 (1916–1917): Introductory Lectures on Psycho-Analysis (Part III), 241–463. Translated by James Strachey. London: Hogarth Press.

———. 1923. "Das Ich und Es." *Gesammelte Werke* 13, 237–289. Imago Publishing Co., Ltd., London. Translation: Freud, S. 1923. "The Ego and the Id." *The Standard Edition of the Complete Psychological Works of Sigmund Freud,* Volume 19 (1923–1925): The Ego and the Id and Other Works, 1–66. Translated by James Strachey. London: Hogarth Press.

———. 1925. "Die Verneigung." *Gesammelte Werke* 14, 11–15. London: Imago Publishing Co., Ltd. Translation: Freud, S. 1925. "Negation," *The Standard Edition of the Complete Psychological Works of Sigmund Freud,* Volume 19 (1923–1925): The Ego and the Id and Other Works, 233–240. Translated by James Strachey. London: Hogarth Press.

———. 1930. "Das Unbehagen in der Kultur." *Gesammelte Werke* 14, 421–506. London: Imago Publishing Co., Ltd. Translation: Freud, S. 1961. Civilization and Its Discontents. *The Standard Edition of the Complete Psychological Works of Sigmund Freud,* Volume 21, (1927–1931): The Future of an Illusion, Civilization and Its Discontents, and Other Works, 1–273. Translated by James Strachey. London: Hogarth Press.

————. 1938. "Abriss der Psychoanalyse." *Gesammelte Werke* 17, vii–153. London: Imago Publishing Co., Ltd. Translation: Freud, S. 1938. An Outline of Psycho-Analysis. *The Standard Edition of the Complete Psychological Works of Sigmund Freud*, Volume 23 (1937–1939): Moses and Monotheism, An Outline of Psycho-Analysis and Other Works, 139–208. Translated by James Strachey. London: Hogarth Press.

Head, H. and Holmes G. 1911/1912. "Sensory Disturbances from Cerebral Lesions." *Brain* 34: 102–254.

Heidegger, M. 1961. *Nietzsche*. Erster Band. Stuttgart: Verlag Günther Neske.

————. 1987. *Zollikoner Seminare. Protokolle–Gespräche–Briefe*. Edited by M. Boss. Frankfurt am Main: Vittorio Klostermann.

Henry, M. 1975. *Philosophy and Phenomenology of the Body*. Translated by G. J. Etzkorn. The Hague: Martinus Nijhoff.

Hobson, P. 2002. *The Cradle of Thought*. London: Macmillan.

Hoffer, W. 1950. "Development of the Body Ego." *Psychoanalytic Study of the Child* 5: 18–23.

Husserl, E. 1952. *Ideen zu einer reinen Phänomenologie und phänomenologische Philosophie. Zweiter Buch: Phänomenologische Untersuchungen zur Konstitution*, ed. M. Biemel. Haag: Martinus Nijhoff. (Hua 4)

————. [1954] 1962. *Die Krisis der europäischen Wissenschaften und die transzendentale Phänomenologie. Eine Einleitung in die phänomenologische Philosophie.* Edited by W. Biemel. The Hague: Martinus Nijhoff. (Hua 6)

————. 1966. *Zur Phänomenologie des inneren Zeitbewusstesens (1893–1917)*. Edited by R. Boehm. The Hague: Martinus Nijhoff. (Hua 10)

————. 1970. *The Crisis of European Sciences and Transcendental Phenomenology: An Introduction to Phenomenological Philosophy.* Translated by D. Carr. Evanston, IL: Northwestern University Press.

————. 1973. *Zur Phänomenologie der Intersubjektivität. Texte aus dem Nachlass. Erster Teil: 1905–1920.* Edited by I. Kern. The Hague: Martinus Nijhoff. (Hua 13)

————. 1973. *Zur Phänomenologie der Intersubjektivität. Texte aus dem Nachlass. Zweiter Teil: 1921–28.* Edited by I. Kern. The Hague: Martinus Nijhoff. (Hua 14)

————. 1973. *Zur Phänomenologie der Intersubjektivität. Texte aus dem Nachlass. Dritter Teil: 1929–35.* Edited by I. Kern. The Hague: Martinus Nijhoff. (Hua 15)

————. 1973. *Ding und Raum. Vorlesungen 1907.* Edited by U. Claesges. The Hague: Martinus Nijhoff. (Hua 16)

————. 2006. *Späte Texte über Zeitkonstitution (1929–1934). Die C-Manuskripte.* Husserliana Materialen 8. Edited by D. Lohmar. Dordrecht: Springer. (HuaM 8)

————. 2008. *Die Lebenswelt. Auslegungen der vorgegebenen Welt und ihrer Konstitution. Texte aus dem Nachlass (1916–1937).* Edited by R. Sowa. Dordrecht: Springer. (Hua 39)

Isakower, O. 1938. "A Contribution to the Patho-Psychology of Phenomena Associated with Falling Asleep." *International Journal of Psycho-Analysis* 19: 331–345.

James, W. 2007. *The Principles of Psychology*, Vol. 1. New York: Cosimo.

Jones, E. 1957. *Sigmund Freud Life and Work, Volume Three: The Last Phase 1919–1939*. London: Hogarth Press.

Leder, D. 1990. *The Absent Body*. Chicago and London: University of Chicago Press.

Lehtonen, J. 1991. "The Body Ego From the Point of View of Psychophysical Fusion." *Psychotherapy and Psychosomatics* 56: 30–35.

————. 1997. "On the Origins of the Body Ego and Its Implications for Psychotic Vulnerability." In *The Seed of Madness. Constitution, Environment, and Fantasy in the Organization of the Psychic Core*, 19–57. Edited by V. Volkan and S. Akhtar. Madison, WI: International Universities Press.

————. 2006. "Infant–Mother Matrix as a Source of Mental Organization in the Infant: Contributions From the Neurophysiology of Nursing." In *Beyond the Mind–Body Dualism: Psychoanalysis and the Human Body*, 201–205. Edited by E. Zacharacopoulou. International Congress Series 1286. Amsterdam: Elsevier.

Lehtonen, J. 2011. *Tietoisuuden ruumiillisuus. Mieli, aivot ja olemassaolon tunne.* Helsinki: Duodecim.

Lewin, B. 1946. "Sleep, the Mouth, and the Dream Screen." *The Psychoanalytic Quarterly* 15: 419–434.

Mahler, M., Pine, F. and A. Bergman. 1975. *The Psychological Birth of the Human Infant.* New York: Basic Books.

Mahler, M. and J. McDevitt. 1982. "Thoughts on the Emergence of the Sense of Self, With a Particular Emphasis on the Body Self." *Journal of the American Psychoanalytic Association* 30 (4): 827–848.

Melle, U. 1983. *Das Wahrnehmungsproblem und seine Verwandlung in phänomenologischer Einstellung: Untersuchungen zu den phänomenologischen Wahrnehmungstheorien von Husserl, Gurwitsch, und Merleau-Ponty.* The Hague: Martinus Nijhoff.

Merleau-Ponty, M. 1945. *Phénoménologie de la perception.* Paris: Gallimard.

Reddy, V. 2008. *How Infants Know Minds.* Cambridge, MA: Harvard University Press.

Schilder, P. 1923. *Das Körperschema.* Berlin: Springer.

Spitz, R. 1955. "The Primal Cavity. A Contribution to the Genesis of Perception and Its Role for Psychoanalytic Theory." *The Psychoanalytic Study of the Child* 10: 215–240.

————. 1965. *The First Year of Life. A Psychoanalytic Study of Normal and Deviant Development of Object-Relations.* New York: International Universities Press.

Stern, D. 1985. *The Interpersonal World of the Infant. A View from Psychoanalysis and Developmental Psychology.* New York: Basic Books.

Taipale, J. 2012. "Twofold Normality. Husserl and the Normative Relevance of Primordial Constitution." *Husserl Studies* 28 (1): 49–60.

————. 2013. "Facts and Fantasies." In *The Phenomenology of Embodied Subjectivity*, edited by D. Moran and R. Jensen, 241–262. Dordrecht: Springer.

————. 2014. *Phenomenology and Embodiment. Husserl and the Constitution of Subjectivity.* Evanston, IL: Northwestern University Press.

Trevarthen, C. 1977. "Descriptive Analyses of Infant Communicative Behaviour." In *Studies in Mother-Infant Interaction,* edited by H. R. Schaffer, 227–270. London: Academic Press.

————. 1979. "Communication and Cooperation in Early Infancy: A Description of Primary Intersubjectivity." In *Before Speech: The Beginning of Interpersonal Communication*, edited by M. Bullowa, 321–347. Cambridge: Cambridge University Press.

11 William James on Consciousness and the Brain
From Psycho-Physical Dualism to Transcendental Philosophy

Richard Cobb-Stevens

INTRODUCTION

In what follows, I shall trace the development of William James's account of the complementary contributions of mind and body to our cognitive and affective modes of consciousness, with particular emphasis on his early *The Principles of Psychology* and his late *Essays on Radical Empiricism*. In these works, James offers a balanced account of the interplay between mind and body and especially between mind and brain while also firmly rejecting various forms of reductive materialism. From the outset, he called attention to the vulnerability of British empiricism to such reductive interpretations and to the inadequacy of Kantian transcendentalism as a corrective response to this weakness. James finally opted for a comprehensive position close to that of Husserl's transcendental philosophy. I shall contend that a Husserlian reading of James's radical empiricism makes for a coherent interpretation of that controversial doctrine. I shall also argue throughout for the merits of James's views on these closely interlocked themes and will conclude with some suggestions about how James's version of the transcendental dimension provides an intellectually compelling alternative to some recent reductionist theories.

1 PSYCHO-PHYSICAL DUALISM

In the Preface to *The Principles of Psychology,* published in 1890, James adopted an explicit dualism according to which conscious experiences (perceptions, memories, judgments, decisions, etc.) are accompanied by parallel bodily processes, especially brain processes. His methodology is also dualistic. Many commentators have called attention to the ease with which James moves in this work from phenomenological descriptions to neurological explanations, sometimes within the same chapter or even in the same paragraph. A "first-person" subjective account of some experience is typically complemented by a "third-person" objective account of relevant processes in the brain and then supplemented by an analysis of laboratory reports of behavioral experiments designed to confirm this parallelism.

In his chapter on the role of habit, for example, having first noted that every pulse of thought is correlated with a brain process, James also contrasts thoughts triggered by reflex responses with freely elected thoughts. The latter type of thinking testifies to a purposive function of mind that operates prior to or in the interval between stimulus and response by freely introducing consciously intended ends. He then draws upon the most advanced empirical research of his time to show how the teleological function of mind may eventually be taken over by neural networks. He concludes, for example, that moral actions at first freely chosen may, after being repeatedly performed, become habitual. As such, their performance no longer requires the same level of consciousness, and they are thenceforth carried out largely under the impetus of energy moving through established neural pathways. In this way, the force of habit diminishes intellectual fatigue and frees consciousness for other tasks.

In his chapters on association, attention, and will, James arrives at similar conclusions. He observes that the direction of much of our thinking may be explained by processes of association that are mainly neurological: "When two elementary brain processes have been active together, or in immediate succession, one of them, on recurring, tends to propagate its excitement into the other" (James 1981a, 534). Indeed, he goes so far as to say that we do not often create new thoughts spontaneously. We are usually limited to emphasizing or reinforcing one thought or another among those that are put before consciousness by the associative machinery of the brain. Our thinking is voluntary only to the extent that it is governed by a present or prior decision to think in a directional way toward a certain end. Guided by this teleological choice, we take an interest in certain ideas or images triggered by associative brain processes. In turn, such acts of interested attention have a feedback effect on the brain's subsequent associative processes: "If, for instance, I think of Paris, whilst I am hungry, I shall not improbably find that its restaurants have become the pivot of my thought" (ibid., 549). James thus suggests that the mind is sometimes free and teleological, whereas the brain tends to be exclusively associative and reactive. He has little to say, however, about the neural processes that accompany the specifically free and teleological dimensions of our thinking. He does remark that "physiologically speaking, we must suppose that a purpose means the persistent activity of certain rather definite brain-processes throughout the whole course of thought" (ibid., 549). Despite this tentative supposition that brain processes play a role even in our free choices, James also consistently makes a case for the irreducibility of our conscious thinking to exclusively physical processes. He points out that just because neural processes are a necessary condition of consciousness, it does not follow that they are a sufficient condition of consciousness, let alone identical with it. Consciousness, he claims, cannot be adequately accounted for in terms of stimulus and response, associative brain processes, or ultimately the particles of physics. He also makes it clear that the only adequate truth about the world is the *total* truth: "The world contains consciousness as well as atoms—and the one must be written down as just as essential as the other. . . . Atoms alone or consciousness alone are precisely equal mutilations of the truth" (James 1981b, 962 n11). Similar criticisms of reductive materialism are often repeated in James's writings. For example, in an essay on Herbert Spencer's evolutionary account of the development of mind in terms of the instinct for survival, James objects that, from the outset, consciousness also has a vote: "There belongs to mind, from its birth upward, a spontaneity, a vote. It is in the game, and not a mere looker-on" (James 1978, 21).

These passages suggest that James was a consistent and unapologetic dualist. However, he sometimes expressed serious doubts about his dualist position. In a significant passage in his chapter on free will in the *Principles*, James first lists compelling reasons for a clear-cut distinction between free volition and resultant bodily movements and between mental and physical processes in general. However, he then qualifies his commitment to this distinction by stating that no amount of introspective evidence demonstrates conclusively that purely nonphysical activities exist, and he finally asserts that the connection between mind and brain is inscrutable: "I do not *fully* understand how we come to our unshakeable belief that thinking exists as a special kind of immaterial process alongside of the material processes of the world. It is certain, however, that only by *postulating* such thinking do we make things currently intelligible" (James 1981b, 1174).

One has the impression that, on a deeper level, James's postulate is founded on reasons that are essentially ethical and pragmatic. At various periods of his life, James struggled with serious depression and even a sense of nihilism, brought on, he later realized, by an intermittent loss of belief in freedom of the will. Despite considerable effort, he eventually became convinced that he could not, on exclusively intellectual grounds, refute the determinism that had become dominant in the theoretical psychology of his contemporaries. He was finally delivered from this depression by reading the reflections on free will by the French philosopher, Charles Renouvier, who defined free will as (in James's translation) "the sustaining of a thought *because* I *choose* to when I might have other thoughts" (James 1920, I, 147). Convinced of the accuracy of this definition, James concluded that it would seem only fitting that freedom's first act should be to affirm itself. He also concluded that we ought not to hope for any other method of getting at the truth about the conflict between determinism and freedom. After all, if we do enjoy first-hand experience of freedom of the will, why should we bother to prove it to ourselves? Given the intellectually seductive character of some deterministic theories, James realized that to enter into debate with them is already to abandon self-evidence that requires no confirmation. The only effective response to determinism is simply to choose freedom. Applying this newly acquired conviction to his own personal predicament, James decided to put Renouvier's theory into practice, by making a firm decision: "My first act of free will shall be to believe in free will" (ibid.). Marilynne Robinson observes that this act was "the beginning of James' convalescence" and of his deliverance from what he called "the entrapment" of the idea of determinism. Commenting on how this conversion was based on the replacement of one idea by another, Robinson concludes that we, "who today live among great libraries and universities," curiously tend to underestimate the influence of ideas upon behavior. We look exclusively to "genetics or chemical imbalance" or to "the complexities of childhood and family" to account for sicknesses such as depression, forgetting that ideas have deep practical and behavioral consequences (Robinson 2010, 12). In contrast, William James understood and emphasized that ideas count; they have a vote—indeed, in many cases, a decisive vote.

Throughout the *Principles,* James is highly critical of British empiricism. He first observes that it might seem that empiricism adheres closely to the evidence, for its proponents claim that their analyses of the nature of mind are strictly based upon introspective observations that may be confirmed by anyone. However, closer analysis, he contends, reveals that the empiricist theory of mind and its processes is in fact hopelessly inaccurate and incoherent. The empiricists generally describe the mind as an interior space containing representations of reality. According to John Locke, for example, the "cabinet" of the mind is empty and dark at birth, and the organs of sensation are windows through which enter "visible resemblances of things without" (Locke 1894, I, ch. 2, sec.17). Perceptions of unified objects are the products of association by contiguity, which assembles into configurations those elementary impressions that habitually occur together. Thus, says Berkeley, "a certain color, taste, smell, figure and consistency having been observed to go together, are accounted one distinct thing, signified by the name apple" (Berkeley 1949, II, 1). If a subsequent impression or complex of impressions is similar to an earlier impression, association by resemblance triggers the revival of the earlier impression, and the mind then possesses earlier and later impressions in conjunction. This is how recognition of the same object occurs.

James makes several criticisms of this theory. First, he notes that the "simple impression" and the "simple idea" of Hume and Locke are both abstractions never realized in experience. Experience from the outset presents us with "original sensible totals"—wholes having focus and fringes, foreground and horizon. Experimental studies demonstrate, James points out, that even the weakest sensations tend to provoke the perception of complex objects as long as they trigger memory's pathways: "All brain-processes are such as to give rise to what we call figured consciousness. If paths are irradiated at all, they are irradiated in consistent systems, and occasion thoughts of definite objects" (James 1981b, 728). By a "figured consciousness" he means what was later called a *Gestalt,* that is, an object that presents itself in a context and against a background. Second, he observes that the empiricists conflate mental processes and their objective correlates: "Mill and the rest believe a thought must be what it means, and mean what it is" (James 1981a, 446). The notion that to know is simply to have a thought within the mind, like a photograph in a bureau drawer, does not explain how the thought means something in the world.

James concludes that the empiricists thus fail to describe sensation and perception accurately. They are intentional functions of mind, not mental contents that somehow represent reality. They present reality; they are not duplicates of reality. He adds that the empiricist notion that, given a repeated stimulus emanating from the outside world, association causes the same sensory impressions to "reappear periodically before the footlights of consciousness" is a myth (James 1981a, 230). What does reappear is the same object in the world taken from a different angle and with a different horizon or backdrop. There is something wrong, therefore, with the description of mind as an enclosure cut off from reality, an inner space filled with representations. There is no evidence, either in descriptive psychology or in the science of the brain, that the primary objects of our experience are intramental pictures of the world. James thus clearly rejects the representational model for mind and emphasizes the intentionality of our cognitive and affective modes of consciousness.

James also calls attention to the ways in which the empiricist representational account of sensation and perception is vulnerable to reductive materialism. He points out that basic themes from empiricism were often taken over by nineteenth-century scientific psychologists and developed into exclusively causal and reductive accounts of perception. For example, James mentions a theory titled "the eccentric projection of sensations" that claimed as a scientifically established fact that sensations are first felt in the brain, initially as simple units or as combinations of units compounded by association, and then projected so as to appear located in the outer world (James 1981b, 678). James's commentary on this theory is terse and decisive:

> It seems to me that there is not a vestige of evidence for this view. It hangs together with the opinion that our sensations are originally devoid of all spatial content, an opinion I am wholly at a loss to understand . . . So far is it from being true that our first way of feeling things is the feeling of them as subjective or mental, that the exact opposite seems rather to be the truth. Our earliest, most instinctive, least developed kind of consciousness is of the objective kind (1981b, 678–679).

In an essay titled "Percept and Concept," James also criticizes Kant's attempt to correct the weaknesses of the empiricist account of our knowledge of objects. He first summarizes Kant's transcendental methodology as follows:

> The account which I give directly contradicts that which Kant gave. Kant always speaks of the aboriginal sensible flux as a manifold of which he considers the essential characteristic to be its *disconnectedness*. To get any togetherness at all into it requires, he thinks, the agency of the 'transcendental ego of apperception'; and to get any definite

connections requires that of the understanding, with its synthesizing concepts or categories (James 1979, 33, n3).

James then observes that he does not accept without qualification Kant's fundamental premise that conception without perception is blind and perception without conception is empty of meaning. He points out that Kant is surely correct to the extent that he calls attention to the complementary roles of perception and conception. His premise is misleading, however, to the extent that it rests on the empiricist postulates that perceptual experience comes to us originally as a chaotic manifold and that there is no intellectual intuition involved in the achievement of conceptual thinking. James maintains, on the contrary, that the field of perceptual experience is replete with inchoatively meaningful patterns and relations. Hence, he says, "We ought to say a feeling of *and*, a feeling of *if*, and a feeling of *by*, quite as readily as we say a feeling of *blue* or a feeling of *cold*" (James 1981a, 238). Moreover, he also suggests that the intuition of particular *thises* by perception is complemented by the intuition of universal *whats* by the "apperceiving intellect," and he concludes that percepts and concepts "melt into each other when we handle them together" (James 1979, 58). In an earlier passage, James adds an important detail: "By those *whats* we apperceive all our *thises*" (ibid., 34). On James's interpretation, therefore, the intuited *whats* are distinguishing features of the object.

James thus suggests that his own interpretation of cognition is more classical than modern. The above description of the interplay of concepts and percepts is decidedly more Aristotelian than Kantian. Aristotle claims that to know any particular object is always to know it by reason of its meaningful form, its *eidos*. The *eidos* is the identifying "look" of a thing, the species-look that determines the predicates that we deploy in its regard (Aristotle *Met.*, VII, 6, 1031b, 17–22). Commenting on this passage, Robert Sokolowski points out that the form of a thing, its look, is not something separate from the thing: it might best be described as *its* "intelligibility" (Sokolowski 2008, 177–180). Alva Noë makes the same point in slightly different language. He points out that there is no reason to think that appearances are exclusively mental items: "How things look, sound, or feel . . . is precisely a feature of the way things are" (Noë 2004, 164).

2   BODY-OBJECT AND BODY-LIVED

In later writings, James gradually moves away from his early emphasis on the psycho-physical parallelism of mind and body toward a greater emphasis on their harmonious interaction in what he now often refers to as the "lived-body," or the "body-lived." Ralph Barton Perry, James's biographer, notes that as early as 1898, when James was preparing the *Principles* for publication, he wrote in his diary that he had failed to distinguish adequately between the brain thought-*of* and the brain thought-*with* and, more generally, between the body as an object of physiological investigation and the body as lived (Perry 1935, II, 369). Commenting on this statement, John Wild points out that in the *Principles*, James had in fact already overcome this dichotomy (Wild 1969, 360). In his chapter on the emotions, for example, James seems at first to give priority to an almost exclusively physiological account of emotion by characterizing emotion as an immediate and reflexive bodily reaction to physical stimuli. On this interpretation, the only conscious activity involved in emotion is the experience of the corporeal disturbances caused by these stimuli. However, James next calls attention to the more complex role played by the lived body in our emotive experiences. First, he distinguishes between "the coarser emotions," in which corporeal disturbances are more pronounced and in which consciousness is mainly reactive, and "the subtler emotions," wherein intellectual, aesthetic, or moral feelings predominate. In the latter instances, our emotions are experienced as accompaniments to predominantly cognitive experiences, especially experiences that involve value judgments. Such emotions, of course, also involve corporeal reactions: "Unless we actually laugh at the neatness of the demonstration or witticism, unless we thrill at the case of justice, or tingle at the act of magnanimity, our state of mind can hardly be called emotion at all" (James 1981b, 1084–1085). In such instances, however, our consciousness is not immediately directed toward bodily disturbances but toward some fearful or delightful aspect of the world. James also suggests that in both types of emotion, there is always a cognitive component, and that in most instances, any reactive corporeal components are subordinated to the lived-body's cognitive intentions and to its power freely to shift its attention. In an essay titled "What Is an Emotion?" he observes that this power makes it possible to limit and contain our emotions. We have the ability, in a moment of fear or anger, for example, to shift our attention to calming thoughts and even to adopt bodily expressions that go counter to the typical bodily expressions of the emotion: "If we wish to conquer undesirable emotional tendencies in ourselves, we must assiduously, and in the first instance cold-bloodedly, go through the *outward* motions of those contrary dispositions we prefer to cultivate" (James 1884, 198). In this way, as Robinson puts it, we discover that "composure *diminishes* fear, and calm *dissipates* anger" (Robinson 2010, 12).

James concludes that our lived bodies are therefore unlike any other objects in our environment. They are part of the world, and yet they are the irreducible focal points of our perspectives on the world: "My body is the primary instance of the ambiguous. Sometimes I treat my body purely as part of outer nature. Sometimes, again, I think of it as mine" (James 1976, 76). James describes the lived body more in detail as follows:

> The world experienced (otherwise called the field of consciousness) comes at all times with our body as its center, center of vision, center

of action, center of interest. Where the body is is 'here'; when the body acts is 'now'; what the body touches is 'this'; all other things are 'there' and 'then' and 'that' . . . The body is the storm center, the origin of coordinates . . . Everything circles around it, and is felt from its point of view. The word 'I' then is primarily a noun of position, just like 'this' and 'here'" (1976, 86 n8).

James thus interprets the lived body both as the locus of stimuli and reflexes and as the functional center of the field of consciousness: "Its sensorial adjustments are my 'attention', its kinesthetic alterations are my 'efforts', its visceral perturbations are my 'emotions'" (ibid., 76). Whenever James refers to the mind-brain relationship in this context, he adopts a language that suggests that mind and brain function as complementary parts of the whole person. They are what Husserl later refers to as "non-independent parts of a whole" (Husserl 1970b, 467; Hua 19/1, 260).

3   RADICAL EMPIRICISM

The priority that James eventually ascribes to the lived body set the stage for his development, in the last decade of his life, of a powerful critique of another form of dualism, the subject-object dualism that had been the default position in epistemology since British empiricism. James gradually developed his position in a series of lectures and essays, delivered and composed in the early 1900s. His notes for his seminars and his correspondence with friends during this period reveal that he looked forward to publishing a book of essays on this topic. Unfortunately, James did not live to see the publication of his book, which was eventually edited and published in 1912, under the title *Essays in Radical Empiricism*, by his friend, Ralph Barton Perry.

As noted above, James's analysis of the stream of consciousness in the *Principles* had convinced him that there was something radically wrong with an empiricism that suggests that our cognitive experiences are objective, only in the sense that British empiricism had ascribed to the status of images and ideas located within Locke's "cabinet" of the mind. Against all such representational theories of cognition, James's later work proposes a more radical empiricism based upon a return to "pure experience." He makes it clear that by a "return to pure experience" he does not mean a return to the intramental world of sensations and ideas but rather a return to our experience *of* the world as it is actually lived rather than as it is theorized by philosophers obsessed by the notion that our experiences must be mediated by intramental representations.

In *The Meaning of Truth*, published in 1901, James had already stated the basic premise of his proposed book: "The postulate of these essays is that the only things that shall be debatable among philosophers shall be things definable in terms drawn from experience" (James 1932, xii). In the *Essays*, James adds some clarifications. An experience is pure, he says, when it occurs prior to being analyzed or conceptualized:

> In its pure state . . . there is no self-splitting of it into consciousness and what the consciousness is 'of'. Its subjectivity and objectivity are functional attributes, solely realized only when the experience is 'taken', i.e., . . . considered along with its two differing contexts respectively, by a new retrospective experience (James 1976, 13).

James's opening essay, "Does Consciousness Exist?", caused quite a stir in the philosophical world, because his initial answer to this question was basically negative. He objects to the vague ways in which philosophers, such as Paul Natorp and Hugo Münsterberg, refer to the "ghostly" or "diaphanous" status of consciousness itself, as opposed to the content of consciousness (James 1976, 3). James responded to these views somewhat acrimoniously: "I believe that consciousness, when once it has evaporated to this state of pure diaphaneity, is on the point of disappearing altogether. It is the name of a nonentity . . . Those who still cling to it are clinging to a mere echo, the faint rumor left behind by the disappearing 'soul' upon the air of philosophy" (1976, 3–4). However, he quickly clarifies these negative remarks as follows:

> To deny . . . that 'consciousness' exists seems so absurd on the face of it—for undeniably 'thoughts' exist—that I fear some readers will follow me no farther. Let me then immediately explain that I mean to deny only that the word stands for an entity but to insist most emphatically that it does stand for a function There is, I mean, no aboriginal stuff or quality of being, contrasted with that of which material objects are made, out of which our thoughts of them are made, but there is a function in experience which thoughts perform. . . . That function is *knowing* (1976, 4).

These comments make it clear, as Gerald Myers suggests, that James's critique of soul-theory is directed at Descartes's interpretation of the soul as a separate ethereal substance somehow linked to a bodily substance (Myers 1986, 61–62).

James attempted to clarify his position in the following remarks:

> I have tried to show that when we call an experience 'conscious', that does not mean that it is suffused throughout with a peculiar modality of being ('psychic' being) as stained glass may be suffused with light, but rather that it stands in certain determinate relations to other portions of experience extraneous to itself. These form one peculiar 'context' for it, while taken in another context of experiences, we class it as a fact in the physical world. This pen, for example, is, in the first instance

a bald *that,* a datum, phenomenon, content, or whatever neutral or ambiguous name you may prefer to apply. I call it . . . a pure experience. To get classed either as a physical pen or as someone's perception of a pen, it must assume a function, and that can only happen in a more complicated world. So far as in that world it is a stable feature, holds ink, marks paper, and obeys the guidance of a hand, it is a physical pen . . . So far as it is unstable, on the contrary coming and going with the movements of my eyes, altering with what I call my fancy, continuous with subsequent experiences of its 'having been' in the past tense, it is the percept of a pen in my mind (James 1976, 61).

Given James's generally negative appraisals of both reductive materialism and Descartes's soul-theory, it is odd that he seems in this passage to have adopted a metaphysical view that Bertrand Russell described as follows: "James's view is that the raw material out of which the world is built up is not of two sorts, one matter and the other mind, but that it is arranged in different patterns by its inter-relations, and that some arrangements may be called mental, while others may be called physical" (Russell 1921, 10). A. J. Ayer later described James's view in this and similar passages as a "neutral monism" and adds that he at first thought that James's view "implies that physical objects are reducible to sense-experiences" (Ayer 1968, 303). After deciding that this interpretation is untenable, Ayer next suggests that James might have meant only that "the positing of physical objects is a means of organizing our experiences in a systematic fashion" (ibid.).

Russell's interpretation is clearly justified by James's comments cited previously. James does seem to be saying that ultimate reality is all of one kind. It does not follow, however, that either of Ayer's interpretations are valid. In the *Principles*, James never suggested that our sensations and percepts are identical with their objects in the world. Neither did he ever suggest that "positing of physical objects" is justified by our conceptual organization of sensory data into more complex representatives of objects in the world. As we have noted above, James explicitly rejects the latter view in his discussion of Kant's relationship between percepts and concepts. There is no indication in the passage cited that James had decided to reject his earlier position on these topics.

John Wild suggests that one may reject James's metaphysical speculations about the ultimate "stuff" of the world while retaining an interpretation of the world of pure experience that is more consistent with James's view in the *Principles* that consciousness is an "intentional" relationship between a personal self and some object in the world rather than an "external" relationship that is found to hold between certain objects within the world (Wild 1969, 362). On Wild's interpretation, when James refers to "the world experienced, otherwise called the field of consciousness," he means a field of intentional relationships wherein objects in the world are presented as known, as objects perceived, remembered, or imagined. In that context we might make a distinction between a pen and the same pen, as known in various ways, or as perceived, as remembered, or as imagined. We might also make a distinction between a pen and the same pen identified as such by reason of its observed objective features ("holds ink, marks paper, and obeys the guidance of a hand"). On this reading of James's remarks, it follows that a distinction between a thing and the same thing as known is not reducible to a distinction between a thing in the world and a representation of the thing in a parallel world, the "cabinet" of the mind. Within what James calls "the world known, or the field of consciousness," it is a distinction between a thing and the same thing, as known, that is, as presented, by reason of *its* look, *its* intelligibility.

4   PURE EXPERIENCE AND THE TRANSCENDENTAL DIMENSION

Many commentators familiar with the phenomenological tradition have called attention to similarities between the works of James and Husserl. The following themes are most often mentioned: James's criticism of traditional empiricism, his emphasis on intentionality as opposed to representationalism, and his description of the status of the lived-body. Some commentators have also called attention to the similarity between James's description of pure experience and Husserl's description of what he calls the transcendental dimension.[1] I propose now to develop the latter theme in some detail.

Permit me to begin with a few remarks about the well-documented influence of the writings of William James on Edmund Husserl. While my intention is to propose a "Husserlian" reading of James's notion of pure experience, it should be noted that historically, Husserl was more influenced by James than vice versa. In his historical survey of the phenomenological movement, Herbert Spiegelberg notes that Husserl had revealed to Dorion Cairns that he had abandoned the project of writing a psychology, "feeling that James had said what he wanted to say" (Spiegelberg 1960, 113–114). According to Spiegelberg, Husserl also made similar remarks in his lecture courses at the University of Halle. Husserl himself confirms these anecdotal impressions when in the *Logical Investigations* he refers gratefully to James's influence as follows: "How little James' genius for observations in the field of descriptive psychology of presentational experiences entails psychologism, can be seen from the present work. For the advances in descriptive analysis that I owe to this distinguished thinker have only facilitated my release from the psychologistic standpoint" (Husserl 1970a, 420 n1; Hua 19/1, 208 n1). I should add that I had occasion to view Husserl's personal copy of James's *Principles* at the Husserl Archives in Leuven. The margins of the pages of several of James's chapters are filled with affirmative notations made by Husserl.

Since my goal is to offer a transcendental interpretation of James's radical empiricism, it will be helpful first to give a brief summary of how Husserl's transcendentalism differs from that of Kant. In modern philosophy, the term 'transcendental' refers to philosophical methods that draw their inspiration from Kant's method of inquiring into the conditions, within the sphere of the human subject, that are requisite for the appearances of empirical objects and relationships. Kant's method was adopted in response to Hume's skepticism concerning the cause-effect relationship, one of the foundational concepts of the physical sciences. Having endorsed the empiricist thesis that human intuition is exclusively sensuous and having thus accepted the premise that sensory impressions caused by external things provide our only intuitive access to the world, Kant could not appeal to the premodern notion of intellectual intuition of the forms of things or of their relations. On the other hand, he does not reduce appearances to Humean impressions. Neither does he reduce appearing to the mere having of such impressions. Kant distinguishes between the matter of appearances that is given to us *a posteriori* by sensations and the forms of appearances that belong *a priori* to the structure of sensibility. The forms of sensibility are space and time, which together enable the discontinuous manifold of sensation to be arranged in an orderly fashion. Without this organization, discernment of identical and enduring objects would be impossible (Kant CPR, B 94/A 69). This achievement would also be impossible without the contribution of the faculty of understanding, which synthesizes perceptions and relevant concepts. Kant distinguishes between empirical concepts, which are derived by abstraction from perceptions, and *a priori* concepts or categories, such as the cause-effect relation, which are inferred as necessary conditions for any possible cognition of empirical objects. Hence, Kant concluded that the way to rescue the validity of the causal laws of nature from Hume's skepticism was to relate them to these more universal conditions for converting subjective perceptions into objective experiences, the *a priori* categories (ibid., A 218/B 265–266).

The judgmental syntheses achieved by the understanding make possible the thinking of organized appearances as objects falling under concepts (ibid., B 137/A 248). The appearances thought in this manner are called "phenomena." Kant opposes phenomena to "noumena" and defines the latter negatively as things insofar as they do not appear to us or positively as things as they would appear to an intelligence capable of intellectual intuition (ibid., A 230/B 309).

Husserl retained the Kantian term 'transcendental' to refer to his own philosophical method but introduced some significant changes. First, he broadened the range of his inquiry so as to include not only the conditions of scientific objectivity but also the conditions of prescientific and even prelinguistic modes of knowing. Second, he contended that transcendental conditions are intuited rather than deduced. According to Husserl, we do not need a complex deduction to experience ourselves as transcendental egos or as rational beings belonging to the kingdom of ends. We enjoy direct intuitive appreciation of ourselves as rational agents of meaning, purpose, and truth. Moreover, mortals that we are, we nevertheless enjoy categorial intuitions, not only of categories applicable to objects in general but also of the conceptual *whats* that permit the meaningful specification of particular perceived *thats* (Husserl 1970b, 778–782). Third, Husserl rejected the distinction between phenomenon and noumenon and developed an interpretation of appearances made possible by the adoption of what he calls the "phenomenological attitude."

Husserl claims that access to this phenomenological attitude requires a bracketing" of the "natural attitude" of everyday life. In the natural attitude, we experience ourselves as having direct acquaintance of a world and of belonging to that world, but we do not ordinarily pay attention to the appearing of the world. As Sokolowski puts it, "We go right through the appearing of the world to the world itself" (Sokolowski 2000, 50). As a result, when we do consider questions about how it is that the world appears to us, we tend to consider modes of causality within the world or products of human ingenuity such as pictures or computing devices as models for understanding how the world appears to us. By bracketing this natural attitude and adopting the phenomenological attitude, we "look *at* what we normally look *through*" (ibid.). We see the world itself as a phenomenon. We do not focus principally on our awareness of the world but rather on the manifold ways in which things in the world and the world itself appear to us.

Husserl describes his methodology most clearly in *The Idea of Phenomenology*, where he claims that his method provides access to a field of experience that "lies in a wholly new dimension" (Husserl 1964, 19; Hua 2, 24). He introduces this theme as a response to what he calls Hume's description of mind as a sphere of "thing-like immanence" (ibid., 35, Hua 2, 36), containing psychic processes and contents that somehow mirror a sphere of transcendent and therefore intuitively inaccessible things-in-themselves. Hume's interpretation, Husserl observes, implies that "cognition is a thing apart from its object, or that cognition is given, but the object of cognition is not given" (ibid., 30, Hua 2, 39). I take it that what Husserl is here suggesting is that Hume's description of the locus of cognition is similar to Locke's description of the "cabinet" of the mind as an enclosure in which there appear sensations and associative clusters of sensations that function as representations of things in the world. The "unspoken assumption" of this theory, Husserl says, is that the immediate objects of our cognition lie within the mind's interiority. This assumption, he concludes, is the "fatal mistake" of modern philosophy (ibid., 28, Hua 2, 37). Hume's fatal mistake was to construct an explanatory theory of how cognition works without first taking into consideration how the world actually appears to us. When we adopt the phenomenological attitude, we bracket not only the world as it is construed in the natural attitude but also the world as described in theories such as Hume's. In either case, we do not lose anything by bracketing these descriptions. On the contrary, by focusing on the actual appearances of things in the world and of the world itself, we acquire a perspective that makes possible a more accurate description of appearances in general. We discover that the appearances of things and their world are not separated from things and world and enclosed within the cabinet of the mind; they are experienced in the world as the manifold looks of things and of the world itself. Husserl calls the locus of this experience the transcendental dimension.

It seems to me that James's decision in the *Essays in Radical Empiricism* to limit all investigation to the realm of pure experience, which he defines as "the world experienced, otherwise called the field of consciousness," is basically the same as Husserl's decision to bracket the natural attitude and replace it with the phenomenological attitude. On this interpretation, James's field of consciousness is equivalent to Husserl's transcendental "dimension" of the appearances of things and world. This interpretation also makes it clear that James rejected both reductive materialism and representationalism. By focusing on the world as experienced, that is, as appearance, James adopted a properly phenomenological approach and thus avoided what Husserl called the "fatal mistake" of modern philosophy, the attempt by Hume and his followers to explain appearances in terms and models borrowed exclusively from cause-and-effect relationships within the world.

According to both James and Husserl, we have only one world, which can be considered in two ways: either in the way that we understand it in the natural attitude of everyday life and in the physical sciences built on that attitude or in what Husserl calls the "transcendental" attitude, which first pays attention to the ways in which the world presents itself and then reflects on these modes of its appearance. James does not develop an explicitly transcendental methodology. Like Husserl, however, he insists that the properly philosophical attitude for the study of cognition is to focus first and foremost on the experience or manifestation of things. When we assume this attitude, we find that the world does not, in fact, present itself by way of the mental pictures that Locke had described as the "visible resemblances of things without" but directly by way of all of its familiar and poetically celebrated intelligible markers. This is why James and Husserl both reject the double-world view implicit in representational theories of cognition.

Having rejected the notion of a parallel world of representation, James and Husserl concluded that the standard empiricist notion of phenomenon had to be revised. This is why Husserl refers to the transcendental realm as "an entirely new dimension." The metaphor of dimension aptly captures the status of the field of appearances or phenomena. In mathematics, a dimension is the number of coordinates needed to specify a point on an object. A rectangle, for example, is two dimensional and a cube is three dimensional. Transcendental reflection does not yield a parallel world that represents or pictures the real world; rather, it considers the real world in the light of its intelligibility as presented in the ensemble of its intelligible markers, its look. Like the coordinates that specify a point, the intelligible markers that comprise the look of a thing reveal its "what," its specific form. As I have suggested above, this revised notion of phenomenon is not really a new idea but rather a renewal of an old idea. Its historical genealogy is aptly summarized by Dan Zahavi in the following remarks about Husserl's interpretation of the notion of phenomenon:

> Husserl operates with a concept of phenomenon that can be traced back to Antiquity. The phenomenon is understood as the manifestation of the thing itself, and phenomenology is therefore a philosophical reflection on the way in which objects show themselves—how objects appear or manifest themselves—and on the conditions of possibility of this appearance (Zahavi 2003, 55).

CONCLUSION: A JAMESIAN APPRAISAL OF CONTEMPORARY NEUROLOGICAL REDUCTIONISM

Recent advances in the study of the human brain have occasioned a contemporary revival of reductive interpretations of our cognitive faculties. This latest version of mind-brain reductionism has had the support of some influential scientists. For example, Francis Crick, who was awarded a Nobel Prize for his work on the structure of the DNA molecule, made the following dramatic claim in his book, *The Astonishing Hypothesis: The Scientific Search for the Soul*: "You, your joys and your sorrows, your memories and your ambitions, your sense of personal identity and free will, are in fact no more than the behavior of a vast assembly of nerve cells and their associated molecules" (Crick 1994, 91). Crick subsequently adopted a more modest and tentative stance, acknowledging that in fact "no one has produced any plausible explanation as to how the experience of the redness of red could arise from the action of the brain" (Crick and Koch 2003, 119). Nevertheless, Crick's original claim remains one of the statements about consciousness and the brain that is most frequently cited both in the academic world and in the popular press.

Several prominent philosophers have lately adopted a position known as the mind-brain identity theory. In an early chapter of his book, *Consciousness Explained*, Daniel Dennett describes his version of this position as follows: "The prevailing wisdom, variously expressed and argued for. is *materialism*: there is only one sort of stuff, namely matter—the physical stuff of physics, chemistry and physiology—The mind is somehow nothing but a physical phenomenon. In short, the mind is the brain" (Dennett 1991, 33). In a later chapter, titled "Consciousness Imagined," he summarizes his position by inviting the reader to imagine a conscious robot:

> My argument is straightforward. I have shown you how to do it. It turns out that the way to imagine this is to think of the brain as a computer of sorts. The concepts of computer science provide the crutches

of imagination we need if we are to stumble across the *terra incognita* between our phenomenology as we know it by introspection and our brains as science reveals them to us. By thinking of our brains as information processing systems, we can gradually dispel the fog and pick our way across the great divide, discovering how it might be that our brains produce all the phenomena (1991, 433).

Dennett acknowledges that his use of language borrowed from computer science amounts to a "replacement of one family of metaphors and images with another" (ibid., 455). Instead of Descartes's mind as a theater, we now have brain as a virtual machine. Dennett justifies the use of metaphors as follows: "It's just a war of metaphors, you say, . . . but metaphors are the tools of thought. No one can think about consciousness without them. So it is important to equip yourself with the best tools available" (ibid.).

Curiously, however, the more recent works by philosophers with reductionist agendas seem to be returning to the Cartesian cluster of metaphors. Raymond Tallis, a British clinical neuroscientist, points out a revealing feature of this new reductionism. Its proponents frequently offer explanations of the brain's functions that are closely linked to traditional representational theories of the mind (Tallis 2011, 44–45). He calls attention in particular to claims made in various recently published works. For example, in *Soul Dust: The Magic of Consciousness*, Nicolas Humphrey, a British psychologist, claims to have solved the "hard problem" of consciousness. A person's consciousness, he says, is a "magical show" staged by one part of the brain to influence another part of the brain (Humphrey 2011, 40–44). Sokolowski also calls attention to similar claims by the American philosopher Paul Churchland in his book, *The Engine of Reason, the Seat of the Soul: A Philosophical Journey Into the Human Brain* (Sokolowski 2008, 211). Churchland refers to "the brain's ongoing portrait of an ever-changing world" and to "the common movie screen at the rear of the brain, which is illuminated simultaneously by two projectors (the eyes) instead of one" (Churchland 1995, 6, 60).

Alva Noë makes a similar point about the tendency, common to many neuroscientists, to describe what goes on in the brain as the construction of an internal representational model of the world. He wonders ironically why we should need an internal model, or picture of the world, when we already enjoy perfectly adequate access to the world itself. "Why not let the world be its own model; its own representation?" (Noë 2009, 142).

Tallis also calls attention to the broadly based cultural effects of the latest mind-brain identity theories. He summarizes the current situation as follows: "The republic of letters is in thrall to an unprecedented scientism. The word is out that human consciousness—from the most elementary tingle of sensation to the most sophisticated sense of self—is identical with neural activity in the human brain and that this extraordinary metaphysical discovery is underpinned by the latest findings in neuroscience" (Tallis 2011, 44). This analysis is confirmed by recent and innumerable essays in the popular press that regularly make extravagant claims about how contemporary neuroscience will eventually offer solutions to ethical and social problems that centuries of philosophical speculation have failed to resolve. For example, an oft-cited essay by David Brooks in the *New York Times* summarizes research that suggests that we have too long been relying on outdated categories. Neuroscience, he says, "will someday give us new categories, which will replace misleading categories like 'emotion' and 'reason' . . . and give us a firmer understanding of motivation, equilibrium, sensitivity and other unconscious capacities" (Brooks 2009, 31).

In my comments on *The Principles of Psychology*, I have several times emphasized James's constant effort to keep abreast of scientific theories that might contribute to his philosophical reflections on our cognitive and affective modes of consciousness. During his entire career, he tried to relate the latest physiological studies of the body and neurological studies of the brain to his first-person descriptions of mind and its powers. He also always took seriously the arguments of various earlier and contemporary philosophers and scientists, even while forcefully criticizing those who in his judgment had espoused reductionist theories that call into question the rationality, freedom, and responsibility that define our humanity.

Hence, I now wonder how William James would have reacted to the latest scientific discoveries about the human brain and how he would have responded to these latest reductionist accounts of the mind-brain relationship. A few comments in response to these questions may, I hope, serve as a brief summary of William James's intellectual itinerary from psycho-physical dualism to the theory of the lived-body and finally to his "transcendental" interpretation of "the field of consciousness."

In the first place, James would surely have welcomed the remarkable progress and great promise of contemporary scientific research on the physiology of the brain and nervous system. However, given his strongly held views in the *Principles of Psychology* on the irreducibility of freely enacted thoughts and decisions to the associative processes of the brain, it is unlikely that he would have accepted these mind-brain identity positions that assert that such free and conscious activities are simply identical to their accompanying neural processes. Second, James's later emphasis on the lived-body as "the center of vision, center of action, and center of interest" is incompatible with the notion that a single part of the body, the brain, or even the entire nervous system would explain every cognitive performance of the whole person, especially if moral visions, free actions, and intellectual and aesthetic interests are included.

However, the main reason James would have rejected these latest versions of materialistic reductionism has to do with an attitude that he shares with Husserl about our dual status as beings in the world and as beings that also have a world. Of course, we share with other conscious beings an awareness of being in a world in the sense of an immediate environment, but we alone seem to be beings that raise questions about the dual status of being in the world and having a world. Why, for example, were both James and Husserl intrigued by the significance of focusing on the appearance of the world as opposed to just observing the world itself? Philosophers reflect on such issues because they wonder about the kind of thinking involved in the recognition of this dual status. Sokolowski points out that Husserl gives different names to the sense of self experienced in these different ways of relating to the world (Sokolowski 2000, 112–119). Husserl calls the self experienced as being part of the world the "empirical ego" and the self experienced as having a world cognitively the "transcendental ego." Many philosophers have also used spatial imagery to distinguish our dual ways of relating to the world. We inhabit the space of the world, but our cognitive powers are exercised within the unique space of mind or consciousness. We have noted that both James and Husserl make use of such images: the field of pure experiences and the transcendental dimension. Other more contemporary philosophers also use spatial images in analogous ways. John McDowell calls attention to the "conceptual sovereignty" that his fellow philosophers, Wilfred Sellars and Donald Davidson, ascribe to the "space of concepts" and the "space of reasons" in their interpretations of the role of conceptual thinking (McDowell 1996, 142). Thomas Nagel raises the dual status question in a particularly lucid and forceful way: "How is it possible that creatures like ourselves, supplied with the contingency of a biological species whose very existence appears to be radically accidental, should have access to universally valid objective thought?" (Nagel 1997, 4). Nagel does not respond directly to this rhetorical question, but he does say that the space of logical reasoning is a space that we cannot either get outside of or explain from the outside (ibid., 34–35).

With the exception of Nagel, who is militantly opposed to reductionist accounts of mind, these contemporary philosophers do not comment extensively on reductionism of the type described. I have the impression, however, that they would agree with James's earlier rejection of theories similar to the current mind-brain identity theories. Philosophers who are committed to some version of the transcendental dimension are not inclined to endorse the metaphor of persons as robotic virtual machines.

NOTE

1. See, for example, Linschoten, J., 1957, *Auf dem Weg zu einer phänomenologischen Psychologie,* Berlin: Walter De Gruyter; Wilshire, B., 1968, *William James and Phenomenology,* Bloomington: Indiana University Press; Wild, J., 1969, *The Radical Empiricism of William James,* New York: Doubleday; and my book, Stevens, R., 1974, *James and Husserl: The Foundations of Meaning,* The Hague: Martinus Nijhoff.

REFERENCES

Aristotle. *Met. Metaphysics*. In *The Basic Works of Aristotle*, ed. Richard McKeon; trans. J.A. Smith, 681–926. New York: Random House, 1941.

Ayer, A. J. 1968. *The Origins of Pragmatism. Studies in the Philosophy of Charles Sanders Peirce and William James*. London: Macmillan.

Berkeley, G. 1949. "A Treatise Concerning the Principles of Human Knowledge." In *The Works of George Berkeley, Vol. II*, ed. A. Luce and T. Jessup. London: L. Thomas Nelson.

Brooks, D. 2009. "The Young and the Neuro." *New York Times*, October 12, sec. A, 31.

Churchland, P. 1995. *The Engine of Reason, the Seat of the Soul: A Philosophical Journey Into the Human Brain*. Cambridge: MIT Press.

Crick, F. 1994. *The Astonishing Hypothesis: The Scientific Search for the Soul*. New York: Charles Scribner's Sons.

Crick, F. and Koch, C. 2003. "A Framework for Consciousness." *Nature Neuroscience* 6 (2): 119–125.

Dennett, D. 1991. *Consciousness Explained*. Boston, Toronto, London: Little, Brown, and Company.

Humphrey, N. 2011. *Soul Dust: The Magic of Consciousness*. Princeton, NJ: Princeton University Press.

Husserl, E. 1964. *The Idea of Phenomenology* (Husserliana II). Trans. W. Alston and George Nakhnikian. The Hague: Martinus Nijhoff.

———. 1970a. *Logical Investigations* (Husserliana XIX/1). Trans. J. N. Finlay. London: Routledge & Kegan Paul.

———. 1970b. *Logical Investigations*, Vol. II (Husserliana XIX/2). Trans. J. N. Finlay. London: Routledge & Kegan Paul.

James, W. 1884. "What Is an Emotion?" *Mind* 9: 188–205.

———. 1920. *The Letters of William James*. Two Volumes. Ed. Henry James. Boston: Atlantic Monthly Press.

———. 1932. *The Meaning of Truth*. New York: Longmans, Green.

———. 1976. *Essays in Radical Empiricism*. Ed. Fredson Bowers, *The Works of William James*. Cambridge: Harvard University Press.

———. 1978. "Remarks on Spencer's Definition of Mind as Correspondence." In *Essays in Philosophy*, ed. Fredson Bowers, *The Works of William James*, 7–22. Cambridge: Harvard University Press.

———. 1979. "Percept and Concept." In *The Problems of Philosophy*, ed. Fredson Bowers, *The Works of William James*, 31–60. Cambridge: Harvard University Press.

———. 1981a. *The Principles of Psychology*, Vol. I. Ed. Fredson Bowers, *The Works of William James*. Cambridge: Harvard University Press.

———. 1981b. *The Principles of Psychology*, Vol. II. Ed. Fredson Bowers, *The Works of William James*. Cambridge: Harvard University Press.

Kant, I. CPR. *Critique of Pure Reason*. Trans. Norman Kemp Smith. Toronto: Macmillan, 1965.

Linschoten, J. 1957. *Auf dem Weg zu einer phänomenologischen Psychologie*. Berlin: Walter De Gruyter.

Locke, J. 1894. *An Essay Concerning Human Understanding*. Oxford: Oxford University Press.

McDowell, J. 1996. *Mind and World*. Cambridge, MA, London: Harvard University Press.

Myers, G. 1986. *William James: His Life and Thought*. New Haven, CT: Yale University Press.

Nagel, T. 1997. *The Last Word*. New York, Oxford: Oxford University Press.

Noë, A. 2004. *Action in Perception*. Cambridge: MIT Press.

———. 2009. *Out of Our Heads: Why You Are Not Your Brain, and Other Lessons From the Biology of Consciousness*. New York: Mill and Wang.

Perry, R. B. 1935. *The Thought and Character of William James*, Two Volumes. Boston: Little, Brown & Co.

Robinson, M. 2010. "Risk the Game: On William James." *The Nation*, December 13, 11–15.

Russell, B. 1921. *The Analysis of Mind*. London: G. Allen & Unwin; New York: Macmillan.

Sokolowski, R. 2000. *Introduction to Phenomenology*. London: Cambridge University Press.

———. 2008. *Phenomenology of the Human Person*. London: Cambridge University Press.

Spiegelberg, H. 1960. *The Phenomenological Movement: A Historical Introduction*. The Hague: Nijhoff.

Stevens, R. 1974. *James and Husserl: The Foundations of Meaning*. The Hague: Martinus Nijhoff.

Tallis, R. 2011. "A Mind of One's Own: The Metaphysical Limitations of Neuroscience." *New Statesman*, February 24, 44–47.

Wild, J. 1969. *The Radical Empiricism of William James*. New York: Doubleday.

Wilshire, B. 1968. *William James and Phenomenology*. Bloomington: Indiana University Press.

Zahavi, D. 2003. *Husserl's Phenomenology*. Stanford, CA: Stanford University Press.

Part IV
Beyond Correlation

12 What Is a Transcendental Description?

Fredrik Westerlund

1 INTRODUCTION

For some time, it seems to me, the question of the transcendental nature of philosophy has addressed us as a problem that concerns the very identity of philosophy.

On the one hand, I think it is no exaggeration to claim that at least since Kant, philosophy has tended to understand its own specific task as transcendental in a wide sense of the word. Philosophy in this respect is seen as an investigation that takes its starting point in our human experience of the world in order to investigate the meaning things have for us there. The mode of investigation here is neither empirical nor logical but instead consists of understanding the general structures of meaning that constitute our experience. On the other hand, the doubts concerning the ambition and possibility of transcendental philosophy have grown steadily during the twentieth century, intensifying and largely triumphing in the last fifty years. The criticisms of the transcendental project have come from many directions—from hermeneutists, deconstructivists, pragmatists, and naturalists as well as from the later Wittgenstein and his heirs—and have taken many shapes. In order to counter the supposed subjectivism, foundationalism, universalism, and essentialism of transcendental philosophy, critics have stressed the linguisticality, historicity, finitude, particularity, and plurality of human understanding. Hence, while the concept of the transcendental still more or less tacitly operates as the basic horizon for our understanding of the autonomous task of philosophy, our ready belief in this concept has collapsed to the extent that for a majority of philosophers—including those who defend it—it has taken on the unmistakable smell of a metaphysical remnant.

The crisis goes deep into our concept of the transcendental. It is not just that philosophy for whatever reasons would have lost sight of the insights already harbored by the tradition of transcendental philosophy so that our task would simply be to recover these insights. Rather, it seems clear to me that the paradigmatic articulations of the transcendental project from Kant to Husserl and onward have all still been burdened with basic problems and unclarities and do not contain ready answers to the most decisive criticisms directed against it. Thus the question arises: Is it possible to sketch a vision of transcendental inquiry that, freed from the metaphysical dogmas of the tradition, is able to open up what we can identify as a genuine mode of understanding for philosophy? Or is the very idea of the transcendental so deeply bound up with metaphysical dreams and prejudices that philosophy had better renounce the transcendental project in favor of other forms of speech and reflection?

In this chapter, I will try to address this question by examining the phenomenological idea of transcendental descriptions originally developed by Husserl and Heidegger, which I consider to be the clearest and most forceful version of transcendental philosophy available to us today. The aim of the chapter is to shed some light on the sense—possibilities and limits—of transcendental descriptions by discussing what I take to be two of the most weighty doubts against this kind of procedure: first, the objection that transcendental descriptions are inherently subjectivist and second, the objection that they are essentialist in nature. In my treatment of the two objections, I will both draw on and critically develop Husserl's and Heidegger's original accounts in order to point the way toward a conception of transcendental descriptions as a genuine possibility of philosophical understanding free from metaphysical dogmas.

The history of transcendental philosophy is of course long and complex, containing a manifold number of different conceptions of the nature of transcendental inquiry. In the twentieth century, the tradition of transcendental philosophy has continued and developed with little interruption in the context of continental philosophy—mainly through the phenomenology of Husserl and Heidegger. The analytic tradition, too, has witnessed an extended discussion concerning the nature and validity of transcendental arguments.[1] In focusing on transcendental phenomenology, I will not only leave aside major parts of the tradition, I will also refrain from discussing the specific questions and problems that transcendental reflection has been thought to apply to, for example, the question—central to Kant and to much of the analytic discussion—whether transcendental arguments can be used to dissolve or answer skeptical doubts. Ultimately, it remains an open question to what extent my account of transcendental descriptions will be able to illuminate the different forms of thinking and argumentation exhibited by the tradition. However, my suggestion is that it not only captures the sense of much of the concrete work done under the heading of phenomenology but also circumscribes a mode of understanding that philosophy has recurrently tended to make use of in more or less misguided and distorted ways. This, of course, does not imply that there could not be other vital forms of philosophical argument and reflection.

2   KANT, PHENOMENOLOGY, AND THE METHOD OF TRANSCENDENTAL DESCRIPTION

Let us begin by going back to Kant, who establishes the idea of transcendental inquiry as the central task of philosophy.[2]

In his *Critique of Pure Reason*, Kant defines the transcendental as follows: "I entitle *transcendental* all knowledge that is occupied not so much with objects as with the mode of our knowledge of objects in so far as this mode of knowledge is to be possible *a priori*" (Kant CPR, A 11–12/B 25). The definition has two main aspects that together articulate Kant's vision of the task of transcendental philosophy. First, Kant's notion that transcendental knowledge is concerned not with objects but with our modes of attaining knowledge of objects is nothing but a reformulation of the Copernican turn at the heart of his critical philosophy. Kant's decisive idea is that we can only attain knowledge of empirical reality as it appears to us—that is, according to the constitution of human subjectivity—while we can know nothing about reality in itself, regardless of how we experience and conceive it. Hence, Kant argued, philosophy must give up its traditional metaphysical ambition to gain knowledge of reality in itself and instead become transcendental: take its starting point in our *de facto* experience of reality and, by way of regressive arguments, determine the basic features and concepts of the human subject that condition our experience and grant it its structure of sense. Second, Kant maintains that the transcendental knowledge of philosophy is *a priori* since it is knowledge of the structures of the transcendental subject conditioning our experience of empirical objects.

However, although Kant for the first time opens up the transcendental self-understanding of modern philosophy, his own elaboration of transcendental philosophy is still beset with fundamental problems and unclarities. Here—anticipating the central themes of this chapter—I especially want to point to Kant's conception of transcendental inquiry in terms of transcendental arguments or proofs, his transcendental idealism, and his essentialism.

For Kant, the transcendental mode of inquiry basically has the form of regressive arguments. It starts by describing some central and obvious aspects of our experience and then goes on to infer the basic features—forms of intuition, categories of understanding—of the subject that constitute the necessary conditions of possibility for the experience. However, in so far as Kant only allows that the transcendental argument takes its starting point in our experience and excludes the possibility of reflectively seeing and describing the structures of this experience, the transcendental argument is bound to come out as a blind and floating construction. There is, for Kant, strictly speaking no experiential evidence that could guide the argument, which means that the only criterion for inferring the necessary structures of subjectivity is that they must be able to function as possible explanations of the possibility of the experience in question. Even fulfilling this criterion does not remove their basic character as arbitrary constructions that could principally have been more or less different. However, the point of this critique is not that Kant's concrete transcendental arguments—or those of other philosophers—would amount to blind constructions or conjectures; rather, it is that in so far as they are illuminating or clarifying, it is because they already draw upon our possibility of reflection in an implicit and denied manner.

What is more, Kant's transcendental mode of argument essentially depends on his already having postulated the forms of intuition and categories of understanding belonging to the transcendental subject as the ontological origin that *a priori* determines the sense structure of the experienced objects. It is only because this origin is presupposed that it becomes possible to argue about what the forms of intuition and the categories of the subject must be in order for us to have the experience we have. Yet there is nothing in Kant's transcendental argumentation itself that grounds his nomination of the transcendental subject to the origin of sense. Hence, the transcendental subject with its capacities and concepts amounts to a dogmatic idealist postulate preceding all other constructions. Finally, Kant's transcendental philosophy is essentialist in a quite naive and uncritical manner. It assumes from the outset that a transcendental investigation of the conditions of possibility of our experience is able to establish the basic features universally conditioning and constituting every particular experience of the same sort as the one investigated—without so much as touching on the question of how we can be sure that there are no other similar or related experiences and situations that are not determined by these features.

Husserl's transcendental phenomenology can to a large extent be read as a critical clarification and elaboration of Kant's transcendental project. This is also Husserl's own view, as he later in his career comes to reflect on and appreciate the Kantian background of his thought. In a letter to Cassirer from 1925, Husserl writes, "I had to realize that this science accruing to me encompassed, in an entirely different method, the entire Kantian problematic (which only now received a deep and clear sense) and that it confirmed Kant's main results through rigorous scientific founding and delimitation" (HuaD 5/3, 4).[3] Husserl thus takes over Kant's transcendental problematic as an as-yet-undetermined and insufficiently grounded insight to be clarified and developed.

In contrast to Kant's mode of regressive argumentation, Husserl insists that transcendental philosophy needs to proceed by way of transcendental descriptions.[4] Indeed, Husserl's entire phenomenology grows out from the basic thought that in order to avoid historical prejudice and theoretical construction, philosophy must take the form of a strict description that does not argue or infer anything but that only describes and explicates what is concretely given and discernible in our *de facto* experiences (Hua 3/1, 51/44). Yet the guiding task of Husserl's phenomenology is not to describe the empirical particularities of our experiences but to examine the transcendental structures of sense constituting our experience of the world.

To make possible a strict phenomenological examination of this transcendental domain of sense, Husserl proposes two basic methodological maneuvers. First, we need to perform the "phenomenological reduction" (Hua 3/1, 106/113), which means that we free ourselves from the object-directedness of our "natural attitude" (Hua 3/1, 56/51)—including all metaphysical theses stemming from this attitude—and perform a reflective turn, allowing us to reflectively observe and explicate the whole experiential context in which the world is given to us as meaningful. Second, we perform the "eidetic reduction," which means that we do not focus on the empirical particularities of our individual experiences but investigate the general structures of sense characterizing these experiences and their correlative objects (Hua 3/1, 6/xx).

At least in principle, Husserl's phenomenologically descriptive approach seems to open the possibility of overcoming what I singled out as the basic problems of Kant's transcendental argumentation—although it remains to be seen to what extent Husserl himself actually realizes this possibility. In contrast to Kant, Husserl's transcendental investigation does not take place as an argumentative construction of the features of the transcendental subject but transpires as a strict description of the structural aspects that we actually find to be basic in our experiences. As a result, there is no reason for Husserl to postulate, as Kant does, the transcendental subject as the universal ontological origin of the structure of the world. Rather, the only way to give a clear and concrete sense to the notion of the transcendental subject is to describe the more or less basic role played—in relation to other aspects— by the experiencing subjectivity in our different experiences. As concerns the problem of essentialism, the phenomenological demand for strict description does not allow us simply to assume the existence of essential conditions and features to be deduced but challenges us to show what it could mean to explicate general structures of sense on the basis of descriptions of concrete particular experiences.

Let me now, on the basis of this brief outline of Husserl's phenomenological project, attempt to sum up the idea of transcendental descriptions in the following formal and open definition: *a transcendental description is a description that, on the basis of a reflective intuitive explication of particular experiences, attempts to articulate the basic general structures of sense constituting the experiences in question.*

Though I cannot argue this convincingly here, I think this minimal definition of transcendental descriptions also captures the gist of what I consider to be the early Heidegger's phenomenological method.[5] To be sure, Heidegger's relationship to Husserl's phenomenology and its central notion of intuitive givenness is extremely ambivalent. From early on, he develops a vision of the historicity of thought that lives in a deep tension with the phenomenological element of his thinking, and that eventually leads him to largely abandon phenomenology in favor of a more radically historical-hermeneutic thinking. Still, I believe the basic method of his concrete investigations in the 1920s and in the existential analytic of *Being and Time* is indeed phenomenological. Even though Heidegger unceasingly insists on the need to reflect on the historical conditions of the analysis and to dismantle the traditional prejudices tending to distort it, his positive concrete investigations principally take the form of transcendental descriptions of the kind defined above. Taking their starting point in *Dasein*'s factical experiences as the place where the world is given to us as meaningful, they try to describe and explicate the basic structures of these experiences: being-in-the-world, care, temporality, historicity.

Obviously both Husserl and Heidegger are complex thinkers and I cannot hope to provide anything like a comprehensive and detailed treatment of their respective takes on phenomenology here. Hence, even though I believe that my explication captures basic tendencies of their thought, it is also clear that the massive work of both philosophers contain analyses and thoughts that transcend and point beyond the horizons I ascribe to them. In any case, since the chief concern of this chapter is systematic, my explications and critical assessments of Husserl and Heidegger should primarily be read as reflections on philosophical possibilities whose exegetical force it remains open for the reader to judge.

3   ARE TRANSCENDENTAL DESCRIPTIONS SUBJECTIVIST?

Earlier we saw that the phenomenological idea of transcendental descriptions seems to imply a potential departure from the Kantian notion of a transcendental subject containing the forms and categories organizing all meaningful being. However, do not Husserl's and Heidegger's accounts of the method of transcendental description still contain essential remnants of subjectivism or idealism? Does not in fact subjectivism belong to the very basic phenomenological notion—common to Husserl and Heidegger—that in order to grasp the meaning of things, we need to turn from the objects themselves to how we experience them? Or is it possible to envision transcendental descriptions as principally free of subjectivism?

Although Husserl and especially Heidegger are certainly concerned with overcoming subjectivism and indeed point the way toward this possibility, I believe both of them, nevertheless, remain ambivalent on this point and exhibit a strong tendency unwittingly to fall back into transcendental subjectivism. Here I can only indicate what I suggest to be the lingering subjectivism of their thought.

Husserl describes the transcendental reduction as a reflective turn in which we free ourselves from our normal directedness at the objects of our experience and instead reflect on how these objects are given in our experiences. This does not—as, for example, Dan Zahavi has pointed out (2003, 44–46)—imply that we turn our attention from the objects of the outer world toward the inner acts of the experiencing subject but rather means that we expand our attention so that we now reflect on the objects in correlation with the acts in which they are given. Indeed, Husserl claims, such a reflective study reveals precisely that our experience exhibits an intentional structure: it belongs to the very sense of our acts of consciousness that they are directed not at inner representations of outer realities but at the things themselves that they intend. Just as it is impossible to understand the meaning of things in isolation from the experiences in which they are given as meaningful to us, it is impossible to understand the acts of the subject in abstraction from the matters and things with which they are concerned. Hence, the reflective turn of the phenomenological reduction should not be understood as a turn to a self-contained transcendental subject but to our experience as a whole in its intentional correlation between our acts of consciousness and the objects as they are given in these acts, between noesis and noema.

And yet, although Husserl's basic idea of the intentional correlation is meant to overcome the notion of a self-contained subject determining the sense of the phenomenal world, I believe this idea in the end remains ambivalent and hides a dogmatic tendency to privilege the subjective acts of experience over the objects experienced.

Husserl's subjectivist bias is in fact already manifest in his articulation of the phenomenological reduction. Even though the reduction is not a turn to the inner sphere of consciousness, it does consist in a reflective turn from the natural direction of our experience—in which we are supposedly only directed at the objects of experience—toward the whole intentional correlation between acts and objects. This description, however, implies that the decisive phenomenological surplus achieved by the reduction in relation to the natural attitude lies precisely in its ability to access the normally hidden sphere of subjective experience, which it only now becomes possible to investigate in its constitutive function. Indeed, this tendency to privilege the acts over the objects is basic to Husserl's guiding notion of the task of phenomenology as constitutional analysis. It involves investigating, through strict description, how different kinds of objects are given and constituted in different kinds of acts and detecting, in these act-systems of transcendental subjectivity, the basic transcendental structures determining our basic possibilities of experience as well as the basic senses of being. Though Husserl stresses that constitutional analysis must take its guiding clues from the object-types whose correlative act-types it wants to examine, this very procedure presupposes a separation and hierarchization of the correlata. It assumes, first, that the object-types can be accessed as clues on the basis of the natural attitude; second, that it is possible to carry out a largely separable analysis of the act-systems of transcendental subjectivity as the hidden basic dimension constituting the givenness and being-senses of the objects.[6]

But what about Heidegger? Is not Heidegger the philosopher *par excellence* who has helped us disengage ourselves from the idea of the transcendental subject as the ground of reality and leveled severe critiques of the lingering subjectivist tendency of Husserl's phenomenology? This is of course true as far as it goes. The aim of the first part of *Being and Time* is precisely to show that the human being is essentially a being-in-the-world. It belongs, Heidegger claims, to the being of the human being to be open toward the world as the historical context of meaning that gives all beings—including the human being—their possible significances. Hence, Heidegger gives up the word 'transcendental' as a designation of his own thinking and, instead of talking about a "transcendental subject," renames the human being "*Dasein*": to be a *Dasein* is to be the open place in which the world and its entities can show themselves to us (SZ, 57, 133/84, 171). Moreover, to ward off the strong traditional tendency of philosophy to reduce the manifold sense structures of our experience to some simple primordial ground, such as the transcendental subject, Heidegger introduces the term 'equiprimordiality' (*Gleichursprünglichkeit*) to accentuate that the different aspects of being-in-the-world—the world, being-in, the who—constitute irreducible codependent moments of a unified structure (SZ, 131/170).

Nevertheless, in spite of Heidegger's hard critique of subjectivism, his own project of fundamental ontology still seems to rest on a basic postulation of transcendental subjectivity as its field of research. Before the commencement of any investigation, Heidegger defines his guiding question as a question concerning the "sense of being" (SZ, 1/19). By "sense," however, Heidegger means the "formal-existential framework" (*Gerüst*) of the disclosedness of *Dasein*, such that this basic framework or structure of *Dasein* constitutes "*the upon-which of the projection in terms of which something becomes intelligible as something*" (SZ, 151/193). Hence, Heidegger's basic methodological idea, that the fundamental ontological investigation of the sense of being has to be preceded by an analytic of the human *Dasein*, rests on the presupposition that an analysis of the basic structure of the human being will confer the ground for an explication of the sense of being as such. Even if Heidegger, in his existential analytic, develops the idea of the essential openness of *Dasein* toward its finite historical world, the analytic itself is carried out as an explication of the basic and universal structures of *Dasein*—being-in-the-world, care, temporality—which can be analyzed prior to and irrespective of any particular historical situation and grant the horizon of sense for every possible experience of meaning. However, conceived as the universal ground determining the sense horizon for every possible experience of the world, *Dasein* does not differ in its philosophical function from the transcendental subject.[7]

Granted that this explication of Husserl and Heidegger is correct, what systematic role does the transcendental subject play in their thinking and why are they—and we—tempted to hold on to it? It seems that postulating the transcendental subject has at least two basic systematic functions. First, by establishing a hierarchical difference between our understanding of the objects of our experience and our understanding of the ways of experiencing them—between the *what* and the *how*—it becomes possible for philosophy to claim to be able to describe the structures of our experience as the *ground* organizing and determining the sense of our object-experience. Second, by conceiving of its descriptions as descriptions of the structures of the transcendental subject, philosophy can claim that its descriptions are *universal* and ahistorical and hold for every possible human experience. Hence, the idea of the transcendental subject could perhaps be said to provide one of the paradigmatic ways for modern philosophy to sustain the ancient ambition of philosophy to attain basic and universal knowledge.

However, if we abide by the concrete possibilities of transcendental descriptions, we will find that it is very hard to give sense to the idea that any such description could ever ground the notion of a transcendental subject. According to the open formal definition suggested earlier, a transcendental description is nothing but an investigation that transpires through descriptions of the sense structures of concrete particular experiences and situations, like experiences of understanding, love, memory, football, natural science, and honor. Still, if the transcendental description takes its absolute starting point in and does nothing but describe concrete experiences, it seems there cannot be some such thing as a transcendental subject to discover here: What could that be apart from the subjective aspects of the specific experience under investigation? Since the only concrete given of our description is the experience that we are dealing with all the possible concepts we might use to articulate the experience—such as subject, act, object, I, you, language, history—can only gain concrete sense in so far as they are able to illuminate different interrelated aspects of the experience in question. Depending on the problem and dialogic situation the description is meant to address, and depending on the experience itself, certain aspects will be given a more or less basic role in relation to others. Still, it is entirely unclear how we could ever be in a position to claim—without yielding to metaphysical dogmatism—that the structure we are describing constitutes the structure of the transcendental subject.

In so far as the transcendental description is freed from every idea of transcendental subjectivity and is radically anchored in the particular experiences it describes, it loses its metaphysical status as a description of the universal traits of the transcendental subject *a priori* grounding all our possible experiences of different matters. This, however, does not mean that the transcendental description would lose all its claims to generality and fundamentality.

As concerns the ambition of transcendental descriptions to explicate basic structures, it seems fully possible—in light of the guiding problem and discursive situation at hand—to describe and articulate the structures of sense constituting different kinds of experience, and without which they could not be what they actually are. Moreover, in such a description, it is quite possible that some structural aspects may come up as more basic, supporting and giving sense to other aspects, but not the other way round. Here are two examples. First, if we want to clarify what is involved in a football player's eye for the game, we can—I think convincingly—try to show that what is crucial to this capacity is a kind of immediate unthematic awareness of the movements of the ball and the surrounding players and a corresponding feel for the momentary possibilities at hand, whereas, for example, the kind of tactical-psychological understanding of the coach or the more theoretical understanding or the football expert come out as secondary intellectual capabilities. Second, if we want to understand the nature of unegoistic love, we can—I think convincingly—try to show that such love cannot primarily be concerned with the general or particular traits and qualities of the other person that make her lovable—but at the same time transform her into an interchangeable object of my interests and desires—but must centrally involve a responsive care for and openness to the other as a you who addresses me in person. As concerns the question of the generality of transcendental descriptions, this will be dealt with in the following section. Suffice to say here that I believe the scope and validity of transcendental descriptions can be more or less general but that this generality cannot be determined in advance, and it ultimately amounts to nothing but the *de facto* capacity of the description to illuminate particular experiences.

The fact that transcendental descriptions can harbor this kind of open nonmetaphysical generality and fundamentality also means, conversely, that the earlier tradition of transcendental—and pretranscendental—philosophy cannot, in spite of its greater or lesser metaphysical predispositions, be rejected out of hand as speculative constructions. To the extent that the philosophical systems and concepts have their origin—directly or indirectly—in explications of concrete particular experiences and situations, which have been generalized and theorized to the extent that they are not readily discernible as what they are anymore, it seems principally possible to deconstruct the metaphysical theories on the descriptions constituting their concrete content. Such a deconstructive approach—in the sense of Heidegger's *Destruktion*—opens the possibility of appropriating, critically delimiting, and articulating anew, for ourselves, the insights—and the play between insight and illusion—of the philosophical tradition.

4   ARE TRANSCENDENTAL DESCRIPTIONS ESSENTIALIST?

For a long time, the most common and to my mind most serious objection against the very idea of transcendental descriptions is that they are inherently essentialist, building on the illusive idea that it is possible to establish, by way of description, the basic features necessarily characterizing given matters, thus constituting their general essences.

Hence, we ask: Is the method of transcendental description developed by Husserl and Heidegger essentialist in a metaphysically dogmatic way? Do transcendental descriptions necessarily involve such an essentialist trait, or is it possible to understand and carry out transcendental descriptions without any speculative stipulations of essences? Earlier I suggested that the phenomenological idea of transcendental descriptions by itself challenges the age-old philosophical belief in essences by opening the question of how a strict description of particular experiences and situations can ever determine the general necessary features of all experiences of the same kind. Still—or perhaps precisely because of this—the problem of essentialism has for a long time been something of a taboo in the literature on phenomenology. It has mostly been dodged, or it has been downplayed and rejected, without much discussion, either as inessential to phenomenology or as a problem that phenomenology has supposedly overcome.[8]

In fact, however, I think both Husserl's and Heidegger's elaborations of the method of transcendental description are permeated by essentialism. In Husserl's case, the situation is quite clear. From beginning to end, Husserl construes his phenomenology as a "science of essences" (Hua 3/1, 6/xx), whose aim is not to discover the empirical particularities of our experiences but to explicate the essential structures constituting these experiences. In *Ideas I*, Husserl defines his notion of "essence" as follows: "*it belongs to the sense of anything contingent to have an essence and therefore an Eidos which can be apprehended purely.* [. . .] An individual object [. . .] has its *own specific character,* its stock of *essential* predicables which must belong to it (as 'an existent such as it is in itself') if other, secondary, relative determinations can belong to it" (Hua 3/1, 12–13/7–8). An essential structure is thus a general structure of sense holding the necessary features constituting a particular kind of being. According to Husserl, phenomenology has access to essences through what he calls "essential intuition" or "eidetic variation."[9] In his description of this method, Husserl oscillates between depicting it as a kind of conceptual analysis and as a process of abstraction. His basic train of thought is the following: in order to explicate the essence of a thing, we perform a variation of a manifold number of particular cases, such that we become able to distinguish what constitutes the basic features of the being in question without which it would cease to be what it is. So far Husserl's procedure could be read as a kind of conceptual analysis dogmatically presupposing the idea that it must be possible to fix the essential features of our concepts. Still, it is Husserl's account of the eidetic explication as a process of abstraction that gives it its distinctive phenomenological character. Thus he also argues that our understanding of essences is ultimately grounded on our direct perception of the similarities and dissimilarities between particular phenomena, on the basis of which we abstract the general features characterizing different kinds of beings. Other problems aside, however, Husserl's conception of the eidetic intuition as an abstraction builds on the dogmatic presupposition that the manifold of possible phenomena and situations we can experience in itself exhibits a rigid order of identifiable essential types and structures that could function as the ultimate ground and measure for our understanding of general concepts.

In Heidegger's case, the situation is more intricate due to his wavering between a phenomenological and a historical-hermeneutic mode of thinking.

However, in so far as Heidegger does not abandon but critically elaborates Husserl's phenomenological method during the 1920s and in *Being and Time,* I believe he also remains trapped in Husserl's essentialism. In fact, I think there is little doubt that Heidegger's investigation of the being of *Dasein* in *Being and Time* fundamentally transpires as a reflective explication of the essential structures determining the experiences under investigation. On the one hand, Heidegger maintains that the descriptive concepts of philosophy gain their substance as articulations of phenomenally given structures of meaning; on the other hand, he claims that the structures explicated by the analytic necessarily constitute *Dasein*'s being: "being-in-the-world is an *a priori* necessary constitution of *Dasein*" (SZ, 53/79). Although Heidegger is highly aware of the extent to which our immediate seeing is guided by our historical concepts, as well as of the tendency of our philosophical concepts to collapse into historical prejudices or theoretical constructs, his own existential analytic is basically an attempt to articulate the fundamental structures—being-in-the-world, care, temporality—necessarily constituting the being of *Dasein.*

Here it might, of course, be argued that even though Heidegger in *Being and Time* might be more or less committed to Husserl's transcendental phenomenology, he is simultaneously engaged in overcoming phenomenology in favor of a radical hermeneutic thinking and that this project also implies a break with the essentialism of phenomenology. Perhaps, but I am not so sure.[10] In any case, I do not think Heidegger's historicist critique of essentialism is so relevant in this context. Provided that it goes hand in hand with a break with the method of phenomenological description, it cannot shed any light on the possibility we are investigating here: the possibility of transcendental descriptions of basic sense structures that are not essentialist.

So what is the systematic function of essentialism? What is it that makes philosophers—us—yearn for it and hinders them from letting it go? Moreover, what is the problem of essentialism and what does it mean to give it up?

Earlier I claimed that the notion of transcendental subjectivity allowed transcendental philosophy to conceive of its investigations as investigations of the transcendental subject as a fundamental and universal ground of meaning. The lure of essentialism is more general and characterizes philosophy from its inception: basically, it is the idea that it is possible to attain *a priori* knowledge of the general essences or concepts determining the possible meaning of particular beings, such that this knowledge is not dependent on our knowledge of individual beings and situations but determines in advance what beings can be for us. Essentialism is thus the idea that upholds the possibility of philosophy as an autonomous *a priori* mode of understanding preceding and grounding all our subsequent knowledge of the particularities of life and the world.

From the point of view of the concrete practice of transcendental description, the problem of essentialism lies in the metaphysical leap that occurs the moment we proceed from explicating the basic features of a certain experience to claiming that these features constitute the necessary determinations constituting this kind of matter or experience. This leap to the essence—which is almost always implicit and which is easily covered up by our will and by philosophical convention—is nothing that can be motivated by a concrete description of a particular experience, thus amounting to a speculative generalization.

How so?

Keeping to the practice of concrete description we can—without, as far as I can see, necessarily yielding to metaphysical construction and dogmatism—attempt to describe the basic features of a particular experience in order to address and illuminate a particular problem-situation, whereby these features can emerge as more or less essential and necessary in the sense that they are constitutive of *this* experience. For example, we can try to comprehend the motives behind our emotional reaction of shame in certain situations, or we can try to describe the kind of awareness involved in Lionel Messi's eye for the game. However, as soon as we proceed from describing the experiences in question to claiming that the features explicated are essential and necessary for *this kind* of experience, we have laid claim to a stronger kind of necessity, namely that there cannot be similar experiences lacking these features. Yet what is it that allows our description of the basic features of the particular phenomenon under consideration—certain experiences of shame, Messi's understanding of the game—to transform into a description of the necessary features constituting *this kind* of shame or *this kind* of understanding, or, perhaps even more generally, shame *as such* or the practical understanding of the footballer *as such?* What is it that guarantees that our explication of the features of these particular experiences has nailed down the constitutive traits of every such experience? The answer is—nothing. There can be nothing in the concrete phenomenological description of one or many experiences that certifies the necessary validity of the description for other similar and related cases. Clearly, our and other people's previous experiences may function as a ground for empirical generalizations and give us good reason to believe that there will be identical and similar experiences whose constitutive structure our transcendental description will be able to illuminate. Moreover, our description may in fact prove illuminating in many cases and situations, perhaps—it is not impossible—in all cases that will ever be experienced. Yet the more or less general *de facto* applicability of a description is not tantamount to the necessity involved in the claim to *a priori* knowledge of kinds and essences.

Let us here, in order to be better able to pinpoint the problem of essentialism in transcendental descriptions, take a brief look at a recent article by Steven Crowell, "Facticity and Transcendental Philosophy," which in my view provides one of the best attempts to specify the claims of transcendental phenomenology. In his article, Crowell argues that Heidegger's concept of facticity should not—as is often done—be taken as a reason for rejecting all transcendental claims to *a priori* knowledge; instead, it can be used to clarify the meaning of transcendental understanding. According to Crowell, the phenomenological description always moves out from and never abandons our concrete factical experiences:

> For Husserl, essences are grasped *in re* through imaginative variation of what is given. Hence their necessity is always conditional: given such and such a thing, it must have these and those features. Where Kant attempts to establish that a certain *type* of experience is necessary by arguing that without it no unified self-consciousness is possible, Husserl can only reflect on the essential features of experiences that the subject *happens* to have. For the same reason, phenomenological necessity differs from traditional metaphysical or absolute necessity. It cannot explain why there *must be* certain things. For instance, phenomenological reflection can establish a necessary connection between memory and perception: the act of remembering something refers necessarily to a previous act of perceiving it. But phenomenology can give no reason why there must be anything like memory, as a Leibnizian might argue that memory is necessary to the best of all possible worlds. (Crowell 2002, 108)

Crowell's central point can be summarized thus: the transcendental understanding can only ground itself on the factical experiences we happen to have; whereas it cannot say anything about the necessity of these experiences—for all we know, they could have been otherwise or they could change in the future—it can explicate the "essential, *a priori,* transcendental structures" (Crowell 2002, 104) characterizing these experiences: "The hermeneutic exploration of our factic situation suffices for insight into necessary connections" (Crowell 2002, 110).

In my view, Crowell's text offers a good formulation of the reliance of transcendental descriptions on our *de facto* experiences as their contingent ground. Even so, it seems to me that his argument still hides a metaphysical leap that allows him to retain his faith in the possibility of transcendental phenomenology to explicate "essential, *a priori,* transcendental structures." Consider Crowell's only concrete example of transcendental knowledge: "the act of remembering something refers necessarily to a previous act of perceiving it" (Crowell 2002, 108). Now, should not this formulation only amount to a conceptual distinction that is simply stipulative or articulates our common concepts of memory and perception, it must grow forth as a description of certain concrete experiences. But then the question arises: How can we know that this description necessarily holds for all our possible experiences of memory? Well, we cannot. Indeed, it seems that the very practice of transcendental description makes it necessary to rid Crowell's account of its last necessity claim. It is not only that transcendental descriptions explicate the structures of our contingent experiences without claiming that the experiences are necessary; it is also the case that these structures do not necessarily hold for all factical experiences of the same kind.

In order to avoid dogmatic essentialism and get a sense of the genuine possibilities and limits of transcendental descriptions, we need to take seriously the fact that a transcendental description can only arise and justify itself as a description of one or many particular experiences and situations. Nonetheless, it belongs to the sense of the transcendental description that it is not just a description of a particular experience but that it articulates general structures and connections of meaning. The upshot of this basic tension—the projection of general structures on the basis of particular experiences—is that the scope and explanatory force of the transcendental description is always bound to remain open and undetermined. There is nothing in our previous experience and in our description of it that could determine in advance that matters will be clarified by our description or in which situations it will be illuminating. Hence, we had better think of the transcendental description as an open paradigm of meaning that is valid for all those experiences and situations that it will *de facto* prove able to clarify and illuminate.[11]

But could it not be argued that both Husserl and Heidegger conceive of our knowledge of essences as fallible and that this fallibilism makes them immune to my criticisms? To be sure, neither Husserl nor Heidegger believes that our understanding of essences is absolutely certain: it is always possible that it can prove false and distortive and be in need of modification. However, this does not free them from dogmatic essentialism. Even though they admit that our understanding of essences is fallible, they both dogmatically presuppose the possibility of an understanding of essential structures that could in principle be true. But this is a dogma. If my argument is correct, the possible understanding gained by transcendental descriptions can never be an understanding of essential features necessarily determining all particular instances of the essence but must be conceived of as an understanding of general paradigms or models of meaning whose range and force lie in their *de facto* capacity to clarify individual cases.

The account of transcendental descriptions developed here also has consequences for how we should understand the aprioricity and autonomy of transcendental understanding and its relation to our understanding and knowledge of particular empirical situations. According to the traditional conception of transcendental phenomenology—shared by Husserl and Heidegger—the transcendental understanding of philosophy precedes and determines our knowledge of empirical particularities in that it grasps the quasi-conceptual patterns of meaning in terms of which we may grasp particular beings as one thing or the other. However, if—as I have claimed—the transcendental description cannot establish any general essences necessarily valid for all particular cases, it loses its principal priority in relation to our understanding of particular situations and phenomena. To begin with, the transcendental description unavoidably originates as a description of particular experiences and is thus dependent on our ability to grasp the sense of these individual occurrences. Moreover, since the transcendental description is nothing more than an open general paradigm of meaning rooted in our better or worse understanding of previous experiences, it cannot determine or delimit in advance what we can see or grasp in new situations—that is, if we do not *let* it do it by leaning back on our general pre-understandings. This, however, means that in every new situation, we are principally faced with the task of understanding anew the particular phenomena we are facing—be it that we find the phenomena in question illuminated by our previous paradigms of meaning or be it that our old general paradigms are put into question and modified through the encounter.

5   SUMMARY

In this chapter, I have argued that transcendental descriptions cannot and need not involve any notion of transcendental subjectivity as their basic field of description or any ambition to establish the essential transcendental structures necessarily constituting different kinds of experience. Instead, I have suggested that what transcendental descriptions can do is to project, on the basis of descriptions of particular experiences, general paradigms of meaning whose range and explanatory force is principally open and shows itself in the *de facto* ability of the paradigms to illuminate the particular experiences and situations we encounter. Still, if I am right in my account of the sense and possibilities of transcendental descriptions—should we then continue calling such descriptions transcendental at all? What speaks for retaining the term 'transcendental' is that such a usage would preserve the continuity with the tradition, thereby sustaining a readiness to critically appropriate the inquiries and insights of the history of philosophy. What speaks against retaining the term is that, on account of its historically sedimented meaning, it will tend to draw us back into misconceptions of the philosophical tasks that lie ahead of us. At the end of the day, this is a strategic decision, and my personal view is that, even though it might at times be clarifying to use the word 'transcendental' to indicate the kind of inquiry we have in mind, it would on the whole be wiser to abandon the term and instead talk about, for example, descriptions of structures, paradigms, or patterns of meaning.

NOTES

1. For some of the central texts of the analytic discussion of transcendental arguments, see Strawson 1959; Stroud 1968; Rorty 1971; Rosenberg 1975; Taylor 1978; Bieri, Horstmann, and Krüger 1979; Schaper and Vossenkuhl 1989; Stern 2001, 2007; Sacks 2005; Kuusela 2008.
2. There is, of course, a massive literature on Kant containing a multitude of diverging interpretations of the nature and validity of his transcendental modes of argumentation. My own brief outline and critique of Kant here does not pretend to offer any substantial contribution to the exegetical discussion. Still, I hope that its very general character will allow it to point to some basic features of Kant's notion of transcendental inquiry, which to some extent are neutral with respect to many of the more specific Kant interpretations on offer.

3. Cf. also Hua 3/1, 133f and Hua 25, 206. For Husserl's two main accounts of the historical background of his phenomenology in Descartes and Kant, see Hua 7, 63–70, 191–199, and Hua 6, 74–104.
4. For a recent discussion of the difference between "transcendental arguments" and "transcendental reflection," see Crowell 2010. See also Taylor 1978 and Sacks 2005.
5. For two qualified interpretations of the early Heidegger as a transcendental phenomenologist who critically yet faithfully carries on and elaborates Husserl's phenomenological project, see Crowell 2001 and Overgaard 2004.
6. For a more detailed discussion of the ambivalence of Husserl's notion of the intentional correlation, see Westerlund 2010, 42–52.
7. In his later thinking Heidegger, as we know, abandons and explicitly criticizes the lingering subjectivist tendency of *Being and Time* in favor of an attempt to think about the *Ereignis*—event or happening—that gives rise to and sustains historical being and that the human subject essentially has to receive and respond to as constitutive of its own being. However, given that Heidegger at the same time largely abandons his phenomenological method, his later self-critique does not seem relevant for our effort to reflect on the possibility of nonsubjectivist transcendental descriptions.
8. It could perhaps be seen as symptomatic of the situation that Dan Zahavi, in his otherwise excellent introduction to Husserl, *Husserl's Phenomenology*, downplays and largely passes over the question of Husserl's essentialism on the ground that "this interest in essential structures is so widespread and common in the history of philosophy that it is nonsensical to take it as a defining feature of phenomenology" (Zahavi 2003, 37). Aside from the fact that Zahavi's formulation certainly misrepresents Husserl's self-understanding, its evasive logic is typical: while dismissing the question of essentialism as an irrelevant and somewhat embarrassing feature of Husserl's phenomenology, it does nothing to articulate a positive vision of how we should understand the scope and validity of the descriptions of general sense structures constantly employed by Husserl and other phenomenologists.
9. Cf. Husserl, EU §§86–93; Hua 9, 72–87.
10. In fact, it seems far from clear to me that Heidegger's move from phenomenology to a historical-hermeneutic thinking explicating finite historical contexts of meaning does by itself imply an overcoming of essentialism. My chapter focuses on the essentialism of Husserl's and Heidegger's method of phenomenological description, where the notion of essence is more or less intimately tied to the possibility of intuitively grasping essences as ahistorical universal structures of meaning. However, the problem of essentialism is not necessarily linked to any notion of the essences being ahistorical and universal or, for that matter, to any specific notion of their ontological domain and epistemological status. If, as I suggest, the problem of essentialism is conceived as the problem of dogmatically postulating that there are general concepts or structures of meaning that can be understood prior to and that necessarily determine our understanding of the particular phenomena instantiating these meanings, then it is another matter whether the essences are universal or historical, linguistic or nonlinguistic, objective or subjective, or whether our knowledge of them is absolute, fallible or necessarily incomplete. As for the later Heidegger, at least this much is clear: even when he abandons the project of fundamental ontology for a radical historical thinking, he retains the ontological difference as a sharp hierarchy between the finite historical formations of meaning explicated by philosophy and all derivative knowledge of empirical particularities.
11. In a recent article—"Transcendental Arguments and the Problem of Dogmatism"—Oskari Kuusela provides a critical discussion of the risk of

dogmatism in transcendental arguments, which in important respects resemble my critique of the lurking essentialism of transcendental descriptions. Taking his main starting point in the analytic tradition and drawing on the later Wittgenstein, Kuusela argues that for a transcendental argument to be nondogmatic, it needs to take the form of an argument that articulates necessary conditions of possibility by reminding the person to whom it is addressed of principles to which she herself is committed by virtue of what she says or thinks: it "operates from within" the interlocutor's own "conceptual system" and does not impose dogmas "from the outside" (Kuusela 2008, 62). However, even in this form, the transcendental argument runs the risk of dogmatism in so far as it dogmatically assumes that the necessary conditions disclosed by the argument universally determine the essential features of the concept in question: "for it does not follow from a condition being necessary for some cases falling under a concept that all the members of the class defined by the concept presuppose the condition" (Kuusela 2008, 63). Hence, Kuusela makes a distinction between "general" and "specific" transcendental arguments, arguing that whereas the former dogmatically involve "universal claims about all cases falling under concepts," the latter "leave open their scope, i.e. how generally a given definition of the necessary conditions of possibility is applicable to the objects of philosophical examinations": "The generality of the definition is, so to speak, relative to the scope of its justified application" (Kuusela 2008, 67–68). Even though I do not share Kuusela's basic characterization of transcendental arguments, including his idea that to be nondogmatic they have to transpire as internal reminders of the interlocutor's own conceptual commitments—an idea that sounds rather dogmatic to me—I believe his central argument about the context-relativity and open scope of transcendental arguments is basically correct and largely parallels my own account.

REFERENCES

Bieri, P., Horstmann, R.-P. and Krüger, L. (eds.). 1979. *Transcendental Arguments and Science*. Dordrecht: Reidel.

Crowell, S. 2001. *Husserl, Heidegger, and the Space of Meaning*. Evanston, IL: Northwestern University Press.

———. 2002. "Facticity and Transcendental Philosophy." In *From Kant to Davidson: Philosophy and the Idea of the Transcendental*, 100–121. Edited by Jeff Malpas. London: Routledge.

———. 2010. "The Project of Ultimate Grounding and the Appeal to Intersubjectivity in Recent Transcendental Philosophy." *International Journal of Philosophical Studies*, 7/1: 31–54.

Heidegger, M. 2001. *Sein und Zeit* [1927], 18th edition. Tübingen: Niemeyer (SZ). Translation: Heidegger, M. 1962. *Being and Time*. Translated by John Macquarrie and Edward Robinson. Oxford: Basil Blackwell.

Husserl, E. 1950. *Ideen zu einer reinen Phänomenlogie und phänomenlogischen Philosophie*. Erstes Buch: Allgemeine Einführung in die reine Phänomenologie. Edited by Walter Biemel. The Hague, Netherlands: Martinus Nijhoff Publishers (Hua 3/1). Translation: Husserl, E. 1982. *Ideas Pertaining to a Pure Phenomenology and to a Phenomenological Philosophy*. Translated by Fred Kersten. Dordrecht: Kluwer.

———. 1954. *Die Krisis der europäischen Wissenschaften und die transzendentale Phänomenologie: Eine Einleitung in die phänomenologische Philosophie* [1936],

Husserliana 6. Edited by Walter Biemel. The Hague: Martinus Nijhoff (Hua 6). Translation: Husserl, E. 1970. *The Crisis of European Sciences and Transcendental Phenomenology.* Translated by David Carr. Evanston, IL: Northwestern University Press.

———. 1956. *Erste Philosophie (1923/4). Erste Teil: Kritische Ideengeschichte.* Edited by Rudolf Boehm. The Hague. Netherlands: Martinus Nijhoff (Hua 7).

———. 1968. *Phänomenologische Psychologie.* Vorlesungen Sommersemester 1925. Edited by Walter Biemel. The Hague, Netherlands: Martinus Nijhoff (Hua 9).

———. 1984. *Erfahrung und Urteil.* Original work published 1939. Hamburg: Felix Meiner Verlag (EU). Husserl, Edmund, *Experience and Judgment.* Evanston, IL: Northwestern University Press, 1973.

———. 1986. *Aufsätze und Vorträge 1911–1921. Mit ergänzenden Texten.* Edited by Thomas Nenon and Hans Rainer Sepp. The Hague, Netherlands: Martinus Nijhoff (Hua 25).

———. 1994. *Briefwechsel. Band V: Die Neukantianer.* Edited by Karl Schuhmann. The Hague, Netherlands: Kluwer Academic Publishers (HuaD 5/3).

Kant, I. 1933. *Critique of Pure Reason.* Translated by Norman Kemp Smith. London: Macmillan (CPR).

Kuusela, O. 2008. "Transcendental Arguments and the Problem of Dogmatism." *International Journal of Philosophical Studies* 16/1: 57–75.

Overgaard, S. 2004. *Husserl and Heidegger on Being in the World.* Dordrecht: Kluwer Academic Publishers.

Rorty, R. 1971. "Verificationism and Transcendental Arguments." *Nous* 5/1: 3–14.

Rosenberg, J. 1975. "Transcendental Arguments Revisited." *Journal of Philosophy* 72: 611–624.

Sacks, M. 2005. "The Nature of Transcendental Arguments." *International Journal of Philosophical Studies* 13/4: 439–460.

Schaper, E. and Vossenkuhl, W. (eds.). 1989. *Reading Kant: New Perspectives on Transcendental Arguments and Critical Philosophy.* Oxford: Blackwell.

Stern, R. (ed.). 2001. *Transcendental Arguments: Problems and Prospects.* Oxford: Clarendon Press.

———. 2007. "Transcendental Arguments: A Plea for Modesty." *Grazer Philosophische Studien* 74: 143–161.

Strawson, P. 1959. *Individuals: An Essay on Descriptive Metaphysics.* London: Methuen.

Stroud, B. 1968. "Transcendental Arguments." *Journal of Philosophy* 65: 241–256.

Taylor, C. 1978. "The Validity of Transcendental Arguments." *Proceedings of the Aristotelean Society* 79: 151–165.

Westerlund, F. 2010. "Phenomenology as Understanding of Origin. Remarks on Heidegger's First Critique of Husserl." *Husserl und Heidegger im Vergleich*, 34–56. Edited by Friederike Rese. Frankfurt am Main: Vittorio Klostermann.

Zahavi, D. 2003. *Husserl's Phenomenology.* Stanford, CA: Stanford University Press.

13 Transcendental Idealism and Strong Correlationism
Meillassoux and the End of Heideggerian Finitude[1]

Jussi Backman

Today, transcendental idealism as a philosophical position is most often seen as a thing of the past, as a historical trend of German philosophy primarily associated with Kant's, Fichte's, Schelling's, and Husserl's very different versions of this approach. At the same time, however, few would disagree that this fruit of Kant's "Copernican revolution" has shaped the course of modern philosophy up to and including Heidegger, perhaps more decisively than any other approach. Its heritage obviously continues to inform contemporary thought in ways that are not always fully acknowledged.[2]

In recent years, a new philosophical upheaval against the persistent predominance of the Kantian transcendental legacy has spread from the French intellectual milieu to the English-speaking world, decisively influenced by a relatively short book by Quentin Meillassoux (2006b), published in French in 2006 and translated into English in 2008 as *After Finitude: An Essay on the Necessity of Contingency*. In his preface to the work, Meillassoux's mentor Alain Badiou maintains that it does nothing less than introduce an entirely new avenue of thinking in the contemporary philosophical context: a new post-Kantian option to compete with the three dominant modern options enumerated by Kant: dogmatic, skeptical, and critical philosophy (Badiou 2006a: 11/vii).[3] Meillassoux calls this option "speculative materialism," with the epithet 'speculative' emphasizing its absolute scope and distinguishing it from other "naïve," "dogmatic," and "historical" materialisms.

One of the great merits of Meillassoux's work is precisely its insightful rearticulation of the main philosophical positions available since Kant's "Copernican revolution." After Hume's skeptical attack on the classical dogmatic metaphysics of the substance and Kant's critical reaction, mainstream philosophical options have arguably consisted first and foremost of the Humean legacy of skeptical antimetaphysical stances (empiricism, positivism, naturalism) on the one hand and of the various developments of the Kantian critical and transcendental heritage (German Idealism, neo-Kantianism, phenomenology and its heirs, structuralism, Wittgensteinian linguistic philosophy) on the other—not to mention creative combinations of these, such as Deleuze's "transcendental empiricism." According to Meillassoux, the Kantian path has basically traversed different forms of what he calls *correlationism*: a general approach that affirms, in different ways, the unsurpassable character of the "idea according to which we only ever have access to the correlation between thinking and being, and never to either term considered apart from the other" (Meillassoux 2006b: 18/5). "Correlationism" is thus a broader and more inclusive category than "idealism," whether the latter is understood in the dogmatic or in the transcendental sense. Unlike the idealist, the correlationist does not necessarily seek to refer being back to acts of consciousness or subjective processes of meaning-constitution but is simply committed to the view that any notion of being without an irreducible correlation with thinking is either epistemically inaccessible or simply incoherent—as is any notion of thinking without an irreducible relation to a being-correlate. Being, for Meillassoux's correlationist, is meaningful givenness to thinking, and thinking is receptivity to meaningful being.

In what follows, I will try to show that "correlationism"—characterized by Graham Harman as a "devastating summary of post-Kantian thought" (Harman 2007, 105)—is precisely the conceptual innovation that allows Meillassoux to portray Heidegger as an ultimate or final Kantian of sorts.[4] For Meillassoux, the Heideggerian hermeneutics of finitude and facticity is a contemporary culmination within the tradition of transcendental idealism, a radicalized position that can itself no longer be characterized in an unproblematic manner as either "transcendental" or "idealist."[5] I will first briefly present Meillassoux's account of the main types of "correlationism"—in particular, of its "strong" variety—and then study the extent to which these labels can do justice to the Heideggerian approach by fleshing out Meillassoux's rather sketchy way of situating Heidegger in the Kantian transcendental framework. Meillassoux follows the Hegelian and Heideggerian maxim that all important philosophical developments require a new articulation of the history of philosophy; I will conclude by showing why his reading of Heidegger as a *strong* correlationist is of key importance to his own speculative systematic thesis, which he presents as a kind of logical *Aufhebung* of Heidegger's position. Meillassoux effectively uses Heidegger as a lever in his attempt to overcome the entire Kantian heritage.

1 CORRELATIONISM, WEAK AND STRONG

Meillassoux distinguishes two main versions of correlationism, a "weak" and a "strong" one; to these, two subsequent modes of speculative thought, speculative (or absolute) idealism and speculative materialism, respectively correspond. In this scheme, Kant's transcendental idealism is presented as a weak form of correlationism according to which we only have access to reality insofar as it is phenomenal and experiential, that is, to the extent that it correlates with the transcendental structures of our cognitive faculties (sensibility and understanding). The notion of a noncorrelational and absolute realm of "things in themselves," of the "transcendental object" as the nonappearing cause of appearances, remains intelligible for Kant, even though it is the fundamental principle of critical philosophy that we have no experiential or epistemic access to any positive content of such a notion—hence the "weakness" of Kant's correlationism (Meillassoux 2006b, 42, 43, 48–49/30, 32, 35–36).[6] However, Kant's position soon lent itself to a speculative absolutization by the German Idealists. While retaining the basic thesis that we have no access to a reality that is not a correlate of thought, speculative idealism added that it need not be construed as a critical thesis on the *limits* of thinking: the very notion of transcendent "things in themselves" is already an intellectual abstraction and inherently immanent to the correlation and must therefore be overcome as ultimately contradictory.[7] Instead, the correlation is itself absolutized: we have access to the absolute through our awareness of ourselves as instances of the conscious and self-conscious, rational and conceptual activity of subjectivity as *spirit*.[8] Interestingly, in addition to Hegel and Schelling, Meillassoux also mentions Schopenhauer, Nietzsche, Bergson, and Deleuze as thinkers who absolutize the correlation under the various headings of will, will to power, or life (Meillassoux 2006b, 26–27, 51–52, 71/10–11, 37–38, 51–52). Certain remarks by Meillassoux suggest that Husserl is also to be included in this category, even though this is left ambiguous (Meillassoux 2006b, 169/122).

The other, "strong" correlationist model is a post-Hegelian and post-Nietzschean development. It agrees with speculative idealism that any notion of a transcendent reality must be given up as unintelligible: "to be" signifies "to be given as a correlate of thinking," if "thinking" is understood in the widest possible sense of any kind of receptivity to intelligibility. However, in addition to this, strong correlationism deabsolutizes even the correlation itself, maintaining, against Hegel, that we are unable to derive the correlational structures of meaning and meaning-constitution from any absolutely necessary principle.[9] They must simply be accepted as an inescapable condition of our finite, situated facticity. Strong correlationism thus denies altogether philosophy's capacity to make statements with a claim to absolutely necessary validity (Meillassoux 2006b, 42, 50–58/30, 36–42). While some strong correlationists will hold on to a notion of nonabsolute, intersubjective universalism (Meillassoux seems to have Habermas's and Apel's theory of communicative rationality in mind), the "postmodern" variant (perhaps most explicitly articulated in Gianni Vattimo's notion of "weak thought") will deny philosophy even the capacity to transcend its own specific historical and cultural situation and to formulate universally valid statements (Meillassoux 2006b, 58–59/42–43). As the leading proponents of strong correlationist models, Meillassoux singles out Heidegger and Wittgenstein (Meillassoux 2006b, 56–67/41–48).[10]

Operating with a Heideggerian notion of "metaphysics" as a mode of thinking reality in terms of an absolutely necessary entity or mode of being—the fundamentally Aristotelian approach that Heidegger terms *ontotheology*—Meillassoux points out that strong correlationism is no longer really a "metaphysical" position (Meillassoux 2006b, 46–68/33–49).[11] Precisely for this reason, it is for Meillassoux the most contemporary and relevant approach, and also the one that he seeks to radicalize and overcome by turning what he takes to be its implicit presuppositions against it in order to explode the correlationist framework altogether. However, let us leave Meillassoux's main argument aside for now and make use of his articulation of the different correlationist positions, especially his rendering of "strong correlationism," as a template for situating Heidegger within the transcendental tradition.

2   FROM TRANSCENDENTAL IDEALISM TO STRONG CORRELATIONISM: KANT, HUSSERL, HEIDEGGER

We should note here that "transcendental philosophy" in the literal sense is not an exclusively modern concept.[12] The expression 'transcendental' has its roots in medieval interpretations of Aristotle's account of being (*to on*) and unity (*to hen*) as coextensive, absolutely universal determinations that apply to every possible instance of "to be" and thus "transcend" even the most general categories and genera of beings.[13] The Scholastics accordingly referred to these transcategorial notions as "transcendentals" (*transcendentia*; in late Scholasticism, *transcendentalia*). Metaphysics, in the sense of the most general study of beings *qua* beings, is, as Duns Scotus puts it, "a transcending science of the transcendentals [*transcendens scientia de transcendentibus*]"[14]—a study that aims beyond all delimited categories and kinds. In this sense, metaphysics has understood itself as a "transcendental" study ever since Aristotle; Kant himself speaks of the "transcendental philosophy of the ancients" (Kant, CPR B 113).[15] The Copernican revolution is first and foremost the turn from the "dogmatic" presupposition of classical metaphysics that all or some of the transcendental structures of objects are structures of an epistemically accessible reality-in-itself to the approach of transcendental idealism, which sees them as structures of the correlation, of the way in which thinking accommodates and organizes what is given to it. Heidegger emphasizes that for Kant, transcendental philosophy remains a name for a critical, nondogmatic and nonspeculative form of metaphysics (Heidegger 1988: 16–17/11). In the first edition of the *Critique of Pure Reason*, Kant (CPR A 11) points out that the study of the *a priori* conditions of possibility of the *experience* of objects is a study of the conditions of possibility of *objects*, that is, that the transcendentally structured experiential reality *is* objectivity as such. Kant's "transcendental object," by contrast, is the preobjective *cause* of the givenness of experience required to account for the receptive and essentially finite nature of human sensibility (Kant, CPR A 494; B 522).

Husserl's account, in *Logical Investigations*, of ideal objectivities and of categorial intuition deviates importantly from the Kantian and neo-Kantian approaches, which tend to limit the realm of intuitive givenness to sensory experience. While Husserl, too, regards sensory intuition as the most basic form of intuition, he shows that the ideal and nonsensuous aspects and structures of experience constitute relatively independent domains that are also intended as objectivities in themselves (Husserl, Hua 19/2, 657–693/271–294). Husserl notes that Kant's basic failure to distinguish between signifying and intuitive acts, that is, between intending an object and its intuitive self-givenness, prevented him from recognizing the self-givenness of categorial idealities (Husserl, Hua 19/2, 731–733/318–319). Moreover, Kant and his followers lack the proper method of phenomenological reduction and therefore fail to base the transcendental project on an adequate descriptive analysis of the constitution of relevant basic concepts and principles.[16]

However, in spite of these fundamental differences, Husserl notes in *Logical Investigations* that he does feel "quite close" to Kant (Husserl, Hua 19/2, 732/319). This solidarity with the Kantian undertaking grew into what is known as Husserl's "transcendental turn" between the *Investigations* (1900–1901) and the first volume of *Ideas* (1913). Phenomenology now becomes increasingly identified with the transcendental project that Kant undertook but, due to his methodological and conceptual shortcomings and traditionalisms, was unable to complete. "Transcendental philosophy" is for Husserl a name for "the original motif [. . .] which through Descartes confers meaning upon all modern philosophies [. . .] of inquiring back into the ultimate source of all the formations of knowledge, [. . .] of the knower's reflecting upon himself and his knowing life" (Husserl, Hua 6, 100/97). Grounded purely in this "knowing life" of the ego as an "ultimate source," truly transcendental philosophy is "ultimately grounded"; the "true being" of the world is thereby known "in my own cognitive formations" (Husserl, Hua 6, 101/98).[17]

For Kant, the transcendental structures of accessibility "mediate" between the inaccessible (transcendent) and the accessible (immanent); for Husserl, the "transcendentality" of subjectivity is related precisely to its capacity for constituting the world *as* relatively transcendent, that is, as a domain that always exceeds immediate and purely immanent presence to consciousness (Husserl, Hua 1, 65/26).[18] The "cause" or "ultimate source" of all knowledge is thus the correlation itself; "a truly radical grounding of philosophy" consists in a return to "knowing subjectivity as the primal locus [*Urstätte*] of all objective formations of sense and ontic validities" (Husserl, Hua 6, 101–102/98–99). Transcendental phenomenology fulfills the requirements of true transcendental idealism by giving up the empirical—anthropological and psychological—vestiges inherent in Kant's weak version of correlationism and by absolutizing the correlation as a "primal locus" of meaning.

> Every imaginable sense, every imaginable being [*Sein*], whether the latter is called immanent or transcendent, falls within the domain of transcendental subjectivity, as the subjectivity that constitutes sense and

being. [. . .] Carried out with this systematic concreteness, phenomenology is *eo ipso* "*transcendental idealism*," though in a fundamentally and essentially new sense. It is not [. . .] a Kantian idealism, which believes it can keep open, at least as a limiting concept, the possibility of a world of things in themselves. (Husserl, Hua 1, 117–118/84–86)

A notion of an *absolute* transcendental subjectivity encompassing all imaginable meaningful being is required in order to accomplish the quest for an absolutely universal science of absolute foundations. This quest, Husserl tells us in *Crisis*, has been handed down to us by the great philosophical tradition of modernity; should we renounce this task, we can no longer remain serious philosophers (Husserl, Hua 6, 15/17). Husserl must therefore be included within the ambit of absolute idealism in the Meillassouxian sense of an absolutized version of Kantian weak correlationism that no longer accepts a transcendent "things in themselves." To a certain extent, this is a concession to Heidegger's provocative claim in "The End of Philosophy and the Task of Thinking" (1964) that even though Husserl's phenomenological method is worlds apart from Hegelian speculative dialectic, the "heart of the matter" (*die Sache selbst*) is for both Hegel and Husserl absolute subjectivity, that is, the absolutized correlation (Heidegger 2000b, 69–71/62–64).

The title of Heidegger's essay, "The End of Philosophy and the Task of Thinking," seems, in fact, to confirm Husserl's admonition that giving up the modern transcendental project would mean renouncing the classical philosophical project as such. For Heidegger, however, the end of classical philosophy by no means signifies the end of thinking. From the Heideggerian point of view, the quest for an absolutely universal science has been only one historical phase of Western thought, a phase whose inherent limitations are now becoming explicit, and Heidegger's later thought is concerned precisely with the possibility of a postclassical "other beginning" of thinking. In order to describe the basic method and motivation of such a potential form of thought, the term 'transcendental' needs at least important qualifications.

Heidegger, as we know, was from the beginning of his independent career critical of Husserl's notions of transcendental subjectivity and of the transcendental reduction.[19] The main reason for this was the concern that these notions risk disregarding the inherent facticity, that is, the historical situatedness, context-specificity, and singularity of human being as *Dasein*. There is, however, a sense in which the "transcendental reduction" designates a move that is indispensable for genuine philosophical study. This is simply the turn from already constituted objectivities to the process of their constitution as meaningful, in Heideggerian terms, from an ontic to an ontological approach, from determinate beings or entities to their being (Heidegger, GA 24, 29/21). With regard to beings (*Seiendes*), being (*Sein*) is "transcendental":

As the fundamental theme of philosophy, being [*Sein*] is not a genus of beings [*Seienden*]; yet it pertains to every being. Its "universality" must be sought in a higher sphere. Being and being-structure lie beyond every being and every possible character that a being may have. *Being is the transcendens pure and simple.* The transcendence of the being of *Dasein* is a distinctive one since in it lies the possibility and necessity of the most radical *individuation*. Every disclosure of being as the *transcendens* is *transcendental* knowledge. *Phenomenological truth (disclosedness of being) is veritas transcendentalis.* (Heidegger, SZ, 38/35–36; translation modified)

Heidegger here seemingly returns to the Aristotelian-Scholastic notion of being as a superuniversal *transcendens*. However, as the quotation marks around the word 'universal' indicate, 'transcendence' and 'transcendental' are used here in a decidedly nonconventional sense. Being does not transcend beings in the way in which the maximally universal transcends particulars; it transcends them in the way in which the temporal horizon or context of a meaningful experience transcends the focal point of presence of that experience.[20] The main aim of the published part of *Being and Time* is to show how the correlation between being and thinking is based on *Dasein*'s ecstatically temporal structure. In its most "authentic" (*eigentlich*) or ontologically primordial mode of relating to its world and itself, *Dasein* encounters the present as a singular "instant" (*Augenblick*) of meaningfulness in the framework of a concrete situation, that is, in terms of a context of specific future possibilities (*Zukunft*) emerging from a specific factical background of already-having-been (*Gewesenheit*).[21] This context-specificity is the "radical individuation" mentioned by Heidegger in the cited passage.[22] The contextual structure of *Dasein,* its "timeliness" (*Zeitlichkeit*), correlates with the contextual structure of being itself, its "temporality" (*Temporalität*; Heidegger, GA 24, 436/307). This temporality was to be disclosed as ultimately identical with the meaning or "sense" (*Sinn*) of being as such. Any meaningful presence is disclosed to *Dasein as* meaningful, and thereby "makes sense," only in the dynamic context of singular temporal situations:

[W]e project being [. . .] upon temporality [*Temporalität*]. [. . .] All ontological propositions have the character of *temporal* [*temporale*] *truth, veritas temporalis.* [. . .] transcendence, on its part, is rooted in timeliness [*Zeitlichkeit*] and thus in temporality [*Temporalität*]. Hence *time is the primary horizon of transcendental science,* of ontology, or, in short, it is the *transcendental horizon.* (Heidegger, GA 24, 459–460/323; translation modified)

These context-specific disclosures of being are not particular instances of any universal "being as such" that would be ideally instantiated in some absolute and ideal being, itself remaining beyond temporal and contextual determinations. Rather, the sense of being *is* the contextualization and singularization that generates singular meaning-situations and thereby lets being (the givenness of meaning) and thinking (receptivity to meaning) belong together—the event or "taking-place" that the later Heidegger famously called *Ereignis*.[23]

In his later work, Heidegger ended up discarding terms such as 'ecstatic' and 'existence,' as well as 'transcendence' and 'transcendental,' as potentially misleading.[24] It is no doubt these expressions he first and foremost has in mind when he later notes that *Being and Time* was still steeped in the language of metaphysics (Heidegger 1996, 328/250). It is Heidegger's fundamental aim to show that there is no primordial point of immediate and immanent presence to consciousness that would subsequently be "transcended" or "exceeded" toward a horizon. Rather, the focal point of a meaningful experiential situation is generated *only* as a singular and situational intersection of the nexus of multiple references that constitutes the unique meaning-context of that situation.[25] Being as *Ereignis* is not a "transcendental" feature of particular beings in the Aristotelian sense. Being and beings are no longer opposed in the sense of a universal and particulars; as Heidegger indicates in several of his latest texts, even the "ontological difference" between being and beings was only a provisional title for the dynamics of being itself.[26] There is *only* the event, the happening of being; there is, strictly speaking, no subject of being, no thing or substance *to which* being is happening. A being is an aspect of being, the focal point in the contextualization of singular experiential situations of meaningfulness, and a focal point is, by definition, something that cannot be conceived apart from a context.[27] The only "universal" feature of the singular happenings of meaningfulness is the structural feature that in their full contextual concreteness, they are unique and singular, even though they do form a historical tradition of inheritance, continuity, and relative transformation.[28]

However, as both Meillassoux and Daniel Dahlstrom point out, there is at least one important sense in which Heidegger does remain an heir to transcendental idealism until the end: *Ereignis* remains a name for the correlation between being and thinking (Dahlstrom 2005, 47–51; Meillassoux 2006b: 22/8).[29] It designates the "belonging-together" (*Zusammengehören*) of being and the human being, their irreducible and inextricable reciprocity. Even the completely desubstantialized event of being, the dynamic process of the temporalizing and singularizing contextualization of meaning, remains an event of meaningful *givenness* and thus cannot be thought independently of a recipient, a receptive dimension. However, as an *event*, the correlation resists absolutization, since "the absolute" literally signifies a purely self-sufficient *self-identity* that is completely "absolved" from all constitutive relations and references to anything other than itself.[30] An event cannot be absolute, since it is never "identical" with itself. When the correlation between being and thinking is conceived as *Ereignis*, neither aspect of the correlation can be conceived of as a permanent self-identity, such as that of the permanently *identical* Platonic Ideas or of the Kantian transcendental subject, of the "I think" implicitly present *as identical* in all possible representations. Rather, being as *Ereignis* is a name for the radical *nonabsoluteness*—the heterogeneity, contextuality, incommensurability, and singularity—of all givenness of and receptivity to meaningful presence.[31] This is what Heidegger strives to articulate in his 1957 lecture "The Thesis of Identity," which is perhaps his definitive statement of being as *Ereignis* and a key text of strong correlationism. All constituted identities are here referred to the fundamental identity indicated by Parmenides, the identity of thinking (*noein*) and being (*einai*). When being is conceived as *Ereignis*, this identity, in turn, is no longer seen as an absolute self-identity but rather as a structural feature of the heterogeneous and singular events of the correlation.

> We must experience simply this lending [*Eignen*] in which the human being and being [*Sein*] lend themselves to each other [*einander geeignet sind*], that is, we must enter into what we call *the event* [*Ereignis*]. [. . .] The word [sc. *Ereignis*] is now used as a *singulare tantum* [i.e., a noun used only in the singular]. What it indicates takes place only in the singular [*Einzahl*], no, not in any number, but uniquely [*einzig*]. [. . .] The event surrenders [*vereignet*] the human being and being to their essential togetherness. [. . .] The doctrine of metaphysics represents identity [*Identität*] as a fundamental feature of being. Now it becomes clear that being belongs with thinking to an identity whose essence [*Wesen*] stems from that letting-belong-together which we call the event. The essence of identity is a property [*Eigentum*] of the event. (Heidegger 2002, 24, 25, 27/36, 38, 39; translation modified)

As the happening of the correlation in which every being, every singular instance of meaningful presence is "grounded" in the sense of being contextualized and thereby made meaningful in a radically singular way, *Ereignis* itself can no longer be "grounded," given further "grounds" or "reasons." *That* the correlation takes place at all, *that* there is any meaningful givenness at all, is radically factical; it resists the question "Why?" which can only be asked of particular things. "The event [*Er-eignis*] and the possibility of the *why!* Can the 'why' still be made into a tribunal before which beyng [*Seyn*] is to be placed? [. . .] Why beyng? From within it itself. [. . .] Groundless [*grund-los*]; unfathomable [*abgründig*]" (Heidegger, GA 65, 509/400; translation modified).

3   FROM STRONG CORRELATIONISM TO SPECULATIVE MATERIALISM: MEILLASSOUX'S ARGUMENT FROM MORTALITY

In articulating his own speculative position, Meillassoux's strategy is to present it as unfolding from an implicit presupposition of Heideggerian strong correlationism. Meillassoux maintains that this approach is ultimately incapable of renouncing absolute principles altogether; on the contrary, it implicitly presupposes one. Just as Kant's weak version fell prey to the absolutization, by absolute idealism, of its basic principle, or the inseparability of thinking and being (termed the 'primacy of the correlate' by Meillassoux), Heideggerian "strong" correlationism falls prey to the absolutization of its additional second principle (the "facticity of the correlation") according to which the happening of the correlation is itself a factical and singular event without absolute grounds.

> [I]f an absolute capable of withstanding the ravages of the correlationist circle remains conceivable, it can only be the one that results from the absolutization of the strong model's second decision—*which is to say, facticity.* [. . .] Accordingly, we must try to understand why *it is not the correlation but the facticity of the correlation that constitutes the absolute.* (Meillassoux 2006b, 71–72/52)

This *absolutization of facticity* is the "nonmetaphysical absolute" speculative materialism is looking for (Meillassoux 2006b, 70/51). The specific argument through which Meillassoux hopes to accomplish it is related to mortality. In Heidegger's fundamental ontology, Kant's transcendental apperception, in the sense of a constantly possible awareness of one's own consciousness, is modified and complemented by being-towards-death (*Sein zum Tode*), that is, by an awareness of the constant possibility of the total absence of one's own experiential horizon. The awareness of the fact "I think" is referred to awareness of the fact "I can die," an awareness that first individualizes *Dasein* as a specific, situated, and finite "I" (Heidegger, SZ, 260–267, 316–323/249–255, 302–309). Mortality thus functions precisely as the "guarantee" of the finitude and nonabsoluteness constitutive of all meaningful thinking.

This *constitutive* relation to one's own death as a possibility most clearly distinguishes Heidegger's strong correlationism from absolute idealism. For Husserl, death can only be an empirical event, the cessation of the factual life of an empirical individual, never a transcendental, constitutive relationship that thinking has to the possibility of its own: "[T]he process of living on, and the ego that lives on, are immortal—*nota bene,* the pure transcendental ego, and not the empirical world-ego that can very well die" (Husserl, Hua 11, 378/467). Heidegger's notion of being-toward-death, however, implies that all "living on" is structured precisely by the constant possibility of its own cessation, of its own absence, and precisely thereby individuated into one's own finite and singular future horizon. Even though this absence is, of course, never experientially given as such and is therefore "unthinkable" in itself, its *possibility*, the possibility of *im*possibility—of the total absence of the horizon of one's own possibilities—as the *ultimate* possibility, is eminently thinkable. Death, for *Dasein*, is a pure, ultimate, and supreme possibility in that it is experienced *exclusively* as a possibility, never as a present-at-hand actuality: it is never actualized *within* existential time but functions precisely as a *limit* of time.[32] In this sense, the account of being-toward-death is an integral part of Heidegger's argument for the ontological priority of the future over the present: death is precisely a future that can never be present, the ever-open extremity of *Dasein*'s futurity as the open dimension of possibilities, a possibility that surpasses all possible actualities.

This is where Meillassoux's speculative argument comes in. It shares the fundamental presupposition of Hegel's critique of critical philosophy that once a limit is acknowledged *as* a limit it has already been transcended: one has already established a relationship to what lies beyond the limit (Hegel, GW 20, §60, 97/107). Experiencing one's own death as the limit of one's own possibilities entails that one has already incorporated what lies beyond that limit, namely, the total absence of one's possibilities. In other words, the constant possibility of death is conceptually dependent on its actualization—which is precisely what Heidegger denies. Just as the German Idealists argued that in thinking the finitude and the limits of thinking, Kant had already in fact transgressed those limits into the absolute realm, Meillassoux claims that in thinking the finitude of the correlation, the strong correlationist has already in fact transgressed the correlational realm of phenomenal meaning into an absolute noncorrelational realm. According to this argument, the only way for the Heideggerian to consistently distinguish herself from the Husserlian—or, more generally, for the strong correlationist to distinguish herself from the absolute idealist—on the question of mortality is by admitting that every thinking ego does indeed have a constitutive relationship to the possibility of an *actual* reality that does not include it and hence cannot be conceived as a correlate of its thinking. There is no transcendental level of egoity from which this possibility could be abstracted away.

> But how are these states [sc. mortality, annihilation, becoming-wholly-other in death] conceivable as possibilities? On account of the fact that we are able to think—by dint of the absence of any reason for our being—a capacity-to-be-other capable of abolishing us, or of radically transforming us. But if so, then *this capacity-to-be-other cannot be conceived as a correlate of our thinking, precisely because it harbors the possibility of our own not-being.* [. . .] if I maintain that the possibility of my not-being only exists as a correlate of my act of thinking the possibility of my not-being, then *I can no longer conceive the possibility of my not-being,* which is precisely the thesis defended by the [absolute] idealist. [. . .] Thus, the [strong] correlationist's refutation of idealism proceeds by way of an absolutization [. . .] of the capacity-to-be-other presupposed in the thought of facticity. (Meillassoux 2006b, 77–78/57)

This, according to Meillassoux, effectively makes the strong correlationist admit that she regards the correlation between thinking and being not merely as factical, that is, as given without any absolute necessity, but indeed as *contingent*, that is, as equally *capable* of *not being*. But to admit this is to admit that one ultimately thinks *everything*, every meaningful disclosure of reality within the correlation *as well as* the correlation itself, as radically contingent, as continually structured by the possibility of its not being as it is. Moreover, logical coherence requires that one actually conceives this contingency itself as absolute, not merely as a matter of fact; to maintain that the contingency of all things is itself contingent would lead to an infinite regress by again invoking an absolute contingency (Meillassoux 2006b, 78–81/57–59). Nothing—so the argument goes—can be conceived as absolute except the radical contingency of all things, which, in fact, must be conceived as *absolutely necessary*. Refusing to absolutize the correlation or any other being or region of being leaves the strong correlationist no other coherent option than to absolutize the *contingency* of the correlation and of every other being and region of being and become a speculative materialist ("materialism" being understood here in the very broad sense of a rejection of correlationism that asserts the accessibility of a notion of being that is not a correlate of thinking). On the other hand, refusing to absolutize contingency would compel the strong correlationist to absolutize the correlation and become an absolute idealist (Meillassoux 2006b, 81–82/59–60). In other words, the postmetaphysical renunciation of the "ontotheological" absolutization of some specific entity or mode of being ultimately entails the thesis that it is *absolutely impossible* that any aspect of reality, other than this impossibility itself, should turn out to be absolutely necessary. All experience of phenomenal meaningfulness entails the total absence of phenomenal meaningfulness as a logical possibility as well as a knowledge that even on this level, the principle of the *absolute necessity of contingency*—whose different aspects Meillassoux names the "principle of unreason (*irraison*)" (according to which nothing has a necessary reason for being the way it is; Meillassoux 2006b: 82–83/60–61) and the "principle of factuality (*factualité*)" (according to which "to be" necessarily means "to be a fact"; Meillassoux 2006b, 107–108/79–80)—is valid.

This, then, is the "end of finitude" indicated by the title of Meillassoux's book. Just as Hegel (and, in a different sense, Husserl) was the end of Kantian "weak" finitude of thinking, Meillassoux presents himself as the end of Heideggerian "strong" finitude. His argument is designed to show that in the end, no attempt to exclude *all* notions of absoluteness from the realm of thinking can be fully consistent. Finitude can never be the final word: in Hegel's words, "the finite is the restricted, the perishable, the finite is only the finite, not the imperishable; all this is immediately part and parcel of its determination and expression" (Hegel, GW 21, 117/102). Strong correlationism's project of deabsolutization paradoxically turns out to be committed to the threefold absolute principle of contingency, unreason, and factuality, and toward the end of the book, it becomes increasingly clear that Meillassoux is constructing nothing less than a new rationalistic *system* in which all principles—such as the logical principle of noncontradiction and the principle that there must be something rather than simply nothing—are logically deducible from the one absolute principle (Meillassoux 2006b, 91–103/67–76). He indeed announces his intention of demonstrating, on the basis of his principle of factuality, that the absolute level of being necessarily conforms to certain axioms of mathematical set theory but postpones this demonstration to later works (Meillassoux 2006b, 152–153/110–111).[33]

This demonstration is a key task since, for Meillassoux, the nonphenomenal and purely formal mode of thinking noncorrelational being is precisely *mathematics*. At the outset of his book, he mentions the necessity of resuscitating the early modern and precritical distinction between primary (e.g., spatial dimensions and number) and secondary (e.g., taste or color) qualities of things, for the familiar reason that the former, as opposed to the latter, are measurable and mathematizable and can thus be conceived in a purely formal way, apart from their phenomenal qualities (Meillassoux 2006b, 13–16/1–3). Meillassoux here reveals the extent of his debt to his mentor Alain Badiou, who famously equates ontology with mathematics, specifically with modern set theory (Badiou 1988, 7–39/1–30). In spite of their differences, the two thinkers share a common goal: to undo the post-Kantian hegemony of phenomenological, experience- and meaning-related categories of thinking and to rehabilitate pre-Kantian rationalism, but *without* the metaphysical notion of an absolutely necessary entity (Meillassoux 2006b, 16–18/3–5).[34] This speculative "end of finitude" seems for them to promise a way out of the final outcome of the heritage of transcendental idealism, or from the contemporary "postmodern" impasse in which the deabsolutization of thinking culminates in its deuniversalization. Phenomenologists and other heirs of Kant will therefore be eager to study the further development of Meillassoux's system and to start considering possible answers to, as well as the legitimacy of, his question: Why—and how—did philosophy "err towards transcendental idealism instead of resolutely orienting itself, as it should have, towards a *speculative materialism*" (Meillassoux 2006b, 168/121)?

NOTES

1. I thank Marko Gylén, Anniina Leiviskä, Simo Pulkkinen, Björn Thorsteinsson, and Gert-Jan van der Heiden for helpful comments on an earlier version of this chapter.
2. It is perhaps telling that Jacques Derrida, for one, urges us to be "responsible guardians of the heritage of transcendental idealism" (2003, 188/134).
3. On Kant's distinction, see CPR B xxxv–xxxvi.
4. On Kantian transcendentalism as the "core" of correlationism, see Ennis 2011a, 2011b.
5. It should be noted that such a reading is not unprecedented. Michel Foucault (1990) presents a similar account of the closure of the modern Kantian episteme in the post-Kantian "analytic of finitude" and anthropologism that

finally lead to the collapse of the distinction between the transcendental and the empirical, or the constitutive and the constituted, aspects of the human being, thus pointing the way toward a forthcoming Nietzschean posthumanism, or to a "death of man." Badiou (1989, 54–55/73–74) considers Heidegger's great accomplishment to be the overcoming of the Kantian subject-object dichotomy. Cf. Žižek (2006, 273): "Heidegger's greatest single achievement is the full elaboration of *finitude* as a positive constituent of being-human—in this way, he accomplished the Kantian philosophical revolution, making it clear that finitude is the key to the transcendental dimension." Chad Engelland (2008) argues that Heidegger sees Kant as a pathway toward overcoming traditional metaphysical rationalism. See also Blattner 1994, 1999, 2007.

6. For Kant's argument for the intelligibility and necessity of the notion of "things in themselves," suggesting that while the validity of this notion is theoretically unknowable, it could be justified on a practical basis, see CPR B xxvi–xxvii. On the transcendental object, tentatively identified with the "thing in itself" and the *noumenon,* see CPR A 288–289, 366, 494; B 344–345, 522–523.

7. See, for example, Hegel, GW 21, 31/27: "In its more consistent [Fichtean] form, transcendental idealism did recognize the nothingness of the spectral *thing-in-itself,* this abstract shadow divorced from all content left over by critical philosophy, and its goal was to destroy it completely." Cf. GW 21, 47/41.

8. See Hegel, GW 9, 18–25/9–17.

9. For Hegel's critique of Kant's failure to derive the categories, see GW 20, §42, 79–80/86. On the impossibility of such a derivation for Kant, see Heidegger 1998b, 55–56/39–40.

10. For readings of Wittgenstein as an heir of transcendental idealism, see, for example, Williams 1973; Tang 2011.

11. For Heidegger's account of ontotheology, see, for example, Heidegger 1998a, 311–315/207–210; 2002, 31–67/42–74.

12. On this, see, for example, Aertsen 1998, 1360–1365; 2012.

13. Aristotle, *Metaphysics,* B.3.998b22–27; I.2.1054a9–19; K.1.1059b27–34.

14. John Duns Scotus, *Quaestiones subtilissimae in Metaphysicam Aristotelis,* prol., n. 5.

15. In Kant's notes, we find 'transcendental' defined in very traditional metaphysical terms: "The determination of a thing in terms of its essence (as a thing) is transcendental" (Kant 1928, 340).

16. For Husserl's critique of Kant, see, in particular, Hua 6, 93–123, 194–212/ 91–121, 191–208.

17. Translation modified.

18. Cf. Carr 2007, 41.

19. See, for example, Heidegger, GA 17, 79–81, 273–275/58–59, 210–211; GA 20, 137–139, 150–151, 157–158/100–101, 109–110, 114. On Heidegger's ambivalent stance toward the Husserlian reductions, see Crowell 2001, 197–202.

20. In *Contributions to Philosophy,* Heidegger makes a clear distinction between "ontological" (i.e., Aristotelian-Scholastic) transcendence and the "fundamental-ontological" transcendence of *Being and Time* as *Dasein*'s exposure to the "openness of beings"—that is, their contextuality (GA 65, 217/170.)

21. On the instant (*Augenblick*), see, in particular, Heidegger, SZ, 335–350/320–334.

22. On *Dasein*'s singularization (*Vereinzelung*) in the instant, see, in particular, GA 29/30, 251/169; cf. SZ, 338–339/323–324.

23. This is stated very compactly in a later marginal note added by Heidegger to *Being and Time:* "*transcendens* of course not—in spite of all the metaphysical resonances—the Scholastic and Greek-Platonic *koinon* [common], rather transcendence as the ecstatic—timeliness [*Zeitlichkeit*]—temporality

[*Temporalität*] [. . .] . However, transcendence from the truth of beyng [*Seyns*]: the event [*Ereignis*]" (SZ, 440n[a] ad 38/36n; translation modified). The obsolete German orthography *Seyn,* which was still used by Hegel and Hölderlin at the beginning of the nineteenth century, is used by Heidegger in his work of the 1930s and 1940s (albeit not in an entirely consistent way) to designate the "postmetaphysical" notion of being as *Ereignis* from being as it was conceived within the metaphysical tradition. Following a now-established convention, I render this term with the equally obsolete Middle English spelling 'beyng.'

24. See Heidegger, GA 65, 322/255: "Even if 'transcendence' is grasped differently than before, i.e., as *excess* [*Überstieg*] rather than as a *super-sensible being,* even then the essence of *Da-sein* is all too easily distorted by this determination. For, even in this way, transcendence presupposes a *below and a hither side* [*Unten und Diesseits*] and is still in danger of being misinterpreted as an action of an 'I,' a subject. Thus in the end even this concept of transcendence is mired in Platonism" (translation modified; cf. GA 65, 217/169–170). "I have deleted the word 'existence' from the vocabulary of the thinking that moves in the compass of the question of *Being and Time.* The seemingly contrary name 'insistency' [*Inständigkeit*] is used instead" (GA 49: 54; my translation). For the later Heidegger's genealogy of the term 'transcendental,' see Heidegger 1997b: 133–143/77–83.

    For an elaborate discussion of the earlier and later Heidegger's ambivalent relationship to the transcendental tradition, see Dahlstrom 2005. Michael Inwood (1999, 227) stresses that Heidegger "rejects the *word* 'transcendence' rather than the concept." Cf. Malpas 2007.

25. This, arguably, is what Heidegger strives to articulate in his lecture on "The Thing": "Each thing arrests [*verweilt*] the fourfold [*Geviert*] into a happening of the simple onehood of world. [. . .] Whatever becomes a thing takes place [*ereignet sich*] out of the ringing [*Gering*] of the world's mirror-play [*Spiegel-Spiels*]" (Heidegger 2000, 173, 174/178, 179; translation modified).

26. See, for example, Heidegger, GA 65, 474/373: "Now what becomes of the *distinction between* [*Unterscheidung*] beings and beyng [*Seyn*]? Now we grasp this distinction as the merely metaphysically conceived, and thus already misinterpreted, foreground of a de-cision [*Ent-scheidung*] which *is* beyng itself [. . .]" (translation modified). In a later marginal note to "On the Essence of Ground," Heidegger speaks of the necessity of "*overcoming* the 'distinction'" between being and beings and of "thinking the 'distinction' as beyng [*Seyn*] itself" (2000: 134n[c]/105n[c]).

27. Heidegger, GA 65, 472, 474/372–373: "The full abidance [*Wesung*] of beyng [*Seyns*] in the truth of the event [*Wahrheit des Ereignisses*] allows us to realize that beyng and only beyng *is* and that beings [*das Seiende*] are *not.* [. . .] beyng *is* unique, and therefore it 'is' never a being [. . .] if beings *are not,* then that means beings continue to belong to beyng as the *preservation* of its truth [. . .]" (translation modified).

28. Heidegger, GA 65, 66/53: "[W]here beyng is conceived as event [*Ereignis*], essentiality [*Wesentlichkeit*] is determined in terms of the originality and uniqueness [*Einzigkeit*] of beyng itself. There the essence is not the general but is rather precisely the abidance [*Wesung*] of uniqueness in each instant" (translation modified). It must be decided "whether beings take being [*Sein*] as what is 'most general' to them [. . .] *or* whether beyng in its uniqueness comes to words and thoroughly attunes beings as singular [*Einmaliges*]" (GA 65, 90–91/72; translation modified). GA 65, 55/45: "*Only what is singular can be repeated*" (translation modified). Cf. Heidegger, GA 26, 128/108: "beyng itself is uniqueness, is singularity [*Einmaligkeit*] [. . .] this singularity does not exclude a 'once more,' but the contrary" (translation modified).

29. The other transcendental vestiges in the later Heidegger listed by Dahlstrom are the notions of being as time-space (*Zeit-Raum*) and of being as "grounding" beings.
30. Cf. Heidegger 2003: 136/102: "The absoluteness of the absolute is characterized by the unity of absolvence [*Absolvenz*] (disengagement from relation), absolving (completeness of disengagement), and absolution (acquittal on the basis of that completeness)" (translation modified).
31. In his 1962 seminar on the lecture "Time and Being," Heidegger makes a comparison between Hegel's notion of the absolute and his own notion of *Ereignis*: "Since for Hegel the human being is the place of the Absolute's coming-to-itself, that coming-to-itself leads to the overcoming of the human being's finitude. For Heidegger, in contrast, it is precisely finitude that comes to view—not only the human being's finitude, but the finitude of the event [*Ereignisses*] itself" (2000b, 53/49). Cf. Agamben 1999.
32. Heidegger, SZ, 261, 262/250, 251: "[W]e must characterize being-toward-death as a *being toward a possibility*, toward an eminent possibility of *Dasein* itself. [. . .] As possibility, death gives *Dasein* nothing to 'be actualized' and nothing which it itself could *be* as something real. It is the possibility of the impossibility of every mode of comportment toward . . ., of every way of existing. [T]his possibility offers no support for becoming intent on something, for 'picturing' for oneself the actuality that is possible and so forgetting its possibility" (translation modified).
33. Meillassoux presumably intends to continue his argument and finalize his system in his forthcoming multivolume work on "divine inexistence" (*L'inexistence divine;* see Meillassoux 2006b, 67n1/132n15). Translated excerpts from the current manuscript of the work have been published in Harman (2011). Some of the central theses of this work are discussed in Meillassoux 2006a.
34. Badiou provocatively maintains that "[t]he critical machinery he [Kant] set up has enduringly poisoned philosophy [. . .] . Kant is the inventor of the disastrous theme of our 'finitude'" (2006b, 561/535).

REFERENCES

Aertsen, J. A. 1998. "Transzendental II: Die Anfänge bis Meister Eckhart." In *Historisches Wörterbuch der Philosophie*, Vol. 10, 1360–1365. Edited by Joachim Ritter and Karlfried Gründer. Basel: Schwabe.

———. 2012. *Medieval Philosophy as Transcendental Thought: From Philip the Chancellor (ca. 1225) to Francisco Suárez.* Leiden: Brill.

Agamben, G. 1999. "*Se*: Hegel's Absolute and Heidegger's *Ereignis*." In *Potentialities: Collected Essays in Philosophy*, 116–137. Edited and translated by Daniel Heller-Roazen. Stanford, CA: Stanford University Press.

Aristotle. 1924. *Metaphysics*. Vol. 1–2. Edited by David Ross. Oxford: Oxford University Press.

Badiou, A. 1988. *L'être et l'évènement*. Paris: Seuil. Translation: Badiou, A. 2005. *Being and Event*. Translated by Oliver Feltham. London: Continuum.

———. 1989. *Manifeste pour la philosophie*. Paris: Seuil, 1989. Translation: Badiou, A. 1999. *Manifesto for Philosophy*. Translated by Norman Madarasz. Albany: State University of New York Press.

———. 2006a. "Préface." In Meillassoux, Q. *Après la finitude: essai sur la nécessité de la contingence*. Paris: Seuil, 9–11. Translation: Badiou. A. 2008. "Preface." *After Finitude: An Essay on the Necessity of Contingency*. Translated by Ray Brassier. London: Continuum, vi–viii.

————. 2006b. *Logiques des mondes: L'être et l'événement 2*. Paris: Seuil. Translation: Badiou, A. 2009. *Logics of Worlds: Being and Event 2*. Translated by Alberto Toscano. London: Continuum.

Blattner, W. D. 1994. "Is Heidegger a Kantian Idealist?" *Inquiry* 37/2, 185–201.

————. 1999. *Heidegger's Temporal Idealism*. Cambridge: Cambridge University Press.

————. 2004. "Heidegger's Kantian Idealism Revisited." *Inquiry* 47/4: 321–337.

————. 2007. "Ontology, the *A Priori*, and the Primacy of Practice: An Aporia in Heidegger's Early Philosophy." In *Transcendental Heidegger*, 10–27. Edited by Steven Crowell and Jeff Malpas. Stanford, CA: Stanford University Press.

Carr, D. 2007. "Heidegger on Kant on Transcendence." In *Transcendental Heidegger*, 28–42. Edited by Steven Crowell and Jeff Malpas. Stanford, CA: Stanford University Press.

Crowell, S. G. 2001. *Husserl, Heidegger, and the Space of Meaning: Paths toward Transcendental Phenomenology*. Evanston, IL: Northwestern University Press.

Dahlstrom, D. 2005. "Heidegger's Transcendentalism." *Research in Phenomenology* 35/1: 29–54.

Derrida, J. 2003. *Voyous*. Galilée: Paris. Translation: Derrida, J. 2005. *Rogues: Two Essays on Reason*. Translated by Pascale-Anne Brault and Michael Naas. Stanford, CA: Stanford University Press.

Engelland, C. 2008. "Heidegger on Overcoming Rationalism through Transcendental Philosophy." *Continental Philosophy Review* 41/1: 17–41.

Ennis, P. J. 2011a. *Continental Realism*. Winchester: Zero Books.

————. 2011b. "The Transcendental Core of Correlationism." *Cosmos and History* 7/1: 37–48.

Foucault, M. 1990. *Les mots et les choses*. Paris: Gallimard. Translation: Foucault, M. 2002. *The Order of Things: An Archaeology of the Human Sciences*. London: Routledge.

Harman, G. 2007. "Quentin Meillassoux: A New French Philosopher." *Philosophy Today* 51/1: 104–117.

————. 2011. *Quentin Meillassoux: Philosophy in the Making*. Edinburgh: Edinburgh University Press.

Hegel, G. W. F. 1980. *Gesammelte Werke*, Vol. 9: *Phänomenologie des Geistes* [1807]. Edited by Wolfgang Bonsiepen and Reinhard Heede. Hamburg: Meiner (GW 9). Translation: Hegel, G. W. F. 1977. *Phenomenology of Spirit*. Translated by A. V. Miller. Oxford: Oxford University Press.

————. 1985. *Gesammelte Werke*, Vol. 21: *Wissenschaft der Logik: Die objektive Logik*, Vol. 1/1: *Die Lehre vom Sein (1832)*. Edited by Friedrich Hogemann and Walter Jaeschke. Hamburg: Meiner (GW 21). Translation: Hegel, G. W. F. 2010. *The Science of Logic*. Translated by George di Giovanni. Cambridge: Cambridge University Press.

————. 1992. *Gesammelte Werke*, Vol. 20: *Enzyklopädie der philosophischen Wissenschaften (1830)*. Edited by Wolfgang Bonsiepen and Hans-Christian Lucas. Hamburg: Meiner (GW 20). Translation: Hegel, G. W. F. 2010. *Encyclopaedia of the Philosophical Sciences in Outline, Part I: Science of Logic*. Translated by Klaus Brinkmann and Daniel O. Dahlstrom. Cambridge: Cambridge University Press.

Heidegger, M. 1978. *Metaphysische Anfangsgründe der Logik im Ausgang von Leibniz* [1928]. *Gesamtausgabe 26*. Edited by Klaus Held. Frankfurt am Main: Klostermann (GA 26). Translation: Heidegger, M. 1983. *The Metaphysical Foundations of Logic*. Translated by Michael Heim. Bloomington, Indiana: Indiana University Press.

————. 1983. *Die Grundbegriffe der Metaphysik: Welt-Endlichkeit-Einsamkeit* [1929–30]. *Gesamtausgabe, 29/30*. Edited by Friedrich-Wilhelm von Herrmann. Frankfurt am Main: Klostermann (GA 29/30). Translation: Heidegger, M. 1995.

The Fundamental Concepts of Metaphysics: World, Finitude, Solitude. Translated by William McNeill and Nicholas Walker. Bloomington: Indiana University Press.

———. 1988. *Kant und das Problem der Metaphysik* [1929], 6th edition. Edited by Friedrich-Wilhelm von Herrmann. Frankfurt am Main: Klostermann, 1998. Translation: Heidegger, M. 1997. *Kant and the Problem of Metaphysics.* Translated by Richard Taft. Bloomington: Indiana University Press.

———. 1989. *Beiträge zur Philosophie (Vom Ereignis)* [1936–38]. *Gesamtausgabe* 65. Edited by Friedrich-Wilhelm von Herrmann. Frankfurt am Main: Klostermann (GA 65). Translation: Heidegger, M. 2012. *Contributions to Philosophy (Of the Event).* Translated by Richard Rojcewicz and Daniela Vallega-Neu. Bloomington: Indiana University Press.

———. 1991. *Die Metaphysik des deutschen Idealismus* [1941]. *Gesamtausgabe* 49. Edited by Günter Seubold. Frankfurt am Main: Klostermann (GA 49).

———. 1994a. *Einführung in die phänomenologische Forschung* [1923–24]. *Gesamtausgabe* 17. Edited by Friedrich-Wilhelm von Herrmann. Frankfurt am Main: Klostermann. Translation: Heidegger, M. 2005. *Introduction to Phenomenological Research.* Translated by Daniel O. Dahlstrom. Bloomington: Indiana University Press (GA 17).

———. 1994b. *Prolegomena zur Geschichte des Zeitbegriffs* [1925]. *Gesamtausgabe* 20, 3rd edition. Edited by Petra Jaeger. Frankfurt am Main: Klostermann (GA 20). Translation: Heidegger, M. 1992. *History of the Concept of Time: Prolegomena.* Translated by Theodore Kisiel. Bloomington: Indiana University Press.

———. 1996. *Wegmarken,* 3rd ed. Edited by Friedrich-Wilhelm von Herrmann. Frankfurt am Main: Klostermann. Translation: Heidegger, M. 1998. *Pathmarks.* Edited by William McNeill. Cambridge: Cambridge University Press.

———. 1997a. *Besinnung* [1938–39]. *Gesamtausgabe* 66. Edited by Friedrich-Wilhelm von Herrmann. Frankfurt am Main: Klostermann (GA 66). Translation: Heidegger, M. 2006. *Mindfulness.* Translated by Parvis Emad and Thomas Kalary. London: Continuum.

———. 1997b. *Der Satz vom Grund* [1955–56], 8th ed. Stuttgart: Neske. Translation: Heidegger, M. 1991. *The Principle of Reason.* Translated by Reginald Lilly. Bloomington: Indiana University Press.

———. 1997c. *Die Grundprobleme der Phänomenologie* [1927]. *Gesamtausgabe* 24, 3rd edition. Edited by Friedrich-Wilhelm von Herrmann. Frankfurt am Main: Klostermann (GA 24). Translation: Heidegger, M. 1982. *The Basic Problems of Phenomenology.* Translated by Albert Hofstadter. Bloomington: Indiana University Press.

———. 1998a. "Die seinsgeschichtliche Bestimmung des Nihilismus" [1944–46]. In *Nietzsche,* Vol. 2, 6th ed. Stuttgart: Neske, 311–315. Translation: Heidegger, M. 1991. "Nihilism as Determined by the History of Being," in *Nietzsche,* Vol. 4: *Nihilism,* 207–210. Translated by Frank A. Capuzzi and edited by David Farrell Krell. San Francisco: Harper San Francisco).

———. 1998b. *Kant und das Problem der Metaphysik* [1929], 6th ed. Edited by Friedrich-Wilhelm von Herrmann. Frankfurt am Main: Klostermann. Translation: Heidegger, M. 1997. *Kant and the Problem of Metaphysics.* Translated by Richard Taft. Bloomington: Indiana University Press.

———. 2000a. "Das Ding" [1950]. In *Vorträge und Aufsätze,* 9th ed. Stuttgart: Neske, 157–179. Translation: Heidegger, M. 1971. "The Thing." In *Poetry, Language, Thought.* New York: Harper & Row, 161–184.

———. 2000b. *Zur Sache des Denkens,* 4th ed. Tübingen: Niemeyer. Translation: Heidegger, M. 2002. *On Time and Being.* Translated by Joan Stambaugh. Chicago: University of Chicago Press.

———. 2001. *Sein und Zeit* [1927], 18th edition. Tübingen: Niemeyer (SZ). Translation: Heidegger, M. 2010. *Being and Time.* Translated by Joan Stambaugh, revised by Dennis J. Schmidt. Albany: State University of New York Press.

————. 2002. *Identität und Differenz* [1957], 12th ed. Stuttgart: Klett-Cotta. Translation: Heidegger, M. 2002. *Identity and Difference*. Translated by Joan Stambaugh. Chicago: University of Chicago Press.

————. 2003. "Hegels Begriff der Erfahrung" [1942–43]. In *Holzwege*, 8th ed. Edited by Friedrich-Wilhelm von Herrmann. Frankfurt am Main: Klostermann, 115–208. Translation: Heidegger, M. 2002. "Hegel's Concept of Experience." In *Off the Beaten Track*, 86–156. Translated by Julian Young and Kenneth Haynes. Cambridge: Cambridge University Press.

Husserl, E. 1950. *Cartesianische Meditationen und Pariser Vorträge, Husserliana 1.* Edited by Stephan Strasser. The Hague: Martinus Nijhoff (Hua 1). Translation: Husserl, E. 1977. *Cartesian Meditations: An Introduction to Phenomenology.* Translated by Dorion Cairns. Dordrecht: Kluwer.

————. 1954. *Die Krisis der europäischen Wissenschaften und die transzendentale Phänomenologie: Eine Einleitung in die phänomenologische Philosophie* [1936], *Husserliana 6.* Edited by Walter Biemel. The Hague: Martinus Nijhoff (Hua 6). Translation: Husserl, E. 1970. *The Crisis of European Sciences and Transcendental Phenomenology.* Translated by David Carr. Evanston, IL: Northwestern University Press.

————. 1966. *Analysen zur passiven Synthesis: Aus Vorlesungs- und Forschungsmanuskripten 1918–1926, Husserliana 11.* Edited by Margot Fleischer. The Hague: Martinus Nijhoff (Hua 11). Translation: Husserl, E. 2001. *Collected Works,* Vol. 9: *Analyses Concerning Passive and Active Synthesis: Lectures on Transcendental Logic.* Translated by Anthony J. Steinbock. Dordrecht: Kluwer.

————. 1984. *Logische Untersuchungen, Zweiter Band, Zweiter Teil: Untersuchungen zur Phänomenologie und Theorie der Erkenntnis* [1901]. *Husserliana 19/2.* Edited by Ursula Panzer. The Hague: Martinus Nijhoff (Hua 19/2). Translation: Husserl, E. 2001. *Logical Investigations,* Vol. 2. Translated by J. N. Findlay and edited by Dermot Moran. London: Routledge.

Inwood, M. 1999. *A Heidegger Dictionary.* Oxford: Blackwell.

John Duns Scotus. 1893. *Opera omnia,* Vol. 7: *Quaestiones subtilissimae super libros Metaphysicorum Aristotelis.* Edited by Luke Wadding. Paris: Vivès.

Kant, I. 1928. *Kant's Gesammelte Schriften,* Vol. 18: *Dritte Abtheilung: Handschriftlicher Nachlaß,* Vol. 5: *Metaphysik, 2. Theil.* Berlin: De Gruyter.

————. 1998. *Kritik der reinen Vernunft* [A 1781; B 1787]. Edited by Jens Timmermann. Hamburg: Meiner (CPR). Translation: Kant, I. 1998. *Critique of Pure Reason.* Translated by Paul Guyer and Allen Wood. Cambridge: Cambridge University Press.

Malpas, J. 2007. "Heidegger's Topology of Being." In *Transcendental Heidegger,* 119–134. Edited by Steven Crowell and Jeff Malpas. Stanford, CA: Stanford University Press.

Meillassoux, Q. 2006a. "Deuil à venir, dieu à venir." *Critique* 62/704–705: 105–115. Translation: Meillassoux, Q. 2008. "Spectral Dilemma." In *Collapse,* Vol. 4: *Concept Horror,* 261–275. Edited by Robin Mackay. Falmouth: Urbanomic.

————. 2006b. *Après la finitude: essai sur la nécessité de la contingence.* Paris: Seuil. Translation: Meillassoux, Q. 2008. *After Finitude: An Essay on the Necessity of Contingency.* Translation by Ray Brassier. London: Continuum.

Tang, H. 2011. "Transcendental Idealism in Wittgenstein's *Tractatus.*" *The Philosophical Quarterly* 61/244: 598–607.

Williams, B. 1973. "Wittgenstein and Idealism." *Royal Institute of Philosophy Lectures* 7: 76–96.

Žižek, S. 2006. *The Parallax View.* Cambridge: MIT Press.

14 "*Die Kehre spielt im Sachverhalt selbst*"[1]

Making Sense of the Twists and Turns in Heidegger's Thought

Niall Keane

INTRODUCTION

The 'turn' or 'turning' (*Kehre*), which is used at various times and with multiple meanings, is without doubt one of the most problematic (and least monochromatic) terms when it comes to understanding Heidegger's work and its lexical horizon. The effective history of its reception stems from the early literature, starting with Karl Löwith, Walter Schulz, and Max Müller, who locate in the *Kehre* a tendency toward a philosophical U-turn of sorts (Löwith 1953; Müller 1949; Schulz 1953–1954). However, with the works of Otto Pöggeler and Friedrich-Wilhelm von Herrmann, to name but two, there emerged the reception and nuanced defense of the idea of a continuity, albeit with qualifications and disagreements, in the development of the question of being, starting from *Being and Time* and running into the so-called later thought (Pöggler 1963; von Herrmann 1964, 1994). Heidegger's editorial self-staging notwithstanding, these interpretations argue that the *Kehre* has little to do with the chronological twists and turns in Heidegger's thought but rather with the matter (*Sache*) of Heidegger's thought. Moreover, it was by means of this abiding concern that Heidegger always defended the unity of his basic question while also being aware that the transitions in his thought attested to moments of great oscillation and upheaval, *Umstürze*. Furthermore, it is precisely these moments of philosophical oscillation and upheaval that forced Heidegger to pursue the unity of the content of his thinking, which both demands and makes possible its own transitions and reformulations. In this sense, any philosophically reconstructive understanding of the *Kehre* as the matter at issue cannot be taken in isolation from the retrospective conviction articulated in Heidegger's 1946 "Letter on Humanism." He writes:

> The adequate execution and completion of this other thinking that abandons subjectivity is surely made more difficult by the fact that in the publication of *Being and Time* the third division of the first part, "Time and Being," was held back (cf. *Being and Time*, p. 39). Here everything is reversed [*Hier kehrt sich das Ganze um*]. The division in question was

held back because thinking failed in the adequate saying of this turning [*Kehre*] and did not succeed with the help of the language of metaphysics. The lecture "On the Essence of Truth," thought out and delivered in 1930 but not printed until 1943, provides a certain insight into the thinking of the turning from "Being and Time" to "Time and Being." This turning is not a change of standpoint from *Being and Time*; but in it the thinking that was sought first arrives at the locality [*Ortschaft*] of that dimension out of which *Being and Time* is experienced, that is to say, experienced in the fundamental experience of the oblivion of being. (Heidegger, GA 9, 327–328/249–250)

In the well-known passage just cited, Heidegger is alluding to a "turn" already promised and projected in *Being and Time*, even if it does or does not correspond to the intensity of his later rethinking of the turn, all of which undermine the impression that the *Kehre* is a drastic psychological and biographical U-turn, caused from without, on the way to something more profound. Yet why was *Being and Time* interrupted, why was it unable to articulate the philosophical significance of the turn, and how is it already operative within the *Sache* itself? What motivates the necessary transition from the openly transcendental approach to the ecstatic-horizonal temporality of the existential analytic of *Dasein* in *Being and Time* to the rethinking of the problem in terms of the history of being? Why should this be understood as a deepening of the transcendental and not simply a rejection of transcendental philosophy? And lastly, even if we are not naïve enough to think of these two ways as incompatible alternatives and that the latter is always already promised in the former, how are they distinct from one another?

1   OUTLINING THE PROBLEMATIC

In an attempt to respond to this decisive network of questions, it is necessary to retrace the essential aims of *Being and Time*, starting with the existential analytic of *Dasein*, which is the modality of access to the question of being in general. The provisional interrogation of the ontological structure of *Dasein* by *Dasein* is, from the beginning, dedicated to the retrieval of an appropriate horizon for an understanding of the sense of being, which in the course of the analysis manifests itself in terms of temporality. This philosophical valence is underlined and reiterated by Heidegger in terms of the provisional nature of the *Daseinanalyse* in the final pages of *Being and Time*, in which he writes:

[O]ur task has been to interpret the *primordial whole* of factical Dasein with regard to its possibilities of authentic and inauthentic existing, and to do so in an existential-ontological manner *in terms of its very basis*.

Temporality has manifested itself as this basis and accordingly as the meaning [or sense] of the Being of care. So that which our *preparatory* existential analytic of Dasein contributed *before* temporality was laid bare, has now been *taken back* into temporality as the primordial structure of Dasein's totality of Being. In terms of the possible ways in which primordial time can temporalize itself, we have provided the "grounds" for those structures which were just "pointed out" in our earlier treatment. Nevertheless, our way of exhibiting the constitution of Dasein's Being remains only *one way* that we may take. Our *aim* is to work out the question of being in general. (Heidegger, SZ, 436–437/486–487)

How is it possible to arrive at such a result, namely, that temporality is the primordial structure of *Dasein*'s totality, and thus locate a transition from the preliminary task (*Dasein* as the way) to that which guides its very how, namely the question of being in general?

The first part of *Being and Time* concludes with the definition of care as the ontological determination of the unitary structural totality of *Dasein*, and hence care proves to be the distinctive delineation of the being of *Dasein*. All in all, it is clear to any reader of *Being and Time* that care is a complex phenomenon, one that unites and one in which sense is bound up with becoming individuated against a horizon that is understandable only as a determining indeterminacy, to invert Husserl's phrase. Division Two of *Being and Time*, "Dasein and Temporality," articulates the analysis of being toward death and resolute anticipation as *Dasein*'s authentic possibility of being a whole and subsequently arriving at temporality as the unitary and constitutive ground of the ontological sense of care. Thus, in *Being and Time* Heidegger reaches the first and second objectives of his previously outlined aims, namely the determination of the horizon appropriate for the elaboration of the genuine question of being. In conformity with the mode of the being of *Dasein*, he was then in a position to proceed with the elaboration of the question of the sense of being in general. If the horizon for an understanding and interpretation of *Dasein* is temporality, temporality as the ontological sense of care, and *Dasein* is that distinct being capable of understanding being, one must assume, accepting the circularity, that it is the same temporality that is the privileged point of departure for an understanding of being. In fact, this was the very task that was set aside for the projected Division Three of part one of *Being and Time*, namely, the performative *Umkehrung* that was to be "Time and Being," the destroyed draft that was to respond to the decisive and concluding question of *Being and Time*: "Does *time* itself manifest itself as the horizon of *Being?*" (Heidegger, SZ, 437/488).

Yet it is precisely this question that did not find a response. In the previously cited passage from the "Letter on Humanism," written some twenty years after *Being and Time*, Heidegger puts the interruption in or rupture of *Being and Time* down to the inability of traditional philosophical language to express or give voice to the uneasy and demanding transition from "being and time" to "time and being."[2] And hence, for the later Heidegger, it is the representative and objectifying nature of the language of metaphysics that impedes access to the genuine truth of being and in fact suppresses any articulation of the operative *Kehre* itself. Yet the experience of the foundering of language as metaphysics does not, as many believe, carry with it the necessity of a new language, the invention of new esoteric terms. On the contrary, this foundering demands on the one hand that we experience the nature of language more profoundly, that we "bring language as language to language" (Heidegger, GA 12, 232/398), and on the other that we retrace that elusive element within the Western metaphysical tradition with a view to attesting to the permanency of its own unthought.

Yet the ineluctability of metaphysics bears witness to the fact that within the linguistic struggle, there continues to dwell the problem of a structural order. Starting from *Dasein*'s preontological understanding or awareness of being and from the possibility of an interpretation adequately oriented to ground temporality and evidently being possessed by and being in possession of an understanding of being, the work must also account for *Dasein*'s ability to comport itself toward entities. In a word, it must also account for *Dasein*'s ability to objectify and conceptually circumscribe the sense of beings or entities.

Much as Heidegger repeats and confirms the provisional, propaedeutic, and methodic orientation of the existential-analytic, there remains the intractable fact that starting from the preontological understanding of *Dasein* always carries the danger—'*Gefahr*' is the term used in *Contributions*—of remaining locked within the will to ground or found and, in doing so, of objectifying thought and its object, perhaps overlooked by Heidegger's own earlier attempts to dismantle this very approach. If it is true that one of the fundamental theses of *Being and Time* and the subsequent *Basic Problems of Phenomenology* is the distinction between being and beings by way of the ontological difference opened up by *Dasein*'s way of being, then the project of fundamental ontology, as Heidegger himself admits in 1927, is still too deeply bound up with the operation of the objectification (*Vergegenständlichung*) of being and beings.

Yet the *Basic Problems of Phenomenology*, the text in which he intended to revisit the question of temporality, and again starting from the way that *Dasein* understands being, signals the first awareness of this danger after Being and Time and the suggestion that a temporal interpretation of being is run though with an insubstantial untruth, the untruth of objectification, which lies hidden within what is seen and projectively (i.e., temporally) interpreted (Heidegger, GA 24, 459/322–323). Here we find Heidegger both wrestling with his own earlier analyses and attempting to defend the unity of his question as the unity of a philosophical itinerary.

It is not by chance, then, that in the 1936 to 1938 *Contributions to Philosophy*, a text that develops the indications, hesitations, and insights of the

Basic Problems of Phenomenology, the awareness of this danger (*Gefahr*) becomes most manifest. If the transcendental temporal horizon of being promised in *Being and Time* had been brought to term, if the projective interpretive horizon proved philosophically sufficient, then one could argue, with the Heidegger of *Contributions*, that the *Seinsfrage* would have lost its *Frage*-like character and would not have unfolded as a question worthy of question. That is to say, transcendental philosophy, understood as an ultimately grounding universal philosophy, arguably reduces being to a constituted or constitutable object, the achievement of transcendental subjectivity and intersubjectivity, and fails to think the dynamic cobelonging of *Da-sein* and the truth of being out of which philosophical questioning first emerges. Or as Heidegger puts it:

> *Being and Time* after all aims at demonstrating "time" as the domain for projecting-opening be-ing. Certainly, but if things had remained that way, then the question of being would never have unfolded as a question and thus as a questioning into what is more question worthy (. . .) Thus at the deciding juncture it was necessary to overcome the crisis of the question of being (. . .), and above all to avoid an objectification of beyng (*eine Vergegenständlichung des Seyns*)—on the one hand by *holding back* the "temporal" interpretation of beyng and at the same time by attempting besides (*unabhängig davon*) to make the truth of beyng "visible." By merely thinking further along the line of the question already set forth, the crisis did not let itself be mastered. (Heidegger, GA 65, 451/317)

Thus, Heidegger is forced to attribute the unfinished Division Three of *Being and Time* not only to a seemingly external factor, that is, the failure of language to get beyond or twist free from its metaphysical determination, but also to the problematic structure and incompleteness of his earlier questions. Hence what we find Heidegger referring to is the pressing need to "refrain from" or "hold off" on (*Zurückhalten*) the temporal interpretation of being and to address the question of the truth of being as it announces its own being-historical. In a way, this move reverses the one present in the penultimate section of Division Two of *Being and Time* that addresses the problem of historicality on the way to addressing the overarching problem of temporality. One could even go so far as to surmise that Heidegger was already responding to the *Kehre* in the penultimate section of Division Two of *Being and Time*, namely, "Temporality and Historicality."

However, it is important to note that this is not a question of moving beyond the temporal-horizonal question set out in *Being and Time*, and neither is it a radical distance taking when it comes to his initial intuition of the intimate rapport between time and being, but rather an attempt to resist making temporality the sole ground of being in the metaphysical sense of the word. In this way, the obstacle to an ecstatic-horizonal approach does not simply come down to a methodic impediment but rather takes its start from the thing itself, namely, that being withdraws in the face of every objectifying or reifying comprehension and refuses to allow itself to be dominated by the hegemonic and overarching enterprises of metaphysics. Importantly, and this should not be overlooked, I would argue that this must hold true for any proposed destruction or dismantling of the history of ontology.

While *Being and Time*, as a necessary and preparatory way, cannot be circumvented for the sake of the later thought and in fact grounds the later work, Heidegger nonetheless affirms in *Contributions* that the crisis of *Being and Time* cannot be resolved, solved, or "mastered" by means of retracing his own earlier steps but only by means of a "leap (*Sprung*) into the essencing of truth itself" (GA 65, 446/314).[3] At the same time, however, this leap is only possible starting from a more originary access to history, in the attempt to arrive at what he terms the 'first beginning' and to shed light on the fundamental term '*aletheia*,' that is, truth as the essential character of being.[4]

2   THE TRANSFORMATIONS OF TRUTH

The possibility of moving forward, which implies moving back through his earlier work, resides in the re-articulation of truth itself, an articulation already operative in §44 of *Being and Time*, which continued to occupy Heidegger in his last Marburg lectures of 1928 and also in the well-known lecture *Vom Wesen der Wahrheit*. Articulated in 1930 but published in 1943 after much reworking, *Vom Wesen der Wahrheit* contains, and especially when one reads the two drafts (the *Urfassung* and *Druckfassung*), the signs of an appropriative transitioning through and beyond *Being and Time* in the direction of thinking the history of being. In fact, laying out the questions surrounding the essence of truth, elaborating ontologically on the question of truth and its origin, signifies, according to Heidegger, speaking to the problem of the *Kehre* itself or at least one of its essential traces, namely the co-appearance in being of concealedness and unconcealedness, of untruth and truth. We are dealing here with the comprehension of *lethe* at the heart of *aletheia*. As Heidegger puts it in *Vom Wesen der Wahrheit*:

> The answer to the question of the essence of truth is the saying of a turning [*die Sage einer Kehre*] within the history of Beyng. Because sheltering that clears belongs to it, Beyng appears originarily in the light of concealing withdrawal. The name of this clearing [*Lichtung*] is *aletheia*. (Heidegger, GA 9, 201/154)

Accordingly, this thinking that turns, as Heidegger puts it in *Contributions*, with "the turning relation of the be-ing to Da-sein" (Heidegger, GA 65, 7/6), a thinking that is capable of the saying of this turning, is a thinking that renounces the classical or dialectical rapport between truth and untruth and is able to offer a new interrogation of negativity understood as a positive hiddenness. In the period between *Being and Time* and the *Urfassung* of *Vom Wesen der Wahrheit*, Heidegger was not in a position to take on this challenge and to think it to completion. Undoubtedly, the co-original reciprocity of truth and untruth was always a central factor in Heidegger's thinking; however, the question of untruth becomes more central and demanding under the weight of its metaphysical heritage, namely as the privation of truth, or absence as the simple other of presence. In the *Druckfassung* of 1943, however, it is precisely this issue that is addressed and modified. In fact, it is illuminating to compare two passages from the original 1930 text and the 1943 redraft. In 1930 he writes, "The concealment of beings as a whole is so old and only as old as the letting-be of beings, which, while disclosing, keeps concealed." In 1943 the co-originality or equiprimordiality appears unequivocally damaged or at least under severe strain, when he writes, "It [concealment] is older even than the letting-be itself, which in disclosing already holds concealment and comports itself towards concealing" (Heidegger, GA 9, 201/154).[5]

Ultimately, it appears then that the entirety of §6 of the *Druckfassung* is concerned with how an interpretation of hiddenness and untruth as privation is unsustainable and how hiddenness is in effect the proper custodian of being, the source of its disclosure, and the condition of the intelligible manifestation (i.e., truth) of beings. From the co-originality of unhiddenness and hiddenness, Heidegger moves to an awareness of an originary plexus in which untruth belongs essentially to truth and in fact determines its movement of disclosure. This very transformation is already announced in *Contributions* when Heidegger writes, "the essential unfolding of truth lies in un-truth" (Heidegger, GA 65, 356/249).

Yet with this insight, aren't we already beyond the ecstatic-horizonal analysis of temporality found in *Being and Time*? If the so-called withdrawal of being is an essential activity of the truth of being, do we not find ourselves compelled to accept that the access to the question of being by means of *Dasein*'s preontological understanding of being, *Dasein*'s affective interpretative capacity, and of temporality as a fundamental and unitary structure of its being, is renounced? Do not the questions of being-historical and the being-historical nature of the withdrawal of being become the new guiding questions? My response to these questions is a hesitant yes and no. I say this because the so-called movement beyond can only take place—and here I would like to stress the continuity of Heidegger's *Grundfrage*—starting from the two basic presuppositions underlying *Being and Time*: (1) the original phenomenological teaching according to which being is taken as that which is self-given, a self-givenness that is run through with absence, and (2) the fundamental intuition that any understanding of being has an original rapport with temporality, a rapport that in 1928 Heidegger defines as "completely obscure and mysterious" (Heidegger, GA 26, 178/141).

However, with a change of intensity and focus, the self-givenness that he later tries to thematize is that of the dispensation or sending (*Schicken*) of the history of being. Again hearkening back to the penultimate section of *Being and Time* and its analysis of heritage, tradition, the constitution of history, and the history of being, Heidegger restates in the second volume of the *Nietzsche* lectures that "The history of Being is neither the history of man and of humanity, nor the history of the human relation to beings and to Being. The history of Being is Being itself, and only Being" (Heidegger, GA 6.2., 489/82). From here the necessity of retracing the occlusion of the history of being in and as metaphysics becomes the pressing question, although the central role of the human being as questioner or seeker, as message bearer, is always preserved.

This does not mean a mere reconsideration of the canonical texts of the metaphysical tradition is in the cards, nor does it mean that he is intent on offering an interpretation of being starting from a consideration of the being whose being is an issue for it or of linking this being that exists understandingly to temporality. Heidegger makes it clear that the guiding intuitions of *Being and Time* do not seem to fully distinguish themselves from those intuitions that have always guided and determined, in diverse ways, the epochs of metaphysics.

3 THE "TURNING" AND THE "OVERTURNING"

What is *Dasein*'s role in this demanding and demanded re- or prethinking the history of being? Some commentators have attempted to address the question of the *Kehre,* incorrectly in my view, starting from the disappearance or dwindling of the fundamental role of *Dasein* and its alleged progressive subservience or self-abandonment to the event of being (Richardson 2003, 624). This reading needs to be corrected—a reading, it must be said, that Heidegger does much to encourage; one need only think of the ambiguity contained in Heidegger's letter to William Richardson, in which he states, "the *Kehre is* a change (*Wendung*) in my thought . . . this change is not a consequence of altering the standpoint, much less abandoning the fundamental issue, of *Sein und Zeit*. The thinking of the *Kehre* results from the fact that I stayed with the matter for thought [of] Being and time, by inquiring into that perspective which already in *Sein und Zeit* was designated as 'Time and Being'" (Heidegger 2003, XVI), and then concluding with a declarative statement, "The *Kehre* is above all not an operation of interrogative thought [. . .] The *Kehre* is at play within the matter itself. Neither did I invent it nor does it affect merely my thought" (Heidegger 2003, XVIII). Leaving aside the potential ambiguity of these words ("the *Kehre* is a change in my thought [. . .] neither did I invent it nor does it affect merely my thought"), Heidegger is intent on thinking *of* the operative *Kehre* itself and not on analyzing his own thinking *after* the

Kehre (Sallis 1992, 202).[6] If anything, he rails against the empty talk of philosophico-biographical shifts.

In the first place, the transition from the ecstatic-horizonal and temporal interpretation to the historical, epochal, or destinal is only understandable and justifiable on the basis of the spadework done in the existential analytic of *Dasein*. I say this insofar as it is instructive to bear in mind Heidegger's own introductory declaration in *Being and Time*, when he writes, "Dasein is as it already was, and it is 'what' it already was. It *is* its past" (Heidegger, SZ, 20/41). Consequently, this means that the understanding of being that belongs essentially to *Dasein* cannot be taken in isolation from the historicality in which it roots itself, nor can it be uncoupled from the authentic temporality through which being gives itself as historical. Already in *Being and Time* the articulation of the *Seinsfrage* in no way makes little of its history and in fact corresponds to a radical interrogation of itself. The historicality constitutive of *Dasein*, the site of the disclosure of being, is what permits the retracing of the history of being in the direction of an origin always already forgotten. In *Being and Time*, the promised dismantling or destruction of the history of ontology takes on the positive sense of an appropriative unbuilding. However, what is perchance undercooked in *Being and Time* is a deeper awareness of the fact that the veils of metaphysics, what the epochs of metaphysics hide, are the veils of the history of being itself, which do not lend themselves to ontological dismantling, no matter how positively appropriating it is.[7]

Hence, even in the self-defined overturning (*Umschlag*) from the fundamental ontology of *Being and Time* to the so-called metontology that Heidegger discusses in the Marburg course of 1928—metontology being the inverse metaphysical ontic horizon of fundamental ontology—which is perhaps the first time that Heidegger uses the term *die Kehre* to define the philosophical problematic, we still find Heidegger rooting his transition or overturning and the motivating content of this overturning in the earlier *Daseinanalyse*. In reformulating the problem of *Dasein*'s transcendence and marking it off from both its Platonic roots and the classical conception of intentionality, Heidegger again proceeds to articulate a sort of synopsis of the principles motivating *Being and Time*.

To avoid the previously mentioned danger of an excessively petrifying methodic or systematic orientation, in 1928 fundamental ontology comes to be articulated according to three steps: (1) the analytic of *Dasein*, that is, "the interpretation of Dasein as temporality; (2) "the temporal exposition of the problem of being"; and (3) "the development of the self-understanding of this problematic, its task and limits—the overturning (*Umschlag*)" (Heidegger, GA 26, 196/154). These steps, which consist in a process of radicalization and universalization of the *Seinsfrage* to include beings in their totality, are described as necessary for the re-articulation and intensification of fundamental ontology. As he puts it in 1928, "The radicalization of fundamental ontology brings about the overturning of ontology out of its very self" (Heidegger, GA 26, 200/157).

But what exactly is concealed behind these terms and these steps, terms that are arguably unusual in Heidegger's lexicon? More than the idea of a simple step forward toward something totally different, what we find being suggested is the necessary doubling-back or return (*Umschlag*) to the ontic or metontological origin and to the metaphysical developments that have guided the history of philosophy and from which the question of fundamental ontology can never be uncoupled. What Heidegger is proposing here is a metaphysics of entities in their totality, an analysis of the different regions of beings already announced, although not carried out, in §3 of *Being and Time*, a theme that is taken up again in *Contributions*. Among the various regional ontologies, Heidegger claims there is need for a metontology of entities, although it is but one region among others (Heidegger, GA 26, 199/157).

However, once again we should not take this as a simple methodological self-correction. The orchestration of fundamental ontology and metontology responds directly, for Heidegger, to the historical duplicity of the object of metaphysics, which he claims has been structured into the polarity of first philosophy and theology, hence into ontotheology. Consequently, the 1928 radicalization of fundamental ontology is not the restitution or remission of the history of ontotheology as the history of the occlusion of the ontological difference. If it is true that this turning or re-turning goes beyond or gets behind the ecstatic-temporal horizon of *Dasein* to include the complex consideration of the hidden manifestation of being, it is also true that this movement beyond or behind must always and necessarily take its start from that particular entity who evinces a preontological understanding of being, namely, *Dasein*. Only with *Dasein*'s understanding can being be brought to the level of a question, and it is this difference that becomes the focal point in the turn, or better re-turn, to metontology. In the end, one is perhaps forced to concede that *Being and Time* already carries within itself a metanthropological structure. However, the critique of anthropologism that Heidegger undertakes starting from the 1929 *Kantbuch* and running all the way up to the Schelling lectures of 1936, in which anthropology becomes synonymous with ontotheology and the metaphysics of modernity, is in reality already a large part of *Being and Time*, all in the name of the metaphysical neutrality of *Dasein*. After all, *Dasein* is not the human being, that is, not the human being as it is understood in the Greco-Christian sense of rational animal. Even the Heidegger of the Davos debate is concerned with restating the original intent of *Being and Time*, which is that of rephrasing the question of the human independently of any possible philosophical anthropology.

However, this does not answer the question as to whether Heidegger, his frequently problematic retrospectives notwithstanding, ever managed to coherently sustain this original intention. In reality, just as the thinking of the history of being involves excavation and the appropriative dismantling of metaphysics, all in the name of recuperating *Fragwürdigkeit*, so too the analytic of *Dasein* represents the dismantling of the traditional and solidified concept of the human being, and this is being carried out in the name of rephrasing the Kantian question of the essence of the human in all of its originality and problematicity.

As Heidegger asserts in his 1950 letter to Hartmut Buchner, the thinking of being, bearing in mind the double genitive, is a comfortless and destitute enterprise, involving the dislocation of the human being's self-privileging, done with an eye to the human being's eventual reconstitution or transformation (Heidegger, GA 7, 186/183). This transformation is hence a displacement of the human being understood as rational animal. It is a manic displacement that responds to the turning of being and that involves risk and danger.[8] Accordingly, once we become aware of this nonidentity at the heart of *Da-sein*, we can affirm that within the overall development of Heidegger's thought, *Da-sein* still remains the site for the disclosure of being. In fact, it is worth mentioning that the very question of *Da-sein* remains central to Heidegger's thought and constitutes, as he puts it in *Contributions*, "the *crisis* between the first and the other beginning" (Heidegger, GA 65, 295/208). Heidegger even goes so far as to say in the text *Das Ereignis*, a private text from 1941 to 1942, that "Da-seyn 'is' the turning" (Heidegger, GA 71, 118). However, if I were to make some concrete claims as to the operative modifications or transitions from *Being and Time* to the later work, and *Contributions* is literally pivotal here, then I would have to say that Heidegger's modified understanding of *Da-sein* is one indexed to a task to come, to a "future humanness" (Heidegger, GA 65, 300/212), as he puts it, and less to a task our humanity gives to itself. And my other claim is that even if the continuity of *Sachverhalt* remains present in the works after *Contributions*, there appears to be a break with the systematic ambitions of *Being and Time*. As he puts it in *Contributions:* "The time of 'systems' is over" (Heidegger, GA 65, 5/4). The question remains, then, should we, following commentators like von Herrmann and Parvis Emad (2007), judiciously prosecute a continuity thesis with qualifications while simultaneously interpreting the "antisystematic" nature of *Contributions* in a systematic fashion? Does not such a systematic interpretation of what are essentially antisystematic ways of thinking run counter to the very matter at stake in Heidegger's thought? The great danger here, however, is that any antisystematic reading of Heidegger's later arguably antisystematic thought might just end up in a form of reductive genuflection, philosophical homiletics, and language mimicry. One thing is sure, though: the limits of *Being and Time*, as Heidegger understands them, namely its methodological attempt to start with *Dasein*'s preontological understanding of being, do not so much consist in the mistaken decision to make *Dasein* central to the project, Richardson's reading (2003) is unsound here, but rather in the decision to make a certain model of understanding central, and with that a certain model of discourse (*Rede*), models that were not radical enough to respond to the essential unfolding of the truth of being, the play of absence and presence. As such, I think it is fair to say that the later Heidegger is attempting to carry out a retrieval of the unsaid and unthought of the earlier *Dasein*-analytic.[9]

The very movement of the *Kehre*, then, and specifically in *Contributions*, reveals itself as the recovery of a loss, the discovery of an essential mediation, namely *Da-sein*, and of a new rapport of cobelonging between the human being and being itself. In a passage from a lecture course given in the *Wintersemester* 1937 to 1938, hence one contemporaneous with *Contributions*, the following is put forward:

> Man is not here the object of any sort of anthropology. On the contrary, man is here in question in the most profound and in the most extensive respect, the one properly foundational; i.e. we are questioning man in his relation to Being, or, after the turning, we are questioning being and its truth in relation to man. The determination of the essence of truth is accompanied by a necessary transformation of man. (Heidegger, GA 45, 214/181)

Consequently, I think it is fair to say that the *Kehre* names both the difference and the essential rapport between being and *Dasein*. This is a rapport that allows, on the one hand, what Heidegger terms the *Wesung* of Being, insofar as being cannot essentially unfold without the human, and on the other, it grounds *Dasein* insofar as the human being can enter into its *Dasein* only thanks to being. This is an insight that was already present in *Being and Time*. The *Kehre*, then, which is again in no way a biographical U-turn, is in fact the very name for this reciprocity and cofounding, undoubtedly paradoxical for traditional philosophy, which has its site in the event of being.

In a word, the *Kehre* is an *Einkehr*, an entry point or turning into the field of oscillation and counter-play (*Gegenschwung*), defined by the reciprocal back and forth between the codependent appropriating claim and appropriated response, between be-ing's needing (*des Brauchens*) of the human being and the human being's belonging (*des Zugehörens*) to be-ing (Heidegger, GA 65, 251/177). In this sense, the *Kehre* is not directly concerned *with* thinking but more with the way in which the truth of being makes a claim *on* thinking and in so doing allows *Dasein* to come into its own.[10] What appears here is the fundamental difference between what von Herrmann calls the originary *Kehre* as a philosophical problematic involving the mutual rapport between the human being and the turning relation in being (von Herrmann 1994, 67–68) and the *Kehre* interpreted as a modification of philosophical position, as a shift in Heidegger's thinking (an *Umwendung* or *Umkehr*).

Moreover, the *Kehre* signals the point of departure from every traditional ontology and anthropology. Neither being nor the human being is capable of grounding independently of one another. Basically, they become reciprocally appropriated in and from *Ereignis*. In other words, *die Kehre im Ereignis*, as Heidegger terms it, is the reciprocal desolidification of the ontological difference in the irreducibility of their coneed or codependency (Sheehan 2001, 195–196; 2011, 59–60).

4   THE *CONTRIBUTIONS* AND BEYOND

Following Heidegger's claims, then, if the *Kehre* has a place in *Ereignis* and *Ereignis* is the theme around which *Contributions* orients itself, it is hence necessary to examine the development of this term in the 1950s and 1960s. As was the case in the previous transition from *Being and Time* to a genuine understanding of the *Kehre*, my attempt now is to examine Heidegger's more explicit claims and what can be read, so to speak, between the lines. The principle published lectures in which Heidegger addresses the theme of *Ereignis* are *Identity and Difference* (1957), *The Way to Language* (1959), and *Time and Being* (1962). In truth, these texts do not perfectly overlap. Albeit within the same horizon, Heidegger's thinking in these texts privileges two approaches that at first sight appear distinct yet on closer inspection belong to the overall constellation of the problem: (1) the cobelonging of being and time (in the 1962 *Time and Being*), and (2) the cobelonging of being and the human being (in the slightly earlier *Identity and Difference* and *The Way to Language*).

The path from *Being and Time* to *Contributions* leads Heidegger to the abiding conviction that, down through the various epochs of Western metaphysics, being (as presence) has always been interpreted starting from temporality and that the manner of the self-givenness of their essential relation has been occluded. Hence, starting from the 1962 *Time and Being* lectures, Heidegger argues that thinking is charged with the task of addressing this unthought relation. However, this task is far from straightforward insofar as being and time are not the ways of being of things or entities, and in truth, we cannot really say that being and time *are* at all. According to Heidegger, we are restricted to such expressions as 'there is/it gives being' (*Es gibt Sein*) or 'there is/it gives time' (*Es gibt Zeit*; Heidegger, GA 14, 20–24/16–20). Yet how are we to understand these expressions? What is concealed in the indeterminable or perhaps overdetermined *Es* that gives time, that gives being? And even more importantly, how does this *geben*, this giving, occur?

The later Heidegger describes the self-givenness of being in terms of a *Schicken*. Being is that which occurs as a destiny, but also as something destined. The characteristic trait of the history of being is the forgetting of what destines in favor of what is destined. The protocol of the 1962 Freiburg lecture introduces the distinction between *Anwesenlassen* as the openness of presence starting from the ontological difference between being and beings and *Anwesenlassen* as the openness of presence itself starting from that which destines this *lassen*, namely the *Es* (Heidegger, GA 14, 45/37). And since in both cases we are concerned with presence as an originary determination of time, one can presume that the *Es* that gives being can in some way be identified.

Here we return to the other fundamental expression, *Es gibt Zeit*. Heidegger tells us that *geben* is here intended as *reichen*, as handing over, reaching toward, or procuring (Heidegger, GA 14, 20–21/16–17). Ever since

Being and Time, it is clear that temporality is not something that *is* but rather something that existentially and constitutively temporalizes. Temporality is hence no thing, no entity; time basically temporalizes itself. Consequently, in the analysis of the givenness of temporalization there emerges an idea of time, in an authentic sense, that is not the simple juxtaposition or isolated accumulation of now moments, a punctuated or perforated present, but rather an expression of the original interwoven unity of the three ecstasies. The givenness of time as *Reichen* is not what coincides with the act of procuring this unity, hence constituting temporality. *Reichen* manifests itself as a kind of fourth dimension that procures time as the reciprocal play (*Zuspiel*) of past, present, and future, whose intimate proximity defines the fourth dimensional space, which is indicated in the 1962 *Time and Being*, and in the earlier *Contributions*, as *Zeit-Raum* (Heidegger, GA 14, 21/16).[11]

Temporality is also the fruit of a givenness that takes its start from the *Es* in *Es gibt Zeit*, which is defined in 1962 as "a presence of absence" (*ein Anwesen von Abwesen*; Heidegger, GA 14, 23/18). The possibility of getting back to this *Es* demands a consideration of the manner of its givenness: *Schicken* as *Reichen*. Taken together, these terms evoke the idea of a carrying toward what is proper, of an appropriation (*Zu-eignen*). In the *Schicken*, the *Es* carries being as its own into presence, while in the *Reichen*, the *Es* carries temporality as its favoring and granting openness, openness in which presence is destined.

Hence, the *Es* that assigns to being and to time what is proper to them and grounds their unified cobelonging is nothing other than *Ereignis*. As Heidegger writes in the 1962 seminar, "What lets the two matters [being and time] belong together, what brings the two into their own and, even more, maintains and holds them in their belonging together—the way the two matters stand, the matter at stake (*der Sach-Verhalt*)—is *Ereignis*" (Heidegger, GA 14, 20/10). Here we are brought back to *Contributions*, in which *Ereignis* is defined as nothing other than the field of oscillation and cobelonging between time and being, which is echoed in the protocol of the 1962 lecture, which defines *Ereignis* in the following terms: "*Ereignis* is to be thought in such a way that it can neither be retained as being nor as time. It is, so to speak, a 'neutrale tantum'; the neutral 'and' in *Time and Being*" (Heidegger, GA 14, 46–47/43).

This theme of *Ereignis* also emerges in his 1957 lecture *Identity and Difference*. Against the horizon of an attempt to reformulate the question of identity beyond a dialectical schema, *Ereignis* is explicitly thematized in terms already present twenty years earlier in *Contributions*, namely as the "*Zusammengehören*" of being and the human being, the constellation of being and the human being in terms of what binds them and holds them together, namely, the event of appropriation as a "*singulare tantum*" (Heidegger, GA 11, 45/36).

In the same way in which being and time, in their co-appropriation, vanish as such, so too, from the perspective of *Ereignis*, do being and the human

being lose much of their traditional metaphysical identity and ontotheological connotations. Yet what exactly hangs on this vanishing? Unsurprisingly,
the response to this question is contained in the late *Time and Being* protocol, in which Heidegger writes:

> At the end of the lecture on Identity [*Identity and Difference*], it is stated
> what Appropriation (*das Ereignis*) appropriates, that is brings into its
> own (*ins Eigene*) and retains as Appropriation: namely, the belonging
> together of being and man. In this belonging together (*in diesem Zusam-
> mengehören*), what belongs together is no longer being and man, but
> rather—as appropriated (*als Ereignete*)—mortals in the four-fold (*Gevi-
> ert*) of world (Heidegger, GA 79, 126/42).

It is worth mentioning that Heidegger's allusions to the four-fold
(a Hölderlinian-inspired theme first developed in the 1950 essay *Das Ding*)
are already an indication of the insufficiency of the positively destructive
appropriation of metaphysical ontology outlined in *Being and Time* (Heidegger, GA 7, 165–187). With this, Heidegger's thinking is a self-confessed
attempt to get to the bottom of what appropriates, and hence his thought
is one that struggles to shake up the fundamental concepts of metaphysics:
being, time, and the human being. In a word, his thinking is both an attempt
to set the history of being free and to make sure that we are not blind to
the history that we ourselves are. This is a possibility, Heidegger tells us in
Contributions, that demands "a courage for the old and a freedom for the
new" (Heidegger, GA 65, 434/306), or as he puts it in the 1924 *Sophist*
course, again attesting to the qualified continuity of his thought, "Ruthless-
ness toward the tradition is reverence toward the past" (Heidegger, GA 19,
414/286). Yet if this is so, is not Heidegger forced to renounce those hard-
won phenomenological insights contained in *Being and Time* and to replace
these hard-won insights with a form of historically mindful deliberation
(*Besinnung*)? Does not the very issue of a philosophical discontinuity come
in here, especially when one thinks of the ineluctability of the history of
metaphysics as that which coincides, without remainder, with the simultaneous givenness and withdrawal of being itself? To answer this question, it is
necessary to consider the nature of the rapport between being and *Ereignis*.

5   BEING, EVENT, AND THE TURNING

The phrase "*Seyn als Ereignis*" appears quite often in *Contributions*. And in
the 1946 "Letter on Humanism," the question of being is expressly assimilated into the *Es* that gives. As I have mentioned, the 1962 seminar *Time
and Being* seems to grant *Ereignis* a sort of priority with respect to being. It
is necessary then to examine the possible identity and difference of the two
terms and to reconsider the formula "*Seyn als Ereignis*" starting from the

"*als*." In the "*als*" there is contained contemporaneously the cobelonging of being and time, of being and the human being, insofar as there is a necessary withdrawal or retraction (*Entzug, Ent-eignis*) of *Ereignis* in favor of that which belongs together. But in the appropriating itself, in *Ereignis* considered in its granting or giving, there is also the disappearance of being, or at least being is taken up (*verwunden*) into the question of *Ereignis* (Heidegger, GA 7, 63). As Heidegger puts it: "It is a matter of seeing that being, by coming into view (*in den Blick kommt*) as *Ereignis*, disappears (*verschwindet*) as being" (Heidegger, GA 14, 46/43). Thus, being is *Ereignis* in its originality, in its ownness, and at the same time, it is also being in its being-given. Against every traditional logic of identity, being finds in *Ereignis* all of its intrinsic *Wesung*, and it is the task of thinking to address its origin. This new task coincides with the recognition of the limits of thinking, limits that exceed all consideration of the historicality of being. In fact, as Heidegger admits in 1962, interrogating the essence of *Ereignis* signifies the end of the history of being and being ceases to become that element that is to be genuinely pursued (Heidegger, GA 14, 50/41).

Ironically enough, the end of the history of being would at the same time appear to signal the sudden disappointment of every attempt at a positive *Destruktion* or *Überwindung* of the history of metaphysics. As Heidegger affirms, the way into the thinking of *Ereignis* inaugurates the simple task of leaving metaphysics to itself and giving up on any attempt to overcome it (Heidegger, GA 14, 25/24). From thinking the history of being, tracing the history of what Heidegger terms the first beginning, by means of *Andenken*, Heidegger passes over to the task of granting a place to the other beginning, to opening up a new horizon that does not simply leave the old behind but rather leaves it to itself. This new thinking comes under the title of *Vordenken*, a pre- or anticipatory thinking. Yet does the essential connection between *Andenken* and *Vordenken* correspond to the structure and task of *Contributions*? There is manifest, in the final analysis, a theoretical issue, more important than chronological concerns, that characterizes *Contributions* and the development of Heidegger's thought. *Contributions* repeats retrospectively the entire movement of thinking from *Being and Time* to the thinking of the history of being and announces and prepares, in an anticipatory sense (*Vordenken*), the thinking of another beginning starting from *Ereignis*. It is precisely this that characterizes Heidegger's later reflections. Yet it is evident that this duplicity does not simply refer to the chronological twists and turns within Heidegger's thought, the twists and turns announced in my title. Such an interpretation is blatantly mistaken. This duplicity refers mainly to both the necessity and difficulty of thinking with and after Heidegger about the necessity of thinking itself. In bringing one history to completion, the only history possible to this day, does Heidegger manage to open up another? And if so, what does this tell us about the so-called *Kehre im Ereignis*? To borrow from Jean Grondin, far from dividing Heidegger's thought into early, middle, and late, perhaps elucidating the problematic of *die Kehre im Ereignis* is the key to unlocking the unity of the *Kehre* as a continuity of *Sachverhalt*, a continuity in relation to the matter at issue.[12]

CONCLUSION

To conclude, these reflections represent an attempt to make sense of the twists and turns in Heidegger's *Denkbewegung* as responses to the twists and turns in being itself, and as such my claims are both well grounded and tentative. Consequently, I would like to end with more questions than I have answers to. It is clear that Heidegger's *Grundfrage* demands a different logic than that of metaphysical thinking and that this different logic is not simply a rejection of metaphysical thinking. Yet how would one know when one has located such a different logic, this logic of the other beginning? How could one articulate this premetaphysical saying or listening? Basically, and I struggle with this question, what would it feel like to succeed or fail in this demanded and demanding anticipatory thinking? And what are the "grounds" upon which one raises this to the level of a phenomenological problem?

In large measure, from the very beginning Heidegger was not inattentive to these questions, although his answers, as he puts it in the WS 1923/24 course, repeatedly turn "back into questioning [and] . . . this questioning turns back into ever new questioning" (Heidegger, GA 17, 76/56). Ultimately, for Heidegger, there is no way of being certain of one's movement along these paths of thinking-otherwise, insofar as they are paths that must be risked for the sake of "something more" or "something other." Consequently, within Heidegger's thought there is no principle of verification in terms of which recourse to "reality" can be made; his is a thinking that seeks the retracting and retracted grounds of the manifestation of what is taken to "be." Or, as he puts it in his 1950 letter to Buchner, "I can provide no credentials for what I have said . . . that would permit a convenient check in each case whether what I say agrees with 'reality'" (Heidegger, GA 7, 187/184). Nevertheless, this recognition makes Heidegger's thinking no less rigorous but in fact renders it both exigent and meager.

I would say that the matter of Heidegger's thinking, the demanding *Kehre* in the matter itself, emerges only when we allow the essence of questioning to come upon us, that is, when we are seized or turned by an essential need for questioning: being both open to the question and simultaneously opened by it. As such, Heidegger's unique style of thinking, his admittedly ambiguous transitional or preparatory vocabulary of elemental terms, is continually at the service of suspending the seductions of metaphysics, yet without simply negating those seductions. His is an attempt to formulate a transitional vocabulary that can aid in a recovery that will always remain incomplete, preparatory, and wayward. In the end, the real significance of Heidegger's analysis of the turn or turning in *Ereignis*, in his indefatigable attempts to get to what he terms in the *Contributions* "the stillest delights at the hearth of be-ing" (Heidegger, GA 65, 177/124), is its demand for an attentive response to the ungovernable ground of our philosophical convictions and seemingly well-vetted metaphysical claims. If one gets nothing else from Heidegger, then perhaps this is enough.

NOTES

1. Heidegger 2003, XVIII.
2. In the 1962 lecture "Time and Being," Heidegger states that "the relation of fundamental ontology to the clarification of the meaning of Being—which was not published—would be analogous to the relation between fundamental theology and theological system. This, however, is not true, although it cannot be denied that this is not yet clearly expressed in *Being and Time* itself. Rather, *Being and Time* is on the way toward finding a concept of time, toward that which belongs most of all to time, in terms of which 'Being' gives itself as presencing. This is accomplished on the path of the temporality of *Dasein* in the interpretation of Being as temporality. But this means that what is fundamental in fundamental ontology is incompatible with any building on it. Instead, after the meaning of Being had been clarified, the whole analytic of *Dasein* was to be more originally repeated in a completely different way" (Heidegger, GA 14, 34/32).
3. Heidegger writes, "Thus at the deciding juncture it was necessary to overcome the crisis of the question of being that was necessarily initially so laid out, and above all to avoid an objectification of be-ing-on the one hand by *holding back* the 'temporal' interpretation of be-ing and at the same time by attempting besides to make the truth of be-ing 'visible' (freedom unto the ground in *Vom Wesen des Grundes,* and yet in the first part of this treatise the ontic-ontological schema is still thoroughly maintained). By merely thinking further along the line of the question already set forth, the crisis did not let itself be mastered. Rather, a frequent leap into the essential sway of be-ing itself had to be ventured, which at the same time required a more originary enjoining into history: The relation to the beginning, the attempt to clarify *aletheia* as an essential character of beingness itself, the grounding of the distinction of being and a being. Thinking became increasingly historical, i.e., the differentiation between what is a historical *[historisch]* observation and what is a systematic observation became increasingly untenable and inappropriate" (Heidegger, GA 65, 451/317–318).
4. "The question of the essence of truth is at the same time and in itself the question of the truth of the essence. The question of truth—asked as a basic question—turns (*kehrt*) itself in itself against itself. This turning, which we have now run up against, is an intimation of the fact that we are entering the compass of a genuine philosophical question. *We cannot now say what the turning means,* where it is founded, since we have hardly entered the portico of the region of philosophical reflection. Only one thing is clear: if all philosophical thought must more unavoidably move in this turning the more it thinks originally, i.e., the more it approaches what in philosophy is primordially and always thought and reflected upon, then the turning must belong essentially to the single focus of philosophical reflection (*Seyn* as *Ereignis*)" (Heidegger, GA 45, 47/44).
5. See also Rosales 1984, 1991, 1995.

6. See also Trawny 2003.
7. "But there was not yet in *Being and Time* a genuine knowledge of the history of being, hence the awkwardness and, strictly speaking, the naïveté of the 'ontological destruction'. Since then, this unavoidable naïveté of the novice has given way to a knowing" (Heidegger, GA 15, 133/78).
8. John Sallis writes, "Thinking requires the most radical loss of self, and it is in this madness that, properly attuned, one is drawn toward, opened to, the gift of Being" (2009, 83).
9. In his 1953 preface to the seventh German edition of *Sein und Zeit*, Heidegger writes, "After a quarter century, the second half could no longer be added unless the first were to be presented anew. Yet the road it has taken remains even today a necessary one, if our Dasein is to be stirred by the question of being" (SZ, xvii).
10. Heidegger writes, "What is this originary turning in enowning? Only the onset of be-ing as enownment of the t/here [*Da*] leads *Da-sein* to itself and thus to the enactment (sheltering) of the inabiding and grounded truth into a being which finds its site in the lit-up sheltering-concealing of the t/here [*Da*]. And *within the turning:* Only the grounding of *Da-sein,* preparing the preparedness for the charming-moving-unto removal-unto the truth of be-ing, brings what hears-and in listening belongs-to the hint of the befalling enownment. When *through* enowning, Da-sein—as the open midpoint of the selfhood that grounds truth—is thrown unto *itself* and becomes a self, then Dasein as the sheltered possibility of grounding the essential swaying of be-ing must in return belong to enowning" (Heidegger, GA 65, 404/286).
11. See also GA 65, 371–388/259–271.
12. "When thinking attempts to pursue something that has claimed its attention, it may happen that on the way it undergoes a change. It is advisable, therefore, in what follows to pay attention to the path of thought rather than to its content" (Heidegger, GA 11, 33/23).

REFERENCES

Emad, P. 2007. "Questioning Richardson's 'Heidegger I, Heidegger II' Distinction and His Response in Light of *Contributions to Philosophy.*" In *On the Way to Heidegger's Contributions to Philosophy*, 186–208. Madison, Wisconsin: University of Wisconsin Press.
Heidegger, M. 1975. *Die Grundprobleme der Phänomenologie* (Sommersemester 1927). Edited by F.-W. von Herrmann. Frankfurt-am-Main: Vittorio Klostermann. (GA 24)
———. 1978. *Metaphysische Anfangsgründe der Logik im Ausgang von Leibniz.* Edited by K. Held. Frankfurt-am-Main: Vittorio Klostermann. (GA 26)
———. 1984. *Grundfragen der Philosophie. Ausgewählte "Probleme" der "Logik"* (Wintersemester 1937/38). Edited by. F.-W. von Herrmann. Frankfurt-am-Main: Vittorio Klostermann. (GA 45)
———. 1985. *Unterwegs zur Sprache (1950–1959).* Edited by F.-W. von Herrmann. Frankfurt-am-Main: Vittorio Klostermann. (GA 12)
———. 1986. *Seminare.* Edited by Curd Ochwadt. Frankfurt-am-Main: Vittorio Klostermann. (GA 15)
———. 1989. *Beiträge zur Philosophie (Vom Ereignis).* Edited by F.-W. von Herrmann. Frankfurt-am-Main: Vittorio Klostermann. (GA 65)
———. 1992. *Platon: Sophistes,* Edited by I. Schüßler. Frankfurt-am-Main: Vittorio Klostermann. (GA 19)

———. 1994. *Einführung in die phänomenologische Forschung* (Wintersemester 1923/24). Edited by F.-W. von Herrmann. Frankfurt-am-Main: Vittorio Klostermann. (GA 17)

———. 1996. *Wegmarken (1919–1961)*, 2nd edition. Edited by F.-W. von Herrmann. Frankfurt-am-Main: Vittorio Klostermann. (GA 9)

———. 1997. *Nietzsche II (1939–1946)*. Edited by B. Schillbach. Frankfurt-am-Main: Vittorio Klostermann. (GA 6.2)

———. 2000. *Vorträge und Aufsätze (1936–1953)*. Edited by F.-W. von Herrmann. Frankfurt-am-Main: Vittorio Klostermann. (GA 7)

———. 2001. *Sein und Zeit*. 18. Auflage. Tübingen: Niemeyer. (SZ)

———. 2003. "Preface/Vorwort" [1962]. In William J. Richardson, *Heidegger: Through Phenomenology to Thought*, 4th ed, vii–xxiii. New York: Fordham University Press.

———. 2005. *Bremer und Freiburger Vorträge*. Edited by P. Jaeger. Frankfurt-am-Main: Vittorio Klostermann. (GA 79)

———. 2006. *Identität und Differenz*. Edited by F.-W. von Herrmann. Frankfurt-am-Main: Vittorio Klostermann. (GA 11)

———. 2007. *Zur Sache des Denkens*. Edited by F.-W. von Herrmann. Frankfurt-am-Main: Vittorio Klostermann. (GA 14)

———. 2009. *Das Ereignis (1941/42)*. Edited by F.-W. von Herrmann. Frankfurt-am-Main: Vittorio Klostermann. (GA 71).

Löwith, K. 1953. *Heidegger—Denker in dürftiger Zeit*. Frankfurt am Main: Fischer.

Müller, M. 1949. *Existenzphilosophie im geistigen Leben der Gegenwart*. Heidelberg: Kerle.

Pöggeler, O. 1963. *Der Denkweg Martin Heideggers*. Neske: Pfullingen.

Richardson, W.J. 2003. *Heidegger: Through Phenomenology to Thought* [1963], 4th ed. New York: Fordham University Press.

Rosales, A. 1984. "Zum Problem der Kehre Im Denken Heideggers." *Zeitschrift für Philosophische Forschung* 38 (2): 241–262.

———. 1991. "Heideggers Kehre im Lichte ihrer Interpretationen." In D. Papenfuss & O. Pöggeler (eds.), *Zur philosophischen Aktualität* Heideggers, 27–38. Frankfurt: Vittorio Klostermann.

———. 1995. "Übergang zum anderen Anfang: Reflexionen zu Heideggers 'Beiträge zur Philosophie.'" *Recherches husserliennes* 3: 51–83.

Sallis, J. 1992. "Language and Reversal." In *Heidegger: Critical Assessments,* vol. 3, 151–167. London: Routledge.

———. 2009. "The Manic Saying of Beyng." In *Heideggers Beiträge zur Philosophie*.Edited byEmmanuel Mejía & Ingeborg Schüßler. Frankfurt am Main: Vittorio Klostermann.

Schulz, W. 1953–1954. "Über den philosophiegeschichtlichen Ort Martin Heideggers." *Philosophische Rundschau*, 1/2–3, 65–93 und 211–232.

Sheehan, T. 2001. "A Paradigm Shift in Heidegger Research." *Continental Philosophy Review* 34, 183–202.

———. 2011. "Facticity and *Ereignis*." In *Interpreting Heidegger*, 59–60. ed. Daniel O. Dahlstrom. Cambridge: Cambridge University Press.

Trawny, P. 2003. *Martin Heidegger*. Frankfurt am Main: Campus.

von Herrmann, F.-W. 1964. *Die Selbstinterpretation Martin Heideggers*. Meisenheim am Glan: Verlag Anton Hain.

———. 1994. *Wege ins Ereignis. Zu Heideggers "Beiträgen zur Philosophie."* Frankfurt: Vittorio Klostermann.

Contributors

Jussi Backman is a university lecturer in philosophy at the University of Jyväskylä and a docent in theoretical philosophy at the University of Helsinki. He is the author of *Complicated Presence: Heidegger and the Postmetaphysical Unity of Being* (forthcoming) as well as numerous articles on Heidegger, ancient philosophy, hermeneutics, and recent currents in contemporary continental thought.

David Carr is a professor emeritus at the Emory University. He has published widely on topics relating to nineteenth- and twentieth-century European philosophy, most importantly Husserl and the philosophy of history. His most important books include *Phenomenology and the Problem of History* (1974), *Time, Narrative and History* (1991), *Interpreting Husserl* (1987), and *The Paradox of Subjectivity* (1999). He is also the English translator of Husserl's *The Crisis of European Sciences*.

Richard Cobb-Stevens is a professor emeritus at Boston College. He completed his dissertation on William James's *Principles of Psychology* at the University of Paris in 1971 under the direction of Paul Ricoeur. More recently, his work has focused on the relationships between the traditions of phenomenology and analytic philosophy, with particular emphasis on the writings of Husserl, Frege, and Wittgenstein.

Steven Crowell is the Joseph and Joanna Nazro Mullen Professor of Philosophy at Rice University. He is the author of *Husserl, Heidegger, and the Space of Meaning: Paths Toward Transcendental Philosophy* (2001) and *Normativity and Phenomenology in Husserl and Heidegger* (2013). He is the author of numerous articles in phenomenology and continental philosophy and has edited several volumes, including *The Cambridge Companion to Existentialism* (2012) and, with Jeff Malpas, *Transcendental Heidegger* (2007). Crowell is co-editor, with Sonja-Rinofner Kreidl, of the journal *Husserl Studies*.

Mirja Hartimo has worked as a researcher or lecturer in several institutions, most recently at the University of Helsinki and University of Tampere. Her work has focused on Husserl's phenomenology and its relationship to the history and philosophy of mathematics. More recently, her research has centered on Husserl's view of norms and scientific rationality. She has published several articles in, for example, *Synthese, Journal of History and Philosophy of Logic, Philosophia Mathematica,* and the *Southern Journal of Philosophy.* She is also an editor of *Phenomenology and Mathematics* (2010).

Sara Heinämaa is senior lecturer of theoretical philosophy and the leader of the research community Subjectivity, Historicity, Communality at the University of Helsinki. Presently (2013–2014), Heinämaa works as professor of philosophy at the University of Jyväskylä. She has served as president of the Nordic Society for Phenomenology since 2008. In her systematic work, Heinämaa has been investigating the nature of embodiment, the mind-body union, intersubjectivity, generativity, and sexual difference. She has published widely in phenomenology, existentialism, philosophy of mind, and history of philosophy. Her most important publications include *Toward a Phenomenology of Sexual Difference* (2003), *Part II: Phenomenologies of Mortality and Generativity in Birth, Death, and the Feminine* (2010), and the edited volumes *New Perspectives on Aristotelianism and Its Critics* (forthcoming) (with Virpi Mäkinen and Miira Tuominen) and *Consciousness: From Perception to Reflection* (2008, with Vili Lähteenmäki and Pauliina Remes). At the moment she is working on a book on personhood and generativity.

Hanne Jacobs is assistant professor of philosophy at Loyola University Chicago. She earned her PhD from the University of Leuven, where she was a member of the research center of the Husserl-Archives. She is the editor of a series of Husserl's lecture courses on the history of philosophy published in the *Husserliana Materialien* series as *Einleitung in die Philosophie 1916–20.* Her current research focuses on Husserl's phenomenology and questions concerning the self and personhood.

Niall Keane is senior lecturer and chair of the Department of Philosophy at the University of Limerick, Ireland. He has published widely in the areas of phenomenology and hermeneutics and is currently working on the emergence and transformation of the self in Heidegger's philosophy. In addition to his publications on Heidegger, Husserl, Gadamer, Michel Henry, and ancient philosophy, he is treasurer of the Irish Phenomenological Circle, executive committee member of the British Society for Phenomenology, and co-founder and coordinator of the Irish Centre for Transnational Studies.

Sophie Loidolt works as an assistant professor at the philosophy department of the University of Vienna, Austria. She completed her PhD in 2007 at Vienna University, and she is the author of *Anspruch und Rechtfertigung. Eine Theorie des rechtlichen Denkens im Anschluss an die Phänomenologie Edmund Husserls* (2009) and *Einführung in die Rechtsphänomenologie. Eine historisch-systematische Darstellung* (2010).

Timo Miettinen works as a postdoctoral researcher at the University of Helsinki. In 2013, he defended his dissertation on Husserl's late phenomenology and the idea of Europe and has published several articles on the relationship of phenomenology to social ontology, political philosophy, and the philosophy of history. He is the author of *Husserl and the Idea of Europe* (forthcoming) and has also written on the topic of contemporary Europeanization and the recent political developments in the European Union.

Bernhard Obsieger is affiliated with the Complutense University of Madrid. He wrote his doctoral dissertation on the phenomenology of time. It focuses on Husserl and on the historical roots of our notions of temporality in the works of Heraclitus, Aristotle, and Augustine. This investigation gave rise to a more general interest in the phenomenological foundations of the ancient and modern conceptions of the natural world. His research also concerns the origin and meaning of Husserl's phenomenological method and its relation to other approaches to intentionality, such as those of Brentano, Meinong, and analytical philosophy.

Simo Pulkkinen is a PhD candidate at the Department of Philosophy, History, Culture and Art Studies at the University of Helsinki, Finland. He is currently working as a doctoral student at the Helsinki Collegium for Advanced Studies and is in the process of finishing his PhD project that examines the idea of transcendental philosophy in Husserlian phenomenology.

Joona Taipale works as a postdoctoral research fellow at the Center for Subjectivity Research, University of Copenhagen. He defended his doctoral dissertation on Husserlian phenomenology in 2009 at the University of Helsinki, and his current research project focuses on empathy and interpersonal understanding. He is also the author of *Phenomenology and Embodiment: Husserl and the Constitution of Subjectivity* (2014).

Laszlo Tengelyi is a professor of philosophy in the Bergischen Universität in Wuppertal, Germany. He has published widely on the topics of modern philosophy, particularly German idealism and phenomenology, and his most important publications include *Der Zwitterbegriff Lebensgeschichte* (1998), translated into English as *The Wild Region in Life-History* (2004), *Erfahrung und Ausdruck. Phänomenologie im Umbruch bei Husserl und seinen Nachfolgern* (2007), and, co-authored with Hans-Dieter Gondek, *Neue Phänomenologie in Frankreich* (2011).

Fredrik Westerlund is a PhD student at the Department of Philosophy, History, Culture and Art Studies at the University of Helsinki, Finland. His philosophical interests include ontology, phenomenology, ethics, and moral psychology. He is currently finishing his doctoral thesis on "Heidegger and the Problem of Phenomenality."

Index

CPSIA information can be obtained
at www.ICGtesting.com
Printed in the USA
LVHW040947021218
598971LV00025B/2799/P

9 781138 210561